FOURTH EDITION

SUPERVISION AS PROACTIVE LEADERSHIP

FOURTH EDITION

SUPERVISION AS PROACTIVE LEADERSHIP

John C. Daresh
University of Texas at El Paso

WAVELAND

PRESS, INC.

Long Grove, Illinois

For information about this book, contact:
Waveland Press, Inc.
4180 IL Route 83, Suite 101
Long Grove, IL 60047-9580
(847) 634-0081
info@waveland.com
www.waveland.com

Printed in the United States of America

7 6 5 4 3 2 1

Contents

❧ PART II
THEORY INTO PRACTICE   57

❧ PART III
THE REALITIES OF SUPERVISION: MOTIVATION,
COMMUNICATION, CHANGE, POWER, AND CONFLICT   131

Preface

The first three editions of this book took the stance that supervision is related to but not the same as administration. In education, this is still a defensible approach that is supported by a good deal of real-world practice. Many school districts still maintain separate supervisory staffs and distinct administrative groups. As is true in many organizations, supervisors report to administrators, but not the reverse. Increasingly, however, this distinction between line (administrative) and staff (supervisory) positions has blurred over the years. It is true that bigger systems retain distinctions of titles. But in fact, there is a very strong and consistent realization that it is neither administration nor supervision which has a positive effect on the quality of teaching and learning that goes on in a school. Rather, it is *leadership*. As a result of this observation, this book makes a strong effort to break away from the tradition of talking about supervision as if it were a distinct and very important area of school organization. The emphasis in this work is on how to increase the quality of schooling by looking at something considerably more important, namely, educational leadership. As was true of the emphasis in earlier editions, this form of leadership is still understood as a proactive process, not an assigned job title.

This edition features an expanded review of some of the more interesting emerging perspectives on school leadership that have appeared in the literature of the past few years. Many authors are now describing the work of leadership according to the extent to which an individual's behavior actually has an impact on the life in an organization. In other words, a leader is not a leader unless she or he has an impact on the quality in a school. And quality of life is defined often in terms of the ways in which a school (or any other organization) is able to reach out effectively to improve society. This fourth edition also includes a discussion of distributive leadership practice as a way to strengthen the quality of interactions that occur within a school. Simply stated, leaders have a responsibility to increase the opportunities for followers to influence organizational goals and outcomes.

Additional information is provided about the world of teachers, particularly in the ways in which teachers look at effective leadership practice. New material has been included, and a good deal of new references have also been added throughout the book.

Readers of this book have consistently commended its readability and attention to real-world issues and practices. This fourth edition attempts to carry on that tradition by explaining clearly the applications of theoretical frameworks to problems and situations that are faced each day by school leaders. As a reader, you will continue to find "Suggested Activities" in each chapter to help you acquire strong appreciation of the ways in which theory can be applied to daily practice. "Cases to Consider" also are presented to help you in applying concepts that are treated in each chapter.

In this edition, a new chapter (chapter 8) has been included that describes the basic assumptions, characteristics, and limitations on the current emphasis on educational accountability in this country. Whether or not educators like it, practices such as high-stakes student testing and expectations that educators would be responsible for demonstrating effective student learning are now a central part of the landscape of educational practice. Proactive leaders need to accept that reality, even when they may not embrace all practices associated with the ways in which successful learning are now carried out.

Finally, a new activity ("Applying the Concepts") has been added to the chapters of this book. In the past five years, most states have devised their own assessments of those who are seeking administrative or supervisory certification. These assessments are typically paper-and-pencil, multiple-choice tests designed to determine if aspiring school leaders are able to apply concepts to actual practice. These are typically reading tests to see if people can "translate" written ideas into real-life applications. In each chapter, brief quizzes patterned after this prevailing testing approach are provided to assist readers in fine tuning their skills at reading for application.

The basic beliefs of the first three editions still endure in this book. More effective educational programs will result from more effective leadership practice. And there continues to be a strong belief that the work of educational leaders can always be enhanced in many different ways. All of these beliefs are inherent in the view of proactive leadership presented in the pages that follow.

Introduction

Imagine two different school leaders facing the same question: What is required to encourage veteran teachers to explore new research on effective teaching strategies? The first supervisor or administrator announces a plan for all teachers to study the topic in inservice workshops, and the experienced teachers immediately and clearly voice their resistance—the program will mean more work, and besides, they are competent and effective teachers already. The leader reacts to this resistance by hastily putting an inservice program together, hiring an outside consultant to run it, and requiring the entire faculty to attend the sessions.

The second supervisor or administrator approaches the issue differently. In fact, the task may not become a problem at all, for this leader has taken time throughout the year to talk with all the teachers on a one-to-one basis. As a result, the leader is neither surprised nor frustrated when some teachers express little interest in the plan to acquaint them with new research on teaching. This second leader already knows where probable sources of dissatisfaction exist among the teachers and constructs the inservice agenda to accommodate this fact. Expert teachers are consulted and given leadership roles; workshops are geared to actual needs; potential resistance is defused.

This brief example illustrates two very different approaches to the exercise of supervisory responsibilities. The first supervisor approaches the job *reactively*. As long as things at the school seemed to be moving along reasonably well, the supervisor left things alone, but conflict erupted suddenly and unexpectedly when experienced teachers were presented with an inservice agenda for which they were unprepared and which they felt was being forced on them. This supervisor, who believed in the need for teachers to keep up with research, was no doubt angry and frustrated because plans for good, professional inservice training had been "sabotaged."

The second leader practices *proactive* supervision. Through constant involvement with staff throughout the year, this person could anticipate and plan for negative reactions to a particular decision. In fact, the second supervisor would probably have avoided making a unilateral decision about a topic for inservice training in the first place and instead would have spent considerable time during the year getting to know the *people* in the organization, and the *nature of the organization*. As a result, the supervisor could *proactively* anticipate problems in advance and minimize their negative consequences for the organization.

This book, which emphasizes the development of skills, knowledge, and attitudes consistent with proactive leadership, makes a number of fundamental assumptions about the nature of supervisory and administrative responsibilities in general. First, the assumption is made that understanding educational supervision and administration must be based on knowledge of historical definitions and perspectives. Second, it is assumed that supervision and administration today represent a blend of many earlier as well as current perspectives. As a result, chapter 1 begins with a review of the development of educational supervision in the United States and some of the most important trends that have guided that development. Finally, and most importantly, the assumption is also made that the most productive and effective way to define educational leadership today is as a *proactive process*. This central assumption underlies virtually all of the arguments advanced in this text.

What is meant by proactive leadership? There are six major components to this approach to practice in schools. To be a proactive leader, you need to:

1. Know your beliefs.
2. Understand the nature and characteristics of organizations.
3. Understand that supervision is not an event or a series of events: it is an ongoing process.
4. Examine and understand alternative perspectives, even those that you do not fully accept.
5. Be consistent in your own behavior: "walk your talk."
6. Be capable of analyzing the people in your organization and their patterns of behavior.

The chapters in this text are not designed to teach you each of these characteristics independently. Rather, these six concepts are woven into a total pattern of leadership behavior throughout the 18 chapters of this book. Effective leaders look at their responsibilities holistically and not as a series of tasks and responses to various emergencies that arise on the life of a school or school district. The effective proactive leader must develop a total understanding of what is being done, to whom, and with what likely consequences.

Leadership, as you will discover by reading this book, is not a neutral or reactive process where things simply "happen." Rather, good leadership changes people and their organizations for the better. Leadership is a critical responsibility in schools, and effective leadership can be extremely rewarding to the educator who chooses to follow the career route of administrator or supervisor. Perhaps this book will assist you in deciding if in fact you want to follow the supervisory or administrative path, and if you do, this text may help you be as good an educational leader as you can be.

PART I

Educational Supervision
Tradition and Context

The single most important attribute for any educator, and particularly for educators who serve as formal leaders, is an understanding of personal attitudes, values, and assumptions concerning both leadership and education in general. This understanding can derive only from knowledge of history and context—how leadership practices have developed in American education—and of alternative theories of educational leadership and supervision.

1

In Search of a Definition

Educational supervision is a field in search of a definition. Although supervision has been a regular school-based activity for as long as there have been schools in America, no absolute consensus has ever been reached concerning what supervision should be or what supervisors should do. Attitudes about schools, teachers, and learners have changed periodically over the past nearly four hundred years. As a result, views of what constitutes proper and effective supervisory practice have also shifted.

In this chapter, you will read about different approaches to supervisory practice that have paralleled changing perceptions of public education and educational management and that serve as examples of the transitory nature of definitions. To clarify the particular approaches that dominated specific historical periods of supervisory practice, some of the basic definitions, assumptions, and characteristics of how supervisory practice has been affected by these assumptions and definitions are provided. Before beginning this review, however, an important reminder is necessary: Although this chapter appears to present an orderly, sequential, and basically rational development of the field of educational supervision, in fact, the history of supervision has never been as clear-cut as it might seem. Overlaps exist from one period to another, and features of most of the early views of supervision are still alive and well today.

One important assumption underlies this review of alternative definitions and also serves as a crucial foundation for the concept of leadership espoused in this text. Educational supervision is greatly influenced by the ways in which individuals and groups define the field on a day-to-day basis. A brief review of past perspectives enables one to see how supervision has developed over time and how some of our present practices and beliefs originated. This understanding will help you make con-

3

sistent choices about supervisory and leadership behavior—an important component of the authenticity that underlies proactive leadership.

The premise of this book is that effective supervisors engage in proactive leadership. This means planning ahead and anticipating proper ways of behaving in advance, not simply reacting after a situation forces a response. It is an easy concept to define, but as the chapters ahead will demonstrate, it is often a difficult one to effect.

❧ SUPERVISION AS INSPECTION

The issue of supervising teachers in American schools is as old as the history of formal education in this country. In fact, the year 1632, when the First Massachusetts School Law was enacted, also marks the beginning of educational supervision in American schools. The first stage of supervisory development lasted until approximately the conclusion of the Civil War in 1865.

During these years, supervisors were primarily engaged in inspection—an approach based on the assumption that an educational supervisor's job was to find out all the wrong things that teachers might be doing in their classrooms. While this description seems rather harsh, one needs to recall some historical facts before judging seventeenth- and eighteenth-century supervisors as insensitive ogres who lacked any compassion or basic respect for teachers. During the earliest days of American education, many teachers were not well-educated and frequently stayed only a step or two ahead of their students in basic skills. Teachers of the time often needed monitoring to make certain that minimal levels of performance were being maintained in classrooms and schools. Individual supervisors did not always agree with their assigned responsibilities. In fact, the judgmental nature of supervision at this time rested in job descriptions, not in personal interpretations. The first stage of supervisory practice (roughly 1642–1865) can be further subdivided into two distinct eras: religious control and a more secular movement. The first years of American education were characterized, particularly in the New England colonies, by the assumption that local religious beliefs and values should be both preserved and transmitted from one generation to another. Supervision, then, was defined largely in terms determined and accepted by religious leaders. The Massachusetts Bay Company in 1642 provided the earliest known description of educational supervision:

> This Court, taking into consideration the great neglect of many parents and masters in training of their children in learning and labor, and other implyments which may be profitable to the common wealth, do hereupon order and decree, that in every town ye chosen men appointed for managing the prudentiall affaires of the same shall henceforth stand charged with the redress of this evill . . . and for this end, they, or the greatest number of them, shall have the power to

take into account from time to time of all parents and masters, and of their children, especially of their ability to read and understand the principles of religion and the capital laws of this country.

These chosen men were typically either ordained ministers or elders in local congregations—an understandable phenomenon in light of the fact that the teaching and learning they reviewed was tied directly to matters of religion. If students were not learning how to read the Bible, their path to eternal salvation was blocked because they would never be able to gain insights into the Scriptures and learn the commands of their God.

After the American Revolution, the duty of monitoring classroom practices was increasingly entrusted to committees of laymen who were not associated with any specific religious group. This switch no doubt occurred as part of the general secularization of American society that was taking place at this time. As the years went on, school officials placed less emphasis on the supervisor's responsibility to verify the quality of religious instruction and more emphasis on the supervisor's responsibility to oversee the quality of instruction. What remained constant, however, was the assumption that teachers lacked basic competency. Two popular definitions of supervision illustrate this shift of purpose. Theodore Dwight (1835) noted the following:

> Visitation and careful examination are necessary to discover the teacher's merits in teaching and governing the attention, deserts, and improvements of the children. To render a teacher, in the first place, to convince him that he can, are the principal objects to be offered by a friend of education. (p. 21)

During this same historical era, James Wickerman (1864) made the following comments regarding the nature of supervision in schools:

> Such visitations [by supervisors] are necessary to secure the caretaking of grounds, buildings, furniture, and apparatus; necessary to secure the most rapid progress on the part of the pupils; necessary to encourage competent teachers and to detect incompetent ones; in short, necessary to ensure the well-working of the whole school machinery. (p. 9)

As these definitions show, the religious orientation in educational supervisory practice had given way to a more worldly and secular view by the middle of the nineteenth century. On the other hand, these definitions continue to demonstrate some striking similarities in supervisory practice derived from a common set of assumptions held by educators throughout the first stage of supervisory development in American education.

Assumption and Related Practices

Teachers were not to be trusted. Perhaps the most basic premise of the earliest descriptions of supervision was simply that teachers were, for the most part, incompetents who could not be trusted to do their assigned jobs. At first this assumption suggested a lack of trust in teachers' abilities to provide instruction in religion. The supervisor's responsibility, then, was to be present in classrooms as often as possible to guard against the spread of any religious heresy, either intentional or unintentional. Instruction was monitored closely, not so much to guarantee proper methods of teaching, but rather to make certain the proper interpretation of the Bible was maintained. Even when this religious focus became blurred and finally disappeared, however, teachers were still viewed as essentially incompetent employees who needed to be carefully watched.

Supervisors had the right to intervene directly in the classroom. During both stages of these early years, supervisors often engaged in activities that were descriptive in their own right; they deliberately tried to catch teachers in the act of making mistakes. Supervisors made frequent, usually unannounced classroom visits, often intimidating even the most confident or competent instructors. Supervisors of the time frequently entered a classroom while a lesson was in progress, and then openly and defiantly debated with a teacher about the accuracy of the information he or she was imparting.

Supervisors were meant to be inspectors. Supervisors were expected not only to monitor instructional processes and correct incompetent teachers in the midst of leading their classes; they were also expected to review the characteristics of the total school, not as consultants or facilitators, but solely as inspectors. They performed functions such as overseeing the upkeep of the school building, instructional materials, and equipment. They were supposed to make sure, for example, that the schoolhouse roof did not leak, that the fire in the stove was well stoked, and that there were sufficient slates and benches for all the pupils.

Current Examples of Administrative Inspection

As we noted earlier in this chapter, the development of educational supervision may be described as if it had gone through several defined phases that ended before the next approach became popular. The fact is, however, that many of the early assumptions and practices of supervision remain alive and well to this day. Supervision as inspection is no exception.

Today, we frequently see educational administrators and supervisors who act as if they are inspectors. Consider, for example, those cases where a supervisor makes extensive use of in-class observations without alerting a teacher to the fact that he or she would be visited. While unannounced drop-in or walk-through classroom observations are certainly an appropriate strategy that might be used on occasion, an administrator who consistently surprises teachers by walking in on classes may be perceived as seeking to find fault with teachers. The reaction of teachers to such an approach will likely be one of distrust and suspicion. The administrator or supervisor who uses this approach will give the impression that he or she believes teachers cannot be expected to perform professionally without a perceived threat that they may be observed when they least expect it.

Some may describe this approach to observing teachers as "intrusive" or an example of micromanagement. But in the current world of education, it may be quite understandable that school administrators might occasionally revert to behavior reminiscent of the "Supervisor as Inspector" era. For one thing, schools now find increasing numbers of relatively inexperienced teachers who may need more intensive observation by principals and other administrators or supervisors. Another factor that may be leading to more intrusive inspection may be the current emphasis on teachers entering the field through alternative teacher certification programs. One can argue that those with solid backgrounds in fields such as mathematics, science, and literature may possess the subject-area content knowledge needed in the classroom, but often alternative certification procedures tend to minimize preparation in such areas as lesson planning, classroom management, and teaching strategies. As a result, in recent years there has been a greater need for administrators to intervene directly in classrooms. These factors, of course, must be understood in light of the increased pressure felt by many educational supervisors and administrators in the current climate of increased accountability.

∂‍ SUPERVISION AS SCIENCE

From approximately the end of the Civil War until soon after World War I (around 1920), teaching procedures and educational practices in general were greatly influenced by experts whose main interest was the improvement of organizational efficiency. William Payne, a school superintendent in Michigan who is often credited as being one of the great early scholars in the field of educational administration and supervision, set the stage for describing important managerial principles with his 1875 definition that reflected the notions of precision and certainty of performance in schools:

> The theory of school supervision . . . requires the superintendent to work upon the school through teachers. He is to prepare plans of instruction and discipline, which requires that teachers must carry it into effect; but the successful working out of such a scheme requires constant oversight and constant readjustments. Hence arises the necessity for conference, instruction in methods, and correction of errors. The teachers of a graded school should be under continual normal instruction. (p. 4)

In 1914, E. C. Eliot offered this view: "Supervisory control is concerned with what should be taught, when it should be taught, to whom, how, and to what purpose" (p. 23).

The views of both Payne and Eliot strongly imply that there is a single right way of doing things in education and that once this path is identified, it is the supervisor's responsibility to ensure that teachers know and follow it. The supervisor is also charged with the responsibility of planning—that is, of finding the most efficient and economical ways to attain organizational goals.

These basic ideas—a single right way of doing things, and responsibility centered on the supervisor—are echoed in the scientific management principles espoused by Frederick W. Taylor (1916) as applied to corporate management (Lunenburg & Ornstein, 2004). Taylor and other writers advocated these principles as a way to ensure good practice in industrial organizations; these same principles also affected the beliefs of educators. A review of Taylor's major tenets provides a context for the discussion of this second period of supervisory thought and practice. Raymond Villers (1960, p. 78) outlined the essential points of Taylor's views:

1. *Time-study principle.* All productive effort should be measured by accurate time study and a standard time established for all work done in the shop.

2. *Piece-rate principle.* Wages should be proportional to output and their rates based on the standards determined by the time study. As a corollary, a worker should be given the highest grade of work of which he or she is capable.

3. *Separation of planning-from-performance principle.* Management should take over from workers the responsibility for planning the work and making the performance physically possible. Planning should be based on time studies and other data related to production, which are scientifically determined and systematically classified; it should be facilitated by standardization of tools, implements, and methods.

4. *Scientific-methods-of-work principle.* Management should take over from workers the responsibility of their methods of work, determine scientifically the best methods, and train the workers accordingly.

5. *Management-control principle.* Managers should be trained in and taught to apply scientific principles of management and control (such as management relying on validated production standards).

6. *Functional principle.* The strict application of military principles should be reconsidered, and their industrial organization should be so designed that it serves the purpose of improving the coordination of activities among the specialists.

These principles of scientific management imply that certain features of organizational life are so predictable that specific laws can be formulated to guide behavior in virtually every circumstance. Thus, in both educational and corporate views of supervision during this time period, it was commonly believed that behavioral formulae, when faithfully followed, would necessarily and automatically lead to predictable outcomes and products.

Scientific management principles clearly influenced the development of educational supervision and administration, but other factors also played a role. For example, many school districts grew rapidly in both size and complexity, to the extent that larger organizational arrangements—districts and systems—were established across the nation, particularly in the industrial North and East. This increased organizational complexity was a major factor in the creation of a segmented view of educational leadership and supervision. Larger school systems began hiring two individuals—a business manager as well as a supervisor of instruction—who would function as equal partners in the hierarchical structure of a school district. Both were responsible to a third person in another newly created role, the district superintendent of schools. The concept of dual administration (business and instruction) greatly influenced the development of modern administrative and supervisory practice. One product of this era in educational history is what may be called the institutionalization and professionalization of the roles of educational administrators and supervisors.

Assumptions and Related Practices

Great faith has been placed in educational laws. Organizations throughout society were awakening to the possibility that rules and principles derived from research could be established to guide practice. School administrators and supervisors in particular were open to this line of thinking, because at this time a variety of problems were emerging from over two centuries of rather confused development. The notion that the educational practices of the past could be understood and even improved upon if some key facts and laws were learned was indeed tempting.

The outcome of this view, in terms of supervision, was that increasingly the educational supervisor became a reviewer who checked to see if employees conformed to procedures that were determined and handed down by experts. The supervisor's job was to make sure that the scientific rules of schooling were being followed. Thus, the emphasis in supervision was on the maintenance of acceptable teaching behaviors, and particularly on ensuring that these were carried out efficiently.

The supervisory staff of a school system would determine the proper methods of instruction. This scientific approach to supervision emphasized a "top-down" orientation to define and communicate information concerning instructional practices, and supervisory personnel of a school or district became the legitimate experts in the field of instruction. Scientific management principles urging the separation of management from employee control made unthinkable the possibility that teachers might work together to influence or define proper instructional techniques. Quite simply, teachers were viewed as the implementers of administrators' policies, and supervisors were around to make certain that policies were being fully and faithfully implemented.

The overriding aim of educational supervisor as it was practiced during this era was to develop teachers who were professionally efficient—that is, capable of self-analysis, self-criticism, and self-improvement in order to conform to stated standards of performance. These standards were determined at higher levels of the school district organization and then transmitted to the teachers. A primary activity of educational supervisors, then, was to provide either commendations or condemnations to teachers after classroom visitations. Compromises between these two extremes were not possible.

Current Examples of Scientific Supervision

The notion of "one right way to do things" might at first seem to have ceased to be the way in which schools or other organizations are to be operated. However, this core perspective of the scientific management era of one hundred years ago has to some extent been resurrected in recent years. In fact, there may be some who would argue that scientific management has never been put aside by many educational leaders.

Consider some examples of how the scientific management principles may still be in use. Today, there is considerable discussion about ensuring that education and educational practice are both consistent with meeting certain standards. These standards may at first seem like benign guidelines, designed to identify some degree of quality to ensure that effectiveness is achieved in schools. But what are the origins of the standards that have been set forth as indicators of quality education? If they have been established largely through a "top-down" action of administrators and supervisors, it is a clear indication that scientific management remains alive and well in schools.

Efforts to define clear, precise, and "scientific" content for school curriculum are increasingly identified as strategies for more effective schooling. Consider, for example, the state of Texas, which has adopted content standards mandated for the basis of all instruction in the state. The Texas Assessment of Knowledge and Skills (TAKS) serve as part of the state's educational code. Specified in state law, the TAKS set forth the learning objectives for all students at all grade levels to learn in all required (core) course areas in public schools. The "scientific" basis of these standards is derived from years of deliberation by committees (which include professional educators, parents, business representatives, politicians, and others) to decide what specific things must be presented in the instructional schema for each grade level of public education.

Similar efforts have been launched in other states, particularly as regards the definition of appropriate teaching behaviors that are assumed to be research-based and related to identified learning standards. In this way, the scientific management philosophy seems clear and unmistakable as a guide to administrative and supervisory practice.

Perhaps the most pervasive theme that has resulted from recent emphases on standards-based education and systems of accountability may be that administrators and supervisors today are to serve as "data-based decision makers." While one might argue that most supervisors have always made use of some forms of data to guide their actions, the current definition of data is increasingly related to the relationships that do (or do not) exist between actions in a school and student achievement data. As a result, before making a valued decision, the leader of today is increasingly expected to ask, "So what will the effect be on student data?" One cannot argue that such a value perspective is correct, and that schools should always be operated by the guideline of student learning impact. However, in the present educational climate "student impact" is increasingly defined ("scientifically") by immediate performance on mandated measures and instruments.

As the move toward greater accountability in public education becomes more powerful in the future, scientific management will continue to serve as a powerful model of administration that will influence the way things happen in schools.

❧ EMPHASIS ON HUMAN RELATIONS

The era of supervisory practice was tightly defined by the attainment of organizational goals and objectives through scientific methods. As a result, there was an increasing sense that the interests and needs of people who work in schools were being ignored and viewed as relatively unimportant parts of the educational enterprise. Scientific management often emphasized the notion that all organizational components—employees included—were best understood as replaceable parts. "One teacher is as good as another" could have been a motto of the time. Predictably, a vigorous reactive movement eventually emerged. In the human relations era (approximately 1920 to 1960), a management and supervisory philosophy that focused on needs of individuals who worked in schools and emphasized satisfying their personal interests took root. Widespread support developed for cooperative group efforts as both an end and a means for change in schools.

Supervisors were encouraged to use every means possible to stimulate and encourage teachers, with the assumed outcome being more effective instruction. Terms found in the literature describing effective supervision during this era included such words as coordinating, integrating, creativity, stimulating, and democratic relationships. Again, a glance at some definitions of supervision from the time provides insights into this era. In 1930, the National Education Association (NEA) stated:

> [The following is a] fundamental philosophy of supervision: Supervision is a creative enterprise. It has for its objective the development of a group of professional workers who attack their problems scientifically, free from control of tradition and actuated by a spirit of inquiry. Supervision seeks to improve an environment in which men

and women of high professional ideals may live a vigorous, intelligent, creative life. (p. 47)

What is truly remarkable about this definition, when compared to those in the earlier era of scientific supervision, is the sudden shift in emphasis from segmentation toward allowing employees to work together to define organizational goals and to create appropriate activities to meet those goals. The top-down emphasis on supervisory control had given way to a more democratic process. Two additional definitions support this view.

> The supervisory function is described not so much toward teachers and their methods as it is toward practices of advisement, student activities, pupil control of defensible subject matter, and personality adjustments of pupils and teachers. (Cox, 1934, p. 33)

> In general, to supervise means to coordinate, stimulate, and direct the growth of every pupil through the exercise of his talents toward the richest and most intelligent participation in the society and world in which he lives. (Biggs & Justman, 1952, p. 21)

Kimball Wiles, often described as the most ardent spokesperson for the human relations school in supervisory practice, provided the following definition of what supervisors should do:

> They [supervisors] are expediters. They help establish communication. They help hear each other. They serve as liaisons to get people into contact with resource people who can help. They stimulate staff members to look at the extent to which ideas and resources are being shared, and the degree to which persons are encouraged and supported as they try new things. They make it easier to carry out the agreements that emerge from evaluation sessions. They listen to individuals discuss their problems and recommend other resources that may help in the search for solutions. They bring to individual teachers, whose confidence they possess, appropriate suggestions and materials. They serve, as far as they are able, the feelings that teachers have about the system and its policies, and they recommend that the administration examine limitations among staff members. (1967, p. 11)

Clearly, there is a great difference between the perspectives of this human development era of supervision and those of the inspection and scientific eras. In the first two centuries of American education, there was little concern expressed about the individual needs of teachers and others in school systems. In Wiles's words, on the other hand, we find little or no concern for the needs and priorities of the organization. The focus had shifted dramatically from things to people.

Assumptions and Related Practices

If people are happy, they will be productive. This is the fundamental premise of this era, and it is the key ingredient of any approach to supervisory or managerial practice that endorses the fulfillment of human needs. If happy employees are better, more effective employees, then supervisors must focus on the needs and interests of the workers. Thus, educational supervisors must spend a good deal of time seeking input from teachers and staff members concerning working conditions and other issues related to the quality of life in organizations. Supervisors must also emphasize discussion groups, shared decision-making activities, and group process skill development.

The improvement of the psychosocial climate of the school is a legitimate concern for supervisors. The human relations movement, which emerged quite forcefully during the 1920s and 1930s, was heavily influenced by the research and theory bases that were increasingly popular in the social sciences. During this time period, the overall tenor of supervision was altered; it became acceptable for educational leaders to expend energy toward effecting positive feelings within an organization. Previously, only the measurable outcomes of organizations were considered to be the legitimate concerns of supervisors and administrators.

The supervisor is an in-between person in school systems. Whether it was a conscious modification is unclear and probably unimportant, but during this time the formal role of the supervisor changed drastically from that of an authority figure to that of a process helper and consultant. In contrast with earlier periods when supervisors were either inspectors or efficiency experts, supervisors became supporters, facilitators, or consultants to teachers. Two reasons may explain this shift. First, educational organizations and curricula were becoming more complex, and increasing specialization took place in many professional roles. The job of the supervisor probably reflected this change more than any other. Increasing demands for more varied curricula in school districts created the need for subject-area specialists—one frequent conceptualization of the role of supervisors—to work with teachers and provide expert assistance to help solve classroom instructional problems.

Second, a prevailing philosophical orientation of human relations management was that teachers and other workers needed supportive people to help them with their jobs. The supervisor's role was ideally suited to that function.

Current Examples of Human Relations Management

Although emphasis on the human side of organizational management and supervision was described as a philosophy popular early in the twentieth century, there are many examples of how this approach to educational supervision remains a part of the landscape today.

For instance, one may rarely find a school district anywhere in the nation without either an individual assigned the role of planning and carrying out staff development—or, in larger systems, whole departments charged with responsibilities related to enhancing the professional growth and knowledge of teacher and administrators. While the present emphasis on defining school success through performance on standardized testing will likely persist in the educational world, there is also recognition that even such a limited definition of success cannot be achieved without the efforts of well-trained and respected professional staff. Human relations management is not a simple frill; it is an essential ingredient in any effective organization.

Even in the climate of standards-based accountability, there is recognition that people and their needs must be addressed. Consider, for example, the following competency developed by the Chicago Public Schools (2004) as a critical expectation for school principals charged with engaging and developing faculty in their schools by:

- promoting teacher leadership within schools;
- supporting staff development strategically to build internal capacity and capability;
- aligning staff development with school goals and district priorities;
- establishing a community of learners;
- recruiting and retaining competent teachers and counseling out low performers.

৶ HUMAN RESOURCES SUPERVISION

In recent years, the prevailing view of supervisory practice and all administration and management has been that it should be an activity of "human resource development." Rather than returning outright to human relations supervision in a way that would resemble a revival of inspection and scientific management as prevailing supervisory philosophies, proponents of the human-resource development approach to supervision have incorporated the basic assumption of human relations (namely, that people in an organization hold the key to more effective supervision or management) into this variation.

As its name implies, human resource development suggests that the single most important responsibility of a supervisor is to help people within an organization—human resources—to become as skillful and effective as possible. The organization will then be improved because its most important features—employees—will be more effective.

There is a good deal of overlap between human relations management and human resource development. Both approaches place tremendous emphasis on the needs of people who work in an organization, and both views hold that organizational effectiveness is a critically important outcome of intervention by a supervisor. In addition, both views suggest that the key to organizational effectiveness is the extent to which workers can feel satisfied in their jobs. Chris Argyris (1971) described the central theme of human resources development and contrasted it with human relations in the following way:

> Happiness, morale, and satisfaction are not going to be highly rele-
> vant guides in our discussion [of human resource development].
> Individual competence, commitment, self responsibility, fully-func-
> tioning individuals and active, viable, vital organizations will be the
> kinds of criteria that we will keep foremost in our minds. (p. 4)

Some important differences keep human resource development from being a mere rehash of the earlier concept. Human relations advocates believed that emphasizing the happiness of an organization's employees would almost automatically guarantee that those employees would work harder, thereby increasing the overall effectiveness and productivity of an organization: "Happy people are productive people." The principal duty of the supervisor, manager, administrator, or leader, then, would be to guarantee that workers are content and satisfied with the workplace and would therefore want to work harder. Thomas Sergiovanni and Robert Starratt (2007) note that the emphasis on employee satisfaction as a primary means to achieve overall effectiveness represents a key difference between the concepts of human relations supervision and human resource development: "Within human resources supervision . . . satisfaction is viewed as a desirable end toward which teachers work. Satisfaction, according to this view, results from successful accomplishment of important and meaningful work, and this accomplishment is the key component in building school success" (p. 17).

While other efforts to conceptualize educational supervision, as noted later in this chapter, have emerged in recent years, human resource development remains as the prevailing view of what many describe as "effective supervision." In all likelihood, the most appealing part of this perspective may be that it presents a balance between a focus on individual employee needs and the goals of the organization.

Assumptions and Related Practices

If people are productive, they will be happy. In contrast to the primary assumption of human relations supervision, with its initial focus on the satisfaction of worker needs above all other concerns, human resource development assumes that if workers achieve the goals set out for their organization they will be satisfied, because the reason people work is to accomplish something of value. As a result, the supervisor becomes primarily interested in bringing about greater organizational effectiveness, thereby creating a setting where employees can feel satisfied through their association with productivity.

Proponents of human resource development criticize the earlier human relations perspective as highly manipulative because it assumed that a supervisor could be nice to employees and thereby make them buy into organizational goals without hesitation.

Workers can be trusted to act professionally. Contrary to earlier approaches to supervision such as the inspection and scientific management eras, human resource development makes a major assumption that workers are more interested in accomplishing personally defined professional goals than they are in simply getting a paycheck every week. They are productive because they want to accomplish certain goals. Traditionally, people have gone into teaching because they want to see children learn, grow, and acquire skills. As a result, the most central motivating factor in the lives of those who work in schools will likely be the extent to which school goals are achieved. While teachers want to be treated with dignity and respect, the supervisor achieves that goal by treating them as vital contributors to the effective school, and not simply by providing short-term compliments and "strokes" in the way that might be seen in a human-relations oriented school.

Human resource development may appear like a return to scientific management at times. Detractors of this approach to management often note that human resource development is really a return to the days of focusing primarily and exclusively on organizational goals. As such, this perspective would actually revert to the practice of the supervisor ignoring human needs, as was the basis for criticism in the days of scientific management. This seems an unfair criticism in that human resource development actually works toward providing a comfortable balance between the organization's needs and priorities and the workers' needs and interests in ways not addressed in earlier descriptions of supervision.

⚘ EMERGING PERSPECTIVES

Supervision as Social Action

For most of the history of American education, teachers and administrative or supervisory personnel were viewed primarily as guardians of the status quo of current pervasive values and practices. Simply stated, children went to school to "learn how to be an American," and to demonstrate skills associated with living a "normal" life in this country. Schools have traditionally been organizations designed to maintain the status quo. Teachers, supervisors, administrators, and others who worked in schools were expected to maintain social order as it was understood to exist.

In the last decade or so, this emphasis on school personnel maintaining past practice and beliefs has started to change, at least in the eyes of some educational reformers. Increasingly, those who work in schools have been encouraged to become critical examiners of the status quo. The purpose of this critical review has been to more clearly identify possible answers to "what" should be learned, and even "why" it should be learned. In the past, teachers and administrators were expected to engage in a process of neatly passing along a knowledge base and beliefs that were uncritically accepted as the central tenets of our society. Carl Glickman (1992) has identified this process of schooling as moving from one paradigm to another in the following terms:

> People are rethinking old ways of doing business, dismantling hierarchies, and formulating new expressions of "life, liberty, and the pursuit of happiness." It is no historical accident that the democratization and decentralization of governments across the world is happening at the same time similar activities are being asked of public schools. Providing administrators, teachers, students, and parents a real voice in educational decisions at the time of perceived educational crisis is a bold attempt to rethink our schools, the ways we teach, and the ways students learn. We know what we will have if we operate as we have in the past—and the prospects are not promising. (p. 1)

As the result of this new socially responsible perspective adopted as a goal of administrative and supervisory personnel in schools, Lynn Beck and Joseph Murphy (1993) have assigned such terms as *social architect* and *moral agent* as descriptive of emerging images of school principals in the late twentieth and early twenty-first century.

The broad terms that have been assigned to those who seek to appreciate the role of educators are critical theory, postmodernism, and the social action perspective. While there is no suggestion at this point that educational leaders are necessarily moving toward the adoption of these perspectives on a wholesale basis, today's literature is filled with efforts to paint the field of educational leadership in ways more consistent with the values espoused by these emerging schools of thought.

Critical theory

One view of the world of educational administration and supervision that has gained considerable attention in recent years is generally referred to as *critical theory* or *critical pedagogy*.

> Fundamentally concerned with the centrality of politics and power in our understanding of how schools work, critical theorists have produced work centered on the political economy of schooling, the state and education, the representation of texts, and the construction of student subjectivity. (McLaren, 1989, p. 159)

Starratt (1996) further explains the world of critical theorists by noting that proponents of this perspective view their task of identifying which group (or groups) have "power over the others, how things got to be the way they are and to expose how situations are structured and language used so as to maintain the legitimacy of social arrangements" (p. 160). In short, the critical theory perspective has implications for those who lead in schools by suggesting that the leader is responsible for interpreting the subtle realities of what is taking place in an organization. It is not enough to "get the job done." Rather, the leader who would engage a critical sense would scan the social and historical context of an organization to determine not only the practical and technical duties associated with his or her job, but more important, the symbolic and cultural meanings associated with practice.

In terms of current supervisory practice, the suggestion of the critical theorists would be that the role of school leader must be expanded to include "reading the map" of what is taking place, not only within a single school but also within the society in which a school is embedded. To respond to apparent crises involving student disorientation and disengagement from school life without also appreciating the nature of the social context in which students in a particular locale might find themselves would be a pointless activity. In addition, the critical theorist perspective requires adherents to engage in a continuing process of questioning and examination of current, past, and even future practice so that what is done in the context of schooling reflects surrounding reality, not commitment to existing models and assumptions. The supervisor who takes on the role of the critical theorist becomes, above all, a value analyst. Further, the critical theorist assumes responsibility for analyzing and ultimately changing the nature of life for those who traditionally have been ignored by educational organizations. As Capper (1995) noted,

> A critical theory would suggest . . . that we develop and shape the knowledge base [of the field of educational leadership] via the deliberate involvement of disempowered people in discussions of education; these people can identify educational "problems," "causes," and "solutions" based on their own experiences with inequity. (p. 287)

Postmodernism

Traditional perspectives of the world of supervisory practice have been largely dependent on one central belief, namely, that the supervisor was to serve as an overseer of organizational life. This was true of the era of inspection, scientific management, human relations and, more recently, in human resource development. It is important for those who would guide the work in organizations to assume that one could predict organizational outcomes. This is true because the prevailing view has been that organizations are rational in structure, practice, and outcome. Carlson (1996) notes that, in response to this traditional view of organizational reality, *postmodernist thought* now "places greater emphasis on lived and deconstructed experience, stresses methodological pluralism built upon a cooperative network, and develops sources of data from art, literature and anecdote, and action research" (p. 12). Postmodernist thought rejects the assumptions of predictability and rationality. As a result, it is a polar opposite of such traditional perspectives as scientific management and the theory movement, which have guided the development of educational administration and supervision since the 1950s.

Janet Littrell and William Foster (1995, p. 35) noted that, as an approach to the analysis of organizations, postmodernism makes the following assumptions:

1. Knowledge is nonfoundational. (There is no such possible thing as a knowledge base to guide all possible actions and behaviors in organizations, since organizational behavior is always based on immediate context).
2. The agreement we develop about what constitutes "true" knowledge is related to the distribution of power in a society.
3. Postmodernists rely on widely accepted stories that construct reality and maintain existing power structures.

As one can see, these descriptions of emerging perspectives on leadership and administration, critical theory, and postmodernism take as a central focus the analysis of organizations and behavioral patterns. They are not efforts to guide how one ought to behave when faced with leading a school in specific circumstances. As a result, these perspectives differ greatly from earlier approaches to supervisory performance. Yet they are included here because they have significant impact on the ways in which individual school leaders may perceive their overall duties.

Limitations on the Social Action Perspective

The literature proposing that educational supervisors and other leaders devote their attention exclusively to addressing broad issues related to the increase of social justice has seemingly had little influence on the world of practitioners. Instead, the topics related to critical theory, postmodernism, and social action in general appear to be directed almost exclusively to the interests of the academic community.

This does not mean that school leaders are not interested in the concerns of those who advocate social justice as the goal of leadership in education. To the contrary, most school principals, supervisors, and others have a keen interest in ensuring that schools have a positive affect on society at large. As an example, few educators would quarrel with the notion that an important goal of education is related to community economic development, and that such development is the foundation of profound social change. The problem, then, is not that there is no value in the perspective of postmodernists. Rather, it is an issue of practicality: Can educational leaders reform society and also run schools and focus on the learning needs of the children in their schools? It is doubtful if anyone can be an effective instructional leader, manager, and social architect all at the same time.

❧ CLIENT-BASED SUPERVISION AND TOTAL QUALITY MANAGEMENT

Another approach to supervision which has gained great popularity over the past few decades has been the concept of Total Quality Management (TQM). This supervisory and management philosophy is sometimes described in the literature as emphasizing the development of organizational plans and priorities with the purpose of increasing the sense of satisfaction felt by the clients or customers of those organizations. In other words, when the external environment perceives that it is satisfied with what happens within an organization, then the organization is, in fact, effective.

Actually, focusing on the need to engage in absolute dedication to customer satisfaction is only one part of the philosophy of TQM. Dan Ciampa (1992, p. 7) noted that TQM is directed toward producing results which fall into the following four categories:

- *Customers* are intensely loyal. They are more satisfied because their needs are being met and their expectations are being exceeded.

- *The time to respond* to problems, needs and opportunities is minimized. Costs are also minimized by eliminating or minimizing tasks that do not add value. Moreover, they are minimized in such a way that they enhance both the quality of the goods or services given to the customer and the way the customer is treated.

- *A climate* is put in place that supports and encourages teamwork and leads to more satisfying, motivating, and meaningful work for employees.

- *There is a general ethic of continuous improvement*. In addition, there is a methodology that employees understand for attaining a state of continuous improvement.

These basic assumptions of structuring organizations to reflect a commitment to the needs of clients and total quality are drawn in large measure from the earlier work of W. Edwards Deming. Deming, prepared academically to be a physicist, has achieved most of his fame as the individual largely responsible for the rebirth of Japanese industry after World War II. He was recruited by the Supreme Command for Allied Powers in 1947 to join a team working with Japanese officials in planning for programs that would bring about national stability after the massive destruction brought on by the war. Deming noted that a complete redefinition of the ways in which people viewed organizational roles and relations would be needed to rebuild the national economy. In short, Deming realized that his role was to foster a new way of thinking about management, perhaps even more importantly than finding new ways to manage.

The result of this initial effort to promote the restructuring of the Japanese management culture has been the identification of Fourteen Points for effective practice (Walton, 1986). These points define Deming's conceptualization of a more effective way in which organizations might operate:

1. *Create constancy of purpose for improvement of product and service.* Effective organizations do not simply try to earn a lot of short-term suc-

cess through immediate increases in profits; rather, they promote long-term success by focusing on organizational maintenance through promoting (and funding) innovation, research, constant improvement, and maintenance.

2. *Adopt the new philosophy.* This new philosophy must be one of intolerance toward poor service and complacency. The goal must be one in which mistakes and negativism are unacceptable.

3. *Cease dependence on mass inspection.* The identification of problems in manufactured products implies that the system of production is designed so that flaws are acceptable. As a result, designing a system dedicated in total to the elimination of errors is more effective than one that is designed to inspect and seek errors as production occurs.

4. *End the business of awarding business on price tag alone.* Selecting products solely on the basis of lowest cost is shortsighted. This often leads to selecting products of low quality: "You get what you pay for."

5. *Improve constantly and forever the system of production and service.* Management is obligated to continually look for ways to reduce waste and improve quality.

6. *Institute training.* It is irrational to expect that people will be able to do their jobs if they are not properly prepared.

7. *Institute leadership.* Leadership consists of helping people do a better job and of learning by objective methods to determine who needs to receive individualized help.

8. *Drive out fear.* It is not wrong to make mistakes. It is a mistake to develop a culture where people believe it is impossible to try without always achieving immediate success.

9. *Break down barriers between staff areas.* Collaboration, not competition, among work groups is the key to success.

10. *Eliminate slogans, exhortation, and targets for the workforce.* The "rah-rah" spirit shown in old movies about great coaches never really helped teams win. Only the skills of individuals did any good. Effective leaders recognize this fact and downplay the reliance on slogans or other "grandstand" efforts to promote "spirit" and a "winning attitude."

11. *Eliminate numerical quotas.* Quotas promote the achievement of numerical goals, which are simply symbols of reality. They do not enhance quality. The effective organization seeks quality, not symbols.

12. *Remove barriers to pride of workmanship.* The fundamental belief is that people really want to do a good job.

13. *Institute a vigorous program of education and retraining.* The only way in which an organization will grow and prosper is if the people who make up the organization continue to grow and learn.

14. *Take action to accomplish the transformation.* People in the organization must function as a team at all times.

For an application of the Fourteen Points to a framework for transforming schools, see Lunenburg and Ornstein (2004).

In addition to these Fourteen Points associated with effective organizations, Deming also noted what he referred to as the "Seven Deadly Diseases of Organizations" that must be addressed:

1. Lack of constancy of purpose.

2. Emphasis on short-term profits.

3. Evaluation by performance, merit rating, or annual review of performance.

4. Mobility of management (i.e., leaders are moved frequently without reason).

5. Running a company on visible figures alone.

6. Excessive medical costs.

7. Excessive costs of warranty, fueled by lawyers who work on contingency fees.

As one reflects on the vision of proper supervision and administration suggested by this emphasis on TQM and the needs of customers, it becomes clear that certain practices are exhibited by those who adhere to this approach. For example, top-down management is no longer valid, nor is any effort to use immediate and visible indicators of effectiveness. As a result, in school settings, it becomes increasingly difficult to imagine successful practice being identified solely in terms of increases in student achievement scores.

There is little doubt that school supervisors and administrators in recent years have been inundated with proposals to improve schools by adopting principles of TQM. The pages of professional journals are filled with stories about how to apply TQM to schools, and dozens of special training sessions are sponsored at professional association meetings each year to describe how to make school more responsive to clients. There is a bewildering array of terms and programs that appear to offer effective strategies to make use of the fundamental principles of Deming's work in schools. Consequently, programs such as site-based management (or collaborative decision making or school-based management) litter the scene as proposed strategies to make school management more consistent with effective practice that is suggested by reformers.

There seems to be no end in sight to school supervisors and administrators attempting to apply TQM principles and techniques. It is unclear whether this trend will continue well into the future and form another major approach to management philosophy in the same way scientific management, human relations, or human resource development have. With respect to the various descriptions of TQM and customer-driven management, at least four areas in which there are inconsistencies between this popular perspective and the reality of schools are noted:

- TQM is not a specific strategy for managing, but rather an overall philosophical orientation to the ways in which organizations and people interact. TQM holds that people are to be heard, valued, respected, and viewed with a degree of importance. This perspective may be novel in many industrial and manufacturing organizations where the historical goal has been to turn out more product at any cost. By contrast, schools (and school personnel) have held a much different set of values concerning their societal roles and responsibilities. Simply stated, school people already view the satisfaction of human needs as central to their vision. As a result, the central belief of TQM is one that has been familiar to most educators for many years.

- The identification of customers and clients is central to TQM. If one cannot specify who the customers of an organization are, how can one develop a set of organizational activities and procedures to meet their needs? In the case of schools, the identification of clients is not a simple task. Are customers pupils? Parents? Teachers? Taxpayers? State legislators? All of the above, or none of the above?

- There are many cases where TQM simply does not fit the reality of public schools. For example, Deming's Point 4 ("Eliminate the practice of awarding business on price tag alone") and Point 11 ("Eliminate numerical quotas") are consistent with the wishes of many educators. Yet are they realistic in today's climate, where public agencies are under constant pressure to become more cost effective and efficient? Would it be likely that many school systems would be able to ignore lowest-bidder provisions when purchasing materials?

- There are many undefined or at least ill-defined concepts and practices associated with TQM. As a result, a philosophical orientation that has power for some might become so open to interpretation by others that its individual concepts become virtually meaningless. Deming is often credited with stating that effective organizations are those which downplay supervision and replace it with leadership, implying that supervision cannot be viewed as an act of leadership. This assertion is dependent upon a much clearer definition of leadership in the first place.

Total Quality Management, in the form of attention to customer needs, has many benefits to offer educational leaders in terms of improving their practice. On the other hand, one is not totally convinced that this perspective is sufficiently articulated at present to make it an enduring or very useful concept.

❧ So, What *Is* Supervision?

In this chapter we have provided a general overview of the development of educational supervision over the years. We noted that the field has been influenced by the tendency to find the worst in people and later by the assumption that people are the most important component in any organization. Currently, several perspectives on the roles and responsibilities of those charged with supervisory duties compete for our attention. Numerous definitions have been offered, but none of them has been endorsed without reservation.

You may find a bias in this book toward the belief that human resource development is a reasonable perspective in most cases. You may also note that critical theory, postmodernist perspectives, and the social action perspective are not endorsed as desirable approaches to supervisory leadership. Perhaps the most fundamental point of view is that anyone with educational leadership responsibilities should understand as many alternative views as possible and then select a perspective that is most consistent with one's own basic set of values. The most important thing to do after making an initial selection of acceptable options, then, is to behave in a fashion that is faithful to that orientation. As noted in the introduction to this section, a key ingredient in the process of proactive leadership is the maintenance of *authentic* and *consistent* behavior. While there are clear strengths and weaknesses inherent in all orientations to supervision, there is probably nothing more damaging to supervisory effectiveness than to pretend to have a particular perspective and then act in a way that suggests an entirely different view. Time and again teachers report great frustration with what they perceive to be behavior that is not authentic or consistent on the part of supervisors and administrators. While it is probably true that few teachers would be overjoyed with the prospect of working for someone who espoused the beliefs of the inspection era, such a condition would be more acceptable than one where a new leader claimed to be a human relations proponent or a believer in Total Quality Management while really being a closet inspector. People value predictable, consistent, and authentic behaviors.

There are probably times and situations in the life of an organization that make different supervisory practices more (or less) acceptable and effective. The prospect of supervisors as inspectors—and the inherent assumption that teachers are not competent—is not typically attractive; on the other hand, there are times when incompetent teachers require greater scrutiny. Human relations supervision may be criticized as manipulative, but there might be a time, for example, after a particularly autocratic administrator has just departed, when an overemphasis on human relations would be effective and important.

Is there, then, a single, acceptable definition of supervision? The ones that are introduced thus far have faults, although they may be useful from time to time. The answer to this question, particularly in this volume's advocation of proactive leadership, is not easy. If proactive leadership calls for the selection of a particular perspective, the espousal of a single definition that is tied too closely to one set of assumptions will contradict a fundamental value of this text. The basic definition here represents an attempt to go beyond educational settings and focus on essential features of supervision in any situation: *Supervision is a process of overseeing the ability of people to meet the goals of the organization in which they work.*

A key feature of this definition is its suggestion that supervisory leadership needs to be understood as a *process* and not as a specific professional role. It is also related to the concept of *proactive leadership*, the foundation of this book, which holds that the best form of educational leadership is based on the set of fundamental values and assumptions held by the individual occupying an administrative or supervisory role. The major characteristic of current supervisory behavior is its undue emphasis on reactive performance orientation—doing things as a result of a crisis—rather than performance based on careful, logical planning and preparation. The remaining chapters of this text are devoted to the idea that effective supervisory leadership is based on the development of a more predictable strategy to guide action, and that strategy must emerge no matter which definition, philosophy, or overall orientation an individual adopts.

❧ SUMMARY

In this chapter, several alternative perspectives of supervisory practice were reviewed to enable you to question your own assumptions regarding the proper definition of supervisory leadership. The hope is that you will begin to formulate a personalized but authentic perspective. Further, it was noted that the development of a personalized understanding of supervision is the first step forward in proactive rather than reactive leadership.

Suggested Activities

1. Interview at least four school leaders to determine their predominant views of supervisory leadership. You might start by asking for personal definitions. Propose a situation, such as "reasons for evaluating staff." Interpret interviewees' responses according to the historical views presented in this chapter. Were there any that leaned toward inspection? Toward critical theory? Toward the human relations philosophy? Toward social action?

2. Look at the job descriptions of supervisors or administrators in at least two different school districts. Can you determine if there are any prevailing views of how such individuals are to behave according to the historical definitions reviewed in this chapter?

Cases to Consider

The brief cases below are based on actual situations which have taken place in schools. Please read each case and consider the following:

- What are the critical issues raised in each case, as they relate to the topics covered in this chapter of the text?
- How do these cases relate to the development of the concept of proactive leadership as it is explained in this chapter?
- In what ways might you suggest a resolution to the issues raised?

Case 1.1   What Do They Want?

Mark Jackson, an assistant principal at Franklin Heights Middle School in the West Yarbrough Schools, had just picked up a copy of the state administrators' association weekly job list and noticed that the El Camino Real Schools were looking for a new principal for one of their middle schools. Mark did not know a lot about El Camino, other than it was located in the northern part of the state, paid administrators quite well, and had a reputation as a really fine school system in terms of student performance on the statewide achievement test each year. Mark decided to do a little investigating to see if it was worth pursuing as a job opportunity. He made a list of people to contact via e-mail or through phone calls and began to search for the reasons he did or did not want to go to El Camino.

One of the first people to respond to Mark's request for more information was Anne Cunningham, a former teacher at Franklin Heights who had moved north two years ago. Anne was a good teacher and Mark respected her candor. It was a bit of a concern when her comments focused almost exclusively on the seemingly never-ending conflict between the school board, the superintendent, and other district administrators. It seemed that the school board was comprised entirely of upper middle-class citizens, most of whom were professionals such as attorneys or physicians. The superintendent had taken a stance that the schools were to become places that would enhance learning for all students, even those who came from more impoverished backgrounds than many board members wanted to admit. The board wanted high test scores and many academic awards, while administrators were committed to equity and service to all learners.

Mark got quite a different feeling based on the information that came from a local realtor, who sent a profile describing the low taxes and the high college placement rates in the schools, as if this were exactly the kind of information that would encourage newcomers to move to the community. In the same day's mail, he got a personal note from one of the other middle school principals in the same district as El Camino's. He had heard from "a friend of a friend" that Mark was looking into the school system. He was very encouraging, but noted that there would be a lot of work for the new principal because "they need someone to go in and get rid of a lot of very complacent, even lazy, teachers."

As Mark now thought about the application process, he was not at all certain what might await him if he went to El Camino.

Case 1.2   I Thought You Said . . .

Mary Witherspoon had just finished her first day as the new assistant principal of Douglas Road Primary School, one of 15 elementary schools in the Hoopstown School District. She has been really excited about taking this position, her first as a school administrator. Although she had interviewed at three other Hoopstown schools, and the word was that she could have had her pick of any of those positions as well, she was particularly attracted to Douglas Road because it provided her with the opportunity to work with Arnie Samuelson, the principal of that school for the past seven years. She had hit it off well with Arnie during the interviews. His statements to her and the interview committee members seemed to be quite consistent with many of Mary's ideas concerning what a campus administrator might be able to do. She particularly enjoyed hearing his views about how the administrative team at Douglas Road worked best when it worked with teachers as equals and colleagues.

It was now several weeks since the interviews were conducted, and Mary had quickly noticed that many of Arnie's earlier statements did not seem to be carried out in practice. For instance, he was always reminding his new assistant of her responsibility to "keep an eye" on the teachers and listen for any sign of teachers refusing to follow school or district policy. Today, the first day of the school year, was another example. When Mary came in this morning, Arnie called an impromptu meeting with her, his secretary, and the guidance counselor. The primary focus of that session was to remind everyone again that the teachers might be competent in their classrooms, but they had to be watched today to make certain that they got things off to a good start with strong discipline with the students.

Mary looked for a bottle of aspirin in her desk drawer.

Applying the Concepts

The following brief quiz is designed to improve your skills in applying some of the concepts discussed in this chapter. Read the brief introductory case and then respond to the multiple-choice questions. You will find the answers in the Appendix.

David Carlisle was happy to learn that he had been selected to serve as the principal of Elm Street School. He had served as an assistant at two other schools in the district, and he had gained a positive reputation as an effective administrator. He knew that some teachers in his former schools were probably happy to see him go. He had established a reputation as a leader who was very direct in the way he worked with staff. He explained his expectations clearly, and he always provided everyone with a rationale for his action based on recent research findings. David knew that many were not always delighted when he reminded them that they were not acting in ways he had identified as the best approaches to make schools more successful and increase student achievement.

He was looking forward to working at Elm Street. He knew that the teachers at the school were accustomed to the approach taken by their previous principal, Mary Green. Ms. Green was regarded as one of the truly "nice people" serving as a district administrator. She retired last spring after being the leader at Elm Street. David heard many stories about how Mary made it a point to get to know each teacher personally. She knew birthdays, the names and ages of all their children, and interesting stories about hobbies, interests, and personal lives. In short, Mary worked hard to ensure that the Elm Street faculty was always like "one big happy family" all the time.

One thing that David knew as assumed responsibility as the new Elm Street principal was that, despite his predecessor's reputation as a caring administrator, the school's performance on the state student achievement tests the last few years was not very good. The school board was demanding immediate improvement. David was now on the "hot seat," but he believed that his management style would lead to direct impact on teacher performance. Scores would rise quickly.

1. David's approach to administration could be described as _____.

   a. administrative inspection

   b. scientific management

   c. human relations

   d. human resource management

2. According to information provided, Mary Green appeared to be an administrator who believed in _____.

   a. administrative inspection

   b. scientific management

   c. human relations

   d. human resource development

3. A management assumption that seems well-suited to David's point of view is:

   a. Teachers are not to be trusted.

   b. The improvement of the school's psychosocial environment is a concern.

   c. Happy teachers are effective teachers.

   d. The duty of an effective teacher is to set standards for employee performance based on solid research, or "laws."

Additional Reading

Deming, W. Edward (1986). *Out of the crisis.* Cambridge: MIT Press.

Dobyns, Lloyd, & Crawford-Mason, Clare (1991). *Quality or else: The revolution in world business.* Boston: Houghton-Mifflin.

Glanz, Jeffrey, & Behar-Horenstein, Linda S. (eds.) (2000). *Paradigm debates in curriculum and supervision: Modern and postmodern perspectives*. Westport, CT: Bergin & Garvey.

Glickman, Carl D. (1990). *Supervision of instruction: A developmental approach* (2nd ed.) Needham Heights, MA: Addison-Wesley.

Leonard, Edwin C., Jr., & Hilgert, Raymond L. (2004). *Supervision: Concepts and practices of management* (9th ed.). Belmont, CA: South-Western College Publications/Thomson.

Sergiovanni, Thomas J. (ed.) (1982). *Supervision of teaching*. Yearbook of the Association for Supervision and Curriculum Development. Alexandria, VA: Association for Supervision and Curriculum Development.

2

Personal Assumptions Guiding Supervisory Practice

Several important assumptions underlie the process of proactive leadership. In the last chapter, we noted that effective supervisors and leaders review and consider many different perspectives concerning supervision but ultimately select one point of view and remain true to it. Such adherence to a particular perspective is encouraged, even if your stance reflects an approach to supervision based on scientific management or some other relatively unpopular view. Of course, you may change or modify a position from time to time, depending on a wide array of reasons. However, your authenticity and clarity in espousing a particular supervisory philosophy are the first important ingredients in effective proactive leadership.

Even more important in developing a framework for successful supervisory practice is an ability to analyze your own personal beliefs, attitudes, and values, as components of a clear philosophy of education. The practitioner of educational supervision who is unable to articulate basic thoughts regarding professional issues will find successful leadership difficult. Equally important, without the capacity to reflect on the beliefs that form the basis of a personal educational philosophy, you will be unable to provide others with modeling and leadership to help them grow and develop in their own roles. Without a personal vision, you cannot expect to assist your colleagues in developing a collective vision for your school.

In this chapter we examine how supervisors build effective practice on personal assumptions, and then translate that personal philosophy into a broader vision for an effective school. First, we review fundamental concepts such as beliefs, attitudes, and values. Second, we develop the concept of a personal educational philosophy as a way to clarify action planning. Third, we briefly examine the concept of reflective practice as it relates to individual philosophy formulation. Fourth, we go through a process of developing a collective vision for a school. Finally, we consider the practical implications of individual philosophy, action planning, and vision building.

❧ BELIEFS, ATTITUDES, AND VALUES

An important first step in defining a personal philosophy is to become more familiar with the meaning of such frequently used words as *beliefs*, *attitudes*, and *values* and to understand the ways in which these affect how a person behaves.

Beliefs

The primary component in a general system of values is a belief or set of beliefs, or what Milton Rokeach (1971) defined as "any simple proposition, conscious or unconscious, inferred from what a person says or does, capable of being proceeded by the phrase 'I believe that'" (p. 61). We all have hundreds, perhaps thousands of beliefs about an equally large number of things, places, people, or ideas. These notions are often short-lived because we find out that they are not correct, or because we simply do not find them important enough to grasp for very long. A person may wake up in the morning, for example, believing that the weather is hot, cold, or any one of dozens of other adjectives. That belief may be shed after hearing the radio report the day's temperature, or when the person goes outside, or when the individual gets sufficiently absorbed in some other belief that the temperature outside becomes unimportant. In schools, much of what teachers and others do is based on beliefs. Teachers are quick to explain their approaches to classroom management issues in terms related to the ways in which they believe students will act under most circumstances.

Attitudes

Attitudes are the next step in the beliefs-attitudes-values hierarchy. Again, Rokeach (1971) provides the definition: "An attitude is a relatively enduring organization of beliefs around an object or situation predisposing one to respond in some preferential manner" (p. 180). Attitudes are clusters of individual beliefs that survive the immediate moment. The belief that it is hot or cold outside may be fleeting, but our belief about temperature may create a particular attitude about the weather. Some people are happy to believe that it is cold outside because their attitude toward cold weather, built on personal beliefs, is positive.

We can certainly have incorrect attitudes based on false beliefs; this does not make the potency of the attitude any less real. Consider, for example, a belief acquired as a child based on an image—seen in a movie or on television—that politicians are corrupt. As the child grows, the belief may unite with other incorrect beliefs to form an attitude of prejudice toward all politicians. The attitude may be wrong, but it is real and may continue to influence the person for a long time unless a deliberate effort is made to change it.

Values

Rokeach (1971) defined values as "types of beliefs, centrally located within one's belief system, that address how one ought or ought not to behave, or about some end state of existence worth or not worth attaining" (p. 202). In many ways, values represent our permanent view of reality, formed and fashioned out of our more temporary beliefs and attitudes as well as the beliefs and attitudes of others in our family, neighborhood, or larger societal environment.

Awareness of some unique characteristics of individual values can increase understanding of this concept. Values represent a person's belief about ideal modes of conduct. They are generally more permanent than attitudes or beliefs, and a hierarchical order exists among our personal values. This order is based on the relative potency, durability, and stability of the values we hold. The values that are more likely to shift over time are lower in the hierarchical order. Values are not typically articulated directly by their bearers; more often than not, behavior is the strongest demonstration of our values.

Recognizing the importance of values is an important skill for those who would engage in proactive leadership. First, if you are aware of values and how they affect human behavior, you will become more appreciative of your own values about a given issue. Even the activity of talking about values tends to make us more sensitive to them and to the role they play in shaping our behavior. Thinking about the fact that people have attitudes, beliefs, and values that differ from our own is the first step toward accepting differences.

Second, educational leaders must examine the issue of values because they will be called upon to analyze the values of people who work in, around, and with schools. Developing personal competency in how to interpret the values, attitudes, and beliefs of the people associated with any organization is a critical skill; a leader who is unable to sense those things that people hold dearest to them will almost certainly be an ineffective leader. All people have absolute points beyond which they will not compromise or change. Attempting to push people beyond those limits is a serious blunder. Appreciating the value orientations of others is necessary for perceiving and dealing with those nonnegotiable issues.

Third (and perhaps most directly related to the overall concept of pro-active leadership), supervisors need insights into many value orientations because organizational leaders are often the most visible people in their organizations. To many people, supervisors represent not only their personal value systems but also the orientation of the entire school or district. Frequently, people think not of the "elementary school down the block," but of "Mrs. X's school," where Mrs. X is the principal. The leader, a values witness, provides the members of the organization with an implicit identity and a sense of "what's right" and "what we do around here."

McGregor's Assumptions

Historically, supervision has been viewed as a means to correct incompetent teachers, to promote better human relations in schools, or to increase the measurable productivity of schools. In this book, none of these three views is espoused specifically, but because each is based on a total value system supported by some people in supervisory roles, each is a legitimate way of thinking. A critical responsibility for those in supervisory positions is to examine personal values and determine how they are aligned with other perspectives. This must be done openly, so that people who work in the school are aware of where their leaders "are coming from." Most people like to work with others who hold similar values; most can work with others with whom they openly disagree; but no one can work effectively with those who attempt to hide their true value orientations.

A useful framework for analyzing individual values regarding leadership responsibility is Douglas McGregor's (1960) Theory X/Theory Y assumptions, which are often used to illustrate how people in organizations can be motivated. Russ Marion (2005) describes McGregor's philosophy as a "man-is-good/man-is-bad" debate:

> The man-is-bad thesis, which he labeled "Theory X," maintains that workers are inherently lazy, indolent, mean-spirited, and opposed to work. . . . [T]he man-is-good philosophy (Theory Y), by contrast, sees workers as basically cooperative, caring, friendly, industrious, and responsible. (p. 51)

A review of McGregor's basic assumptions is a good starting point for the leader intent on forming a personal and honest view of what leadership implies.

Theory X Assumptions

1. People are naturally lazy; when faced with a choice, they normally prefer to do nothing.
2. People work mostly for money and status rewards.
3. The main force keeping people productive in their work is fear of being demoted or fired.

4. People remain children grown larger; they are naturally dependent as learners.

5. People expect and depend on direction from above; they do not want to think for themselves.

6. People need to be told, shown, and trained in proper methods of work.

7. People need supervisors who will watch them closely enough to be able to praise good work and reprimand errors.

8. People have little concern beyond their immediate motivational interests.

9. People need specific instruction on what to do and how to do it; larger policy issues are none of their business.

10. People appreciate being treated with courtesy, even when that courtesy is not provided.

11. People are naturally compartmentalized; work demands are entirely different from leisure activities.

12. People naturally resist change; they prefer to stay in the same old ruts.

13. People are formed by heredity, childhood, and youth; as adults they remain static.

14. People need to be "inspired" through pep talks; they must be pushed or driven.

Theory Y Assumptions

1. People are naturally active; they set goals and enjoy striving to attain them.

2. People seek many satisfactions in work; pride in achievement; enjoyment of process; sense of contribution; pleasure in association; stimulation of challenges, and so forth.

3. The main force keeping people productive in their work is their desire to achieve their personal and social goals.

4. People are normally mature beyond childhood; they aspire to independence, self-fulfillment, and responsibility.

5. People close to the situation see and feel what is needed and are capable of self-direction.

6. People who understand and care about what they are doing can devise and improve their own methods for doing work.

7. People need a sense that they are respected as capable of assuming responsibility and self-direction.

8. People seek to give meaning to their lives by identifying with nations, communities, companies, or causes.

9. People need ever-increasing understanding; they need to grasp the meaning of the activities in which they are engaged; they have cognitive hunger as extensive as the universe.

10. People crave genuine respect from others.

11. People are naturally integrated; when work and play are too sharply separated they deteriorate.

12. People naturally tire of monotonous routine and enjoy new experiences; in some degree everyone is creative.

13. People constantly grow; it is never too late to learn; they enjoy learning and increasing their understanding and capability.

14. People need to be encouraged and assisted.

Two general observations can be made about the pairs of items shown in the above lists. First, most people will not agree with every item under either Theory X or Theory Y; one list will be preferable, but a few statements from the other list will probably seem more accurate. Second, true professional feelings about a particular item may not be reflected in the statements of either list; a middle ground may be preferable. Very few people could be classified as absolute Theory X or Theory Y leaders. However, considerable insight can be gained into personal values by determining which of these items seem more accurate and acceptable. Such insight is the first step toward developing a personal educational philosophy.

✑ INDIVIDUAL ACTION PLANNING

Each person has an established set of beliefs and attitudes that shape individual values. The next step is to put these concepts together into a meaningful statement to guide behavior in a leadership role. In this section, some ways are suggested to help you to assemble your most important value statements into a working personal philosophy, one that can be translated into an individual action plan.

Construct Theory

The assumptions that underlie individual action planning come from a body of theory that has had a significant impact on the ways in which teachers are initially prepared. This body of thinking is referred to as *construct theory*. Developed by George A. Kelly (1965) as a way to explain actions in terms of mental constructs, it attempts to explain how people derive signs used in making decisions about how they conduct their lives.

Antoinette Oberg (1986) said of construct theory:

> It is the major premise of Construct Theory that people's actions are based on the ways in which they anticipate future events. . . . Future events are differentiated on the basis of constructs that are attributes or qualities the events are expected to exhibit. (p. 57)

Construct theory can help us understand why effective supervision is not always "knowing all the answers" but rather developing a way of thinking through problems and asking the right questions. Donald Schön (1983), in *The Reflective Practitioner,* observed that the critical responsibility of a professional is often to recognize the nature of problems and not always to determine perfect solutions to all problems. Construct theory and the concepts of reflection-in-action by Schön are important bases for the development of personalized guides to leadership.

Educational Platform Development

The educational leader's platform, developed by Sergiovanni and Starratt (2007), is a model designed to help professional educators assess their views in a straightforward manner, akin to the platform statements made by political candidates in an election campaign. The major difference between a politician's and an educator's platform is that the latter is structured to communicate the educator's deepest and truest beliefs, attitudes, and values, even if these are contrary to the sentiments of the public.

There is no single, perfect format for an educational platform. For example, Bruce Barnett (1991) has suggested that a platform may consist of a written statement which articulates an educator's views on issues ranging from desired student outcomes to preferred school climate to expectations for community involvement in schools. Sergiovanni and Starratt's model (2007) for formulating a supervisor's educational platform includes twelve major elements. Ten of these deal with general educational themes, and as a result they can serve as the basis for any professional educator's platform. The last two are linked directly to the role of the supervisor.

1. The aims of education
2. The major achievements of students this year
3. The social significance of the student's learning
4. The supervisor's image of the learner
5. The value of the curriculum
6. The supervisor's image of the teacher
7. The preferred kind of pedagogy
8. The primary language of discourse in learning situations
9. The preferred kind of student-teacher relationships
10. The preferred kind of school climate
11. The purpose or goal of supervision
12. The preferred process of supervision

The following excerpts from two well-developed statements—the first by an experienced classroom teacher contemplating a supervisory career and the second by a beginning elementary school principal—illustrate how writing a platform helps define personal views.

Aims of Education

(Teacher) The aims of education are threefold. First, the schools must help each student to acquire a sense of self-fulfillment and self-worth in which all children can discover and realize their own unique talents, gifts, and abilities. . . . Secondly, our schools must help students create and maintain meaningful relationships with others. They must help students learn how to communicate . . . their needs, attitudes, concerns, and appreciation. . . . Finally, educators should enable students to become productive, responsible citizens in our society. Schools need to impart the basic knowledge, develop creative expression, and provide a variety of experiences that will enable each student to assume a role within one's community, one's country, and one's world. . . .

(Principal) I believe it is the responsibility of education and educators to develop students' self-esteem and self-worth, creating the situations and/or environment when necessary . . . we must use extra effort to improve students' self-esteem when the home situation or personal environment is abusive, unnurturing, or uncaring; develop students' ability to get along in society . . .; give all students the opportunity to build a foundation of basic knowledge and develop strategies to enable them to achieve future goals; help students understand the advantages of developing a lifelong learner attitude.

Major Achievements of Students This Year

(Teacher) The major achievements I would hope to have my children display by the end of the year include both academic achievements and personal achievements. As a first grade teacher, I hope that my children will acquire the basic skills, concepts, and information that they will need in order to continue in their educational pursuits. . . .

(Principal) I believe that a major achievement of a student at any age is to be satisfied with his or her learning accomplishments and yet to strive to do his or her best. As students mature, education must put more emphasis on the process of setting learning goals or life goals and to develop certain attitudes and beliefs toward the learning process. . . .

Social Significance of the Students' Learning

(Teacher) Our children are our future. Therefore, student learning profoundly affects us in that students' views of the world begin to take shape during the school years. Out of the student population will come the future leaders and decision makers of our country. . . .

(Principal) I believe that part of what students are expected to learn in the educational setting involves societal behaviors, and there are certain requirements that society dictates. Education is partly responsible for developing productive individuals. . . . I believe we all need to do a better job helping students understand the importance of developing interpersonal relationships with a variety of different personalities. . . .

The Image of the Learner

(Teacher) Children are unique. Therefore, their ability to acquire and retain new knowledge and skills is unique. One method of instruction, although it may be appropriate for a percentage of the children within a classroom, cannot adequately meet the individual needs and learning styles of the remainder of the children. Thus, in order to motivate children to greater degrees of personal success, it is necessary to provide a variety of learning strategies within a classroom. . . .

(Principal) Educators perceive the learner in a variety of situations and in a variety of performance modes. Through experience and observation, educators make assumptions of students' visual, auditory, tactile, and kinesthetic learning styles and should help students understand their most preferred learning style. Educators see students as individuals who want to gain knowledge or understanding through study, instruction, and experience. Adjectives that describe the learner are responsible, enthusiastic, inquisitive, attentive, hard working . . . and the opposite of each adjective as well. . . .

Value of the Curriculum

(Teacher) In essence, the curriculum is a composite of all experiences, planned and unplanned, that constitute the learning of the individual. These learnings occur both within and outside of the classroom. Those experiences which children encounter through the interaction with their families and peers, through the mass media, such as television, radio, magazines, and newspapers, and through social and religious organizations strongly impact the curriculum that is presented in schools. Therefore, in designing and developing curricula for schools, this "hidden" curriculum needs to be recognized, acknowledged, and planned for specifically. In so doing, the teacher can be proactive rather than reactive in providing the optimal learning experiences for each child. . . .

(Principal) By articulating the curriculum (the vision, mission statements, proficiencies, outcomes, objectives, etc.) the focus and direction of the school becomes evident. The curriculum is a means through which educators can reflect on the value or importance of the information taught, make recommendations for adjustments, and be more accountable for the results. The curriculum is also a means to communicate to parents and communities the nature of desired educational goals.

The Image of the Teacher

(Teacher) A teacher is an individual with a specific purpose or mission. The teacher with a mission has a deep underlying belief that students can grow and attain self-actualization. Teachers believe that they have something of significance to contribute to other people, especially students, and believe with every fiber of their being that they can "make a difference." Teachers believe that children can and want to learn and are driven from within to find the technique or strategy that will assist each child to learn. . . . Teachers also achieve high personal satisfaction and inner joy from the growth of their students. They seek out the resources necessary to stimulate and activate learning with the student and are excited when students think, respond, and learn. . . . A teacher is also a contributing member of the larger school setting and should value working closely with the principal and other staff personnel.

(Principal) Since teachers work with . . . our children, I expect them to:
- Possess a certain set of high standards and moral values.
- Be caring and concerned about the education and welfare of students.
- Be service-oriented and have a high sense of achievement.
- Have a positive attitude about people, especially children.
- Be a dispenser of knowledge and a translator of culture.
- Be knowledgeable, enthusiastic, and hard working.
- Be challenging and understanding.
- Be a friend, advisor, and counselor.
- Be an observer, facilitator, and role model.
- Work miracles.

Preferred Kind of Pedagogy

(Teacher) As a first grade teacher, I employ a multitude of ideas, materials, and experiences when helping my children to learn. Because of age, experiences, and socialization of first graders, at the beginning of the year I find it necessary to assume a more directive role within my classroom. I feel this is appropriate and necessary in order to help six- and seven-year-olds feel safe and secure in their new environment and to help them make a transition from a more home-centered world into a more school-centered world. . . . As I work within my classroom, . . . I also utilize the larger resources of the school. These include other students, the principal, the media specialist, the special area teachers . . . the guidance counselor, the psychologist, and our teacher aides. I believe that it takes many caring and concerned individuals to help a child learn and grow into a healthy, productive adult. . . .

(Principal) I am discovering that personality styles and temperaments affect all that we do. I can't state that one teaching style is preferable over another. Different kinds of pedagogy can be effective depending on . . . situations, subject areas, skills to be taught, educator style, and temperament of student groups. The important issue is how educators use their own temperament to establish and maintain a facilitative relationship with the differing temperaments of the student groups. . . .

Primary Language of Discourse in Learning Situations

(Teacher) Children learn best when they are involved and when the material presented is relevant to their interests and needs. Therefore, the language within the classroom should foster communication. This communication can take many forms: discussion, lecture, questions and answers, dialogue, and role-playing. But whatever form that it takes, it should have at its base the interests and needs of the child. . . .

(Principal) Communication is the essence of education, possibly in all industries. Communication can be orderly and thought provoking, imaginative and open, feeling and nurturing, or conflicting and confusing. Communication involves sending and receiving messages. An educator must give praise; give instructions; ask and answer questions; deal with conflict and emotions; and be friendly, positive, stern, caring, and aware of students' needs. With the interests of the child in mind, we need to improve our skills in active listening, observing, interpreting messages, using appropriate acknowledgements, using door openers, paraphrasing; giving feedback, and maybe sometimes just being silent. Communication is both verbal and nonverbal. The educator must realize the importance of nonverbal communication and be consistent in the conveyed messages. Effective communication is a vital and complex process and not easily accomplished.

Preferred Kind of Teacher-Student Relationships

(Teacher) The relationship established between the teacher and the student has a profound effect upon the child's ability to function and learn to his or her optimal level. A teacher's priority is to foster a safe environment in which each child feels a sense of belonging, importance, and acceptance. If this is established, the child is able to channel his or her energy into positive . . . learning rather than withdrawing from the learning situation in a negative way. . . . It is important for the teacher to understand that each child is unique and that a teacher's expectations for one student might not be the same for other students. . . .

(Principal) The interpersonal relationships that occur and the bonds that are formed between teacher and student are very special. We must admit that our children spend a great deal of time at school. In addition to the time involved in daily academic instruction, we have to consider all the extracurricular activities, practices, and athletic events which contribute to the overall growth and development of the . . . child. By nature, people become involved in such activities to satisfy the need for group belonging and interpersonal relationships. Students often look up to educators with admiration. Educators who give praise and encouragement might be the only positive influence in some students' lives. It is not surprising that strong bonds and relationships are formed.

Preferred Kind of Climate

(Teacher) An atmosphere of trust and safety must be created within a classroom. Within this environment, each child's unique needs and interests can be met. Because all students are different, they have different requirements for openness and structure, for movement and control, for an opportunity to work in groups, or for the need to work alone. It is important to meet these differences, and to help children create an awareness and understanding of the similarities and differences that they share. . . .

(Principal) The school climate is affected by educator attitudes, how staff relates to administration, the amount of collegiality that exists, teacher-student relationships, and school-community relationships. I believe that attitudes might be the key to a positive climate. The students are unable to feel the general attitudes of the staff, which will be filtered to the parents and into the communities. The teachers will produce a more comfortable and safe climate for the students if these attitudes consist of openness, trust, and honesty. Likewise, when community groups are not positive about school issues or staff members, this will have an effect on the students and staff and their climate as a whole. Educators need to be continually aware of the relationship between school and community and present an open-door policy at all times. Schools need the support of parents and communities and should do what they can to nurture and develop this relationship.

Purpose of Supervision

(Teacher) The purpose of supervision is to maximize children's learning. This is accomplished by directly improving the quality of a teacher's instruction within the classroom. A supervisor, therefore, is an individual whose responsibility and desire are to help teachers recognize and capitalize on their strengths. A supervisor must also understand and assume responsibility for the goals and priorities of the organization as a whole. This requires that the supervisor often bridge the gap between the interests and needs of the teachers and those of the administration. Thus, the supervisor's role often entails effective communication and advocacy—advocacy of the teacher and advocacy of the administrator. The supervisor must clearly visualize how each separate part of the organization fits together for the benefit of the whole and be able to take the steps necessary to accomplish this end. The supervisor must be genuinely concerned and comfortable with each group and be able to effectively merge their varied concerns and transcend the difficulties to a level of greater excellence for the total organization. In order to accomplish this, supervisors must clearly understand their personal platforms. This has the potential of creating a climate of trust and credibility between supervisors and all parties involved. When this is achieved, the needs of the child are enhanced, and that is our primary focus as educators.

(Principal) I have some administrative colleagues who really believe that supervision should be a way to find out what's wrong with a school. They use it as a kind of quality-control process that can help them weed out teachers and staff who are not doing the job. I disagree with that perspective. Instead, I think that the real purpose of supervision should somehow be to identify the strengths that people have and to build on those. If people make mistakes and need help, that should also be something which occurs in the supervisory process. Dealing with mistakes can be done in a way that promotes growth and professional development, not simply with finding fault with others' performance.

Preferred Process of Supervision

(Teacher) As I grow in my understanding of supervision . . . , I believe that there is no one best way to supervise. I realize that each institution is different and that each individual is unique. It is my responsibility as a supervisor to evaluate and to respond to each condition by gathering and accessing the data surrounding that particular situation.

I would respond to the inherent worth and value of each individual, and this belief would be a strong guide as I interact with colleagues. I believe that growth is attained when the strengths of an individual are determined and those strengths are developed and encouraged. By identifying and developing strengths, I believe that the personal dignity of the individual is preserved and that this is the foundation upon which change and growth can occur. I feel that as I would direct and encourage teachers to utilize their strengths to their greatest potential, they would, in turn, direct their abilities to more productive instruction of the children.

I see myself as applying the human resources philosophy. When members of an organization understand the goals of that organization, and they become agents by which those goals are achieved, then growth within those members is attainable to a higher degree. Personal self-attainment is energizing, both to the individual and to the organization, and creates an atmosphere of good will, trust, and greater cooperation. This has a cyclic effect. Within the organization, participation should be encouraged at the level at which an individual is capable; understanding that each person has his or her own personal "timing" and will develop accordingly. It would be necessary to stimulate learning for each staff member by offering many opportunities for personal and professional growth, such as inservices, workshops, conferences, and involvement in specific interest groups. . . . In this way, supervisors can, by acknowledging the control of the growth of the teachers as their colleagues, internalize and expand the ownership in the goals of the district.

(Principal) The main challenge that I face as an educational leader is to promote learning in my school. That learning, of course, is most directly related to children. However, it also includes the promotion of effective learning among all who work in our school. . . . As a result, the kind of supervisory process that I believe that I follow is one that does not emphasize making judgments about others' competence. Instead, what I hope that I emphasize is always a supervisory style that encourages individual growth and development. In other words, I encourage people to do what it takes to become all that they can be . . . even if that means making mistakes from time to time.

Others who have engaged in the platform preparation process have written their beliefs in ways much different than the two models shown here, which followed the outline presented earlier. Consider, for example, some of the comments made in the following statement prepared by an experienced school building administrator who left campus leadership after serving as a successful assistant principal and principal for a number of years and now works in a central office position. Note that, instead of responding to individual issues, this person has made a general statement about his role as an administrator:

I was an English teacher for 19 years in two different states. I have been an administrator for 11 years. My core beliefs as an administrator have been influenced by my years as a teacher. For instance, my core belief that a principal's main objective should be to keep his or her teachers happy is founded in my experience as a teacher. A happy teacher is able to keep students happy, and happy students keep parents happy, and happy parents help keep the school staff happy and on and on.

A definition of happy is necessary. The happy of which I speak is a feeling that is based on one's internal state exhibited externally. A happy person feels good about him- or herself, is caring, sees a bright future, is constantly seeking to improve, and is self-evaluating. A person cannot be "happy" all the time, but a happy person exhibits the above most of the time.

The goal of keeping teachers happy has helped me grow as an administrator, not only in my professional reading, but also in the way I supervise and administer. I believe that all employees must be given room to grow, which involves trust on my part as an administrator which I believe leads to employees trusting their administrator. I believe I am to provide a variety of means for success, and then let my employees seek the ones in which the employee can grow. . . .

I also believe that I must be prepared to change and take risks if I expect my employees to do both. Therefore, I must model what I say I believe in. I should admit mistakes, take criticism, self-evaluate and improve in all my areas of my professional life. I should always consider the effect of any decision that I make. I should therefore be willing to listen, communicate and encourage, for I know that many employees look to their administrator for the mood of the workplace. . . .

Shared decision making is a must if anyone is to take ownership. Therefore, my role as an administrator is to involve employees in the decision-making process. I must be willing to truly listen and make changes in my thinking as long as the students are considered. A core belief that drives this thinking is that all decisions are based on the ultimate good of the student. . . . What I model for the teachers, I want the teacher to model for the student. . . .

As administrator, it is my responsibility to make sure that all are doing quality work. It is not easy; quality is not easy. The result is well worth the effort, however. Not to strive, persuade, teach, and model quality is not to live life fully. The satisfaction of a job well done is a singular reward worth pursuing, for it brings the inner joy that makes external happiness authentic.

Preparing and periodically revising an educational platform is useful for a number of reasons. Writing a formal educational platform requires a person to articulate many of the ideals taken for granted as a person goes about business in a particular role. Highly experienced educators praise the platform-writing process because it is a disciplined way to express sets of beliefs, attitudes, and values they may have forgotten over the years; it results in a formal agenda that allows one to see and then confront ideas that are rarely stated; and it allows one to make values more visible to others. It is not recommended to circulate copies of a personal platform as a standard practice, but a well-prepared platform can be a useful tool for sharing important personal feelings with others who need to know those beliefs. In addition, a formal statement can help a person gain greater insights into fundamental nonnegotiable values.

Finally, the articulation of a personal educational platform can be a most valuable experience for anyone who may be contemplating a career shift into the field of school administration or supervision. This is consistent with the recommendation of the National Policy Board for Educational Administration (1989), which noted that it is important for aspiring educational leaders to explore their personal values and attitudes as they consider new career options.

> . . . students [of educational leadership] must be pushed to examine their own belief systems, their reasons for wanting to be administrators, their images of the missions of schooling as a social process. The curriculum should be designed to provide frameworks and tools to assist students in assessing the moral and ethical implications of administrative decisions in schools. They must come to understand the concept of public trust and to realize how values affect behaviors and outcomes. (p. 9)

Everyone who works in any organization wonders from time to time whether or not to stay in a particular position. Sometimes an organization changes to the extent that it no longer seems to represent values that were once appealing. A formal platform statement is a visible and constant reminder of what an educator holds in great esteem. Its real value may to help answer the question, "What is so important to me that I would quit rather than compromise?"

Reflective Practice and the Action Plan

Articulating an educational platform is an extremely powerful activity for reviewing professional and personal values, but it is little more than an exercise unless it is combined with an action plan. An action plan need not be a formal statement with a predetermined number of elements as in a platform, but it should list actions that will enable a person to look at a present role and determine how personal behavior actually matches both the platform and the characteristics of the job.

The earlier excerpts from the platforms of the principal and the teacher also included statements of analysis and commitments to personal action. For example, consider how the teacher moved from her initial platform to a statement of analysis, and then to a personal action plan:

Platform Analysis

> The writing of my platform has been a challenging and valuable undertaking. I feel these beliefs and assumptions, but have never articulated them until now. This has been an affirming exercise, but at the same time, I realize that I am also in process. I am not the same person today that I was yesterday. Nor will I be the same person tomorrow as I am today. . . . I know that should I ever step out of the process, I will stop growing as a person and will lose any effectiveness that I may have as a teacher and a supervisor. . . . I found as I placed my thoughts on paper that there was an element of interrelatedness among the different themes. In order to achieve one aspect of my platform, I need to build upon the others. As a result, I sense a unified direction for myself. It is as though I have developed a focus, and that the confusion that accompanies indecision is removed. As a

teacher I know what I am about and feel that what I do is valuable. Yet, as I began to express my thoughts regarding supervision, I found myself searching for clarity. My experience in personnel, in facilitating student and adult groups . . . has given me a background of understanding. There are still gaps in this understanding. This is what is directing me to get a better understanding of the field of supervision.

Personal Action Plan
I plan:
1. To exercise my belief that learning is a lifelong adventure. This would include my present goals.
2. To become a more effective classroom teacher, and to continually seek the resources that will permit children to reach their greatest potential.
3. To encourage and assist in the development of staff within my particular school and within the district. To plan and implement with my principal a specific plan for staff support and supervision.
4. To evaluate my growth and needed areas of growth with my supervisors and the participants involved in my experience.
5. To continually clarify my educational platform by asking the question, "What is best for children?"

The principal concludes with the following statement of actions that she wishes to carry out for her professional development in the future:
1. Work on becoming more of a visionary leader who can pull the group together for a common goal.
2. Improve my evaluation techniques, time management skills, and legal knowledge.
3. Improve my communication skills and interpersonal skills.
4. Be a good model for the students and the staff.
5. Develop trusting and open relationships with students and the staff.
6. Spend more time expressing appreciation and acceptance of the staff and students.
7. Become a proactive leader.

These two action plans allow the teacher and the principal to examine the major non-negotiable issues described in their original platform statements and to seek a series of important personal professional development objectives. Action planning allows the platform writer to come full cycle from an original statement of philosophy to a statement of action.

One additional issue regarding the development of an educational platform is an important item to remember. It is relatively easy to fill a platform statement with many commendable, nice-sounding, or even politically correct items. One example might be the stated belief that "all children can learn." While there is no disagreement with the essence of that statement, the doubt arises when that type of commendable view is not supported by apparent behaviors. Can we see the teacher or supervisor acting in a daily way to engage in active support of the espoused beliefs? It is important for a person to state a philosophy as a way to guide action, and to share values and beliefs with others. However, statements of belief need to be honest and consistent with actual practice. Nothing could be worse than saying one thing and not "walking the talk."

DEVELOPING A VISION FOR THE SCHOOL

It should be evident that a central feature of effective, proactive leadership involves the ability of the individual to develop a sense of what she or he wishes to do as a leader. Beyond that personal developmental process, there is also a duty of the leader to extend the logic of articulating core beliefs and values to the organizational level through the process of leading the school toward a common vision, or "organizational platform." In recent years, writers have stressed the importance of "visioning" as a central duty of leaders in many settings. In the following section, a strategy for the educational leader to follow in working with a staff in developing a group vision, or platform, is outlined.

The Ideal School

According to Lunenburg and Ornstein (2004), "Vision that reflects only the leader's view is bound to fail, since it lacks motivational appeal with which people can identify" (p. 355). The first step in establishing a vision in any organization involves the process of bringing together people who work in that organization, to do a bit of dreaming. In essence, when a vision is established, it represents a collective value of what is the very best that can possibly happen. Some may even say that the best vision is something that is unattainable, although simply beginning the discussion of how to envision a desirable end state as a kind of unrealistic "exercise in futility" is not a good starting point. On the other hand, setting sights on things which may be easily obtained with little effort, is rarely going to move an organization onto greater accomplishment.

Often, the process of establishing a collective vision in a school might begin with a general question posed to the entire faculty, or at least to a critical mass of individuals who represent the diverse views of the larger group:

> *Think about the kind of school you would want your own child to attend. Think about some of the things that would be seen in that school.*

This question serves several purposes as a starting point for the discussion of a vision set for a school. First, it asks participants to personalize the process. While it is relatively easy to talk about something in "the third person" or as some sort of inanimate institution, asking people to consider something as personally important as their own child's education moves the discussion to a more emotional level. Suddenly, participants in the vision-building process are engaged in considering something with high stakes and important outcomes.

Inevitably, this first question results in discussions that provide a rich description of the ideal school. Under most circumstances, participants move well beyond "scientific" or "political" statements regarding achievement test scores or statistical data regarding dropout rates. Instead, what often appears at this first stage are statements such as "a school where people care about each child as an individual," or "a place where everyone feels involved," and so forth.

Operationalizing the Ideal

While the first step can involve imagining and considering the very best scenario possible, it is critical that the vision-building process move quickly toward a more concrete stage. Joel Barker (1996), the well-known futurist, has noted that a "vision without action is only a dream." Unfortunately, schools cannot function effectively as dreamworlds. As a result, the process needs to consider a series of questions about this ideal school, to take the discussion to the next level:

- What are some student behaviors you would observe in the classroom? In the halls? On the playground? In what types of activities would students be engaged?
- What teacher behaviors would you expect to see? How would the teachers act? What would their interactions with students be like? What would you expect to see in faculty meetings?
- What behaviors and practices would you expect of the principal and other administrators in the school? How would they interact with students? With teachers?
- What kinds of behaviors would you expect to see in an ideal school on the part of the other adults who work in the school, such as the custodians, clerks, cafeteria workers, and others?
- What would the school district administration be doing to support the vision of the school?

Responding to these questions moves the process to the level of operationalization very quickly. No longer is it possible to say simply that, "In our ideal school, everyone cares for everyone else." Rather, it is now important to consider how "care" is actually played out. Does it mean that teachers do not reprimand or discipline students? Probably not, but in the "caring" school environment, there may be a way of disciplining students in a very different way than one might see in other settings.

Similarly, the interactions between principals and teachers might be one where respect is evident through the nature of dialogue. In other schools, principals might treat teachers as adversaries who need to be "talked down to." In the ideal, caring school, dialogue among professional colleagues might be the rule, as evidenced by the principal talking informally with many teachers, staff members, and others throughout the course of a typical day. In the caring school, custodians might never be ordered to "clean up my office" or classroom as if they were present only to attend to the chores teachers and others did not wish to do. Instead, they might be treated with respect and dignity, as true members of the school's team of professionals. Even that observation prompts further discussion about "how" things might look in a school where professional respect was present.

The critical thing at this stage is not that every possible answer to every question listed above is answered. Rather, the critical issue is the nature of dialogue and the brainstorming that occurs with respect to issues often overlooked in schools because "things are too busy."

Sharing Values

Simultaneous to the consideration of questions noted above, conversation must take place involving a review of mutually held values and beliefs by those who would participate in the "ideal school."

What do we believe about schools, students, teachers, administrators, and staff who work in the ideal school? Why are these beliefs important? What would be accomplished by putting these beliefs in place?

As described in the section dealing with personal platform development, the foundation for any action must be beliefs and values. That is as true for a school staff as it is for the individual educator. Dreaming about the ideal, noting a "wish list" of desirable practices and behaviors, and a great deal of conversation is not likely to result in actual behavioral change or commitment if these activities are not founded on a core belief system. All the descriptions in the world concerning "caring" in a school will be hollow if teachers do not trust and respect their students. Teachers and principals can appear to work in harmony but will not do so in reality if they view each other as enemies. Talking respectfully to secretaries may be a good show, but it will never change the way a school really operates if teachers look down on the staff.

Translating the Vision into Action

Discussions of the ideal school are important conversations that need to take place among the leader and the other members of the school community. In and of themselves, these sessions serve to open lines of dialogue and enable people to learn more about other platforms. However, the discussions themselves must move forward to another level of action if they are to have an effect on the school.

In describing the individual platform-building process, it was noted that the most important step was the personal commitment to action through a statement of an individual action plan. The same is true of a larger organization. After a review of ideal vision, values, and desirable behaviors, the last step in the vision-development process must be a public statement and a commitment to action so that the organization lives up to its internal promises.

Often, the term used for the public declaration of an organization's vision and commitment is *mission statement*. The schema suggested in figure 2.1 may serve as a kind of blueprint to be followed in writing a mission statement for a school.

The mission of this organization IS TO . . .

> . . . IN A WAY THAT . . .

> . . . SO THAT . . .

Figure 2.1.   Framework to be followed in writing a mission statement

What is critical to note here is that, while we often see rather detailed statements of mission hanging on the walls of schools (and hotels, restaurants, insurance companies, etc.), the actual mission statement is a simple and straightforward response to: "What do we want to do, how do we do it, and why do we do it?" In figure 2.2, some of the blanks from the earlier diagram are completed.

The mission of this school IS TO . . .

> *Provide all children with a comprehensive high school educational program*

> . . . IN A WAY THAT . . .

> *encourages the pursuit of high academic goals and the development of personal interests and skills*

> . . . SO THAT . . .

> *students may be well prepared for whatever goals they have after high school graduation.*

Figure 2.2.   A basic mission statement for a high school

This hypothetical mission statement for an imaginary high school could be criticized because it is rather simple, or because it includes neither details about how it will be achieved nor specific goals. It is meant to serve only as an illustration of fundamental issues that may be addressed. In a real setting, greater detail would no doubt be included about the relationship of the individual school to district goals, special needs of students, or the ways in which the school is designed to serve the unique features of a particular community.

One final part of the vision and mission-building process that must be understood is that, like the individual platform statement, the words selected are never set in concrete. Periodic reflection and review of what an organization says it does or wants to do are critical to ensure that the mission statement remains reflective of current reality.

⚮ Summary

This chapter introduces the most critical and basic aspect of supervision as proactive leadership: To be most effective, educational leaders must be aware of their personal assumptions, beliefs, attitudes, and values.

Beliefs and values change frequently during a person's life, with values being more permanent. However, values can be modified over time. Personal values can be put together in a coherent statement to guide leadership practice, using procedures involving two separate but related tools: an individual educational platform and an action plan. Writing these as a formal activity helps individual educators to understand and demonstrate their most important values.

Similarly, schools as organizations need to reflect on their "platforms" from time to time, since the values shared by everyone in the school form the overall sense of what a particular school is all about. As a result, it is recommended that the entire school community go through a periodic process of considering its vision, values, and behaviors. Further, these characteristics need to be shared openly and publicly in the form of a thoughtful mission statement.

Becoming aware of personal values will benefit individuals and the organizations in which they work. Awareness of shared values and beliefs held within a single organization has a similar positive benefit on what others know about and understand in terms of the overall school as an organization.

Suggested Activities

1. Formulate your own educational platform, using any format presented in this chapter, or through a design of your own creation. As preservice students, many of you will not be able to address every element suggested here, but try to define your feelings about as many important educational issues as possible. What do you consider to be the primary aims of education? What is your image of the learner? What pedagogical methods do you prefer? Why should people be supervised?

2. Review the educational platform that you have developed. In what ways can your values and beliefs about education be put into action in

supervisory practice? Make a brief, informal list of actual behaviors or objectives that would enable you to put your beliefs into action.

3. As you review your platform, write down one or more observable behaviors you demonstrate, allowing others to recognize that you consistently put your beliefs into action. By contrast, identify any of your value statements in the platform that are often contradicted by your normal practice and behavior.

4. Share your platform statement with someone who knows you quite well and ask him or her to provide a critique. Is what you say you believe reflected in what you do on a regular basis?

5. Collect the public mission statements offered by at least three different organizations. These organizations need not be schools. Review the mission statements in terms of their ability to provide the reader with a sense of what the organization does, and what values it espouses. If you are familiar with the organization, also critique the mission statement in terms of its accuracy—that is, does it really state what the organization is all about?

Cases to Consider

The brief cases below are based on actual situations which have taken place in schools. Please read each case and consider the following:

- What are the critical issues raised in each case, as they relate to the topics covered in this chapter of the text?

- How does each case relate to the development of the concept of proactive leadership as it was defined in chapter 1?

- In what ways might you suggest a resolution to the issues raised?

Case 2.1   It's All in the Numbers

After nine years as a teacher, and now five more years as an assistant principal in the Rio Verde Schools, Tom Watkins believed that it was time for a first principalship. He had received a lot of praise from colleagues, parents, students, teachers, and others regarding the ways he had been able to work effectively with his principal at Julio Marquez Middle School. Together with the teachers, they had developed a new program designed to focus on the needs of all students. They called the program "The Whole Child," and its focus was on making certain that academic performance was high, as well as ensuring that attention was placed on all other areas of development such as social skills and self-esteem. The program was something in which Tom took great pride because it truly reflected values he had for his entire career. It was time to look for a principalship, but Rio Verde simply did not have any openings, and given its small size it was unlikely that Tom would find a position in the district in the near future.

Tom applied for the principalship that was posted for the Hawkins Intermediate School in the neighboring Waterville Local Schools. From what he knew about the place, it sounded like a terrific opportunity. After all, Hawkins School, like all the schools in the Waterville district, had received a recent award from the state department of education as a result of its performance on the statewide student achievement test. Tom went through a series of interviews involving teachers, the assistant principals, parents, and the Campus Decision Team at Hawkins. Their recommendation was unanimous and positive: They liked Tom and wanted him to be their new leader. A recommendation was sent forward to the superintendent of schools for Waterville, Carl Ashby.

When Tom went to meet Mr. Ashby, he was extremely enthusiastic about the probability that he would soon be a principal. But after about 20 minutes of conversation with the superintendent, he was no longer so sure about the move. After a few minutes of general conversation, Ashby leaned over his desk and looked Tom directly in the eye. "Let's be honest. The thing I like best about your background is that it's clear that you get teachers to follow you. They seem to like you, and that's what we need—someone who can get in there and make sure that the teachers keep working with the kids on the state tests each year. We have to keep those scores up. I'm sure you know, Tom, that it's all in the numbers here."

Case 2.2   The First Job

Mary Ann Callahan was really excited about the phone call she just received. The superintendent of the Climbing Vine Schools had called her to say that he and the assistant superintendent had decided to offer her the job as an elementary principal in their school system. Mary Ann, a primary teacher for 16 years, had worked hard to complete the courses needed for administrator certification at her local university. Now she was eager to leave the classroom and put her ideas to work as a real-life principal.

Her first inclination was to accept the position at Climbing Vine. The pay was good, it wasn't far from home, and the building where she would work was only three years old. As she got into her car to drive over to the superintendent's office to discuss some of the details of the new job, she started to think again about her readiness to take the job.

When the superintendent called, he made no mention of any of the input he had gotten from the people who had interviewed her last Monday. In fact, there was no mention of any of the ideas that she shared with the interview team or any of the other central office administrators with whom she had talked. And what about the feedback the superintendent must have received from other district principals? Surely there must have been some concerns about a few ideas that Mary Ann had shared in her discussions with that group. She knew that there were at least two other elementary principals who disagreed with some of her views concerning teacher professional development. In short, the district administrator acted as if he had received no feedback from anyone else when he made his decision.

As Mary Ann reflected on the interview process that she had gone through, she recalled how careful she had been to point out that she would always seek input concerning any important decisions she would make as a principal. Fostering a strong sense of community in her building through promoting consensus would be at the heart of her approach to leadership and problem solving.

Applying the Concepts

The following brief quiz is designed to improve your skills in applying some of the concepts discussed in this chapter. Read the brief introductory case and then respond to the multiple-choice questions. You will find the answers in the Appendix.

When Clarence Witherspoon became the principal at Crestview Street Middle School, he quickly recognized that one of the issues he would be facing concerned the fact that many of his teachers who had worked in the school for several years were witnessing major changes in the neighborhood around the school. Less than ten years ago, the Crestview community was described as middle- to upper-middle class, and few minority students had attended the school. In the last few years, however, Crestview Middle School had enrolled many students of color who came from homes that could be described as impoverished. An increasing number of students had limited proficiency in English. In short, it was a very different Crestview than the place where many of the teachers had begun their work. Clarence heard from his teachers that the lower achievement scores now being seen were due to "the type of students we now have. They come from backgrounds where they simply cannot learn and perform as well academically."

1. One way to describe the belief systems of many of Clarence's teachers is to note that _____.
   a. they do not care about students any more.
   b. they have developed faulty personal theories of educational achievement by poor, minority students.
   c. they are racists who do not want children to succeed.
   d. they are not very effective teachers, and they should be dismissed immediately.

2. An inservice strategy that Clarence could try in working with his teachers is _____.
   a. to lecture to his teachers on the importance of not being biased and racially prejudiced.
   b. to invite an expert in sensitivity training to ensure that teachers are no longer prejudiced against minority students.
   c. to work with teachers in examining disaggregated test data to identify where groups of students seem to be experiencing difficulties and develop a plan of action to assist those students.

d. to provide training that would reinforce teachers' recognition of the deficiencies that some children have because of their backgrounds.

Additional Reading

Ackerman, Richard H., Donaldson, Gordon A., Jr., & Van Der Bogert, Rebecca (1996). *Making sense as a school leader*. San Francisco: Jossey-Bass.

Alvy, Harvey B., & Robbins, Pam (1998). *If I only knew: Success strategies for navigating the principalship*. Thousand Oaks, CA: Corwin Press.

Argyris, Chris (1982). *Reasoning, learning, and action: Individual and organizational*. San Francisco: Jossey-Bass.

Barth, Roland (1990). *Improving schools from within*. San Francisco: Jossey-Bass.

Deal, Terrence E., & Peterson, Kent D. (1994). *The leadership paradox*. San Francisco: Jossey-Bass.

Fullan, Michael (2001). *The new meaning of educational change*. New York: Teachers College Press.

Kottkamp, Robert (1982). The administrative platform in administrator preparation. *Planning and Changing, 13:* 82–92.

Osterman, Karen F., & Kottkamp, Robert B. (1993). *Reflective practice for educators*. Thousand Oaks, CA: Corwin Press.

Raven, J. (1981). The most important problem in education is to come to term with values. *Oxford Review of Education, 7* (2): 50–67.

Sanders, Donald P., & McCutcheon, Gail (1986). The development of practical theories of teaching. *Journal of Curriculum and Supervision, 2* (1): 253–272.

Schön, Donald A. (1987). *Educating the reflective practitioner*. San Francisco: Jossey-Bass.

Sergiovanni, Thomas J. (1987). *The principalship: A reflective perspective*. Boston: Allyn & Bacon.

Thorpe, Ronald (ed.) (1995). *The first year as principal: Real world stories from America's principals*. Portsmouth, NH: Heinemann.

West, Sylvia (1993). *Educational values for school leadership*. London: Kogan Page.

PART II

Theory into Practice

Throughout Part I, the argument was made that the most practical way to understand educational leadership and supervision is as a set of process skills, rather than as simply a specific job or role. Part II presents and analyzes a series of analytic "tools"—theories advanced by various perspectives in the social sciences—to help those who are engaged in leadership activities. Only through this use of theory to guide action can educational leaders function in a dynamic, proactive way.

3

The Role of Theory in Improving Supervisory Practice

An important assumption throughout this text is that an understanding of theory in the social sciences represents a critical step toward enhancing our appreciation and understanding of effective supervisory practice: It is a way to gain important insights into how things work in organizations. One very practical consideration serves to support this assumption. When our perspectives are rooted in theory, we also have access to a way of guiding our behaviors in everyday problems and situations. As a consequence, our actions will be based on something other than the same tired answers to the same tired questions. Developing a basic understanding of what theory is and how it can be applied to local school settings will greatly contribute to your mastery of proactive leadership.

BACKGROUND OF THEORY IN EDUCATIONAL LEADERSHIP

The belief that looking at theory grounded in the social sciences is an important foundation for understanding educational leadership and administration is not new. Since the 1870s, there have been numerous attempts to develop a set of principles to guide the training and preparation of future educational administrators in this country. In the 1940s, this effort seemed to find an established foundation, not in education but in other related social science fields. A half-century ago, scholars and practitioners began turning to work in organizational psychology, sociology, and other social sciences as a way to understand what those who direct the work of schools should do. This is often referred to in the literature as the beginning of the *theory movement in educational administration*. Jack Culbertson (1988), in his review of the development of school administration as a field of practice and scholarship, noted that this era of trying to identify specific approaches to a science based on existing theories has served as the basis for research and practice in the field for many years. Culbertson (1988) noted the following as a critical moment in administrative history:

> Perhaps the most influential social science book of the 1940s was Herbert Simon's *Administrative Behavior* (1945). Innovative in its design, the book influenced administration in far-reaching ways. Early in the book, Simon noted he had not elaborated "first principles" but had used the tenets of logical positivism "as a starting point" for his decision-making theory. His work provided the most direct conduit in the 1940s for the flow of "administrative science" into educational administration. (pp. 12–13)

The 1940s, 1950s, and 1960s became known as the period of educational administration as a function of social science theory. Among the greatest contributors of that time were noted scholars such as Roald Campbell (1957), Andrew Halpin (1957), and Daniel Griffiths (1982), all of whom have left a powerful legacy wherein the field of educational supervision and administration moved from a job related to responding to immediate school crises to a field built upon serious research and vision.

As noted in the first chapter, there are now proponents of a very different view of the nature of educational supervision and administration. With the advent of critical theory and the work of postmodernists and others with a sincere interest in learning how schools function, the visibility of the "old guard" is often diminished, along with its adherence to the principles of long-standing "science" of administration based on validated theory.

The purpose here is not to dissuade you from any interest in the more current perspectives of management. Rather, it is to introduce a set of beliefs which have endured for many years and which now continue to serve as the basis for much of what may be called *educational supervision* and *administration practice*. Be aware, however, that there is undeniably a bias present in this which suggests that the theory movement continues to offer much to those who would be "proactive educational leaders." The theory movement was born in a time when the scholars were also practitioners of educational administration in public schools. They had recently tasted the frustration of real-world practice, which often demands decisions and responses to immediate crises "in the trenches." Often, those who eschew the theories of the past have not faced the same dilemmas of actual school practice. One of the purposes of this book is to offer readers a discussion of the usefulness of theory as a legitimate tool in becoming proactive leaders ready to deal with the demands of daily practice, not to prepare them as philosophers who view schools as laboratories, where they can study reflective responses from a safe distance.

◌ࣷ DEFINITION OF THEORY

What is theory? To many, a standard and rather negative view of what theory is prevails in the field of education. Discussions with numerous school practitioners suggest that educational theory is often viewed as a synonym for speculation or supposition or as an attempt to represent some ideal with little relevance to the real world. For many people actually working in schools, theory is anything that does not possess an immediate, practical value.

There are many things that theory is not. It is not, for example, a part of axiology (the branch of philosophy that deals with values)—although you may develop a personal theory based on your own values to guide your supervisory practice, as discussed in chapter 2. In the strictest sense, mixing "theory" with "values" and "philosophy" represents an incorrect application of all these terms. Nor is the theory simply the individualized application of one person's common sense. The problem faced whenever one talks about common sense is that what we label with this term is often neither "common" nor "sensible" to everyone at the same time; common sense is, in fact, often a fiercely individualistic and personal view of reality. We need only think of the bit of sense commonly held in the Middle Ages that the earth was flat. Ultimately such commonsense views are of little practical use to any decision maker.

What is theory, then? *Theory* is an attempt to describe phenomena and interrelationships found in the real world in terms that reflect the true nature of the world. In its most fundamental form, theory is an attempt to collect elements of knowledge and truth from multiple sources—authority, tradition, intuition, common sense, observation, structured empirical research—to guide practice by informing decision makers of likely (if not always certain) consequences of their actions under certain conditions. The view of theory in the field of educational supervision, consistent with the view in the wider field of social sciences, holds that theory is a type of generalization based on observable and verifiable reality. The assumptions of theory in the social sciences, then, have been borrowed extensively from the physical sciences.

For educational supervision in particular, the contemporary literature provides several useful definitions. Thomas Sergiovanni and Robert Starratt (1988), for example, define theory as "a mode of thinking that leads to the generation of propositions amenable to testing either in the laboratory or in practice. It is a systematic, conceptual framework to be used in understanding present phenomena and in gaining insights into how to behave in the future, when faced with the same phenomena" (p. 121).

Wayne Hoy and Cecil Miskel (1988) offer a similar, related definition by noting that theory is "a set of interrelated concepts, assumptions, and generalization that systematically describes and explains regularities in educational organizations" (p. 155). This second definition is particularly interesting because it suggests three important characteristics of social science theory: First, that theory is logistically composed of concepts, assumptions, and generalizations; second, that the major function of theory is to describe, explain, and predict the nature of regularities in human behavior; and finally, that theory is heuristic—it stimulates and guides the further development of knowledge. Both definitions suggest that theory is based on present reality, but usable in building future understandings. These notions are consistent with and applicable to the view of proactive leadership.

It would be misleading to suggest that theories always appeal to us because of their clarity and precision as descriptions of present reality. They are, in fact, frequently full of terms and concepts difficult for us to grasp. Theories are, by their very nature, general and somewhat abstract, and more importantly, they are never absolutely true or false. A theory is always open to some individual interpretation.

❧ FUNCTIONS OF THEORY

Based on the definitions of theory cited above, certain specific outcomes to be accomplished through the application of theoretical perspectives to educational leadership can be identified.

Ultimately, the function of a theory in the social sciences is to provide generalizations and, eventually explanations of the ways in which phenomena appear in the "real world." As a result, theory often serves as the basis for further empirical research in which "theory testing/theory verification" is a stated goal. One function of theory has traditionally been to set up future research questions and to provide suggestions about which research results may be relative to a defined, specific issue. Consider, for example, the researcher who conducts a study based on an established theory of motivation, such as Abraham H. Maslow's (1970) view of needs satisfaction, which holds that people will be motivated only as their lowest levels of need are met. If the researcher finds that people seem to be motivated in this way, Maslow's view is supported. If people do not respond in the way predicted by the theory, further studies with different assumptions will be carried out.

A second widely accepted function of theory is to provide an integrating, common feature in the further development of the knowledge base in the given field. Theory often leads to the generation of research; the findings of research lead to action; action leads to further theory refinement, and so on. Marion (2005) offers the cautionary view that "Theory is not reality; it is our best shot at describing reality" (p. 4). He describes theory building as "a process of building and rebuilding, with each cycle illuminating different corners of the darkness" (p. 5).

Research emerges from a theory base, and this often stimulates the researcher to build upon the assumptions and generalizations of an earlier theory and research base. The use of theory in this type of clarification and building process often leads to new issues. Researchers might investigate, for example, how a certain theory is reflected in the ways teachers think about instruction. As research is conducted, the researcher will see an increasingly clear picture of how thinking takes place. As a result, the theory may be reviewed to reflect this research finding, and new and separate issues discovered in the process may be reserved for further study.

Finally, and perhaps most relevant to supervision as proactive leadership, theory in the social sciences often guides action. Theory can help us make wise, reality-based decisions. Theory often allows us to make sense out of the complex and often contradictory behavioral patterns that we so often see in the real world. While the first two functions of theory related primarily to the needs of most educational practitioners engaged in systematic research in schools, this last function is a cornerstone for effective practice, which reflects proactive rather than reactive or crisis-oriented behavior. The third function of theory captures present conditions and events in a most accurate and economical fashion and predicts the likelihood of the same conditions and events occurring in a similar, predictable way in the future. A teacher who is aware of child development theory that suggests that children learn best when they are personally ready to learn, for example, may design a classroom environment where children with varying personal interests can find a variety of things to do.

❧ STEPS IN THEORY DEVELOPMENT

Another way to clarify how theories are used to link present reality with future practice is to consider how they develop over time. Most theories appear to develop as a result of a movement through at least three identifiable, sequential steps: (1) the discursive treatment of a topic; (2) the development of a simple listing of characteristics; and (3) the creation of a juxtaposed taxonomy of observed events. These first three steps are often followed by the building and sharing of theoretical models, also known as graphic depictions of theoretical statements. These steps will be reviewed in the next few pages to examine how they fit together and how they may be used by the practitioner of supervision interested in the improvement of practice in schools.

Discursive Treatment of a Problem or Topic

This step, usually considered a starting point in the theory development cycle, consists of brainstorming, or even "idle chitchat" about some specific issue, topic, trend, or event. No attempt is made to offer any connection between and among random, disjointed observations.

As an example, consider the type of talk that can be heard in teachers' lounges in schools across the nation. Dozens, even hundreds, of random observations are made each day about how a particular group of students behaves, about the latest memo from the administration, or about the policies formulated by the school board at a recent public meeting. This kind of real-world, random discussion might well serve as the beginning for the theory-development cycle.

Imagine that a group of teachers makes some random observations about how the students in their classes tend to behave. Most teachers may comment that "the kids are pretty good here," while a few might note that some students "cause a lot of problems" in the school. Names of individual students will probably emerge. Comments from other staff members range along a continuum stretching from "the kids here are angels" to "the kids are terrors." These comments come fast, without advanced thinking; they are not offered in any specific order, but they randomly represent what at least a subset of the teaching staff in a particular school believes about the nature of students in their care. They are "true" statements insofar as they represent the honest beliefs of people; they derive from each teacher's perceptions of the reality that he or she experiences each day. Theory in the social sciences often begins this way, even when the participants have no realization (and certainly have no conscious desire in that direction) that they are laying the groundwork for a theory in any formal sense.

Development of a Simplified Listing

Eventually, observations made in a random fashion begin to be repeated with enough frequency that a list becomes apparent. Although this activity is the second step in a linear theory-building process, it is actually quite similar to and often simultaneous with the "discursive treatment" stage. Listings of phenomena begin to take shape almost immediately from random observations.

As suggested above, random observations about student behavior are virtually nonstop in most teachers' lounges. The same general observations occur with sufficient frequency to suggest that simplified listings of observed characteristics could easily be compiled. Unfortunately, the random observations of professional educators are not generally recorded in any systematic manner; therefore, a relatively small amount of formal theory is actually built upon the observations of classroom teachers, but a very personal informal level of theory building is in fact continually going on in schools. What rarely takes place is the type of codification and formalized listing described as the characteristics of this step in the formal theory-building cycle.

Formulating a Juxtaposed Taxonomy

At a certain point in the theory-building cycle, the random limited observations of existing phenomena are placed in relationship to other features of the observed environment. In other words, discursive treatment is placed in context, and a juxtaposed taxonomy is created.

Returning to the teachers and their observations of student behavior, simple statements such as "The kids are terrors" are usually quickly followed by qualifying statements such as "right before spring break." Teachers frequently make use of context-based statements to guide their own professional behavior. Within a relatively short time, beginning teachers note that students tend to behave one way on Monday mornings, somewhat differently in the afternoon on Wednesdays, and in a completely different fashion on Friday afternoons. One year "in the trenches" is usually time enough to show a teacher that students will react to directions differently before a long vacation break from how they act after that break. This series of random observations of student behavior, then, when placed in the context of the school year calendar, provides considerable guidance for the teacher who is planning instructional activities. Most instructors learn quickly that a major examination on the last afternoon before spring break will result in low grades and high frustrations for students. For years, teachers have tended to search for hands-on activities that call for high physical involvement when they know students are preoccupied with thoughts of an upcoming week away from school.

A good theory must be able to describe the present with a high degree of accuracy; more importantly, it must be useful in terms of suggesting and predicting future events. The fact that students tend to be disengaged from classroom activities on days before vacations is in itself an interesting piece of descriptive information. However, this information is much more important in terms of what it offers to the classroom teacher for lesson planning at vacation times. The observation placed in context allows teachers to change their behavior to accommodate what they have learned. The real value in understanding theory is not simply that a theoretical perspective offers a novel way to describe real situations. Rather, the long-term value is that theory enables us to engage in proactive practice.

Model Building

Although the steps just covered constitute the basic theory-building cycle, one additional activity is often included in this process, namely, the building of a theoretical model. This may sound like a mysterious activity, but this means simply that the interrelationships of variables or factors in a theoretical statement are depicted graphically. Although not an absolutely essential part of theory development, models are nonetheless an integral part of most conceptualizations that influence practice in the social sciences.

◈ CHARACTERISTICS OF "GOOD" THEORY

A good, usable theory in the social sciences—that is, one which ful-fills the assigned functions of events occurring in the future—should have at least some of the following identifiable characteristics:

- A "good" theory must be based on observed (and observable) events that are grounded in reality. Theories cannot be so concep-tually abstract or divorced from common reality that no one besides the individuals who formulate the theories can understand what is meant. Theories must communicate bits of reality to a rela-tively wide audience. Thus, "good" theories cannot be mere suppo-sitions of a chosen few; they must be born of and tested in a reality that is shared by many at a time.

- A "good" theory should explain things found in reality in a com-plete, yet succinct fashion. A statement that must use many qualifi-ers to explain exceptions to the rule is probably not a particularly "good" theory. A theory should say much in a few words, or in the case of a theoretical model, in as simple a graphic design as possible.

- A "good" theory must be amenable to some type of systematic ver-ification, validation, or testing process. It is not enough, for exam-ple, for a small group of teachers to note the behavior patterns of the students in a single elementary school. Someone else needs to be able to witness the same behaviors; in a sense, a person must be able to walk in off the street and verify whether or not students do behave as the teachers claim. More important, a good theory must "hold up" when it is transported to other settings. Is it true that students do not behave seriously the day before a vacation? If this question can be answered similarly in a wide variety of different sites, then this theoretical assumption is likely to be a "good" one.

- A "good" theory must have a future-time orientation, because it ultimately needs to be an accurate predictor of the way things will probably be. As mentioned throughout this text, understanding and applying the theories of the social sciences to educational supervision will be of little value unless the understanding some-how improves practice in the schools at some point in the future.

One way of thinking about social sciences theory is to conclude that a good theory is like a pair of glasses worn to aid our vision. Theory should help us see the relationships between the goals of the organiza-tions more clearly. We wear "glasses" to get a better look at things—the situations and events that might occur from time to time in the world of practice related to educational supervision. The corrective lenses of a good theory help us develop generalizations and reactions, and, more importantly, to aid in future planning and anticipation of events. The application of good theories does indeed permit more proactive, less reactive behavior. The ultimate importance of theory, and perhaps its stiffest test of goodness, is that it provides consistent ways of looking at similar, but not wholly alike, events that are part of the world at work. Theory in this sense can be viewed as an important part of an educational leader's "bag of tricks."

❧ RESTRICTIONS ON THE USE OF THEORY

There are some important cautions that need to be voiced about reliance on and usage of theory in the field of educational supervision. These cautions are in no way meant to detract from the value of theory as an ongoing guide to practice in supervision; rather, they are listed only to suggest potential problem areas to those who might develop too great a reliance on theoretical formulations as guides to all behavior.

- Although many elements of current supervisory practice date back to the origins of American public education in general, the field of educational supervision as currently practiced is an emergent discipline. As a result, the events from which the initial observations and assumptions come are highly limited. There is no long-established history from which we can draw sufficient inferences for use in formal theory-building processes.

- We need to recognize that biases are a constant threat to objectivity in the collection of sound observations. Idiosyncratic interpretation of reality is bound to enter the field of theory development at one point or another, and listings will remain the products of personal observation, wherein we can never be sure that the observers are totally free of prejudice.

- Educational supervision is a complex and widely interpreted field. As a result, the totality of educational supervision can never be represented by one finite set of theoretical assumptions and models.

The chapters that follow will underscore this point by selecting for intensive review a handful of theoretical perspectives that might prove useful to you in guiding supervisory practice. There are many other perspectives, models, and theories that might be useful to those who serve as educational leaders; no one theory can answer all our questions.

We have focused our discussion of theory up to this point almost exclusively on formal theoretical formulations in the social sciences. Before moving on, we should glance quickly at the applications of less formal, more personal theories to the enhancement of supervisory behavior and proactive leadership practice.

❧ DISTINCTIONS BETWEEN FORMAL THEORY AND PERSONAL PHILOSOPHY

Much of what was just stated about the functions and characteristics of formal theory, along with the steps followed in the theory-building cycle, has relevance to the development of a personal philosophy as a guide to improve supervisory practice. While the tendency has been to suggest that theories are developed in a more or less conscious fashion by those who wish to contribute to a widespread clarification of practice in the social sciences, theory also emerges in a considerably less visible and grandiose way. Most people periodically observe events in their personal reality, form simple lists, and then place their observations in a context that enables them to behave in a more or less predictable way over time. We can cite again our examples of the individual teacher who, after some experience, knows that students tend to behave one way at certain times and differently at other times. The ability to accumulate such theories to guide personal practice is often considered a characteristic that differentiates between "average" and "good" teachers. We can use the knowledge accumulated in one year to help us improve the next year—or we can simply repeat the same year, over and over. *Cumulative learning* is another way to describe what we refer to as the development of personal philosophies, theories, platforms, or guides to action.

Structurally, then, great similarities exist between the steps followed in formal theory building and individual or personal philosophy construction. Perhaps the greatest single difference is the extent to which we can generalize from the initial random observations made by many different individuals in numerous settings over a long period of time; our own observations, on the other hand, are simply that—our own.

A potential danger exists in developing too rigid a stance toward personal theory. There is a fine line between taking a stance on a particular issue, based on highly personalized observations that are not necessarily shared by many in the general population, and closed-mindedness. Personal observations can produce prejudices and biases. A teacher whose classes have included only a few Hispanic children might generalize based on observed behavior that Spanish-speaking students are (1) very ambitious, (2) very lazy, (3) very talkative, (4) very shy, (5) very bright, or (6) any one of thousands of other characteristics that might be assigned to all students based on the same witnessed behavior of a very few in a highly limited setting. (Of course, merely increasing the number of observations does not guarantee that a theoretical formulation will be free of bias. For example, during the earliest days of our nation, "theories" of witchcraft were "proven" by a multitude of "observations" reported by reliable citizens about their neighbors).

Formal theory, then, does not differ from personalized, informal theory solely because observations are made by many people rather than one. Other distinctions need to be recognized. Formal theory, for instance, is open to ongoing testing and verification in an objective fashion. If those subscribing to the theories of witchcraft had been open to a dispassionate review of their assumptions, their theories might have had a much smaller audience. The theories used as the basis for much of our thinking in the social sciences are formal; they have been tested through empirical research and, as a consequence, have undergone periodic modifications. In addition, what are most often classified as important theories in educational supervision have been generalized across many different settings. A review of Hage's theory of organizations in the next chapter, for example, demonstrates that it is as usable in schools as it might be in hospitals or private industry. To be sure, there is considerable value in developing individualized, personal, and informal theory, and it is a process that occurs with or without recognition. However, there are limitations in allowing our behaviors as leaders to be guided too much by informal patterns. We also need knowledge of formal statements of theory.

❧ SUMMARY

This chapter explored the role of theory in the social sciences as a way to improve supervisory practice. As an introduction to this concept, we considered how theory has been accepted as foundation for the improvement of administrative practice in schools for many years. We also offered a number of definitions for theory and noted that theory is not, as often described, solely abstraction or philosophy. Rather, *theory attempts to reflect the nature of reality based on observable phenomena.* Steps in the theory-building cycle were described and related to the major functions and characteristics of "good" theory in the social sciences: the description and explanation of present events and the prediction of the likely occurrence of future events and behavior. The chapter concluded with the review of some typical restrictions and limitations associated with the use of formal and informal theory. It was noted that both informal, personal theory development and formal theory building in the social sciences are important tools for use in educational supervision. However, formal theory makes use of widespread generalizations of observable phenomena and is normally subjected to some degree of objective testing and verification. As a result, some special features of formal theory make it particularly appealing to those who need to understand "the way things work" in organizations.

Understanding and relying on theories is certainly not the only way for practitioners of educational supervision to function. There are many unfortunate examples of supervisors living solely in the world of theory who are very ineffective when faced with making decisions regarding "real world" issues. On the other hand, we firmly believe that an appreciation of theory is an important characteristic of successful followers of proactive leadership.

Suggested Activities

1. Analyze the way in which you or a colleague deals with parents, students who have discipline problems, or some other situation faced by school teachers to determine how your approach is guided by the development of a personalized theory as described in this chapter.

2. Interview a supervisor or school administrator concerning the way in which he or she handled some sort of recent "critical incident." In your analysis, try to determine the steps that were followed by the person. Was there a similarity between his or her expressed behavior and the steps in the theory-building cycle described in this chapter?

3. Ask a number of people how they would define "theory." Determine from their responses the extent to which these individuals have a positive or negative view of theory.

Cases to Consider

The brief cases below are based on actual situations. Please read each case and consider the following:

- What are the critical issues raised in each case, as they relate to the topics covered in this chapter?
- How does each case relate to the development of the concept of proactive leadership?
- In what ways might you suggest a resolution to the issues raised?

Case 3.1   That's The Way Things Are Around Here

Michael Carlucci, the new principal of the 125th Street Elementary School, had just finished his first day walking around his new school building on the "Teacher Report" day for the new school year. He had been assigned to this campus after having spent six very successful years at another elementary school on the east side of town, where he had gotten a deserved reputation as a principal who could change a lot of attitudes very quickly. His former school had a horrible reputation when he got there; most teachers seemed to dislike pupils, distrust parents, and disrespect the staff. Michael spent most of his time during the first three years of his last principalship working to change the attitudes in his school, and it had worked. Now, the superintendent had sent him to another difficult assignment.

While walking around 125th Street Elementary, Michael overheard quite a few conversations that disturbed him. For the most part, the teaching staff was extremely experienced and had worked together at the school for many years. If a single comment could summarize the mood of most people that he heard, it was one made by Rita Finn, the librarian, who had spent virtually her whole career at the school: "When he works in this neighborhood long enough, the new principal will find out what it's like to really earn his paycheck. We all know that the kids here on the west side have no respect for schools, adults, or just about anything else. I've seen them come and go over the years, and it's always the same. Give me this and give me that, but no one is really interesting in working or learning."

Michael reflected that this new school would likely be even more difficult that his last.

Case 3.2   I Thought I Knew . . .

The faculty of Mountain State University, a major research institution with a strong national reputation for the quality of its academic program in educational administration and supervision, was universally happy with one of its recent graduates, Dr. Peter Greene. Pete was one of those rare students who came along only once every ten years or so. He was someone who really stood out as an outstanding scholar, even at a place as prestigious as MSU. It was not surprising that he was able to land a principalship at Olive Tree Elementary School, one of five highly regarded elementary schools in the Peaceful Branch District, a well-respected system near the campus of Mountain State. It took a little bit of work on the part of the MSU faculty to convince Bob Davidson, the Peaceful Branch superintendent and another graduate of their doctoral program, to hire Pete, even with his strong academic record. Pete had only three years of prior experience as a primary school teacher in a small private academy in another state. For the past six years, he had been enrolled as a full-time graduate student at MSU where he completed his masters and doctoral degrees. The faculty convinced Bob that Pete was a bright young star who could truly bring a fresh perspective to the system. Besides that, it was hard to dispute the fact that over the years, MSU had produced so many examples of first-rate administrators like Bob.

Pete had been on the job for less than a month, but the signals were already becoming clear that something was not right. Bob Davidson was starting to hear a number of complaints by parents, and he noted on his calendar that he was meeting with Shirley Kincaid, the president of the Peaceful Branch Teachers' Association and building rep at Olive Tree. His secretary's notes indicated that Shirley was coming to express some faculty concerns about the way in which this school year had started. Beyond that, Bob had been hearing some concerns regarding the fact that Pete did not seem to be able to make decisions very quickly. Even relatively simple things seemed to be taking longer than they should to be resolved. The other principals were beginning to make comments to Bob about the "rookie" at Olive Tree.

Pete was aware that there was some tension in his building, but he was not really concerned. After all, he felt confident that the findings of his doctoral dissertation which dealt with the micropolitics of education would help him in his work. He would be able to tell exactly what the issues were in his community. Further, he had learned quite a bit from Dr. Jackson's excellent class in conflict resolution and Dr. Rosella's course in qualitative research back at MSU. Finally, he had been reading a number of other studies conducted by researchers all over the country on the issue of community unrest and its impact on staff morale. Pete felt confident that, as he studied and analyzed the problems that were emerging on his campus, he would be able to provide a reasonable explanation for what was happening, and the rest of his principalship would be quite successful.

Applying the Concepts

The following brief quiz is designed to improve your skills in applying some of the concepts discussed in this chapter. Read the brief introductory case and then respond to the multiple-choice questions. You will find the answers in the Appendix.

Franklin Perez was just named principal of Walker Elementary School, a well-respected school on the east side of Desmond City. The school was almost always at the top of the county schools in terms of student scores on the annual student achievement tests. Mr. Perez was looking forward to getting to work with a new group of colleagues, so during the summer after he was appointed, he sent out personal notes to each of the teachers and invited people to stop by his office for coffee and a chance to get to know the new principal. More than half of the staff responded that they were eager to take him up on his offer.

After two weeks of coffee sessions, Franklin was getting a bit concerned. He began hearing the same themes expressed by several teachers. Specifically, the view seemed to be that Walker was a really good school, as demonstrated by the test results. The thing that disturbed the new principal was that the reason for success that was often shared was the fact that the school had virtually no minority students, and even the few African American and Latino students were good because "they came from good homes." Finally, when Anna Spencer, an experienced third-grade teacher, came in to meet the new leader and began to talk about how good the children at the school were, Mr. Perez interrupted her to inquire why she believed that to be the case.

"Well, Mr. Perez," explained Anna, "most of us have been here a long time. We are experienced teachers and we have seen a lot in our many years of professional experience. We know that we have good families in this neighborhood, and that parents care about their kids. Walker is different from so many other schools in the county, where parents are poor, without jobs in many cases, and so often have a tendency to not provide proper home modeling for their children. Here at Walker, we have children who are clearly better prepared to learn because they have families who care."

1. If you were Mr. Perez, what might you suggest that teachers might do as a way to change some of their perceptions of the needs of students in their school?

   a. Ask the current teachers to start thinking about seeking teaching positions at other schools.

b. Openly criticize the teachers who hold the beliefs that poor minority children cannot learn.

c. Suggest that teachers begin to visit other schools and get to recognize that there are factors beyond race or economic level that contribute to children's abilities to learn and succeed.

d. Hire a consultant to begin sensitivity training with the teaching staff as soon as possible.

2. In terms of theory development, what might be noted about the collective "vision" of schooling that had been created by the teachers of Walker School over the years?

a. The vision would have been different if there had been more minority students enrolled in the school.

b. The faculty members made use of an incomplete picture of student achievement and family backgrounds in making up their theoretical perspective.

c. No test results should ever be used in guiding theoretical perspectives.

d. The faculty should have never shared their collective visions with a principal before he had a chance to really see the school in action.

Additional Reading

Carr, David (2003). *Making sense of education: An introduction to the philosophy and theory of education*. London: RoutledgeFalmer.

Getzels, Jacob, Lipham, James M., & Campbell, Roald F. (1965). *Educational administration as a social process*. New York: Harper and Row.

Griffiths, Daniel (1959). *Administrative theory*. New York: Appleton-Century-Crofts.

Halpin, Andrew (ed.) (1958). *Administrative theory in education*. Chicago: Midwest Administrative Center, University of Chicago Press.

Hubbard, Bill (1995). *A theory for practice*. Cambridge, MA: MIT Press.

Owens, Robert G. (1987). *Organizational behavior in education* (3rd ed.) Englewood Cliffs, NJ: Prentice-Hall.

❧ 4 ❧

Analyzing the Structure of Schools

Practitioners of proactive leadership must be involved in the continuous monitoring of the structure of the school as a complex organization. As a response to that challenge, this chapter reviews the theory-based analysis of organizations through two analytic approaches. The first is called *formal analysis*, and the second *informal analysis*. Formal organizational analysis refers to the structure of organizations, including their stated and institutionally defined purposes and objectives. Informal organizational analysis deals with the characteristics of people who work in the institutions, along with the less visible and tangible features of the organization such as the psychosocial climate or "feel." The practitioner of effective and proactive supervisory processes needs to be aware of both the formal and informal levels of analysis.

The first part of this chapter presents some theoretical perspectives that describe and predict behavior associated with formal organizations. Included are Jerald Hage's axiomatic theory of organizations, Jacob Getzels's social systems, Gareth Morgan's organizational metaphors, and Lee Bolman's and Terrence Deal's organizational frameworks. In the second part of the chapter, two perspectives in informal aspects of organizations, Matthew Miles's view of organizational health, and organization climate as conceptualized by Andrew Halpin and Donald Croft, will be described. Throughout the discussion, it is indicated how these theoretical perspectives offer opportunities for the educational leader to improve his or her practice, and more importantly, the quality of life in schools.

⚜ HAGE'S AXIOMATIC THEORY OF ORGANIZATIONS

An enduring theoretical analysis of the formal characteristics of organizations was proposed by sociologist Jerald Hage (1965). While the term "axiomatic" (i.e., so obvious as to be self-evident) may be open to some debate, this framework is included for two reasons. First, the development and application of the *axiomatic theory of organizations* directly follow the rational, linear theory-building cycle set forth in chapter 3. Second, the theory offers some important insights into the operation of organizations to the extent that supervisory behavior can be greatly enhanced through an understanding of the assumptions and properties found in this theory.

Historical Development

Hage's focus throughout his work as a sociologist has been to determine how societal institutions function. He began by looking at a wide array of organizations—hospitals and nursing homes, private companies, and educational institutions, among others. By reviewing the characteristic components in diverse locations, Hage and his colleagues were able to note conceptually similar features that existed in all types of organizations. Thus, the process of the discursive treatment of a topic (random observation) and the development of a simplified listing of phenomena were completed as nearly simultaneous activities. In this earliest phase of the historical development of Hage's theory, then, the first descriptive function of a theory was completed.

Structural and Outcome Variables

Hage's examination of complex organizations yielded a primary, simple finding: All organizations, regardless of their type and purpose, have two basic characteristics: *structural variables* (or the varying ways in which they are put together) and *outcome variables* (the characteristics or organizations that describe the means of meeting their goals). Further analysis indicated that all organizations have at least four common structural components. These may be defined as follows:

- *Centralization.* A measure of the proportion of jobs in an organization that participate in decision-making processes. An organization where only a few people tend to make all or most decisions is highly centralized, whereas an organization where there is widespread and broad-based involvement in decisions is low in centralization.

- *Complexity.* The number of occupational roles and specialties, and the level of training required of people in an organization to fulfill the roles and specialties needed. Organizations with many complicated jobs requiring advanced training are high in complexity.

- *Formalization.* The proportion of jobs that are codified, along with the range of individual variation and interpretation that is allowed in the performance of jobs. An organization where people are expected to comply with the features of a very specific job description is high in formalization. If there are opportunities for many employees to do many different tasks without regard to official responsibilities, an organization is low in formalization.

- *Stratification.* The differences that exist in income levels and prestige found within an organization. When there are gaps between employees in terms of salary levels and other forms of organizational rewards, there is high stratification.

A few additional comments need to be made concerning these structural variables. First, some organizations are typically relatively high or low in terms of each factor. For example, a large modern hospital is normally very high in complexity, given the tremendous amount of specialization now found in the field of medicine. Moreover, hospitals are also institutions with high stratification: Cardiac surgeons make more money and have greater prestige and visibility than do general surgeons, emergency-room physicians, or radiologists; physicians stand far apart from nurses, orderlies, or any of the other scores of jobs found in most hospitals. By contrast, consider the characteristics of another type organization, the mom-and-pop grocery store. Here, decision making is highly decentralized, there is little complexity, and stratification does not exist. In many instances, when something needs to be done, everyone (owner or employee) pitches in to get the job done. We should be aware, however, that there could be gradations in each of these structural components in the same types of organizations. For example, not all hospitals are the same; some are more stratified than others.

As do hospitals, schools have different gradations of structural components or structural variables. While schools might, in general, fall somewhere around the middle on a continuum of all organizations, some schools are obviously different from others in terms of centralization, complexity, formalization, and stratification. Some schools feature opportunities for greater teacher participation in school-wide decision making. Other schools have greater job specialization and, perhaps as a result, more levels to increase discrepancies in terms of prestige. In fact, the nature of the size and grade levels served by a school has a good deal to do with the relative degrees of any of Hage's structural elements that might be present. High schools, particularly those with a strong departmental structure and many specialists on the staff (nurses, guidance counselors, librarians, and so forth) are much higher in their degree of complexity than are the majority of elementary schools. On the other hand, some elementary schools serving many students across a range of several grades will be more complex than elementary schools enrolling students in only two or three grades. In addition, the degree of formalization and stratification will vary in schools where there are many specialized roles, as contrasted with a setting where there is but one administrator and, perhaps, no more than ten classroom teachers.

Organizations also may be understood through their outcome characteristics or outcome variables. Hage described four: production, efficiency, job satisfaction, and adaptiveness.

- *Production.* In most organizations, production is defined simply as the number of things that are produced during a given period of time. High production means that many things are created or built in a relatively short period of time, and low production occurs when a small number of items are produced during a certain time frame.

- *Efficiency.* This outcome variable is a measure of the cost associated with the production of the items produced. High efficiency results when the ratio of cost-per-item or unit is low. Low efficiency is the reverse; an individual item costs a great deal to produce. Incidentally, cost here is defined as the amount of any resource—money, time, labor, and so forth—that is expended.

- *Job satisfaction.* This was originally indicated by the rate of turnover of employees. However, people often tend to stay on their jobs whether or not they like them. Thus, in many institutions job satisfaction might currently be viewed as a condition where there is a continuous, deliberate focus on the needs and interests of employees.

- *Adaptiveness.* Also referred to as "innovativeness," adaptiveness describes the number of new products developed within an organization during a given period of time. A manufacturing company would be considered high in adaptiveness if it introduced many new products in a calendar year. By contrast, a company that tended to "stand pat" and stay with the same merchandise year in and year out would be low in adaptiveness.

As was true of structural variables, organizations may also be generally high or low in these four outcome variables. Employees in a manufacturing company might not enjoy the daily routine on the assembly line but experience job satisfaction because the company's policies reflect a caring attitude. For example, the company might provide pay-increase incentives, insurance benefits, and profit-sharing plans, as well as display a caring attitude—all factors which can affect job satisfaction. On the other hand, an employee working for a small firm, performing challenging tasks that vary every day, might feel isolated and unappreciated by coworkers and management. The firm might not provide extra benefits or other incentives. Job satisfaction, in this case, might be low. A research and development institute might place great emphasis on adaptiveness because the company was created primarily to develop an abundance of new ideas and products. A very "old line" and stable producer of one identifiable product line, such as high-quality watches or writing instruments, might never be inclined to bring out something "new and different." Variations may occur, however, even among organizations with similar titles and interests.

Similarly, individual schools differ significantly in terms of the outcome variables. One school may have a reputation for very high standardized test scores (an indicator of productivity), while a neighboring school system has a history of much lower scores. One system may produce X number of National Merit Scholars at a per-pupil expenditure of $4,800, while another district, spending only $4,500 per student, boasts of even more scholars—a difference in efficiency.

Mechanistic Versus Dynamic Organizations

After Hage analyzed organizations in terms of structure and outcome, he essentially finished the stage of the theory development cycle referred to earlier as the *simplified listing*. In the next stage of theory formulation, Hage related two prototypic organizational structures that could be described in terms of the structural and outcome variables. These two organizational types are defined as *dynamic* (open to constant change) and *mechanistic* (tending to maintain existing practice). Table 4.1 indicates the relative degree of structural and outcome variables possessed by each type.

Neither the mechanistic nor the dynamic organization should necessarily be viewed as better or worse than the other: these two designations serve only to describe two polar-opposite organizations. Table 4.2 compares two opposite organizational structures by Richard Wynn and Charles Guditus (1984). If we ask, "Should a school tend to be a dynamic

---

Table 4.1. Dynamic vs. mechanistic organizations*

Dynamic Organizations	Mechanistic Organizations
Structural Variables	*Structural Variables*
High complexity	Low complexity
Low centralization	High centralization
Low formalization	High formalization
Low stratification	High stratification
Outcome Variables	*Outcome Variables*
High adaptiveness	Low adaptiveness
Low productivity	High productivity
Low efficiency	High efficiency
High job satisfaction	Low job satisfaction

* as described according to the relative amount of four structural variables and four outcome variables

Source: Reprinted from An axiomatic theory of organization, by Jerald Hage, published in *Administrative Science Quarterly, 10(3)* (December 1965) by permission of *Administrative Science Quarterly.*

Table 4.2.   Comparison of two models of organizations (dynamic vs. mechanistic) in terms of 10 selected criteria

	Mechanistic (Bureaucratic)	Dynamic (Professional)
Decision Making	Centralized	Widely participative
Work	Individual jobs are self-contained and isolated	People function in face-to-face groups collaboratively
Control	Through hierarchical structure	Through interaction of involved persons
Tasks	Specialized and differentiated with precise specifications of jurisdictions	Continuously enlarged through consensus in context of total organization
Authority	Determined by hierarchical status	Shared and determined by consensus
Relationships	Unilateral management action based on passive conformance	Emphasis on mutual dependence and cooperation based on trust and confidence
Mood	Competition and rivalry	Cooperation
Nature of Organization	Rigid	Flexible
Commitment	To superiors	To the task and "ethos of progress"
Climate	Closed	Open

Source: Wynn, Richard, and Guditus, Charles W. (1974), *Team management: Leadership by consensus*. Copyright ©1984. Reprinted by permission of the authors.

or mechanistic organization?" two answers are possible. First, individual schools are already best understood as dynamic because they emphasize widespread involvement in decision making (low centralization), few distinctions among staff members in terms of prestige or income differences (low stratification), but many special technical skills demonstrated by teachers and other staff (high complexity). Other schools typify the mechanistic model because they have the opposite structural characteristics.

Second, perfection for schools, as for any organization, depends largely on the goals of that particular school. Different structural characteristics yield different outcomes. If a school's goals include stability (low adaptiveness), high test scores (high productivity), without spending too much money (high efficiency), but without concerns for the needs of staff (low job satisfaction), the appropriate model would be the mechanistic organization. Other goals might suggest that the dynamic model is more appropriate. As the nature of organizations tends to change in the twenty-first century, some of the assumptions of Hage's theory might change. For example, we note that in many cases smaller businesses now tend to be less formalized, demonstrate less centralization, and show virtually no stratification. Nevertheless, they show great productivity while remaining efficient. It could very well be that the economies traditionally associated with large-sized organizations drove Hage's analysis of organizations in the 1960s and 1970s, while we now operate from a different paradigm. Those who make policy regarding schools, however, tend to remain driven by traditional views that suggest that "large is better."

Illustrations of Actual Applications

The ultimate educational value of any theory is that it can help us make decisions that improve the quality of what takes place in schools. Hage's axiomatic propositions listed below represent little more than an academic exercise unless they serve to direct our leadership behavior so that we can more effectively guide school district personnel to achieve their goals. Following the list of propositions is an example of how an understanding of this theory might lead to a more proactive approach to leadership in schools.

- The higher the centralization, the higher the production.
- The higher the formalization, the higher the efficiency.
- The higher the centralization, the higher the formalization.
- The higher the stratification, the lower the job satisfaction.
- The higher the stratification, the higher the production.
- The higher the stratification, the lower the adaptiveness.
- The higher the complexity, the lower the stratification.
- The higher the complexity, the higher the job satisfaction.

Suppose that an educational supervisor is assigned the task of working with a school where there has been a long history of low staff morale, and where little attention has been paid to the human dimension of the organization. In Hage's terms, the school would be described as *low in the outcome variable of job satisfaction.* If the supervisor's goals include increasing the variable so that teachers and staff feel their personal needs are being addressed, the axiomatic theory suggests a number of avenues for change, all in the structural characteristics of the school. Job satisfaction can be increased by raising the level of complexity in the organization, or by lowering stratification, formalization, or centralization. While any of these changes is likely to have a positive effect on the job satisfaction variable, the most readily modified structural variable of a school is probably the extent to which people believe that they are involved in organizational decision making. Thus, the proactive leader interested in increasing satisfaction among school employees might increase opportunities for teachers and staff to participate in making important relevant decisions. Many successful educational leaders make the kind of structural shift to achieve different outcomes almost intuitively. Effective supervisors need not make use of Hage's technical, theoretical language to act in this way. The essential understanding of the principle that job satisfaction tends to be higher when people are involved in making relevant decisions is all we really need.

If Hage's theory is valid, however, modification of one structural component might cause undesirable effects in terms of other outcomes. Remember, for example, that the productivity and efficiency levels of organization are generally lower in organizations where centralization is lower. The net effect of involving people in a school's decision-making processes might indeed be a happier staff, but one that does not "produce" as much or as efficiently as a staff in a school where one person makes most of the decisions. The reason for this is simply that, when many are involved in a consensus-making approach to decision making, it takes longer to reach a decision. It is not an efficient approach. When one makes all decisions alone, it takes little time. However, note that this is only a statement about the *ease* of decision making, not an assessment of the *quality* of decisions that might be made.

The real practical value of a theoretical framework such as Hage's, then, is not that it tells us what we are supposed to do in all cases. No theory is meant to serve as a cookbook. To the contrary, understanding a given theory should provide us with an awareness of the possible outcomes of a set of actions that we might follow. In the case we just examined, no one can say whether it is better to have a "satisfied staff" or a "productive and efficient staff." Such a choice must be made by the leader in a way that is consistent with goals, objectives, vision, values, and individual philosophy.

∂ Getzels's Social Systems

Jacob Getzels developed another theoretical model that educational leaders might find useful in understanding what takes place in formal organizations.

Historical Development

Getzels's initial work was carried out largely in the years immediately after World War II and involved the analysis of such diverse settings as the military, hospitals, universities, private businesses, and public schools. Getzels isolated essential properties of all these different organizations and was able to conclude that, regardless of the organizations' stated purposes, all such units possess two common dimensions, one that describes the structure of the organization and the other that provides a review of the people who work in it. Observing and analyzing the interaction of these two dimensions helps us understand much of the human behavior in organizations.

The Structural Dimension

The dimension of social systems that deals with the structure of organizations is referred to in Getzels's theory as the *nomothetic* (normative, or sociological) *dimension*. "*Nomothetic* structures refer to things that have something in common; . . . generalizations that tend to be true across a wide variety of people" (Marion, 2005, p. 98). The component elements of this dimension are the institution, roles, and expectations (Getzels & Guba, 1957).

Society has created many different *institutions*, each of which is theoretically designed to carry out some identified and required function. Because society requires that there be ways of helping sick people, hospitals (and other health care organizations) have been created. Schools exist largely because society has indicated that there shall be organizations that educate people. Police agencies have been created to deal with the need to protect people and their property.

When institutions are thus formed, the *roles* within them are also created and institutionally defined. "Roles represent dynamic aspects of positions, offices, or statuses within the institution" (Lipham & Hoeh, 1974, p. 66). Schools have a number of standard roles: students, teachers, and administrative personnel. In fact, institutions and roles form an intense interrelationship: Institutions would not exist without the presence of certain roles (e.g., schools would not exist without students), and roles are meaningless without institutions (e.g., a teacher would be lost, to some extent, without a school).

The third component element of the nomothetic dimension of Getzels's social systems model is the *expectation* that exists for the performance of any particular institutionally defined role. Teachers, students, and others serve in roles within the school, which is a social institution, and each of these roles evokes certain types of behavior. Teachers act in certain ways (with some limited variation allowed); students do other things to play out their institutional responsibilities, and so forth.

The "People" Dimension

The second dimension of the social systems model is concerned with the nature of people who serve within organizations. This aspect is called the *idiographic* (personal, or psychological) *dimension*. "*Ideographic* describes phenomena that cannot be generalized and that are locally defined and locally meaningful" (Marion, 2005, p. 98). The ideographic dimension is also composed of three elements: the *individuals* (corresponding to the institution in the nomothetic dimension) who belong to the organizations, each of whom has a unique *personality* that, in turn, is defined largely in terms of particular *needs*. The two dimensions of the social systems model are represented in the model in figure 4.1.

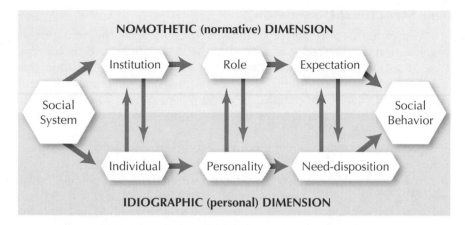

Source: Social Behavior and the Administrative Process, by J. W. Getzels and E. G. Guba, from *School Review, 65,* 429. Copyright © 1957. Used by permission of the University of Chicago Press.

Figure 4.1.   Representation of the social systems model of Getzels showing the two component dimensions and their elements

The pictorial representation of Getzels's model illustrates a number of concepts that are useful to the educational leader. The congruence demonstrated between the component elements of the two dimensions of the model suggests a neat, parallel alignment of individual personalities and institutionally defined roles. As the model suggests, this type of clear overlap is a strong indication of organizational effectiveness because people who work in the organization are doing what they want, and their jobs are fulfilling their needs. Unfortunately, in many organizations and at many times, the definition of a role is far from consistent with the personality and needs of the person who fills it. At such times conflict occurs, and the extent to which this conflict is serious is a critical indicator of whether or not a particular organization will achieve the kind of balance between institutional demands and human needs that leads to effectiveness.

Illustrations of Actual Applications

Understanding Getzels's central ideas allows the educational leader to be more effective, particularly in the context of the definition of supervision presented in this book: Supervision is the process of overseeing the ability of people to meet the goals of the organization in which they work. Supervision has a legitimate stake in maximizing the match between people and organization. As suggested by Getzels's model, people who are involved with and interested in their jobs will do their jobs better, and the organization will benefit through increased productivity and effectiveness.

Examples are plentiful in most school settings of the mismatches between institutional roles and individual personalities. Teachers are often assigned duties such as "cafeteria patrol," which are at best tolerated and at worst seen as totally opposed to their view of professional responsibility. Many teachers define their role as working constantly with highly motivated students, whereas in fact the role of the teacher in most schools today requires working with some kids who do not want to come to school, let alone learn. Frequently a lack of congruence exists between assigned roles and individual responsibilities. The value of a theoretical model such as the social systems paradigm is not that it tells the leader that conflicts will occasionally occur, but that it allows a person to predict such conflicts in certain cases, conflicts that can make the operation of a school or district likely to fail. Once again, the model of organizations as social systems has the potential of increasing more proactive behavior on the part of the supervisor.

⚘ Morgan's Organizational Metaphors

Yet another perspective of formal organizations is that of Gareth Morgan (1996), who attempted to provide managers, supervisors, and other leaders with a way to learn how to "read" what is going on in their organizations. He suggested that metaphors provide a useful way of understanding the subtle differences among the purposes, practices, policies, and underlying philosophies of organizations.

> It is easy to see how this kind of thinking has relevance for understanding organizations and management. For organizations are complex and paradoxical phenomena that can be understood in many ways. Many of our taken-for-granted organizations are metaphorical. . . . For example, we frequently talk about organizations as if they were machines designed to achieve predetermined goals and objectives, and which should operate smoothly and efficiently. And as a result of this kind of thinking we often attempt to organize and manage them in a mechanistic way, forcing their human qualities into a background role. (p. 127)

Listing of Major Metaphors

Morgan suggested eight predominant metaphors that describe organizations.

1. *Organizations as machines* derives from the era of scientific management and suggests that organizations resemble machines because of the prevailing expectations for reliable, durable, and predictable behavior. People who work in such organizations are seen as expendable and wholly interchangeable components. The usefulness of this metaphor is that it suggests we can design organizations to maximize predictability, especially in designing problem-solving strategies. Its major shortcoming is that creative approaches to problem solving are

destroyed, and the people who work in such settings participate in a dehumanized environment that provides little opportunity for individual creativity.

2. *Organizations as organisms* suggests that organizations have needs, interests, and life cycles, just as living organisms do, and that we can better understand the workings of organizations by considering them in terms of features like cellular structure. The usefulness of this metaphor is that we become increasingly aware of such things as the "social ecology" in which organizations exist. This metaphor emphasizes our need to appreciate the dynamic nature of the relationships between organizations and their environments. This organization as a living, breathing organism dissolves, however, as we realize the level of abstraction necessary to create it.

3. *Organizations as brains* emphasizes the organization's capacity to be guided by conscious rationality while still safeguarding such characteristics as flexibility and creative action. Its usefulness lies in its suggestion that organizations are capable of learning and self-organization—of creating, for instance, a series of appropriate responses to problems and "storing" that creation for future use. The major shortcoming is that, in its emphasis on rationality, it may prevent us from recognizing the important reality that much of what occurs, especially in the struggle for power and control of organizations, is in fact irrational.

4. *Organizations as cultures* suggests that we can best understand organizations by examining them in the context of culture. Understanding value components is thus a critical factor in organizational analysis; we cannot understand how Toyota operates, for example, without also understanding how Japan operates. This perspective places a premium on subtle behaviors, but it is limited in that understanding a culture is impossible. Cultures are fluid, their values, beliefs, and traditions constantly changing; we are prevented, then, from ever entirely understanding the working of an organization.

5. *Organizations as political systems* suggests that we can best understand organizations by recognizing that they represent ongoing attempts to gain control over finite resources. The analyst must discover the nature of special interests, conflict, power, and authority because it is these processes—and not more rational or logical ones—that finally lead to organizational action. This is a particularly realistic view of what takes place in organizations, but its danger is that too much emphasis placed on political agendas may increase the amount of political activity within an organization. Hidden agendas can become operating practice, and honesty and openness abandoned.

6. *Organizations as psychic prisons* suggests that organizations frequently construct views of reality that cause their members to be trapped, because they lose contact with larger, more accurate visions of reality.

Organizations often create their own assumptions about what is and what is not possible for members to attain, and these assumptions limit the extent to which members feel free to explore new avenues of behavior. Examples of this kind of *groupthink* occur regularly in politics, as for instance in the Watergate or Iran-Contra scandals, where "those on the inside" were convinced by the assumptions of the group that their behaviors were appropriate, even though those same behaviors seemed entirely inappropriate to virtually all outside observers. The metaphor's strength is that it encourages critical analysis of what the organization considers "real." Its weakness is that it suggests that members of the organization are often trapped when in fact they have consciously selected the view of reality that underlies their actions. We must ask, then, who controls "reality?"

7. *Organizations as emblems of flux and transformation* suggests that organizations constantly change and must be understood as symbols of a larger, unending evolutionary process. Traditionally, change has been viewed as a process that organizations must endure; this metaphor suggests that organizations are proactive and create their own constant change. The weakness of this view is that organizations, like people, in fact frequently change in reaction rather than proaction; people do not always create their own vision of change.

8. *Organizations as instruments of domination* suggests that organizations can best be understood in terms of elites that use organizations to promote selfish interests through the manipulation of others. It serves as the basis for a radical critique of organizations. The constant danger in this metaphor, however, is that it can move us toward cynicism by suggesting that conspiracies of elite, controlling classes abound, and that the control of lower classes is the sole focus of organizations. In short, a belief inheres in this metaphor that organizations (and the people who control them) are entirely rational in both purpose and action.

Practical Applications

Morgan's organizational metaphors represent another tool that leaders may use to increase their personal insights into how organizations function. As Morgan notes in his work, the metaphors provide a "road map" that leaders may use to "read and understand" strengths and weaknesses in various organizations. For those in supervisory roles that require working with many different organizations (i.e., different school buildings, districts, or multiple educational agencies such as state departments of education, universities, and so forth), the ability to sense the nature of differences among these organizations can be critical to successful relations. You will no doubt find some metaphors more appealing than others. Those in control of organizations make the same choices; they often view their organizations as one (or a mixture) of Morgan's models. The reality of a description comes largely from a leader's perceptions of its characteristics. Whether or not the supervisor likes it, therefore, some organizations must be understood as "political systems" or even "systems of domination." You may find this awareness useful in understanding why things happen as they do in different settings.

You may also find Morgan's framework useful in assessing your own personal assumptions regarding the nature of organizations and building an individual philosophy and action plan. When we pause to consider basic views concerning the "goodness" or "badness" of organizations, "rationality" versus "irrationality," "openness" or "closedness," or any of the other issues that are raised through the metaphors, we become involved in an important reflective process that may lead to increasing the clarification of our beliefs and the identification of non-negotiable values.

Finally, as Morgan noted, examining competing metaphorical descriptions of organizations encourages us to confront the paradoxes that exist in the world around us and to think in new and more expansive ways about them. We can "imaginize" or attempt to see the world in completely untested ways, and our creativity may lead to the formulation of new metaphors. Only through this type of thinking can more creative solutions to existing problems be found, a process entirely consistent with proactive leadership.

◈ BOLMAN AND DEAL'S ORGANIZATIONAL FRAMEWORKS

The review of the ways in which the formal properties of organizations have been applied has included the ideas of Hage, Getzels, and Morgan. Over the years, there has been a decided movement away from a technical-rational approach to the analysis of organizational structure to an increasingly artistic perspective. Whereas Hage developed an analytic perspective wherein aspects of the organization could be measured and counted, Morgan moved to the use of literary techniques such as metaphors as a way to describe reality.

Even more recently, Bolman and Deal (1991) advanced the artistic approach to organizational analysis through their conceptualization of four alternative interpretations of organizational structures and processes that they refer to as *frames*. As was true of the theorists listed earlier, Bolman and Deal developed their schema after studying numerous public and private organizations. An awareness of the four frames has considerable potential value to any educational leader.

Alternative Frames

The four alternative frames developed by Bolman and Deal (2002, pp. 15–16) are explained in the following terms:

1. *Structural frame*. This perspective emphasizes the understanding of organizations through an appreciation of formal roles and relationships. In terms of other approaches reviewed here, this perspective would be quite consistent with those who believe that scientific management, or perhaps Morgan's metaphor of organizations as machines, might be the most useful way to understand and explain what is happening in a particular institution.

2. *Human resource frame*. Here, the emphasis is on the people who inhabit the institution. An underlying belief in this perspective is that it is critical to understand the needs and feelings of people, rather than what an organization looks like on a formal line and staff chart. This view is similar to the human relations and human perspectives to management discussed in chapter 1.

3. *Political frame*. In this approach to the analysis of organizations, the emphasis is on developing an understanding of the ways in which competing groups tend to strive for control over power and scarce resources. The assumption is made that conflict is a normal and expected reality in all organizations. In terms of Morgan's work, this perspective is similar to viewing organizations as political systems.

4. *Symbolic frame*. This frame is the most unique perspective offered by Bolman and Deal, and it differs greatly from any other view reviewed in this chapter. The symbolic frame "treats organizations as tribes, theater, or carnivals. . . . [Organizations] are cultures that are propelled by rituals, ceremonies, stories, heroes, and myths than by rules, policies, and managerial authority."

Practical Applications

There are at least two reasons for learning more about this approach to organizational analysis. First, each frame makes extensive use of a variety of established social science disciplines as a way to describe what is taking place in an organization. For example, the structural frame borrows greatly from sociology, the symbolic frame is related to anthropology, the human resource frame is based on ideas from social psychologists, and political science defines the political frame. Thus, the supervisor who would use the alternative frames is able to rely on several well developed paradigms that have long histories of use in studying a variety of social issues.

The Bolman and Deal perspective warrants our attention, if for no other reason than it introduces the concept of the symbolic frame as a usable part of the leader's analytic "tool kit." The symbolic frame legitimizes the use of many subtle signs of organizational life which exist, but which often become ignored because they do not "fit" established social science descriptions. Yet we know that cultures, traditions, and even myths often drive much of what takes place in schools and school districts. Bolman and Deal provide words and a framework to appreciate these real features of the world of education.

ᘔ Miles's Organizational Health

The theoretical perspectives of Hage, Getzels, Morgan, and Bolman and Deal differ considerably from one another. However, they are similar in the sense that they all represent descriptions of the formal characteristics of organizations with an emphasis on structure and predictable interrelationships rather than sensations or feelings. In the following sections, we look at the contributions of Matthew Miles, Andrew Halpin, and Donald Croft, all of whom examined informal features of organizations.

Matthew Miles is not the only theorist to suggest that organizations can be seen as healthy or unhealthy. Chris Argyris (1965) used this construct and suggested that, in order to be effective and healthy, an organization must accomplish the following core activities:

- Achieve its goals
- Maintain itself internally
- Adapt to its environment

Miles (1965) built on these characteristics and defined a healthy organization as one that

> not only survives in its environment, but continues to cope adequately over the long haul, and continuously develops and extends its surviving and coping activities. Short-term operations on any particular day may be effective or ineffective, but continued survival, adequate coping, and growth are taking place. (p. 162)

The analogy exists, then, with healthy people who are able to respond positively to whatever barriers occur in their pursuit of long and prosperous lives. Healthy people are not always without illness; rather, they are able to avoid prolonged stages of being incapacitated. The immune system remains intact because of overall good health.

By contrast, the unhealthy person has numerous, recurring encounters with illnesses, some of which are relatively minor, some life-threatening. The long-term prognosis for such individuals is poor; they will probably enjoy shorter life spans than other, healthier people. Robert Owens (1987) described "unhealthy" organizations in much the same way:

> The unhealthy organization . . . is steadily ineffective. It may cope with its environment effectively on a short-term basis with a "crash program," a concentrated drive to meet a particularly threatening situation, or "administration-by-crimes" techniques, but in the long run the unhealthy organization becomes less and less able to cope with its environment. Rather than gaining in its ability to cope with its situation, it declines in this capacity over time and it tends to become dysfunctional. (p. 218)

The unhealthy organization is one with a continually ineffective "immune system." The unhealthy organization uses crisis organization just as the ineffective leader engages in reactive behavior.

Miles identified ten dimensions that indicate the relative health of an organization:

1. *Goal focus* is the extent to which people in an organization understand and accept the goals of an organization. In a healthy organization, these goals are further defined as being appropriate, achievable, and well accepted by organizational members.

2. *Communication adequacy* is the ease and facility of communication that takes place within the organization and its external environment. In healthy organizations, the flow of information is not constrained from one level to another, and shared information is accurate.

3. *Optimal power equalization* is the balance among organizational members that ensures that no one party can coerce and corrupt other members. Healthy organizations demonstrate a relatively low degree of influence-seeking behavior by their members.

4. *Human resource utilization* is the effective use of organizational personnel, to the end that they feel as if they are growing, developing, and being satisfied in their jobs. In healthy organizations there is evidence that members are working as hard as they can and, more importantly, are experiencing personal and professional pride in this effort.

5. *Cohesiveness* is the extent to which members like their organizations and want to remain a part of them. Healthy organizations are those in which all members make a firm commitment to invest personal energy toward the goal of increasing the strength of the total organization.

6. *Morale* pertains to feelings of well-being and satisfaction expressed and demonstrated by organizational members. People express happiness at being part of healthy organizations.

7. *Innovativeness* is the tendency of an organization to grow, develop, and become "better" over time, as demonstrated by a general willingness to try new programs and procedures. Healthy organizations are those that indicate openness to new ideas that may be tried as a way to stimulate continued growth toward meeting external environmental changes.

8. *Autonomy* is the tendency of an organization to determine its own standards and behaviors in harmony with external demands but without acquiescing to those demands. Healthy organizations show a consistent independence from other organizations, but without rebellion or other potentially destructive behaviors.

9. *Adaptation* is the ability of an organization to anticipate changes in environmental demands and engage in self-corrective behaviors that indicate an ability to adapt to these demands. Healthy organizations

provide evidence of ongoing sensitivity to changes in environmental pressures, and they make change accordingly with great regularity.

10. *Problem-solving adequacy* involves the maintenance of strategies for sensing problems, along with techniques for regularly dealing with organizational crises in a rational fashion. When a healthy organization has problems (as all organizations do, from time to time) it has established ways of dealing with these issues.

Practical Applications

The concept of organizational health has some useful applications in educational supervision. For example, there is probably no organization that is high in all areas at all times. In other words, there probably has never been and never will be a completely healthy organization. Schools will never be perfect, just as no human being will be without periodic bouts with illness. The value of a conceptual frame of reference such as the one proposed by Miles is that it permits the proactive leader to serve as a diagnostician by reviewing the nature of some critical features of schooling. Are people communicating openly? Are obvious involvement and commitment being demonstrated by teachers to the stated goals of the school? Is there a spirit present suggesting that people want to try new approaches to instruction? If the answer to these questions is yes, the leader has a fundamentally healthy organization. If most questions yield a no response, there is a lot of work to do.

✧ ORGANIZATIONAL CLIMATE

A frequently discussed characteristic of organizations in recent years is *climate*, or the *psychosocial feel* of an organization, and one of the earliest and most familiar attempts to gain a handle on this characteristic was the work of Halpin and Croft (1963).

Halpin and Croft based their work on the simple notion that schools and other organizations have unique personalities, just as do human beings. The researchers developed an instrument, the Organization Climate Description Questionnaire (OCDQ) (Halpin, 1967), to measure the relative absence or presence of eight factors determined to have an impact on the informal feel, or climate, of a school. These factors, or dimensions, were grouped into two categories: one descriptive of teachers' behavior, and the second of principals' behavior. The individual dimensions related to teachers are *disengagement* (tendency to be uninvolved in school activities); *hindrance* (sense of being burdened by too much inconsequential work); *esprit* (morale); and *intimacy* (friendly social relations). The behaviors of principals include *aloofness* (formal and impersonal actions); *production emphasis* (preference for tight monitoring of staff performance); *thrust* (effort to "move the organization"); and *con-*

sideration (tendency to treat the staff in a warm and humane fashion). Through the interpretation of the OCDQ administered to teachers and principals, the climate of these dimensions is measured as "high," "medium," or "low."

Halpin and Croft suggested six different profiles of organizational climate, which reflect the degree to which and organization is high or low in the eight dimensions reviewed in table 4.3.

1. *Open climate.* An energetic organization that is moving toward its goals while its staff members are satisfied in their personal needs.

2. *Autonomous climate.* An organization in which leadership emerges primarily from the groups, and the formal leader exerts little control over staff.

3. *Controlled climate.* A climate that is impersonal and highly task oriented.

4. *Familiar climate.* A highly personal, but undercontrolled environment in which personal needs are satisfied, but with little attention paid to task accomplishment.

5. *Paternal climate.* An organization in which the formal leader tries consistently to constrain leadership emerging from the group: the leader tries to do it all.

6. *Closed climate.* An organization that demonstrates considerable apathy by all members.

The Ideal Managerial Climate (IMC) (Redding, 1972) is composed of five components: *supportiveness, trust, openness, emphasis on high-performance goals,* and *participative decision making* (Cheney et al., 2004).

Table 4.3. Profiles of six different organizational climates, based on OCDQ criteria

Climate	Disengagement	Hindrance	Esprit	Intimacy	Aloofness	Production Emphasis	Thrust	Consideration
Open	low	low	high	med.	low	low	high	high
Autonomous	low	low	high	high	high	low	med.	med.
Controlled	low	high	med.	low	high	high	med.	low
Familiar	high	low	med.	high	low	low	med.	high
Paternal	high	med.	low	low	low	high	med.	high
Closed	high	high	low	med.	high	high	low	low

Source: Andrew W. Halpin and Donald B. Croft (1963, March), The organizational climate of schools, *Administrator's Notebook, 11,* 1–2.

Practical Applications

Halpin and Croft's organizational climate concept is not meant as a tool for judging the quality or lack of quality of a particular school, even if some climate profiles may seem more appealing than others. For example, a closed climate is not necessarily less desirable than an autonomous climate or an open climate. Rather, the true value of the organizational climate conceptualization rests in the useful perspective it provides for analyzing the organization and understanding how to introduce new concepts to school groups and how to compel school employees to engage in more goal-related behavior. For example, if you determine that a particular school reflects the paternal climate (where the principal tries to do everything), you will probably need either to seek ways to help the principal delegate some activities or to be satisfied with a limited set of goals and objectives. By contrast, in an autonomous climate you will be well advised to work directly with individual staff members interested in engaging in particular types of work.

❧ SUMMARY

In this chapter we provided several theoretical models for leaders who want to become more proactive through the use of organizational analysis. Organizational analysis is but one of a number of theory-based perspectives which educational leaders may find useful.

The first part of the chapter reviewed four theories that describe the formal nature of organizations. The first, Hage's axiomatic theory of organizations, suggests that complex organizations are best understood as mechanistic or dynamic, depending on the relative amounts of eight different variables, four related to structure and four to outcomes, The major relevance of this theory is that, while changes in structure may be a part of daily organizational life, such modifications have a great likelihood of altering much of what goes on in an organization.

The second theory, Getzels's concept of social systems, suggests that organizations must be understood in terms of a constant, dynamic interaction that takes place between two dimensions: nomothetic (institutional), and idiographic (personal). A congruence between institution and individual, role and personality, and expectations and needs is a strong indication of overall organizational effectiveness. Getzels's concept encourages leaders to look at practices in their schools or districts to determine if a sufficient "fit" exists between the system and the people who work in it. An absolutely perfect match can never be achieved, but an awareness of serious discrepancies can help leaders head off major, dysfunctional conflict.

Morgan's eight organizational metaphors are designed to help us gain a more complete understanding of the ways in which institutions function. The metaphors are useful in that they provide some important insights into the assumptions held by others concerning organizational behavior and purpose.

We also considered some possible applications of Bolman and Deal's four alternative organizational frames as yet another way to assist proactive leaders in carrying out their duties. These themes stem from social sciences that have long been studied and used to understand the interrelationship so people and organizations.

Theories of organizational analysis based on informal perspectives were also included. First, we reviewed Miles's description of organizational health, which focuses on the relative presence of ten different dimensions such as goal focus, communication adequacy, resource utilization, and so forth. We noted that no school is likely to possess equally high amounts of these characteristics. However, an appreciation of the ten dimensions can help the proactive leader who seeks to engage in an ongoing diagnosis of the schools and districts in which she or he normally works.

The second construct related to informal organizational behavior was developed by Halpin and Croft, who suggested that schools have identifiable climates analogous to the personalities of individual human beings. These climates, which range from "open" to "closed," are the products of behaviors demonstrated by the teachers and principal in a school. Again, the value of this perspective is that it offers the leader yet another tool in understanding the complex behaviors and relationships that impact the effectiveness of schools.

All these perspectives, quite different on the surface, have some common aspects. First, all may be used by leaders to understand succinctly an enormous amount of subtle and complex information about organizational behavior: Formal theory can describe "a lot in a few words." Second, all the models avoid the tendency to provide complete answers. Each attempts to analyze organizations, but none provides recipes for behavior. Finally, none of the models is an absolute unto itself. They are presented as but a few examples of frameworks which educational leaders might consult as they engage in proactive and analytic—and therefore effective—supervision.

Suggested Activities

1. Make use of the constructs of Hage's theory and prepare a questionnaire to be distributed to the staff of a school to determine their perceptions of the strengths of the various structural variables. Distribute the questionnaire in two or three schools. Are there differences in terms of structure? What about differences in terms of outcomes? (With this or any other activity involving research in schools, make sure to obtain permission from the necessary people before beginning and follow all required procedures.)

2. Obtain a copy of the Halpin and Croft OCDQ instrument for measuring school climate, or any other similar scale used to measure this quality in schools. Administer it in two or more schools to see if there are obvious differences.

3. Using either Morgan's organizational metaphors or Bolman and Deal's frames as a guide, interview four or five teachers from your school to see if they reach any consensus regarding the type of organization apparently represented by your school.

Cases to Consider

Read each case and consider the following:

- What are the critical issues raised in each case, as they relate to the use of theoretical constructs to analyze organizational structures and processes?
- How does each case relate to the development of the concept of proactive leadership?
- In what ways might you suggest a resolution to the issues raised?

Case 4.1 Tipping the Balance

The Mill Valley High School had gained a reputation in recent years as one of the most innovative and exciting secondary schools in the country. There were so many visitors coming to the school each year that a policy was adopted to prohibit observing the school except on Thursdays, a fact that prompted Mill Valley students to refer to that day each week as "Zoo Day."

There were many factors contributing to the innovativeness of Mill Valley. For one thing, it was truly a school where everyone was involved in the decision-making process. Chuck Stowe, the principal, always described himself as the "facilitator of the school" rather than as an administrator. That was characteristic of another feature of the school: There appeared to be no differences among the staff in terms of authority. The principal, assistant principals, teachers, classified staff, and instructional aides all referred to themselves as equal members of the Mill Valley Team.

Everything at Mill Valley seemed to be working very well, for the most part. The biggest problem that was developing was that, recently, new homeowners from out of state were beginning to complain about some of the features of the school that did not match the expectations that they brought into the Valley. For example, longtime residents of the community were proud of their school and were content that their graduates seemed to be happy and well-adjusted community members. Some went on to college, others to trade schools or the military, and some simply went directly to work in businesses located in Mill Valley. The new residents, however, were expressing grave concerns about the fact that they believed that local high school graduates were not really being prepared for the kinds of post-secondary school experiences desired by their parents. New residents expected most students to proceed to prestigious colleges and universities.

At a recent parent information night, Chuck Stowe came under considerable fire from many new community members who indicated that they were displeased with the kind of high school program that was being offered. One consistent complaint was that things were simply "too loose." Chuck's first inclination was to let this fire burn out and protect the current practices at the school. But the attack was well organized, and the school board was now directing the superintendent to do something before the disgruntled parents (who tended to be the wealthiest residents of the district) started to hurt other district programs by voting against the annual district budget, school taxes, and other funding proposals. Chuck knew that he would have to act quickly. He now sat in his office thinking about some possible changes. He was also thinking about the consequences that those changes might have at Mill Valley. Would the school continue to need a weekly "Zoo Day," or might the place simply be turned into a zoo?

Case 4.2   This Isn't What Brought Me Here

Frank Castillo had been recognized as an extremely effective secondary school principal in the Puente del Norte school system for several years. He had taken over two of the roughest schools in the city and, through aggressive discipline, policy enforcement, and new programs designed to serve all students, he has cleaned up schools where gangs and other problems had been a plague for many years. After his work at Jackson High School, he was placed in a new position as assistant director of high schools for the district. Although the pay was better, he soon realized that he missed the "action" of a school. Within six months of taking the central office position, Frank found himself at Cortez High School, a well-respected school where the previous principal had just announced his decision to retire.

Cortez was a great school. Frank found few of the problems that he encountered at Jackson. In addition, there was strong community and parent involvement. For the most part, that was a positive feature; however, at times the "support" bordered on efforts to control the educational agenda that Frank wanted to implement in the school. For example, while most kids at Cortez went on to college, a large minority did not. In the past, these students appeared to be ignored for the most part. The parents who were most visible and involved did not seem to really care about the kids who did not conform to the majority expectations. Frank vowed to serve that "forgotten minority" as well.

Frank loved to spend most of his time out in the building, with the students and teaching staff. It was no wonder that the recent school board election was now causing him a great deal of frustration. The new board members had engaged in a spirited campaign to rid the district of several former board members who had supported the superintendent and who had also tried to stay in the background with regard to educational policies in each school. They were supporters of principals. The new board majority promised the voters to "bring the schools back to community control—away from the bureaucrats 'downtown' in the Ivory Tower." Part of that promise involved carrying out many small group meetings where parents could express their wishes directly to board members "without fear of censorship from the overpaid administrators." Needless to say, one of the more fertile areas in the city for parental involvement was with the Cortez parents who now had advocates on the school board who could "bring sanity back to their school."

Frank looked at his calendar for tomorrow and noted that, instead of attending a special debate among students in one of the school's social studies classes, he would now have to appear in his office to entertain two of the new board members who called to indicate that they had "several urgent matters to discuss." Frank knew that the new Integrated Social Studies and English program that he had launched at Cortez needed the full support of the school board. He knew that the meeting tomorrow was critical for a lot of reasons, none of which had seemed too important to him a few years ago.

Applying the Concepts

The following brief quiz is designed to improve your skills in applying some of the concepts discussed in this chapter. Read the brief introductory case, and then respond to the multiple-choice questions. You will find the answers in the Appendix.

Mary Macy, the new principal of Longfellow Middle School, has a tough task ahead of her. Longfellow has long been identified as one of the most desirable schools in which to work in the Green Valley School District. Even in these days of teacher shortages, the school has enjoyed the enviable reputation as one of the places to which people wanted to apply when openings appeared. It has a reputation as a very "happy school," where teachers were always shown great respect by being invited to become involved in suggesting ways to improve the school.

Jane Fields, the former principal, was widely recognized as the person who had created the conditions that now exist at Longfellow. She served the school for 19 years, and most say that if it were not for some recent health concerns, Jane would probably have been around for another 19 years. Several years ago, Mary had been a teacher at Longfellow, and her first administrative assignment had been as Jane's assistant principal nine years ago. After having served as a Longfellow assistant principal, Mary had become the principal at Oak Street Middle School.

It was no surprise that Mary was selected to return to Longfellow after Jane tearfully announced her retirement last May. When Mary came to the school as the new principal, Jane made it a point to appear with her at her first faculty meeting to assure the teachers that they "were in good hands with their new principal." Mary was most appreciative of a public vote of confidence in her ability to maintain the "Longfellow tradition."

However, during her principalship at Oak Street Middle School, Mary had gained a different perspective about Longfellow. Perhaps the most critical insight that she had acquired was the fact that the "perfection" of Longfellow was not what it appeared to be on the outside. Specifically, she had found that the students of the "happy Longfellow teachers" had some of the lowest state achievement test scores in the district for four consecutive years. Green Valley district (home of both Oak Street and Longfellow schools) had an excellent reputation across the state, so having one middle school below the norm was not seen by many as a cause for great alarm.

While Jane Fields had been principal of Longfellow, she had been considered such a community hero that the district had not wished to appear critical of her work. Nevertheless, Mary has now become aware that the superintendent and several board members are concerned with Longfellow's performance in the district. As the new principal, Mary has been told that her time as principal there would be limited if the 7th and 8th grade math and reading scores did not improve dramatically—and soon.

1. Which of the concepts derived from an analysis of Hage's axiomatic theory of organizations represents a strategy that Mary might use in order to increase achievement scores at Longfellow?

   a. Increase opportunities for teachers to be involved in making decisions at the school.

   b. Decrease opportunities for teachers to be involved in making decisions at the school.

   c. Decrease any sense among staff that differences exist for teachers who are more effective than others by giving some individuals preferential treatment.

   d. Decrease the number of teachers who were called upon to serve in specialized roles in the school.

2. By following the strategy selected in your response to the preceding question, Mary might also expect the following outcome at her school as she strives to increase productivity:

   a. The teachers would be more satisfied.

   b. More new programs would be initiated.

   c. The teachers would be less satisfied.

   d. Test scores might go down.

Additional Reading

Bolman, Lee G., & Deal, Terrence E. (2002). *Reframing the path to school leadership.* Thousand Oaks, CA: Corwin Press.

Bolman, Lee G., & Deal, Terrence E. (1993). *The path to school leadership: A portable mentor.* Newbury Park, CA: Corwin Press.

Senge, Peter M. (1990). *The fifth discipline.* New York: Doubleday.

❦ 5 ❧

Leadership

For many, leadership is synonymous with supervision in school settings. The literature is filled with suggestions that educational administration represents the maintenance of past practice, whereas leadership, or supervision, involves bringing about organizational change. Unfortunately, the implication is that supervisors are the "good guys" who wear "white hats," while administrators block innovation and creativity and are generally nonprogressive. This is too simplistic a notion to describe the complex processes associated with leading schools. Here, the belief is that *effective proactive leadership and supervision are compatible with effective administration*. Good supervisors need highly refined administrative skills. And good administrators must be able to lead. Leadership, however, is a quality required of both supervisors and administrators. In fact, leadership is a characteristic increasingly required by all educators—teachers, administrators, supervisors, and staff.

In this chapter, a broad view of leadership is developed by first seeking a definition that applies to a variety of contexts and then reviewing theoretical perspectives. The chapter concludes with an examination of the concept of instructional supervision.

❦ ALTERNATIVE DEFINITIONS

When people talk about how an organization works, conversation almost immediately is directed toward leadership. The presence or absence of this characteristic has a strong and direct impact on the effectiveness of an organization. Nevertheless, organizational analysts struggle to find a basic definition for the concept of leadership. This section reviews several definitions in an attempt to determine some basic features needed in analyzing leadership in schools.

101

Gary Yukl (1997) pulled together a number of different definitions of leadership in his comprehensive review:

- Leadership is "the behavior of an individual when he is directing the activities of a group toward a shared goal" (Hemphill & Coons, 1957, p. 7)

- Leadership is "interpersonal influence, exercised in a situation and directed, through the communication process, toward the attainment of a specified goal or goals" (Tannenbaum, Weshler, & Massarik, 1961, p. 24)

- Leadership is the "initiation and maintenance of structure in expectation and interaction" (Stogdill, 1974, p. 41)

- Leadership is "an interaction between persons in which one presents information of a sort and in such a manner that the other becomes convinced that his outcomes (benefits/cost ratio) will be improved if he behaves in the manner suggested or desired" (Jacobs, 1970, p. 232)

- Leadership is "a particular type of power relationship characterized by a group member's perceptions that another group member has the right to prescribe behavior patterns for the former regarding his activity as a group member" (Janada, 1960, p. 358).

- Leadership is "a process whereby O's actions change P's behavior, and P views the influence attempt as being legitimate and the change as consistent with P's goals" (Kochran, Schmidt, & DeCotiis, 1975, p. 285).

- Leadership is "the influential increment over and above mechanical compliance with the routine directives of the organization" (Katz & Kahn, 1978, p. 528).

- Leadership is "the process of influencing others to achieve mutually agreed-upon purposes for the organization" (Patterson, 1993, p. 3).

Although these definitions represent a wide range of ideas about organizational leadership, they display some common themes. First, all suggest that the central feature of leadership is an interpersonal relationship where one individual influences, guides, or controls the behavior of another person. Second, most of the definitions suggest that leader behavior implies some sort of change—that leaders promote movement in the organization or in the behaviors of people in the organization.

Lipham and Hoeh (1974) provided yet another definition of leadership that is appealing largely because of its emphasis on the responsibility of a key actor to promote and sustain positive and needed change. For them,

> leadership is that behavior of an individual which initiates a new structure in interaction within a social system, it initiates changes in

the goals, objectives, configurations, procedures, inputs, processes, and ultimately the outputs of social systems. (p. 196)

Recent research on leadership has emphasized a simple observation: Leaders must have followers. As a result, an entire set of behaviors is often described in the literature as "followership." This concept will be revisited later in this chapter when the discussion turns to the characteristics of effective instructional leaders who empower their followers.

Regardless of the definition, leadership is a critical issue both in schools and in other organizations. In their study of leadership behavior in many different settings, Warren Bennis and Burt Nanus (1985) noted that this issue has particular relevance for at least three reasons:

1. Organizations are suffering from a "commitment gap": people do not believe in what their organizations stand for because leaders have not developed that sense of belief in their followers.

2. The level of complexity in modern society is higher than it has ever been before. Predictability and stability are characteristics that are virtually absent from most organizations today.

3. Organizational credibility is disappearing. Generally accepted authority figures are being questioned and challenged more often today because so many leaders have disappointed their followers in recent years.

Bennis and Nanus suggest that leadership is no longer a simple academic term to be understood by social scientists but a very real concept that has meaning for everyone. The proactive leader has a special interest in learning more about leadership and must develop a genuine and personal definition about this concept.

❧ HISTORICAL DEVELOPMENT OF LEADERSHIP

If any single topic can be considered a staple of management and administrative studies over the years, it is the search for a better understanding of what constitutes the best way to study the central concept of leadership. The analysis of leadership in organizations has proceeded through at least four major stages: the "great person"; traitist; situational or sociological; and behavioral. These are all *descriptive approaches*.

"Great Person" Approach

The *"great person" perspective* is a psychologically based approach that suggests that leadership is determined primarily by the personality of an individual. If we wish to understand what characteristics comprise leadership, then we should look to how a particular individual, or "great person," demonstrated leadership in the past.

A famous practitioner of this theory of leadership was General George Patton, who often determined how to deal with a problem by reviewing what famous historical characters had done under similar circumstances. An avid student of military history, Patton often charted a path for the American army during World War II based on the strategies of Caesar, Hannibal, or other great military leaders. The "great person" approach to leadership analysis (sometimes called "heroic leadership" [Marion, 2005]) is seen more frequently than we might at first assume. Young children, for instance, have long been advised to read the biographies and autobiographies of famous people in order to learn the ways in which such people lived. If you learn about Thomas Edison, Martin Luther King, Jr., Helen Keller, or some other famous "great person," the implication is that by following their example you might also grow up to be famous, inventive, brave, or wise.

While this approach to understanding leadership is temptingly simple, it has severe drawbacks that limit its usefulness as a guide to the development of leadership skills. For one thing, we can never find a single "great person" as a role model, because the exact circumstances of two lives will never be the same. Reading about the life of Abraham Lincoln does not enable us to follow in his footsteps, because so much of Lincoln's career and behavior was shaped by conditions in early nineteenth-century Illinois. Marion (2005) points out that "great persons" are also limited by timing:

> Heroic leadership is powerless when the timing is wrong—it is doubtful, for example, that Dr. King would have made much impression 50 years before his time, or that Horace Mann could have launched the common school movement in 1750, 100 years before his time. It's all a matter of timing.

A second limitation to the "great person" view is that the "person" has historically been defined in male terms. The net effect of this sexism has been that women who aspire to leadership roles have been forced, usually in subtle ways, to find male role models; they have been trained to "act like a man." Ultimately this ignores natural differences between ways in which men and women might function most effectively in leadership positions, a major problem identified by Charol Shakeshaft (1987) in her analysis of gender differences in school administration.

Finally, "great person" approaches to leadership limit the creative behavior of present leaders. Instead of asking, "What would Caesar have done under these circumstances?" the modern leader might more profitably explore new ways of facing a problem. By relying exclusively on the past behaviors of others for guidance, people in leadership roles will rarely bring about changes so often needed in dynamic organizations.

Traitist Approach

The "great person" approach suggests that we study individual leaders; a related view suggests that to understand how leaders behave, we should examine several individuals to determine common characteristics or traits. The student of leadership, for example, might note that leaders of successful corporations are generally tall, attended Ivy League universities, and drive big cars. We might conclude then that a way to the top of a major company would be to enroll at Penn, buy a Cadillac, and, if possible, grow a few inches (or at least buy a pair of elevator shoes!).

Once again, the *traitist approach* to the study of leadership is appealingly simple and straightforward. It suggests that an educational supervisor who wants to be perceived as an effective leader might constructively spend time finding out which of her or his predecessors were viewed as effective and then identifying and copying traits found in all those individuals. While the realization that "dressing for success" sometimes produces an executive and thus may make trait analyses seem like reasonable strategies, there are some obvious drawbacks.

Traits analyzed in this approach are frequently characteristics over which we have little control. A short follower wishing to acquire leadership characteristics cannot, of course, suddenly become tall. Additionally, there is a danger in generalizing widely from limited examples. The lives of Abraham Lincoln and Lyndon Johnson might reinforce the notion that physical height has a relationship to leadership ability, but how then do we explain the abilities of Napoleon in both the military and political spheres?

Finally, traitist leadership approaches are restrictive. When people focus on specific, similar traits of past leaders, there is a tendency to be unduly biased toward those traits. Perhaps the traits of the leaders even overshadow the other components necessary to run the organization. Thus, traits of new leaders should not necessarily be restricted to the traits of past leaders. Consider the following example: If we were to select school superintendents and principals based on traits common to past holders of these positions, we would limit our search to white, married males who had previously been coaches. The fact that the majority of present school administrators possess these traits is probably testimony to the popularity of the traitist perspective. Popularity, however, is no excuse for the maintenance of a delimiting practice. Cheney and his colleagues (2004) identified another disadvantage of the traitist approach:

> Traits research was more consistent in identifying the characteristics associated with leadership *emergence* than leadership *effectiveness*. Certain traits seem to predict fairly well who will be chosen or viewed as a leader, but not necessarily whether that person will get good results. (p. 187)

Situational Approaches

In sharp contrast to the "great person" and traitist approaches that emphasize physical and psychological characteristics in the study of leadership, the *situational* or *sociological approach* (Hersey & Blanchard, 1996) maintains that leadership is determined less by the characteristics of individuals than by the requirements of the group or the setting in which the individual works. According to this view, acts of leadership are the direct result of situations that arise in groups or organizations that call for those acts. Thus, an individual's exercise of leadership is brought about by the demands of the group with which that individual must interact. John Hemphill (1949) conducted a comprehensive sociological study of the impact of leader according to differences of groups. He found such variables as viscidity (the feeling of cohesion in a group), hedonic tone (the degree of satisfaction of group members), size of the group, homogeneity of group members, and intimacy among individuals within the group to correlate significantly with leadership effectiveness. Inevitably, however, researchers realized that is the study of leadership focused purely on such situationally specific issues as how particular groups react to particular individuals, then the study of leadership, per se, would end.

A good deal of situational leadership analysis is found in the actions of the World War I hero, Sergeant Alvin York. York might never have been recognized in history had he remained a poor Tennessee farmer. As a result of the war, he enlisted in the army. He then was in the right place at precisely the right moment to capture more German prisoners of war than any other soldier. The clear limitation on this theory that situation alone evokes leadership is that it ignores almost completely the individual's characteristics as a leader. Alvin York would not have been a military leader without World War I, but his leadership potential might have been realized in some other field. We have no way of knowing.

Behavioral Approaches

Recent analyses of leadership examine the behavior of the leader and balance elements of both the psychological ("great person" and traitist) and the situational approaches. This perspective, reflected in Lipham and Hoeh's definition cited earlier, recognizes that a leader's behavior is the result of a blend of both personal characteristics and situations in which the leader must act. The basic assumptions of the *behaviorist approach* are:

- People behave according to different leadership styles. This occurs because people differ in how they perceive a situation, accomplish tasks, interact with others, and make decisions.
- People behave differently, depending on contextual circumstances. Consequently, behavior changes.
- There is no single "right way" for people to behave.
- What is comfortable and "right" for one person may feel uncomfortable and "wrong" to another.
- An organization functions best when it capitalizes on the strengths of each individual, encouraging the recognition and celebration of differences.

If any single approach to the study of leadership might be classified as the prevailing perspective of the last 25 or more years, it would be the behavioral approach. As a result, the following descriptions are offered of the work of three influential theoretical perspectives that have been widely adopted in studies of educational practice.

Halpin and Winer's Two-Dimensional Theory

According to Andrew Halpin and A. J. Winer, a leader's behavior is composed of two basic dimensions: Initiating structure and consideration. These two concepts reflect Getzels's nomothetic and idiographic dimensions (see chapter 4). Halpin (1957) defined them as follows:

- *Initiating structure.* Behavior that delineates the relationship between the leader and members of the work group and endeavors to establish well-defined patterns of organization, channels of communication, and methods of procedure.

- *Consideration.* Behavior that indicates friendship, mutual trust, respect, and warmth in the relationship between leader and the staff.

Bowers and Seashore's Four-Factor Theory

D. G. Bowers and S. E. Seashore (1966) suggested that leadership behavior consists of goal emphasis, work facilitation, support, and interaction facilitation. These four dimensions are defined in the following way:

- *Goal emphasis.* Behavior that stimulates enthusiasm for meeting the group's goals or achieving excellent performance.

- *Work facilitation.* Behavior that helps goal attainment by scheduling, planning, and coordinating.

- *Support.* Behavior that enhances someone else's feelings of personal worth and importance.

- *Interaction facilitation.* Behavior that encourages members of the group to develop close, mutually satisfying relationships.

House's Path-Goal Theory

Robert House (1973) developed three terms derived largely from the work of Halpin and Winer for describing leadership behavior: instrumental, supportive, and participative.

- *Instrumental (or directive) leadership.* Behavior that delineates the relationship between the leader and members of the work group and attempts to clearly define patterns of the organization without autocratic or punitive control.

- *Supportive leadership.* Behavior that indicates friendship and warmth toward the work group by the leader.

- *Participative leadership.* Behavior that allows subordinates to influence decisions by asking for suggestions and including the subordinates in the decision-making process.

Table 5.1 suggests some obvious similarities among these three theoretical perspectives derived from the behavioral approach to the analysis of leadership. Subtle distinctions can be found in the individual component dimensions suggested in each model, but the overlap is significant.

Table 5.1   Three descriptive theories of leadership showing the comparability of their component dimensions

Halpin and Winer	Bowers and Seashore	House
1. Initiating structure	1. Goal emphasis	1. Instrumental
2. Consideration	2. Work facilitation	2. Supportive
	3. Support	3. Participative
	4. Interaction facilitation	

No matter what approach one uses to analyze leadership, certain basic issues must be considered: *locus, frequency, potency,* and *scope* of leadership. The locus of leadership is the social system in which leadership occurs—be it classroom, school, school district, or entire community. The frequency of leadership, or how often a leader engages in certain behaviors, is also important. Leaders may attempt too many acts of leadership too often without actually implementing or evaluating all of the elements necessary for achieving effective outcomes. On the other hand, some people in leadership positions may rarely engage in any active leadership attempts at all. There is no consensus as to what constitutes the optimal balance between "too frequent" and "not often enough." Potency refers to "the extent to which an initiated change by a leader represents significant departure from that which exists, i.e., the magnitude of the initiated change" (Lipham & Hoeh, 1974, p. 186). Finally, scope or range of leadership is significant. Leadership may be functionally diverse or functionally specific; some leaders have defined and virtually unlimited responsibilities and obligations, whereas for others, the obligations, breadth, and depth of the leadership role are limited and functions circumscribed.

Contemporary Popular Leadership Theories

In addition to the theoretical frameworks presented here to illustrate behavioral perspectives, there have been several recent popular attempts to describe the nature of leadership in organizations. Among the most popular have been Peters and Waterman (1982), Bennis and Nanus (1985), and Kouzes and Posner (1987), whose perspectives represent a blend of analysis reflecting the traditional traitist view of leadership, although each work is careful to note that leadership behavior must be appreciated in light of a specific contextual reality. As a result, it might be argued that many current descriptions of leadership are also behavioral in nature.

Covey's Principle-Centered Leadership

The example of popular leadership analysis selected for a brief review here is the work of Stephen Covey (1991). His work is founded on many of the same basic assumptions identified as central to proactive leadership. Covey notes eight characteristics of *principle-centered leaders* (pp. 33–38):

1. *They are continually learning.* Principle-centered leaders are constantly educated by their experiences.

2. *They are service-oriented.* Principle-centered leaders view their roles as providing for the needs of followers, as career stops.

3. *They radiate positive energy.* Principle-centered leaders are happy and enthusiastic people.

4. *They believe in other people.* Principle-centered leaders endeavor to find the best in others, not the faults of others.

5. *They lead balanced lives.* Principle-centered leaders are not "married to their work"; they enjoy a full range of social, intellectual, familial, and work-related experiences.

6. *They see life as an adventure.* Principle-centered leaders see things that occur in their lives as challenges, not problems.

7. *They are synergistic.* Principle-centered leaders are able to pull together the vast resources of talent and energy found in people and events that surround them so that they can make organizational life more productive, as the sum of many individual parts.

8. *They exercise for self-renewal.* Principle-centered leaders engage in regular exercise to strengthen themselves physically, mentally, emotionally, and spiritually.

Each of these theoretical perspectives related to the description of leadership can help us understand some of the basic characteristics of leadership behavior.

ℰ₰ NORMATIVE PERSPECTIVES OF LEADERSHIP

To this point, previous analyses and models of leadership have had one thing in common: They were all *descriptive* models. In other words, each of the theories presented was developed specifically to explain *what leadership is*. There were no efforts made to identify *how leaders ought to behave or act in order to be effective*.

In the following sections, we review several additional models of leadership. While each has a unique focus, the common ingredient is that they are meant not only to describe, but also to give direction to effective leadership behavior. In this way, all of the following models may be defined as *normative models* of leadership.

The Leadership Grid

As is true of most conceptualizations of leadership, the *leadership grid model* of Robert Blake and Anne Adams McCanse (1991) suggests that leadership consists of two attitudinal dimensions: a concern for people (or interpersonal relationships) and a concern for tasks, production, or things. This conceptualization of leadership is based on earlier work by Blake and Jane Mouton (1985), who developed the *managerial grid*. Blake and Adams McCanse's leadership grid, depicted in figure 5.1, particularly resembles Halpin and Winer's two-dimensional managerial theory.

The leadership grid allows us to analyze leadership attitudes in terms of both concern for people and concern for product, on a continuum of 1 (low) to 9 (high). According to Lunenburg and Ornstein (2004) and Robert Owens (1987), Blake and Mouton made it clear in their earlier work that 9.9 (high in both areas) is the leadership attitude pattern likely to be most effective in most organizations to achieve the best results. Owens (1987) remarked:

> "Results" means that effectiveness of the organization in (1) achieving its goals and (2) maintaining a high level of morale. Goal achievement might be measured by such indicators (in schools) as test scores, rate of dropouts, percent of graduates going on to further education, employee-management relations, community support for bond issues, and feedback from employers on the performance of graduates. Morale may be indicated by such things as absenteeism, number of grievances, employee-management relations, and cohesiveness of the group. (p. 134)

The leadership grid model does not simply provide more terms to describe leadership approaches; rather, its implications about the relative effectiveness of certain behaviors provide useful directions for any individual seeking to perform as an effective educational leader. A grid rating of 1,1 (Impoverished Management), for instance, would hardly be an appropriate pattern approach for a supervisor or administrator called upon to provide direction to a school staff. A 9,9 rating (Team Management), on the other hand—where equivalent emphasis is placed both on the needs of teachers, students, and staff and on school outcomes—would be optimal. Variations on this most desirable level are likely, of course; a supervisor who is a proponent of the human relations philosophy would probably come closer to a 1,9 (Country Club Management) attitude rating—high concern for people, low concern for production—while a supervisor who believes in scientific management might achieve something closer to a 9,1 (Authority-Compliance)—low concern for people, high concern for production.

The leadership grid is widely used in both public and private management circles not only as a diagnostic, descriptive device to help individuals understand their attitudes, but also as a way to appreciate places where one set of attitudes may be more or less appropriate than others.

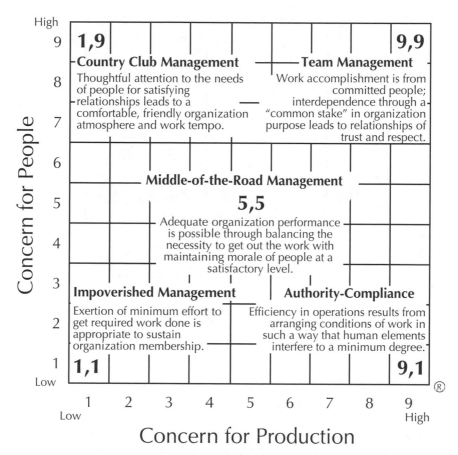

The Leadership Grid® Figure from *Leadership Dilemmas—Grid Solutions* by Robert R. Blake and Anne Adams McCanse (formerly the Managerial Grid Figure by Robert R. Blake and Jane S. Mouton). Houston: Gulf Publishing Company, p. 29. Copyright © 1991 by Grid International, Inc. Reproduced by permission of the owners.

Figure 5.1. The Leadership Grid©

Reddin's 3-D Theory

The normative 3-D theory of leadership developed by W. J. Reddin (1970) goes a step beyond the leadership grid yet builds on the same logic (concern for people versus concern for tasks). The major distinction between Reddin's view and that of the leadership grid is that, at its most basic level, Reddin's model does not suggest that any one single combination of behaviors is necessarily better than any other combination. Figure 5.2 demonstrates Reddin's basic model, which simply provides descriptive classification in four quadrants: *separated* (low in concern for people and task); *related* (high in concern for people, low in task orienta-

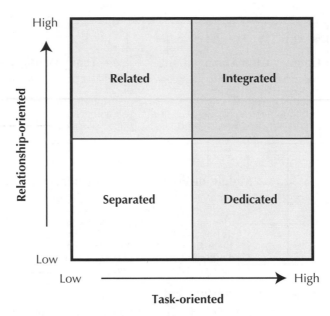

Figure 5.2.   Reddin's 3-D theory of leadership

tion); *dedicated* (low in concern for people, high in task orientation); and *integrated* (high in concern for people and task). The critical point to remember is that, at this basic stage, Reddin's quadrants are purely descriptive; none is better or worse than any other.

Reddin's theory becomes normative, however, when it goes on to suggest that the basic four behaviors are more or less appropriate depending upon the unique characteristics of the situation that exists in the leader's organization (Lunenburg & Ornstein, 2004). As the model in figure 5.3 suggests, for example, the leader who demonstrates an "integrated" style might appear to be inappropriately compromising in some circumstances; in other situations, the "high in concern for both people and task" style might be perceived as truly "executive." The "separated" leader (low in concern for people and tasks), viewed as disconnected and a "deserter" in some situations, might be an effective and organizationally needed "bureaucrat" in other cases. Sergiovanni and Starratt (2007) summarized the overall value of Reddin's 3-D theory of leadership:

> At first glance the theory seems complex and the labels chosen by Reddin confusing and on occasion inappropriate. But the language system is worth deciphering, for the concepts and ideas basic to the theory are powerful and important. A key to this theory is the notion that the *same style* expressed in different situations may be effective or ineffective. (p. 183)

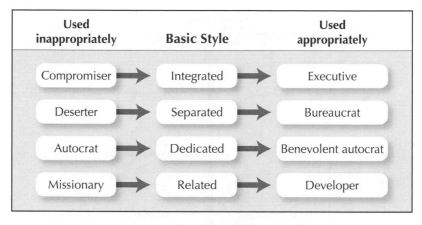

Used inappropriately	Basic Style	Used appropriately
Compromiser ➡	Integrated ➡	Executive
Deserter ➡	Separated ➡	Bureaucrat
Autocrat ➡	Dedicated ➡	Benevolent autocrat
Missionary ➡	Related ➡	Developer

Figure 5.3   Effective and ineffective expressions of leadership style according to Reddin's 3-D theory of leadership

The basic problem with Reddin's theory is that "appropriate" and "inappropriate" situations are not clearly defined. Nevertheless, Reddin's view of effective leadership behavior as a dynamic and situational, rather than static, phenomenon is important.

Behavioral Matrix

The final normative view of leadership behavior considered here is the *leadership behavioral matrix* developed by researchers at the Northwest Regional Educational Laboratory for Educational Development in Portland, Oregon. This model suggests that two dimensions comprise leadership behavior. The major difference between this perspective and the others reviewed earlier is that the Northwest Laboratory Matrix suggests that a person is *either* task-oriented or people-oriented and *either* introverted or extroverted in terms of how he or she works with others. Figure 5.4 depicts the basic leadership matrix model, which classifies the behavior of an individual according to four distinct styles:

1. *Promoters.* Extroverted and people-oriented, these individuals get involved with others in active, rapidly changing situations. They are typically outgoing and friendly and can get things going, but may settle for less than the best results. Promoters are highly competitive.

2. *Supporters.* Introverted, people-oriented types who value interpersonal relations, these individuals try to minimize conflict and promote the happiness of others.

3. *Analyzers.* They are introverted, task-oriented people who are problem solvers and like to have all the data before making a decision. Thus, some people get frustrated with their slow decision making.

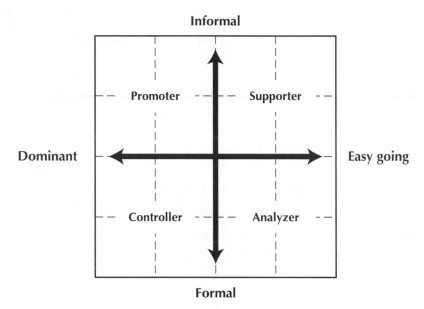

Informal

Promoter   Supporter

Dominant   **Easy going**

Controller   Analyzer

Formal

Source: Northwest Regional Educational Laboratory, Portland OR. Reprinted by permission of the publisher.

Figure 5.4.   Leadership behavioral matrix

4. *Controllers.* Extroverted and task-oriented, these are individuals who love to run things and have jobs done in their own way. These people will make sure the task is completed on time and to their satisfaction.

The critical observation in this description is that no one leadership style is better than others; there are no "right" or "wrong" styles. Individuals in each of the four quadrants of the behavioral matrix have strengths and weaknesses that may be called upon in different situations to create more effective organizational outcomes.

The leadership behavioral matrix is particularly useful in analyzing potential conflicts which are most apt to occur along the diagonals of the quadrants depicted in figure 5.4. Thus, the most powerful conflicts tend to take place between promoters and analyzers and between controllers and supporters. Consider, for example, the possibility of conflict between a patient, thoughtful analyzer who wants more and more facts before acting, and the more impulsive promoter. Moreover, the action-oriented controller will no doubt have a difficult time dealing with the more laid-back supporters. Conflicts are clearly going to take place in schools where all of these various behavioral styles are represented, and they will be increasingly visible and powerful as people become more wedded to the predominant behavioral characteristics of a particular quadrant. More extreme promoters will probably have even more direct problems in deal-ing with more extreme analyzers.

The behavioral matrix, like Blake and Adams McCanse's leadership grid and Reddin's 3-D theory of leadership, is a behaviorally-based, norma-tive model of leadership analysis. All three, properly understood, can pro-vide direction and guidance for effective supervisory leadership practices.

In the next section, other approaches to the analysis of leadership in school settings are offered.

ও EMERGING LEADERSHIP PERSPECTIVES

In recent years discussions of leadership in the context of educa-tional organizations have built upon the behavioral theories of leadership reviewed here. However, these theoretical bases have been directed increasingly toward three specific themes: The supervisor or administra-tor as an instructional leader (Austin, 1979; Brookover & Lezotte, 1980; Lipham, 1981; Andrews & Smith, 1991), the supervisor or administrator as moral and ethical leader (Etzioni, 1990; Hodgkinson, 1991; Barnett et al., 1991), and the cognitive development of leadership on the part of supervisors and administrators (Leithwood, 1989).

Instructional Leadership

Despite the amount of discussion about, as well as support for, the concept of instructional leadership, little has been done to define the concept operationally. Few studies have been undertaken to determine the specific behaviors of supervisors and administrators who serve as instructional leaders. Early efforts tended to define leadership behavior in very narrow terms. As a result, most early descriptions focused only on the ways in which school principals became directly involved with instructional activities, and the perception quickly grew that only those principals who spent nearly all of their time either teaching classes or observing teachers were legitimately serving as instructional leaders.

This view has been more recently rejected for at least two reasons. First, we now recognize that individuals other than principals (e.g., superintendents, supervisors, department chairs, lead teachers, etc.) might engage in instructional leadership behaviors. Second, we have increasingly realized that instructional leadership can take forms that go well beyond direct intervention in classroom activities (Henson, 2006; Jensen, 1989; Weber, 1989). The definition of instructional leadership suggested by Ching-Jen Liu (1984) is useful in describing this concept. "Instructional leadership consists of direct and indirect behaviors that significantly affect teacher instruction and, as a result, student learning" (p. 33).

Liu divided the tasks of instructional leadership into two catego-ries—direct and indirect. In very broad terms, we might classify *direct leadership* activities as staff development and teacher evaluation and supervision, and *indirect leadership* as instructional facilitation, resource acquisition, building maintenance, and student problem resolution. Examples of specific behaviors related to each of these categories are shown in the following list.

Factor I: Staff Development

- Work with a committee to plan and implement the staff development program.
- Survey staff members to determine topics and activities for a year-long staff development plan.
- Provide in-service training for the support staff on how their roles relate to the instructional program.

Factor II: Resource Acquisition and Building Maintenance

- Acquire adequate resources for teaching.
- Allocate resources on the basis of identified needs according to a priority ranking.
- Maintain the building in order to provide a pleasant working condition for students and staff.

Factor III: Instructional Facilitation

- Establish priorities so that, by the amount of time directed to it, instruction is always first.
- Work according to the belief that all students can learn and achieve at high levels.
- Support teachers who are implementing new ideas.

Factor IV: Teacher Supervision and Evaluation

- Involve all staff members and people from the community in setting clear goals and objectives for instruction.
- Work according to the belief that all teachers can teach and teach well.
- Have conferences with individual teachers to review their instructional plans.

Factor V: Student Problem Resolution

- Assist teachers in dealing with discipline problems.
- Enforce school attendance policies to reduce tardiness and absentee rates.
- Interact directly with students to discuss their problems about school.

Using these classifications and descriptions of instructional leadership, Liu studied two groups of high school principals, one "effective" and another "not effective." He found that the effective group engaged in instructional leadership behaviors more often than the other group and that those behaviors reflected both direct and indirect instructional leadership. As a result, we now recognize that the analysis of instructional leadership is considerably more complex than first thought and that supervisors and administrators who strive to exhibit instructional leadership must be prepared to engage in a wide range of activities that support the instructional priorities of the school. Instructional leadership is as much a product of a personalized instructional philosophy as it is of any particular activities that a person follows.

One of the most comprehensive recent efforts to gain a better understanding of what behaviors comprise instructional leadership was carried out by Jerry Patterson (1993) for the Association for Supervision and Curriculum Development (ASCD). This study looked at the work of numerous principals who had been identified as instructional leaders. Five behavioral patterns were identified in those individuals who were viewed as effective leaders.

1. *They provide a sense of vision to their schools.* They demonstrate the ability to articulate what a school is supposed to do, particularly in terms of what it should do to benefit children. Effective instructional leaders leave little doubt that the purpose of the school is to find ways in which children may learn successfully. This vision, or mission, guides all other activities.

2. *They engage in participative management.* They encourage a better organizational climate in the school by allowing teachers and staff to participate meaningfully in real decision making and not merely in an effort to "play at" getting people to be involved when decisions are already made. The staff senses greater ownership in the priorities and programs that are available to help children.

3. *They provide support for instruction.* Instructional leaders are committed to maintaining quality instruction as their primary organizational focus that when decisions must be made concerning priorities, instruction always comes first. These individuals make it clear that energy will be expended to assure that resources are available to enable the instructional program of the school to proceed unabated.

4. *Instructional leaders monitor instruction.* They know what is going on in the classrooms of their schools. This monitoring may take several forms from direct, in-class, intensive observation to merely walking around the building and talking with students. The critical issue, regardless of the particular procedures followed, is that instructional leaders are aware of the quality of instruction being carried out in their schools.

5. *They are resourceful.* Instructional leaders rarely allow circumstances in their organizations to get in the way of their vision for quality educational programs. As a result, they tend not to allow a lack of resources, or apparently prohibitive district policies, or any other factors, to interfere with the goals of their schools.

Instructional leaders carry out these behavior patterns very differently. Thus, people with different personalities, philosophies, values, and attitudes can be equally effective educational leaders. In addition, entirely different schools can serve as settings for instructional leadership identified through the ASCD work.

Effective school leaders share many behavioral patterns, predictably, with leaders in other organizations. Bennis and Nanus (1985), in a study of a wide variety of effective organizations, discovered five strategies followed by successful leaders:

- *Strategy I: Attention through vision.* Leaders create a focus in an organization or an agenda that demonstrates an unparalleled concern for outcomes, products, and results.

- *Strategy II: Meaning through communication.* Effective communication is inseparable from effective leadership.

- *Strategy III: Trust through positioning.* Leaders must be trusted in order to be effective; we trust people who are predictable and whose positions are known. Leaders who are trusted make themselves known and make their positions clear.

- *Strategy IV: The deployment of self through positive self-regard.* Leaders have positive self-images, self-regard that is not self-centered, and they know their worth. In general, they are confident without being cocky.

- *Strategy V: The development of self through the "Wallenda Factor."* Before his death, the famous aerialist Karl Wallenda was said to have become more preoccupied with not falling than with succeeding. Leaders are consistently able to focus their energies on success rather than on simply avoiding failure.

Other researchers have created other lists by successful leadership behaviors parallel to these efforts by Liu, ASCD, and Bennis and Nanus. Such lists typically feature overlap with what is noted here. What is highly significant about all of these efforts is that they represent attempts to move the study of leadership to levels of analysis not found in most past treatments. For educational supervisors, this is good news. It offers the possibility that specific, effective leadership behaviors may now be identified in greater numbers than they were in the past. While such efforts should never be viewed as gospel to be followed for leadership or as panaceas to cure the absences of direction often found in schools, they do provide practitioners with a road map to follow in search for more effective educational programs.

Moral and Ethical Leadership

A new perspective on leadership behavior is appearing in the literature. This view, referred to here as moral and ethical leadership, appears to have two different ways of looking at the duties of organizational leaders. One characterizes the leader as the model of moral behavior—as the person who works to set a proper ethical tone for the organization. The other is related to the leader becoming a servant to meet the diverse needs of those who work in the organization (Greenleaf, 1977).

With regard to the leader as a moral role model, there is an increasing recognition that, contrary to many conventional images of leadership, it is not sufficient to believe that leaders are simply those who bring about organizational change. Instead, there is now an increased emphasis in the quality and nature of the types of changes that an individual might promote. This view might serve as a response to those who have often claimed that the mere ability of an individual to promote massive societal change (e.g., Hitler or Stalin) made that person a leader. There is now an assumption by many (Sergiovanni, 1990; Hodgkinson, 1991; Barnett, et al., 1991) that a key feature of leadership is that it promotes change toward morally and societally redeeming goals. Etzioni (1990) contends that what means most to people is what they believe, how they feel, and the shared norms, values, and cultural symbols that emerge from groups with which they identify (Lunenburg & Ornstein, 2004)

An understanding of leadership in these terms is highly dependent on the acceptance of a clear vision of the nature of education. Hodgkinson (1991), a proponent of leadership as a moral activity, noted the following:

> Education is not the art of training and subjugating people to serve at the profit of others. It is the art of helping people to know themselves, to develop the resources, judgment, and skills of learning and the sense of values needed on facing a future of unpredictable change, to understand the rights and responsibilities of adults in a democratic society and to exercise the greatest possible degree of control over their own fate. (p. 16)

Educational leadership, then, is the art of promoting this view of value-based and "value-added" (Sergiovanni, 1990) education.

The second vision of moral and ethical leadership is related to a view which states that the primary goal of the leader is to serve the needs of followers. An example of this perspective is found in the notion of stewardship defined by Block (1993):

> Stewardship is the umbrella idea that promises the means of achieving fundamental change in the way we govern our institutions. Stewardship is to hold something in trust for another. Historically, stewardship was a means to protect a kingdom while those rightfully in charge were away, or more often, to govern for the sake of an underage king. (p. xx)

By separating these two branches of moral and ethical leadership, there should be no confusion: value-added leadership is not a contradiction to stewardship. To the contrary, these concepts are quite compatible. Each of these areas will likely see greater development in the near future, and the proactive leader would be well advised to remain aware of this development.

Cognitive Development Models of Leadership

A most promising recent direction in the area of leadership analysis has taken a different path from earlier descriptive and normative approaches. In the past, the focus of researchers has been to discern what leadership is by looking primarily at what leaders do. To understand leadership in organizations, we must recognize that it has largely been tied to looking at the external evidence or outcomes of leaders and their work.

An approach which has been gaining in popularity among leadership researchers looks at the issue of how leaders think, or how they engage in cognitive processing of information (Hallinger, Leithwood, & Murphy, 1993; Prestine & LeGrand, 1991). Simply stated, do leaders process information differently than nonleaders? Even more critical is whether *good* leaders think differently than *less effective* leaders.

A particularly well-developed research agenda following the notion of cognitive processing by educational leaders was developed by Kenneth Leithwood and his colleagues at the Ontario Institute for Studies in Education. One set of studies has looked into the ways in which *expert* principals solve everyday school problems in ways that are markedly different from practices demonstrated by *novice*, or *typical*, principals. The designation of individual administrators as either *expert* or *novice* (*typical*) principals is derived from scores achieved on an instrument known as the *Principal Effectiveness Profile* (Hallinger, Leithwood, & Montgomery, 1993).

The ways in which expert principals handle problems is quite different from that of their novice colleagues. For example, when novice principals prioritized the handling of problems, the criterion that they used focused on "consequences for school and academic growth of large numbers of students," while their typical or novice colleagues were "more concerned about consequences for themselves" (Leithwood & Steinbach, 1995, p. 51). Expert principals used detailed prior planning and consultation with others in their schools as a way to get important information about problems; novice principals gave little attention to planning and consulted less frequently with fewer specific purposes (Leithwood & Steinbach, 1995). Information concerning these and other differences was obtained through lengthy interviews and repeated observations which enabled researchers to gain insights, not only into observable differences in behaviors but more significantly into the thought processes followed by the two different groups.

While there are many interesting implications that may be derived from this current approach to studying leadership in schools, perhaps the most significant issue has an air of optimism attached to it. For years, there has been a tendency to note that some people who hold administrative roles are leaders, while others have titles but do not demonstrate the kinds of skills and behaviors which make them effective leaders. The implication from that observation is simple: Some people can be leaders, while others cannot. The analysis of leaders' ways of thinking offers hope to the possibility that, with care and over time, those who are now classified as novice or typical principals can acquire skill at approaching the problem-solving process with different outlooks and insights. Indeed, this recent approach suggests that being a novice may not be a lifelong sentence. Expertise can be acquired as a leader.

Distributive Leadership

Recent analyses of effective leadership practices in schools suggest that, contrary to other views presented in this chapter, leadership is not necessarily found in only the actions of a single person. Too often, there is a lack of recognition that what schools (and all organizations) need in order to be successful is strong *leadership*, but such leadership may not necessarily be something attributable to the role of a single leader. This view, while becoming more popular in recent years (Southworth, 2004), actually has its roots in many earlier observations of organizational behavior. For example, Peter Drucker (1967) observed in his classic work, *The Effective Executive*, that one of the perennial realities in organizational life is simply that, even without formal leaders, leadership will always exist. To test this proposition, you may wish to reflect on your experiences in a school that did not have a principal or anyone else clearly exerting leadership in a formal way. The fact that these types of "leaderless organizations" are able to persist and even thrive is strong evidence that someone (or many "someones") are providing leadership, even if the principal or other chief executives appear to be disengaged.

Several authors have tried to explain the importance of the concept of distributive leadership throughout schools as a critical ingredient of success. Nigel Bennett and his colleagues (2003) defined *distributive leadership* as "leadership seen as the product of concertive or conjoint activity rather than as a phenomenon which arises from the individual" (p. 3). What this suggests is that the true skill of a great leader is not so much the ability to do everything needed to operate an effective organization alone. Rather, good leaders are able to draw out the latent leadership ability of everyone (or at least many) who work in a school so that the sum of all individual efforts truly goes beyond what an individual might be able to accomplish. James Spillane (2006) carried out an in-depth study of the Chicago Public Schools and concluded that some of the best schools feature strong and effective principals who were able to distribute leadership effectively throughout their staffs and communities.

> Distributive leadership means more than shared leadership. Too frequently, discussions of distributive leadership end prematurely with

an acknowledgment that multiple individuals take responsibility for leadership: that there is a leader *plus* other leaders at work in the school. Though essential, this leader-plus aspect is not sufficient to capture the complexity of the practice of leadership. From a distributive perspective, it is the collective interactions among leaders, followers, and their situation that are paramount. The situation of leadership isn't just the context within which leadership practice unfolds; it is a defining element of leadership practice. (pp. 3–4)

Philip Woods, Nigel Bennett, Janet Harvey, and Christine Wise (2004) further explained the concept and noted the following essential qualities that distributive leadership must include:

• Must highlight leadership as an emergent property of a group or network of interacting individuals. This contrasts with leadership as a phenomenon which arises from individuals.

• Must suggest openness of the boundaries of leadership. It is predisposed to widen the conventional net of leaders; it raises the question of which groups and individuals are to be brought into leadership or seen as contributors to it. Teachers, administrators, staff members, parents, and students can all be classified as leaders in this view.

• Must embrace the view that varieties of expertise are distributed across the many, not the few. Numerous perspectives and capabilities can be found in individuals spread throughout the organization and its surrounding community.

What these observations suggest is that while school principals are certainly important people, they are not solitary heroes who must transform schools on their own. In itself, this is not a remarkable finding. As we saw in descriptions of effective leadership presented earlier in this chapter, participative management, also referred to as *shared leadership*, is now identified as a critical element in successful schools. This creates the image of school leaders serving as the people who give others permission to join in influencing decisions that the leader ultimately makes. This is clearly a central theme of standards adopted in many states to guide the licensing or certification of school principals and other administrators. At the national level, the importance of shared leadership has been adopted by the Educational Leadership Council (ELCC), an organization focused on improving the ways in which school principals are prepared and developed (Wilmore, 2002).

As an example of the ways in which shared leadership has been envisioned as an effective tool in efforts to improve schools, Wilmore (2002) provides the following description of the value of inherent in creating learning communities where collaborative leadership occurs:

Ms. Watson began the year with open discussions pertaining to the development of the [school] vision, inviting faculty and staff, parents, and interested community members to take part. Committees were formed with members of the campus-based decision-making team serving as coordinators. Through this process, stakeholders in the campus developed a vision of where they wanted their school to go academically. This included increasing parental involvement in the success of all students and finding strategies that would motivate parents and other community members to become actively involved in the school. Ms. Watson empowered individuals within the public arena to have a voice in the direction the campus was taking and selecting the steps to get there by involving them in the decision-making process, promoting collaboration, and facilitating ownership in both the vision and the school. By not making top-down, directive decisions but empowering the stakeholders of the school community, Ms. Watson was able to plant the seeds for shared stewardship of the school vision that she would continue to nurture throughout the year. (p. 25)

This description of one principal's successful efforts to create a sense of community within a school represents a strong argument in favor of a leader creating a climate that allows and enables stakeholders to engage in determining how a vision of effectiveness can be supported. However, proponents of distributive leadership note that while simply encouraging formal leaders to create structures to encourage greater involvement by many within schools to participate in decision making is good, it is only a start toward creating more effective learning communities (Thurston, Clift, & Schacht, 1993).

The greatest difference between shared leadership and distributive leadership is based on the extent to which a formal leader is able to allow followers increasing degrees of freedom in exercising their involvement in the decision-making process of a school. Shared leadership is activity that is controlled largely by the leader who "allows" teachers, staff, parents, and others to engage in the process of directing the activities of the school. As a result, committees are formed (by the principal), school-wide decision-making groups are formed (by the principal), and in general, input regarding issues that have been defined (largely by the principal) as needing involvement by others is sought, and people are specifically invited to lend their ideas and expertise. The key to this type of sharing and participation is that the parameters are clearly identified and controlled by the formal leader *prior* to the invitation for involvement. Distributive leadership, on the other hand, is a much more "organic" and free-flowing form of ongoing engagement by stakeholders. In a sense, it is not a specific action (e.g., forming a school-wide decision-making group), but rather the development of an organizational culture that honors the input and capabilities of all who have a stake in the affairs of the school.

The vision of schools where formal leaders not only allow for participation but also create conditions that lead to continuous engagement in leading organizations has many advantages. It suggests an environment that goes beyond "allowing" people to participate in decision making. Some of the important advantages gained by practicing distributive leadership include:

1. An increase in the likelihood that needed changes may occur in schools, since the base for any change in practice is shared by many rather than by a select few who endorse a single leader's ideas.

2. The creation of a culture that enables the staff to feel empowered and committed to a sense of collegiality that will extend beyond the term of a single principal. In short, having people involved increases the likelihood that change becomes "the way we do things here" rather quickly.

3. An increase in the number of opportunities for true leadership skill to emerge. In these days of declining interest by educators to serve as school administrators and supervisors, early opportunities to demonstrate leadership skill may increase the opportunity for future career paths to evolve.

✑ GENERAL COMMENTS ABOUT LEADERSHIP

While we have tried to present an ordered view of the nature of leadership as it has been analyzed in school settings, we have only scratched the surface of a very complex topic. The search for precise understanding of what contributes to effective organizational leadership has been at the center of virtually every analysis of organizations. People always have been and will continue to be fascinated with determining "Who leads?" and "How do they do it?" People will always try to put into some kind of order the notions they have about leadership.

Researchers have only gotten a very brief glimpse into the process of leadership. Many facets of this critical topic have not yet been explored. For example, researchers have tended to look almost exclusively at leadership as demonstrated by those who have formal leadership roles in schools and other organizations. The roles of principals, supervisors, and superintendents have been examined to the virtual exclusion of the study of others. Anyone who has ever worked in or around schools will recognize that leadership is not the exclusive property of administrators (Playko, 1991), and anyone who assumes that it is could be making a terrible error in judgment.

A second area where more research is needed is the phenomenon of "followership" and the nature of the dynamic relationships that occur between leaders and others in their organizations. The concept of "transformative leadership" (energy directed toward enabling others to sustain needed change), first described by James McGregor Burns (1978) and expanded into an emphasis on empowerment by Bennis and Nanus (1985) and Block (1989), appears to hold promise for increasing understanding of how leaders interact with others. Leaders must have followers, and interest must be directed toward that fact.

Finally, a discussion of leadership often includes some views that Bennis and Nanus call the "myths of leadership." The following is a list of these myths and notes as to why the myths should not be viewed as limitations.

- *Myth 1—Leadership is a rare skill.* In fact, virtually everyone has some leadership potential, and opportunities are great for many people to assume formal and informal leadership roles in a variety of settings.

- *Myth 2—Leaders are born, not made.* As noted earlier in the discussion of "great person" approaches to leadership, the major capacities and competencies of leadership can be learned if there is a basic desire to learn them. Acquiring the knowledge and skills for effective leadership is not easy, but most people have the fundamental capacity to become powerful leaders.

- *Myth 3— Leaders are charismatic.* Most leaders are quite human, and they rarely possess any magical talents that are unavailable to the rest of us. In fact, some evidence indicates that what we call charisma is the result of leadership, not the reverse. Good leaders often gain respect and admiration from their followers because of the ways in which they demonstrate leadership qualities.

- *Myth 4—Leadership exists at the top of the organization.* As noted in the review of instructional leadership, successful leaders strive to increase opportunities for staff members to take active roles in schools through conscious efforts at participative management. Leaders are not threatened by allowing others to have some control over their organization.

- *Myth 5—The leader directs, controls, prods, and manipulates.* Leadership is not the exercise of absolute power, but rather the empowerment of others to make use of their full potential. As a result, any effort at control for its own sake might not be an activity of leadership at all, but rather an effort to dominate. Ultimately, organizations that are faced with this type of strangling behavior will either cast out the leader or die as organizations.

❧ SUMMARY

This chapter reviewed a theory base typically associated with the analysis of educational supervision, that of leadership. Leadership is often referred to as the single most important area to be developed by anyone interested in pursuing an administrative or supervisory role. Supervisors can be neither proactive nor effective without considering some of the basic issues of leadership presented in this chapter.

The chapter began with a consideration of a variety of definitions of leadership found in the literature. Basic differences between descriptive and normative conceptualizations were also reviewed because this has represented a subtle shift in the ways which leadership has been studied in recent years.

In the next section, we considered four historical frameworks for the analysis of leadership, including the "great person," traitist, situational, and behavioral approaches. We noted the major limitations of each of the first three approaches and suggested why most current explanations of leadership use the behavioral perspective, which emphasizes the relationships that exist between individual characteristics and the context in which people work.

Next, we considered several descriptive and normative leadership theories. We also reviewed the concepts of instructional leadership, moral and ethical leadership, cognitive development and processing by effective leaders, and distributive leadership.

The chapter concluded with some general concepts and observations on the nature of the complex phenomenon of leadership in schools, including the debunking of several popular myths concerning leadership.

Suggested Activities

1. Interview a group of teachers to determine their perceptions of what leadership should be. Compare the definitions that are presented with the alternative perspectives of leadership discussed in this chapter.

2. Using the list of "leadership myths" described by Bennis and Nanus, compose a rating scale that may be used to collect data concerning perceptions of whether people agree or disagree with each of the stated myths.

3. Talk with people who are not in professional education to determine their perceptions of what leadership is. Compare their statements with the "great person," traitist, situational, and behavioral perspectives.

4. Interview at least five practicing school administrators or supervisors to determine their personal definitions of "instructional leadership." How successful do these individuals feel about actually engaging in behaviors that are part of their definitions? What prohibits people from serving as instructional leaders? What contributes to their ability to serve in this capacity?

Cases to Consider

Read each case and consider the following:

- What are the critical issues raised in each case, as they relate to the use of theoretical perspectives of leadership?
- How does each case relate to the development of the concept of proactive leadership?
- In what ways might you suggest a resolution to the issues raised?

Case 5.1   But I Don't Get It!

Mary Spencer was really frustrated. She just got a phone call from the assistant superintendent for operations, Bob Cresswell, who told her the bad news—again: She didn't get the principalship she applied for at a middle school in the district. This marked the fifth time in the past three years that Mary—an assistant principal with seven years of experience at Jefferson Middle School—had been passed over for a building of her own. She got along very well with Milton Marowsky, her principal. Milton was generally recognized as a really effective principal, although there were times when Mary found his way of dealing with problems to be quite contrary to the ways in which she would have dealt with the same issues. Still, Mary always listened when Milton spoke, but she prided herself in presenting her own views when she went out on interviews for principalship. After all, Mary was a realist; she knew when things would simply not work in a school, and she wasn't afraid to indicate that to interviewers, who surely would recognize her ability to react to problems caused by the many constraints that were part of everyday life in her school district. Milton was the type of person who seemed to look past the constraints and ignore the reality of not being able to do certain things. Although she would never say it publicly, Milton was a really nice guy who didn't seem to be connected to a lot of the reality Mary saw each day.

People always seemed pleased and comfortable in the interview sessions, but Mary was finally becoming convinced that she just wasn't going to be successful in a district that always seemed to put more stock in administrative candidates who were as unrealistic as was Milton. She was now ready to start looking around at jobs in what she believed to be higher quality school systems.

Case 5.2   But I Thought They Liked Me!

Bob Cleveland had looked forward to his first principalship for several years. He had completed a master's degree and the administrative certification program at the local university three years ago and had taken a position as an assistant principal in one of the district elementary schools as a way to learn even more about the job he eventually wanted. He worked with Ruth Martinez, a principal who had a well-deserved reputation as a very strong leader who really controlled the teachers and the students in her school. Bob gained a reputation as a great listener, particularly to those who believed that Ruth had not been sensitive to their needs. Bob considered himself to be a great team player with Ruth; their styles and personalities complimented each other.

This past year, Bob got his wish and became the principal of Big Bend Elementary School, a small but new building. The school's extremely experienced teaching staff moved to Big Bend primarily because it was a beautiful new facility and also because Bob had gained the reputation as a "nice guy" who would not bother teachers, unlike many of the other principals in the district.

As everyone predicted, Bob took on his role as principal with many of the same behaviors that he demonstrated as an assistant principal. He rarely confronted teachers. Rather, he took pride in his ability to remain cool under pressure and simply wait for teachers to come to him with their problems. He truly viewed his role as that of a facilitator and supporter of the teachers, and he announced his view at all staff meetings at the beginning of the school year.

What Bob did not see at first, however, was that parents were starting to complain to the central office that they were disappointed at what was going on at Big Bend. "You spent all that money on carpeting and new equipment at the new school, but it looks like we got a bunch of retired teachers to work in it," was one of the more direct comments made to the superintendent after a recent board meeting. Then Bob had a personal revelation that something was seriously wrong when he walked into the teachers' lounge one night after everyone had left and found a reference to "Bob the Wimp" on a cartoon someone had drawn on a piece of paper.

Applying the Concepts

The following brief quiz is designed to improve your skills in applying some of the concepts discussed in this chapter. Read the brief introductory case and then respond to the multiple-choice questions. You will find the answers in the Appendix.

For many years, the teachers at Jamestown School earned a reputation as a very strong group. They worked together as a team to implement many changes over the years. They were seen as extremely competent, but also as "mavericks" within the school system. Since the school opened ten years ago, five different principals had worked at Jamestown. The general perception was that the turnover was based on the teacher behavior at the school.

The school board and its new superintendent, Dr. Carlos Juarez, decided that they would need to "take control of Jamestown." As a result, the latest principal is Ernie Carter, a former successful football coach and most recently an assistant principal at the high school. He was seen as someone with a strong will who could "get tough and straighten out those teachers."

Ernie came on board in August and immediately scheduled numerous meetings where he instructed the teachers on procedures and practices that he expected to see implemented. Although he never made any threats, it was clear to all who observed his presentations that Ernie meant business. Anyone who did not follow his direction would be better off at another school, or maybe even out of the teaching profession entirely. As the school year began, the board and the superintendent were pleased to note that the Jamestown teachers already seemed more "under control" than they had been in the past. Ernie was doing the job. No grievances were being filed, and phone calls with complaints from teachers were now almost nonexistent.

As the year progressed, things continued to change at Jamestown. A few years ago, it was common to hear about teachers talking directly to representatives of the local media about their dissatisfaction with things at Jamestown. In the past, parents had reported that teachers often spent conference time lobbying for parental and community support for some of their causes. All of that seemed to be changing with Ernie in charge.

The change at Jamestown Elementary School continued into May and June of the school year. However, Dr. Juarez became aware that the results were not necessarily positive. First, he was shocked to see that student scores on the statewide achievement test had fallen dramatically at Jamestown this past year. Second, he was now receiving at least three requests for transfers each day from teachers at Jamestown. Even Ruben Whitlow, one of the most respected and quiet teachers in the school district (and State Teacher of the Year two years ago) had stopped in to share that he was filling out the papers needed to begin his retirement within the next few weeks.

1. Based on the information presented here, the new principal at Jamestown seems to have ignored which of the behavioral patterns associated with effective instructional leadership?

   a. engaging in participative management

   b. providing support for instruction

   c. monitoring instruction

   d. being resourceful

2. In terms of Stephen Covey's research, Ernie Carter might want to learn about the following skill if he wants to work more effectively with the teachers at Jamestown:

   a. radiating positive energy

   b. believing in other people

   c. seeing life as an adventure

   d. exercising for self-renewal

Additional Reading

Acheson, Keith A., & Gall, Meredith Damien. (2002). *Clinical supervision and teacher development: Preservice and inservice applications*. New York: Wiley/Jossey-Bass Education.

Balch, B., Frampton, P., & Hirth, M. (2006). *Preparing a professional portfolio: A school administrator's guide*. Boston: Pearson Allyn & Bacon.

Bennis, Warren (1990). *Why leaders can't lead*. San Francisco: Jossey-Bass.

Bolman, L. G., & Deal. T. E. (2006). *The wizard and the warrior: Leading with passion and power*. San Francisco: Jossey-Bass.

Buckingham, M., & Coffman, C. (1999). *First, break all the rules*. New York: Simon and Schuster.

Deal, T., & Peterson, K. (1999). *Shaping school culture: The heart of leadership*. San Francisco: Jossey-Bass.

Deal, T. E., Peterson, K. D., & Deal, T. E. (2000). *The leadership paradox: Balancing logic and artistry in schools*. San Francisco: Jossey-Bass.

DePres, Max (1989). *Leadership is an art*. New York: Dell.

Duke, Daniel L. (1987). *School leadership and instructional improvement.* New York: Random House.

Duignan, P. A., & MacPherson, R. J. S. (eds.) (1992). *Educative leadership: A practical theory for new administrators and managers.* London: The Falmer Press.

Fink, Elaine, & Resnick, Lauren B. (2001). Developing principals as instructional leaders. *Phi Delta Kappan, 82:* 8, pp. 598–607.

Jacobson, Stephen L., & Conway, James A. (eds.) (1990). *Educational leadership in an age of reform.* White Plains, NY: Longman.

Marzano, Robert J., Waters, Timothy, & McNulty, Brian A. (2005). *School leadership that works: From research to results.* Alexandria, VA: Association for Supervision & Curriculum Development.

Maxwell, John C. (1995). *Developing the leaders around you: How to help others reach their full potential.* Nashville, TN: Thomas Nelson Publishers.

Norris, Cynthia, Barnett, Bruce, Basom, Margaret, & Yerkers, Diana (2002). *Developing educational leaders.* New York: Teachers College Press.

Oliva, P. F., & Pawlas, G. E. (2004). *Supervision for today's schools* (7th ed.). New York: Wiley.

Owens, Robert G., & Valesky, Thomas (2006). *Organizational behavior in education: Adaptive leadership and school reform* (9th ed). Needham Heights, ME: Allyn & Bacon.

Parker, Stephanie A. (1993). So now you're a leader—What should you do? *Phi Delta Kappan, 75:* 3, 229–230.

Rost, Joseph C. (1993). *Leadership for the twenty-first century.* Westport, CT: Praeger.

Shapiro, Joan Poliner & Stefkovich, Jacqueline A. (eds). (2005). *Ethical leadership and decision making in education: Applying theoretical perspectives to complex dilemmas* (2nd ed.) Mahwah, NJ: Lawrence Erlbaum Associates.

Starratt, Robert J., (1996). *Transforming educational administration: Meaning, community, and excellence.* New York: McGraw-Hill.

Wheatley, Margaret (1992). *Leadership and the new science: Learning about organizations from an orderly universe.* San Francisco: Berrett-Koehler Publishers.

PART III

The Realities of Supervision

Motivation, Communication, Change, Power, and Conflict

Part III discusses many ongoing issues and concerns that face the effective proactive leader. Among these are how to motivate teachers, deal with conflict, and manage change. In addition, the section will review the nature of organizational communication and how leaders deal with power, authority, and control.

◊ 6 ◊

Motivation

Regardless of how individual supervisors and leaders look at their work (for example, as "inspectors," or disciples of human relations), and regardless of whether they subscribe to the assumptions and practices of the proactive leadership process, a key leadership responsibility is inevitably the fostering of employee motivation. In this chapter, a number of alternative theoretical models of motivation are presented. First, there is a definition of motivation presented, along with an overview of differing perspectives. The chapter concludes with a discussion of the relationship among the personal philosophy of education developed by an individual to guide professional supervisory behavior, the implementation of proactive leadership processes, and employee motivation.

◊ DEFINITION OF MOTIVATION

Motivation is one of the most important and challenging supervisory responsibilities undertaken in schools or any other organization. Unlike the concepts explored in earlier chapters, however, motivation can be defined in a relatively simple way. John Lovell and Kimball Wiles (1983) defined motivation as the "level of effort an individual is willing to expend toward the achievement of a certain goal" (p. 50). In attempting to motivate people, we must look for answers to the following three questions, which have been faced by managers, supervisors, and administrators in many different types of organizations throughout history:

- What makes some people work hard, while other people hardly work at all (or at least work as little as possible)?
- How can certain people—educational leaders, for example—positively influence the performance of the people who work for them?

- Why do some people leave organizations, show up late for work, refuse to be committed, or generally "tune out" of their job responsibilities, while other people tend to go to work early, stay late, and engage in all types of behaviors indicative of a strong commitment to their labor and "go the extra mile?"

Each of these questions is a legitimate aspect of the overall issue of how to increase human motivation. Clearly, there are no "perfect" answers to all, or perhaps to any of these three questions. There is no way to ensure commitment by all employees all the time. Neither is there a way to guarantee that any single employee will remain highly motivated and committed at all times. The search goes on, however, for the most appropriate motivational techniques. Several theoretical perspectives have been offered to aid in this search. The basic assumptions and features of four of these conceptualizations are reviewed in the following pages.

NEED SATISFACTION THEORIES OF MOTIVATION

Theorists most closely associated with *need theories* are Abraham Maslow and Frederick Herzberg, each of whom has developed a slightly different scheme for analyzing motivation in organizations.

Maslow's Hierarchy of Needs

The basic assumption underlying Maslow's *Motivation and Personality* (1970) are familiar to many. One primary belief is that people are motivated by their individual needs to address certain natural concerns. These concerns, in turn, can be rank-ordered hierarchically in terms of potency.

We need to recognize two important premises in order to understand Maslow's perspective more completely. First, human beings are best defined as "wanting creatures" who are motivated by a consistent desire to satisfy certain needs; second, individuals pursue needs in a linear, sequential progression according to the following levels of intensity and potency:

1. *Physical/physiological needs*—oxygen, food, warmth, rest, activity, and other basic essentials necessary to maintain life
2. *Safety needs*—routine, rhythm, and order in life; protection from physical danger
3. *Love/belonging needs*—desire for affectionate relationships with people and acceptance by others; the need for affection, affiliation, friendship, and love
4. *Esteem needs*—receiving recognition and acceptance among one's peers as a worthwhile individual, a sense of worth, self-confidence
5. *Self-actualization needs*—striving to fulfill one's potential, satisfaction with achievements

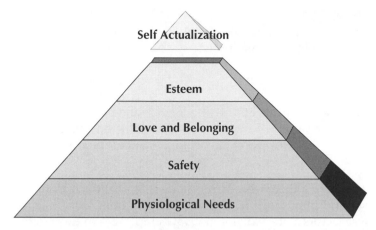

Figure 6.1.   Maslow's hierarchy of human needs

The key concept in Maslow's model is that the needs indicated in the pyramid must be addressed in a hierarchical fashion. Individuals will not be motivated toward a higher level of concern and performance until lower needs are satisfied. If they are not, tension, rather than a positive sense of motivation, is created within individuals. There is little sense, for example, in trying to motivate people by focusing on esteem (professional recognition) while they are hungry or physically insecure.

Herzberg's Need-Satisfaction Theory of Motivation

The work done by psychologist Frederick Herzberg is based largely on the same assumptions about need-satisfaction promoted by Maslow. In fact, Herzberg's (1966) motivation theory represents a natural refinement of Maslow's basic hierarchical framework. Instead of needs originating in the individual, Herzberg identified work-environment factors that cause motivation (Lunenburg & Ornstein, 2004).

Two major premises or assumptions serve as the basis for Herzberg's theory:

Hygiene factors are those job-related elements that can affect satisfaction. These factors cannot, in themselves, motivate a worker; they can only prevent dissatisfaction. Hygiene factors are generally defined as those tangible elements such as wages, fringe benefits, and working conditions (see the list below). When an employee's pay is low, for instance, he or she will probably be dissatisfied; raising the pay, however, will not necessarily raise satisfaction (and therefore motivation) proportionately.

Motivators are factors whose presence in a worker's life leads to satisfaction, but whose absence does not necessarily lead to dissatisfaction. Among these are achievement, recognition, responsibility, and advancement.

Hygiene Factors	Motivators
1. Work environment (organizational climate and physical conditions)	1. Achievement
	2. Advancement
2. Type of supervision	3. Characteristics of the
3. Salary and fringe benefits	work itself
4. Job security	4. Growth (personal
5. Attitudes and policies of the administration	and professional)
	5. Responsibility
6. Status	6. Recognition

If Herzberg's theory is correct, it implies that such things as salary increases and improvement of fringe benefits must not be ignored, but that these factors alone will not motivate employees to excel in that work.

Three basic criticisms have tended to follow the work of both Maslow and Herzberg and their views of human motivation. First, critics suggest that both Maslow and Herzberg suffer from not providing clear definitions, which in turn hinders the ability to make predictions from their theories. A classic question, asked particularly of Maslow, is "What is self-actualization?" If we cannot adequately define the term, how can we determine if a person has attained this level? How can we even direct our behavior toward attaining it? It is relatively simple to appreciate the attainment of lower-level goals such as those associated with physiological and safety needs. Higher-order needs such as esteem and self-actualization, on the other hand, are unclearly defined.

Second, the work of both Maslow and Herzberg is criticized as insufficiently dynamic. Inherent in both views is the assumption that individuals wait for needs to arise in their lives before they respond: people do not actively seek ways to increase their effectiveness. These views, then, suggest that needs manipulate people rather than that people control needs.

Third, critics find in Herzberg's theory no clear-cut distinctions between hygiene factors and motivators. Factors classified as motivators by one organization may be referred to as hygiene factors by another organization, or even by other people who work in the same organization.

Implications of Need Theories for the Supervisor

Educational supervisors can find at least two major values in the concepts defined by need-satisfaction theories. One is the implication that supervisors, administrators, and others engaging in educational leadership should be responsible for creating a climate in their schools or districts conducive to the ongoing process of personal growth and self-fulfillment by employees.

A second value is that a supervisor's knowledge of what might satisfy or dissatisfy teachers and other staff members can be an important tool to improve their effectiveness. One major supervisory responsibility is to increase employee motivation: the danger, however, is that the power to motivate might be manipulative. That is, supervisors often have the authority to withhold as well as dispense many of the elements that satisfy staff members' needs.

✑ EQUITY THEORIES OF MOTIVATION

Equity theories suggest that the most important factor in employee motivation is the extent to which workers perceive a sense of equity in the work environment. If workers believe that they are being treated fairly, they will be more satisfied and work harder toward achieving personal and organizational goals.

Implications of Equity Theories for the Supervisor

If the assumptions on which equity theory are based are correct, then supervisors must determine ways to ensure that their employees believe they are being treated fairly on the job. Employee perceptions of a given situation are important, because "fairness" cannot be entirely based on any objective reality. The supervisor's duty, then, is to make sure people perceive the treatment they are receiving as equitable; to do this requires that the supervisor first determine what people perceive as fair. Equity theories tend to place considerable emphasis on the use of monetary and other tangible rewards, because it is easier to distribute equitable dollars in recognition of valued performance than it is to distribute equitable recognition or esteem. For the supervisor, then, equity theories suggest the need to seek tangible or visible rewards for employees.

One issue that we need to understand in this discussion of equity theories is the difference between "equitable" and "equal." *Equality* implies the need to provide every employee with exactly the same rewards; everyone is treated the same. *Equity* is the concept of finding the fair or right amount of reward for each individual according to need. An equitable workplace is not one in which every employee receives the same treatment, benefits, and rewards. We emphasize this because supervisors frequently attempt to provide equity in the workplace through equal treatment, and this is not what equity theories advocate.

✑ REINFORCEMENT THEORIES OF MOTIVATION

When we talk about motivation through reinforcement, we immediately think of the contributions of B. F. Skinner. Skinner's assumptions are quite simple. *Reinforcement theory* assumes that human behavior can be engineered, shaped, or altered by manipulating the reward structures for various forms of behavior. This manipulation is called *positive reinforcement*.

In this approach, performance standards are first clearly set. Improvement results from the application of frequent positive feedback linked to the attainment of stated performance objectives.

Implications of Reinforcement Theory for the Supervisor

Reinforcement theory probably makes more demands on supervisors than any other popular approach to supervision. The supervisor is largely responsible for manipulating and altering a number of features of the work environment. For example, supervisors must clearly set standards and inform their employees as to which behaviors are desirable in reaching these standards and which are not. The leader who bases practice on reinforcement theories would probably spend a considerable amount of time at the beginning of the school year defining rules and procedures and explaining the consequences of violating these rules. Breaking policy would bring a swift reprimand, and adherence to policy would be rewarded openly.

In addition, reinforcement theory assumes that performance can be improved by providing continuous feedback to employees concerning the nature and quality of their work with regard to the established goals and standards. In a school setting, then, this suggests that a supervisor would engage in a good deal of monitoring behavior to evaluate teacher performance as a way to start the feedback process. In other words, the supervisor must live by the motto, "When people do good jobs, tell them so."

Reinforcement theories of motivation stand in direct contradiction to equity theories. According to reinforcement theories, leaders should work to ensure that all employees are not rewarded equally. Instead, they should always be rewarded differently according to their levels of performance. Again, leaders should be aware of the possibility that their behavior might be overly manipulative or exploitive of teaching staff.

❧ EXPECTANCY THEORIES OF MOTIVATION

According to expectancy theories of motivation, when people value something, they will be motivated to engage in actions based on the strength of that valuing. Victor Vroom (1994) and Porter and Lawler (1965) have been most closely associated with this view of organizational motivation. They offered the following observations concerning the nature of expectancy theories:

- Behavior is determined by a combination of forces in the individual and forces in the environment.
- People make decisions about their own behavior in organizations.
- Different people have different needs, desires, and goals.
- People make decisions among alternative plans of behavior based on their own perceptions or expectations of the degree to which a given behavior is likely to lead to some desired outcome.

Implications of Expectancy Theories for Supervisors

Because employee behavior ultimately derives from forces in the person and in the environment, a supervisor who subscribes to expectancy theories of motivation must first know the organizational and personal outcomes that each employee tends to value most. The supervisor would therefore need to spend time talking with staff to determine what outcomes have the greatest value. Without such knowledge, the supervisor would be unable to seek a motivational focus. In addition to determining the staff's desired outcomes, the supervisor needs to assess what behaviors and outcomes he or she desires from the staff. To do this the supervisor needs to have a well-articulated personal educational platform to provide guidance and a plan of action.

Expectancy theories of motivation also imply that supervisors must make certain that the goals, behaviors, and outcomes they desire are actually attainable and that the desired outcomes are linked directly to desired levels of performance.

The supervisor adhering to this theoretical framework would need to determine the exact reward structure most likely to ensure that employees will continue to make progress toward the attainment of organizational goals and objectives. The supervisor first needs to analyze the nature of the total work environment to locate any potentially conflicting expectancies. Does one part of the organization value one type of employee behavior while another department suggests rewards for an entirely different behavior? If such conflicts exist, the supervisor might need to make some adjustments to reduce the number of mixed messages being transmitted to the staff.

The supervisor would also need to make certain that, where possible, the changes in organizational outcomes are large enough to motivate and positively change the behavior of employees. Trivial changes and rewards will automatically result in trivial changes in levels of employee performance. This will, in turn, result in trivial outcomes for the organization.

Using expectancy theories for motivating employees also will probably result in some modifications in organizational policies and procedures. For example, pay and reward systems might generally need to be redesigned, with more effort put into rewarding people for organizationally desirable performances. Consequently, extremely precise employee appraisal and evaluation systems would be needed to guide the distribution of employee rewards.

Expectancy theory requires careful reexamination of tasks, jobs, job descriptions, and the roles of employees within the organization. Supervisors must understand the importance of formal and informal employee group structures, because such structures are important determinants of ultimate employee performance.

The final implication for supervisors who buy into the concept of expectancy theory is that they must pay considerable attention to individual employee needs, concerns and interests. Such sensitivity to individual issues is not found in many organizations, but it needs to be developed and maintained if expectancy theories are to be employed with any consistency.

❧ INDIVIDUAL PROFESSIONAL PHILOSOPHY AND APPROACHES TO MOTIVATION

In the previous section we reviewed four alternative theories about how people are motivated. Ideally, we could settle on one "best" way to encourage greater commitment to organizational goals and objectives in all structures, but no such satisfyingly simple solution exists. The motivational strategy you select as an educational leader will depend largely on your own educational philosophy. In particular, how you view the role of teachers and others who work in schools will determine to a large extent how you try to motivate them. If, for example, you believe that teachers are fundamentally nothing more than employees of the school district and that they need much direction to control their behavior, then your approach to motivation might well be based on reinforcement theory, which suggests that people can be "conditioned" to operate in a desired manner. If, on the other hand, you view teachers as a highly skilled group of professionals, then you might approach motivation through the needs-satisfaction theory. In particular, Herzberg's views might appeal to you.

Your personal educational platform also comes to play in determining to what extent you support McGregor's Theory X or Theory Y, described in chapter 2. Do you, for example, begin with the assumption that people are basically lazy? If so, your attempts at motivating them would differ significantly from those you would make if you believed that most people really do wish to work hard.

Finally, we point out that no one ever truly motivates another person. There is no causal relationship between your selection of a motivation theory and an outcome of greater staff commitment. Ultimately, whether or not a person works harder rests in that person's own choice. More important, a supervisor's motivational effectiveness depends not on the specific tactic used but on the extent to which the staff believes in the supervisor and on the consistency of the supervisor's performance. In order to achieve the kind of consistency that employees admire, educational supervisors must operate from a foundation of principle and belief about education; again, the development of a personal educational platform is vital ingredient in effectiveness.

Motivation for What?

Regardless of the approach that might be taken to encourage teachers and other school staff members to strive for excellence, the issue that cannot be ignored is the goal which "motivated" educators might be expected to achieve. Too often, those who speak about the importance of motivation seem to suggest that there is some value in making people work harder for its own purpose: Motivating for the sake of being motivated. As an educational leader, your job is to ensure that, above any particular purpose that might be served through your work with teachers, the single most critical issue that must always be addressed is the ability of students to learn, grow, and achieve their goals through their experiences in school. Therefore, make no mistake that whether you make use of reinforcement theory, need-satisfaction, expectancy, or equity theory, the goal must be the improvement of education for your clients, namely, students in schools. There is no question that having satisfied teachers, happy parents, or proud local community members may be desirable, but the focus can never shift from the core goals of a school.

SUMMARY

This chapter reviewed a number of theories concerning the motivation of employees in organizations. We noted that motivation is yet is yet another example that reflects how important theory can be in effective supervisory practice, but we also pointed out that motivation is a critically important supervisory responsibility. We stressed that motivation is ultimately the responsibility of those who are to be motivated, but that knowledge of alternative theoretical perspectives can serve as a critically useful tool for effective educational leaders.

Four theoretical approaches to motivation were offered in this chapter; the popular *needs-satisfaction* theories of Maslow and Herzberg; *equity* theories, which suggest that fairness in the workplace is the most important motivational factor; *reinforcement* theories as developed by B. F. Skinner and others; and *expectancy* theories, which suggest that employees respond favorably to conditions that they value. The chapter concluded with a review of the relationship between motivational strategies and the educational supervisor's individual philosophy.

Suggested Activities

1. List the things that someone could do to make you want to work harder than you already do. To what extent are those motivation factors compatible with any of the theories reviewed in this chapter? Are you likely to respond to the satisfaction of needs? Describe your sense of fairness or equity. Also, list the things that make you feel unmotivated. Is there a pattern present in the same way as for motivating factors?

2. Interview three or four teachers in a school and determine the kinds of motivational factors reviewed in the exercise above.

3. Watch several television commercials for a number of different products and services. Try to classify the approaches that are used in an effort to motivate you buy the advertised goods or services.

4. "Motivation" is used very ambiguously in daily discussions. Whenever you hear a reference to this concept, think about whether the person

using the term is really referring to the concepts described in this chapter. If the term is being used precisely, classify the strategy for motivation that is being suggested, according to the theoretical models described in this chapter.

5. Observe a teacher's class and keep a record of the motivational strategies that are used with students during a one-hour period.

Cases to Consider

Read each of the cases below and consider the following:

- What are the critical issues raised in each case, as they relate to the use of theoretical constructs to analyze motivation?
- How does each case relate to the development of proactive leadership?
- In what ways might you suggest a resolution to the issues raised?

Case 6.1   This Will Fix Those Teachers!

"It's perfectly absurd to think that every teacher should get paid the same as every other teacher. As many of my teacher neighbors and friends have told me, some people simply deserve more because they work more!" Those were the words that were heard during almost every campaign debate and rally in which Hank Gottschalk appeared this past fall. Apparently, his views made a lot of people believe in him, because he won the election. Since taking his seat on the seven-member board of education for the Grovedale Schools, Hank has continued with his drive to reward teachers for hard work. After all, he saw such a practice work well in his very successful concrete business for many years. "If you expect more, you get more. And when you get more, you pay more."

As the current school year progressed, further discussions took place regarding the possibility of the board implementing a new pay system for teachers that would be based on demonstration of merit. For the most part, teachers were firmly against the plan and noted that implementing such a system would be inherently unfair. No one could distinguish precisely the nature of the kinds of things that would distinguish really outstanding teachers from others who simply worked hard at their jobs without necessarily attracting a lot of attention from outside reviewers. The school board, however, with very vocal support from a large percentage of the community, persisted with its vision of more effective ways of getting "better results" from teachers. Paying people for extra effort seemed to make a lot of sense. Test scores on the state achievement exams had to be maintained or increased, student dropout rates had to decrease, and schools in general had to become more effective places. The board felt that the only way such outcomes could be attained would be to reward teachers and other staff members with a pay system that recognized their excellence. After all, they were not going to take anything away from those who were not associated with more effective outcomes—yet.

Case 6.2   Good Breakfasts, Bad Motivation

Dan Kaiser, an elementary principal for the past two years at LaMer Middle School, always had a great reputation when he worked as a high school and middle school science teacher for 15 years before going into administration. In particular, he was known all over the Jetson City Schools as a teacher who had the rare ability to "get the best out of" every student in his class, whether or not the student was really very strong academically. One of the things for which Dan was well known was his ability to provide emotional and inspirational talks to groups of kids who were never tuned into school expectations before. In fact, his reputation as a motivational speaker to kids was so well known that he received several requests to serve as a keynote speaker at school district meetings both in his own school system and in other settings around the state. In addition, Dan had been featured in a "People in the Community" segment on WWLL TV Channel 19 a few weeks before he got his principalship at LaMer.

Hopes were really high when the school board approved the superintendent's appointment of Dan as a new middle school principal. LaMer was an old school in an economically distressed part of the city. Many of the teachers in the school had been there for at least 20 years, and the general sense was that they had given up because "they couldn't work with a bunch of poor kids" who had little support from their parents at home. Dan knew that people wanted him to change this situation around almost immediately, but he was wise enough to know that he would not be able to change all the negative attitudes overnight. The strategy he took was quite low-key; once a month, he would sponsor a breakfast for the staff. In addition to the bagels, coffee, juice, and fresh fruit, teachers were typically treated to a brief "Kaiser Talk," often a spin-off of one his famous motivational speeches that he used with the kids. At first, Dan was quite happy with the reaction from his veteran staff. He knew that he was experiencing the traditional "honeymoon period," and that most staff would be polite enough to listen to his new approach. Besides, the coffee and bagels were really good—and free.

Over the last two years, the teachers and Dan had developed a fairly strong bond. Most faculty members genuinely liked the new principal, and the breakfasts had become a kind of tradition at LaMer. Still, Dan was now at a point of depression. His faculty liked him, his speeches were clever (if he did say so himself!), and there was a pleasant feeling in the school that was not there when he first came. But the relationships between teachers and students were not much improved, and the achievement tests the past two springs were as low as ever. While teachers were careful about saying so in public, Dan knew that there was still a strong sense that the kids at LaMer could not learn. Maybe it was time for a new strategy for motivating his teachers.

Applying the Concepts

The following brief quiz is designed to improve your skills in applying some of the concepts discussed in this chapter. Read the brief introductory case, and then respond to the multiple-choice questions. You will find the answers in the Appendix.

Rich Sokorski enjoyed a great reputation as an effective high school football coach for six years. Everyone in the Apple Blossom School District seemed to know him and respect his accomplishments. As a result, it was not a great surprise when the local school board named him as the new principal of Troy Middle School last year. Troy was always seen as a school with a lot of great potential, but it was also seen as a place with a lot of problems. Specifically, the teachers at the school were referred to as "prima donnas" by many who believed that, even with a lot of talent, they did not seem to produce the kind of educational results for which the Apple Blossom Schools were striving. Instead, the teachers had a reputation for being committed only to their own agendas. They had made life miserable for the last three principals in the school, none of whom lasted more than two years in the position.

When Rich was offered the middle school principalship, he was asked by the superintendent how he planned to work with the teaching staff. "I don't look at this as a problem. Instead, I believe this is a real opportunity to accomplish some important things. After all, when I took over as the football coach at the high school, they hadn't won more than two games in a season in over ten years. I know how to get the most out of people, and I'm going to put that know-how to work at the middle school."

The first staff meeting saw Rich taking a strong stance with regard to his plans for the next school year. His game plan included implementing a wide array of practices that were associated with effective schools, but the Troy teachers had not supported these in the past. Multi-age grouping, team teaching, and teacher advisor programs were all going to be part of the new vision of the way things would be at Troy. After all, the school would be recognized as "one of the best middle schools in the state within five years," according to the new principal in his opening-day comments to the teachers. The former coach concluded by enthusiastically remarking, "The only way this dream won't happen is if we all don't get together and work as a team." With that, he walked off the stage to the sound of eerie silence. This job might not be as easy as he thought.

1. Rich Sokorski was clearly trying to make use of which model of motivation with his staff?

   a. need-satisfaction

   b. reinforcement

   c. equity

   d. impossible to tell from this scenario

2. If Rich had spent time with each teacher before making his speech to motivate people, he might have been able to determine each teacher's personal views regarding the kinds of things that he or she valued. Then, he would have used this information as the basis for his efforts

to persuade people to make changes at Troy. This would have been an example of using which theory of motivation?

a. need-satisfaction

b. reinforcement

c. expectancy

d. equity

3. On the other hand, had the new principal first identified each teacher's potential contributions to the new school vision, and then rewarded each person who made use of that potential for helping the program, that would be an example of _____.

a. need-satisfaction

b. reinforcement

c. expectancy

d. equity

4. A general strategy that Rich might have used to make certain that he had more "buy-in" by the teachers would be to :

a. Begin by bringing in a guest speaker to introduce the changes instead of making the presentation himself.

b. Introduce the desired changes to small groups of teachers rather than addressing all teachers at one time.

c. Simply cancel the whole plan before sharing it with teachers.

d. Begin by creating the opportunity for teachers to become involved in creating a new vision for Troy Middle School.

Additional Reading

Alderman, M. Kay (2004). *Motivation for achievement: Possibilities for teaching and learning.* Mahwah, NJ: Lawrence Erlbaum Associates.

MacIver, Douglas J., Main, Samuel R., & Reuman, David A. (1995). Social structuring of the school: Studying what is, illuminating what could be. *Annual Review of Psychology, 46*, pp. 126–159.

Vroom, V. (1994). *Work and motivation.* San Francisco: Jossey-Bass.

Communication

A discussion of organizational communication ties directly into an analysis of proactive leadership in schools. After all, communication takes place daily on many different levels and within various subsystems. For example, teachers communicate with each other as well as supervisors, students, and parents; administrators share information with community and staff members; there is student-to-student communication. Examples of the levels and groups participating in the communication process include many different combinations.

Communication clarifies an organization's goals, procedures, and rules for people who are both inside and outside of the organization, bringing to light the unique identity of the organization—what it stands for. Maintaining that identity over time is carried out through ongoing intraorganizational communication patterns. Open channels of communication allow for feedback—information that can be used by an organization to alleviate any blurring of its identity or to implement corrective measures. Feedback helps the organization adapt to changing needs.

Basically, communication is the "glue" that holds the organization together. We often hear that a school or other institution has suffered a "breakdown in communication," or that "people aren't communicating with one another." By contrast, when a school is particularly effective, we rarely notice anything related to communication patterns. The need for open and consistent communication in organizations is great, and we automatically assume that people in effective organizations are communicating. Only when an effective process is disrupted is its importance fully understood.

The proactive leader needs to look constantly at the importance of communication. Supervisors who desire to lead rather than simply react to crises profit greatly from identifying, understanding, and ultimately joining into patterns of communication employed by their school staff. In addition, it is important that school leaders have the ability to comprehend where barriers to effective communication exist and how those patterns might be removed.

⚛ DEFINITION OF COMMUNICATION

Communication is defined here simply as the effort on the part of an individual or group to transmit information to another person or group. This transmission process, which is often extremely difficult to implement in a satisfying and effective manner with any degree of regularity or clarity, is nonetheless simple to describe and to depict graphically, as in figure 7.1.

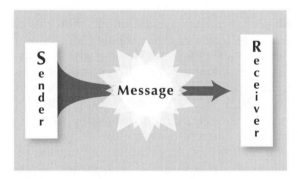

Figure 7.1.   The basic act of communication, or the transmission of a message (M) from a sender (S) to a receiver (R)

As the figure indicates, communication involves two major actors, a sender (or speaker) (S), and a receiver (R). The contact between these two ends of the communication process is established by forwarding a message (M) across some recognized channel. As seen in the subsequent discussion of the different types of communication that exist in organizations, the basic diagram can be modified to reflect other communication processes, such as two-way communication. In addition, the description of available modes of communication will reveal a variety of channels available to senders of messages.

⚛ TYPES OF COMMUNICATION

In a review of the characteristics of communication patterns and their implications for school administrators, Russell Spillman (1975) noted that there are essentially three types of communication processes that take place in any organization. The educational leader needs to be aware of the strengths and limitations of each type, because all will be required at one point or another in the life of a school. The three types of communication are one-way communication, one-way communication with feedback, and two-way communication.

One-Way Communication

Here the speaker, or communicator, sends a message through some channel or mode directly to a receiver (see figure 7.2). Although there are likely to be effects from the message, one-way communication strongly implies that the sender is not concerned with the effect and that there is no provision made for the relay of the effect from the receiver back to the speaker.

Figure. 7.2.   One-way communication (Information proceeds directly from the sender (S) to the receiver (R) and concludes at that point.)

One-way communication occurs in all organizations from time-to-time. Someone must occasionally "tell" others some information, regardless of what those others might wish. Nevertheless, there are problems associated with one-way communication, stemming from the quality of the initial transmission of the message at the sender's level. The nature of "what" is to be communicated must be absolutely clear; once the sender transmits the message to the receiver, there is no way to clarify any misconceptions that may occur. One-way communication might be compared to a person firing a rifle shot into the air—not a dangerous practice in itself, but potentially dangerous because no one can be absolutely certain where the bullet will eventually land.

Examples of one-way communication are plentiful in schools. Public address announcements, memos in teachers' mailboxes, and PTA newsletters are all examples of a message going from the sender to receivers without any chance of immediate response. One-way communication is not "bad" in itself; it is a highly efficient way for schools to share information because it is economical in terms of both time and money spent in preparing the initial message. People in schools often need bits of information presented to them, and one-way communication is highly appropriate in such cases. Problems may arise, however, if there is virtually total reliance on this limited type of communication. Other methods are needed.

One-way Communication with Feedback

In this variation on one-way communication, the receiver transmits a verbal or nonverbal response to the sender, giving the sender the opportunity to modify the message (see figure 7.3).

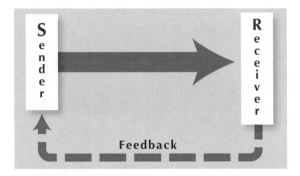

Figure 7.3. **One-way communication with feedback (The sender (S) transits information directly to the receiver (R) and no direct response is expected; however, feedback is provided from the receiver to the sender, although the sender may do nothing with this feedback.)**

One-way communication with feedback takes place constantly in the classroom. When teachers use formal lecture techniques to instruct students in their classes, there is no dialogue with students. This is essentially one-way communication. However, in most cases, even when students are not deliberately asked to participate, they will exhibit clues suggesting the extent to which they understand the content of the lecture. A puzzled look on some faces will typically nudge a teacher to restate or elaborate upon the phrase just presented. In communication terms, then, the receiver conveys a message—in this case a subtle, nonverbal one—to the sender that, in turn, transforms the nature of the initial message. Good teachers make use of this process constantly.

Utilizing this type of communication to the exclusion of others can, however, have negative consequences. Even if the sender relies on subtle feedback almost exclusively as a way to receive messages from the receiver, the sender is still in control of the act of communication. True learning involves dialogue. On the other hand, as we saw earlier, one-way communication even without feedback is entirely legitimate in some circumstances. If the content and nature of the message being transmitted is such that no adjustment is needed or wanted, feedback is not truly appropriate. We should note, however, that soliciting feedback when you have no intention of modifying the original message is much worse than not providing for feedback in the first place.

Two-Way Communication

This type of communication is characterized by the presence of two or more communicators or speakers, each of whom sends messages, and each of whom also receives messages. Diagrammatically, we can see that what takes place in two-way communication is a continuous shifting of the individual's role from sender to receiver to sender, and so forth (see figure 7.4).

True open dialogue where all participants talk and share ideas with one another is the essence of two-way communication. The most important feature is that, although one party may initiate the communication activity, no one controls the dialogue, and each message is transferred on an equal basis from sender to receiver. True parity is achieved between the senders and the receivers.

Two-way communication with true open dialogue occurs in school settings where there is shared decision making. Team-teaching situations, or administrative councils where all staff members have input into school policies and procedures, often exemplify this process. It may also be seen in individual classrooms where open student-teacher discussion and dialogue take place.

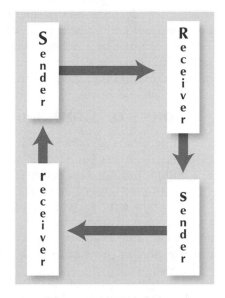

Figure 7.4.
Two-way communication (Initial message is transmitted from the sender (S) to the receiver (R). At that point, the receiver becomes a sender (s) and transmits either a new message or a modification of the original message to the initial sender, who now plays the role of receiver (r). The process of communication may end at this point, or it may continue through the same loop again, or with additional senders and receivers added.)

Communication processes will break down and be ineffective, however, if two-way communication is "played at" rather than truly enhanced as a valued activity. Token openness—when open, two-way communication is publicly espoused, but one or more parties in the process fail to listen and hear accurately the messages sent by others—probably does considerably more harm than good.

Two-way communication, of course, is not always the best way to achieve a specific goal. When nonnegotiable information must be shared with a school staff (e.g., the school district's newly adopted policy regarding students' involvement in field trips), two-way communication is probably not appropriate. The formulation of the policy may have indeed already involved considerable open dialogue. Once formulated, however, that policy needs to be announced in a straightforward manner. The key is not using two-way communication in all circumstances but rather knowing how to use this process at the appropriate time to enhance overall organizational communication.

❧ FORMS OF COMMUNICATION

Three means or modes of communication are present in most organizations. These may be listed as verbal (or spoken) communication, written communication, and nonverbal communication. All three of the communication approaches reviewed below are found in all organizations, and the effective educational leader cannot hide behind one type to the exclusion of others. Instead, the leader must be able to discover the advantages and disadvantages, as well as the likely consequences to the organization, of consciously making use of one means of communication or another.

Verbal Communication

The most prevalent form of intended communication in organizations, verbal communication, is used in a deliberate way to send messages between speakers and receivers. This involves certain advantages and disadvantages.

Spillman (1975) noted that verbal communication is spontaneous and reflects the immediate needs of the speaker. We need no advance preparation to articulate an idea verbally, although verbal communication can be planned in advance. One advantage of verbal communication is that a need can be made known "on the spot." In addition, verbal communication takes little or no additional effort by its speakers and receivers, and other than the time that may be expended in the actual process of talking; it uses no greater organizational resources. Verbal communication is momentary. Words shared in haste are, fortunately, hastily forgotten; permanent scars are less likely when no record exists of what has been communicated.

Obviously, these same advantages can also become disadvantages. For example, the fact that verbal communication leaves no permanent record can be an advantage *unless* what is said is worth remembering. Temporary statements are soon forgotten. Moreover, verbal communication is easily misunderstood by receivers who might actually believe they heard one message when something else was actually being said. A final disadvantage is that closure of the verbal communicative act may be difficult, if not impossible, to achieve. There is no exclamation point, question mark, or final period to signal the close of a verbalization.

Patricia Hayes Andrews and John Baird (2005) remark upon yet another disadvantage of verbal communication: semantic pitfalls. Sometimes the same words mean different things to different people. Other problems include *allness* (applying a label to someone by using the word *is*, as in "She is a manager"; thus implying that she is that, and nothing more) and *stereotyping* (labels we affix to people when using the word "is"). *Polarization* can occur when the words we use cause us to think in dichotomous or polarized terms. *Signal responses* can occur when we react to words not as symbols, but as things in and of themselves (if using emotionally-charged words such as "terrorist," our response is typically immediate and unthinking). According to Andrews and Baird,

> The language we use is riddled with imperfections and inadequacies, and semantic breakdowns occur too often. By recognizing the traps language poses, ... we can minimize this barrier to communication and improve the flow of messages throughout organizations. (p. 134)

Written Communication

Written communication is a staple of organizations. In schools, all manners of written notes, forms, and memos are used routinely and extensively. Included in this category are electronic messages such as those transmitted from person to person via e-mail and Web pages. Schools and other organizations increasingly are moving toward "paperless" communication. However, the communication mode still employed, whether in the form of a message on a computer screen or as a memo in the teachers' mailboxes, is written communication.

One of written communication's most powerful advantages is that it provides a permanent record. Minutes of meetings and letters can be filed and referred to at a later date. In addition, written documents serve to accurately preserve information that may be crucial to the operation of the organization. Policies, procedures, and other guidelines that need to be followed to ensure efficient operation are logically kept in a written format so that all members of an organization have a constant reference point from which to clarify activities. Another advantage is that written methods are a good way to transmit complicated information about hard-to-remember facts or concepts. Imagine providing oral directions for assembling a detailed electronic gadget. Quite a few Christmases would have been ruined if bicycles had not been assembled by parents (and Santa, of course!) following printed *instructions*.

A major disadvantage of written communication is its impersonality. Think of a time when a memo was slipped into your mailbox, rather than a message being transmitted through face-to-face confrontation. Traditional written communication can also be relatively slow and expensive to prepare, although that problem is less likely to occur with the near-instantaneous ending and receiving capabilities of electronic messaging. However, whether information is sent via printed memo or online, the speaker or sender can never be entirely assured that the message has been received, understood, and acted upon. There is no guarantee that any form of written communication will be read.

Nonverbal Communication

Too often we assume that spoken or written words are the only means we have of communicating. These measures are clearly the most widely used in organizations, but increasingly we are realizing the importance of the process of nonverbal communication. In fact, there is a general recognition today that up to eighty percent of all meaningful messages among humans are transmitted not through planned words, but rather by subtle signs, signals, and nonverbal clues (Argyle, 1994; Benthal & Polkemus, 1975). Because there are so many nuances associated with nonverbal communication, a more lengthy discussion of this mode is necessary.

Nonverbal communication is the subtle expression of attitudes, emotions, and even the physical state of the sender or speaker (Spillman, 1975) through voluntary or involuntary gestures. It is "communication without words: it is anything someone does to which someone else assigns meaning. It may be structured . . . but is more to be unstructured" (Furnham, 1999, p. 1). Winces, a smile, a glance off into space, or toe tapping are all examples of powerful, nonverbal signals of what we are feeling or thinking. Nonverbal communication also greatly modifies the words that we utter; it either affirms or denies what is being said. Throughout the history of schooling, for example, students have been masterful in determining if teachers "mean business" by watching *the ways* in which things are said.

It is a major advantage for proactive educational leaders to have the ability to sense and analyze nonverbal messages accurately. This means of communication is almost constantly present in all environments, including schools. While nonverbal messages are constantly present, how they are interpreted can be extremely difficult to control. For example, John might interpret Nancy's abrupt exit from a room where they were conversing as an angry reaction to something he said. She, on the other hand, might have realized that she was late for an appointment and rushed out, consumed with the desire to be on time. At that moment, Nancy had no control over the effect her nonverbal message had on John.

Nonverbal messages can and often do contradict what we say in verbal or written form. As a result, receivers tend to use nonverbal cues to judge the accuracy and honesty of verbal statements (Furnham, 1999). If a difference exists between nonverbal and verbal cues, people tend to place more trust in the nonverbal behavior; the old maxim "Actions speak louder than words" is very true.

Nonverbal messages establish the status and honesty of the speaker in the mind of the receiver, who tends to make unconscious decisions about the speaker and his or her intentions (Ekman, 1976). Receivers tend to judge quickly if speakers are egotistical and self-serving or sensitive and caring. Nonverbal messages might disclose hidden agendas and may be held by speakers as well as significant messages about the sender's feelings and attitudes toward the receiver. For instance, a receiver may "hear" that the sender has trust in him or her, but see that the personal is actually suspicious or even hostile because the speaker makes no eye contact, drums two or three fingers on the table while talking, and so on.

⚛ POTENTIAL BARRIERS TO COMMUNICATION

Proactive leadership involves a constant effort to reduce the potential barriers to effective communication that might be categorized in four groupings. These are barriers related to the person, barriers based on the role of the speaker, barriers found in the role of the receiver, and barriers caused by situations that inhibit the receiver's accurate perception of the message.

Personal Barriers

The sources of personal barriers, or barriers derived from the speaker, may be classified as *egocentric* limitations, *personality* limitations, or *self-concept* limitations. Egocentric barriers can never be totally overcome. All individuals are somewhat restricted in their ability to communicate absolutely and completely, because each person must judge the world from a unique and highly idiosyncratic perspective. Personality limitations grow out of individual characteristics; some people have difficulty as speakers, for instance, simply because they are shy or timid. Finally, our own self-concepts can serve to prevent us from being completely open, honest, and effective in instigating communication.

Barriers Based on the Role of the Speaker

Roles are normally defined as socially ascribed statuses within the organizational environment. People tend to have preconceived notions about certain roles, which are independent from the notions about the individuals who are assigned to the roles. The characteristics of the role, whether resented or revered, can become serious barriers to the degree of open communication possible in an organization. The role of the educational leader is sometimes symbolically more powerful, for example, than the person who fulfills the role might want it to be. Thus, the designation of someone in a role might very well in itself constitute a barrier to communication. For example, we could point to what happens when a person who has been a teacher for several years is suddenly named to the principalship of the same school. The individual may begin to lose contact with former colleagues simply because he or she is now the "boss," or an administrator.

Receiver Barriers

Sometimes the effectiveness of the communicative act is affected negatively by the receiver, not the speaker. There are a number of ways in which this occurs.

Receivers sometimes simply lack interest in the message being sent; they see no relevance in it. Part of this might derive from the fact that the receiver is not sophisticated enough to appreciate the message or lacks the necessary background or knowledge base to understand it. Also, receivers often have biases that serve to filter out what they really do not want to hear and which, in fact, sometimes prevent the communication process from beginning in the first place. Barriers such as differences in age, sex, social position, or cultural heritage often serve to screen out the real meanings needed for effective communication.

Situational Barriers

Finally, communication may be hindered by specific situational circumstances that screen out a message as it proceeds from speaker to receiver—too much noise, not enough time, additional external distractions, and so forth. Think of the last time you tried to concentrate on a lecture given in a room which was either too hot or too cold, for example. In fact, many people question whether much real communication can take place at all in our modern world because it is so cluttered with what appears to be an overwhelming number of such situational barriers.

ᘓ Skills to Improve Communication

Regardless of the barriers to carrying out effective communication, people *can* talk to one another. However, understanding and enhancing the communication process is also largely dependent on the development of a set of specific skills employed to increase its accuracy. Richard Gorton (1986) suggested some useful strategies for this important effort:

Paraphrasing. Restate the main ideas of others to clarify more ideas. ("In other words, what you're saying is . . .")

Perception checking. Check to see that your perception of what has been said is accurate. ("If I understand what you're saying . . .")

Relating things to personal feelings. Communication can break down because receivers have a negative reaction to statements: what we say offends, often unintentionally. Confront such negative feelings openly when they occur. ("When you say that, I feel like . . .")

Use objective descriptions. The use of highly subjective terms that imply personal value statements hurts open communication. Use objective terms, when possible, to describe behaviors so that people are less likely to say, "It's not what you're saying that I reject, but rather *how* you're saying it."

Feedback. Give, and accept in return, constructive and honest feedback to keep communication channels open between and among all parties.

SUMMARY

A major responsibility of the educational leader must be to keep communication going in both the school and district. The explicit assumption was made at the beginning of this chapter that organizations generally will not be effective if people do not know what is going on. Further, the effective leader is committed to open communication. As Warren Bennis and Burt Nanus (1985) noted, leaders communicate at all times, and the more effective the communication, the more effective the leadership.

In this chapter, we began by noting some basic definitions and concepts of the communication act. Next, we reviewed types and modes of communication and noted that, depending on circumstances and setting, different modes may be more appropriate than others, even when we generally feel more negative toward some approaches. For example, e-mails or written memos (one-way communication) might not seem highly desirable, but there are times when this strategy is in fact the most appropriate. The important issue is that a variety of techniques must be used to keep communication channels open.

The chapter concluded with a review of typical barriers to effective communication and skills that the supervisor may develop in an effort to reduce the barriers when they occur.

Suggested Activities

1. Observe the class of a colleague and keep track of how often each of the major types of communication described in this chapter is used. After the class, ask the teacher to estimate the percentage of time that she or he spent using both one-way communication and two-way communication; then compare your findings with the teacher's estimate.

2. Carry out the same analysis as above, but follow a practicing school administrator for a part of a school day instead of watching a teacher. Again, compare your findings with the administrator's self-perceptions.

3. Conduct a survey to determine why people believe there are barriers to effective communication. Next, question people about the ways in which they believe communication is enhanced. Put together a brief overview of your findings in a way that may be presented to a teaching staff during an inservice day. Make sure that you ask people for some suggestions regarding the possible improvement of communication in your school.

Cases to Consider

Read each case and consider the following:

- What are the critical issues raised in each case, as they relate to the use of theoretical constructs to analyze organizational communication processes?

- How does each case relate to the development of proactive leadership?

- In what ways might you suggest a resolution to the issues raised?

Case 7.1   What Happened to My Buddies?

Lonnie Timmons was a good teacher in the district for several years before he had his first chance as a school administrator. Toward the end of last summer, he received the welcome news that he would be the new assistant principal at Marcus White Elementary School, a school with a good reputation, mostly because the teaching staff had been there for many years. In fact, Lonnie had spent his first six years as a teacher in the building. He knew most of the teachers fairly well. In fact, he was very excited about being able to work with Thelma Grayson and Martha Pleshkowitz, two teachers from whom he learned so much when he started in the profession.

Mary McDade was the principal at Marcus White, a fact that was not the best possible news for Lonnie. She had been the assistant principal a few years ago at Mitchell Manor School, and Lonnie had been a fourth-grade teacher in that building. While there was never any major negative encounter involving the assistant, Lonnie never really felt at ease with her. She seemed to be quite aloof and stayed away from the teachers most of the time. Lonnie vowed to himself that, as a new assistant principal working with Ms. McDade, he would take on the role as a mediator between the principal and the group with whom he still felt close—the teachers. Thelma and Martha would be the first people he would spend time with in order to build the communication bridges he felt were so crucial.

As the school year progressed, however, Lonnie became increasingly disappointed with his failure to live up to his promise. He kept trying to find an opportunity to visit with his former colleagues and allow them to begin to confide in him. He knew that there probably had been several instances where teachers would have liked to talk to him on the side; after all, Mary McDade had made several very unpopular decisions about classroom assignments and student placements at the beginning of the year, and Lonnie knew that teachers were upset. Still, no one came to him. Wasn't he a colleague anymore?

Case 7.2 Doesn't Anyone Here Know How to Read?

For several years, the Upper Elroy Schools were known as one of the premier school districts in the state. National test scores, state achievement scores, and large numbers of students receiving scholarships at top-notch universities across the nation were all evidence of a school district with educational programs that were far superior to any other districts in the area. It was no wonder that the board of education regularly rewarded Dr. Mark Andrews with his contract as superintendent, along with significant raises in salary. After all, it would not be good to lose a person of his caliber in Upper Elroy.

Dr. Andrews was generally satisfied with his work in Upper Elroy. He enjoyed the community, and he had made many good friends in the business community as a result of his regular participation in the Rotary Club and many other local programs. Last year, he was named as one of three "Outstanding Leaders of Upper Elroy." The only thing that he never really understood was the fact that teachers and building administrators often appeared to be quite distant from him. He often visited schools and frequently sent out cards that noted specific accomplishments of different staff members. Further, when he took over the superintendency in the district nine years ago, he immediately instituted the practice of sending out a weekly "Superintendent's Newsletter" where he praised individual accomplishments of teachers and other staff members.

It was truly frustrating for the superintendent to hear, through some feedback that he recently received from one of his assistant superintendents, that he was viewed as quite distant and aloof by the teachers and principals. The thing that was most frustrating for Dr. Andrews was the fact that he truly believed he was communicating with the staff through his newsletter and notes. In fact, he had recently added a special "tear-off" section on the last section of the newsletter so that people could send him notes from time to time. It was, after all, nearly impossible for him to get out to really talk with teachers. Yet, it seemed reasonable to assume that they could read his statements each week.

Applying the Concepts

The following brief quiz is designed to improve your skills in applying some of the concepts discussed in this chapter. Read the brief introductory case and then respond to the multiple-choice questions. You will find the answers in the Appendix.

Dave Spencer spent twelve years as an elementary school teacher in the Post House School District. He was generally regarded as a very effective teacher, and many administrators in the district had encouraged him to think about a career as a principal. With that support, he enrolled in graduate courses in educational administration at State University. Soon he was certified as an elementary principal. In a short time, he received his first appointment as a campus administrator in the Post House Schools.

Dave was extremely happy to learn that he was assigned to Old Hickory School. He had worked there for nine years, so he knew quite a few of the teachers as well as community members. He was aware of a lot of the issues that would face him as the principal. Despite these facts, however, he quickly recognized that he really did not have as good a handle as he believed on how to be an effective leader for Old Hickory.

One of he first things that he began to realize was that the teachers, many of whom he had known for several years, looked at him very differently now that we was a principal. As he walked into the teachers' lounge one day, he noticed that all conversations appeared to either cease or at least shift in tone. In the past, he had been the "life of the party" in many lounge conversations. As a teacher, he was always telling jokes, sharing gossip, and serving as the center of attention. As principal, he recognized that his presence had created a chilling effect on the tone of the group. In short, he felt as if the group with whom he used to talk openly was now talking about him.

1. Dave was discovering that there was a barrier to effective communication with regard to his relationship with teachers. The barrier was one that could be described as _____.

   a. a personal barrier

   b. a barrier based on the role of the speaker

   c. a receiver barrier

   d. a situational barrier

2. If you were to advise Dave in this case, a reasonable approach would be _____.

   a. to apply for a transfer to another school

   b. to spend a good part of his day getting the teachers to look at him as "one of the gang" again

   c. to let this situation take care of itself by letting time go by and letting teachers get to know him as a principal, not as a former teacher

   d. to announce that rudeness to the principal would not be tolerated in the school

3. The fact that teachers made their feelings known to Dave when he walked into the teachers' lounge was an example of the effectiveness of _____ communication.

   a. nonverbal

   b. written

   c. verbal

   d. indirect

4. The best way for Dave to begin to reduce the tension between him and his teachers might be to engage in _____.

   a. one-way communication

   b. one-way communication without feedback

   c. two-way communication

   d. two-way communication without feedback

Additional Reading

Ekman, P., & Friesen, W. (1972). Hand movements. *Journal of Communication, 22:* 253–274.

Hackman, M. Z., & Johnson, C. E. (2004). *Leadership: A communication perspective, 4/E.* Long Grove, IL: Waveland Press.

Katz, Neil H., & Lawyer, John W. (1992). *Communication and conflict resolution skills.* Dubuque: Kendall Hunt Publishing Company.

Malandro, L., Barker, L., & Barker, D. (1989). *Non Verbal Communication.* New York: Random House.

Addressing Accountability

For many years, public schools in the United States operated on some very basic assumptions. Perhaps the most central of these was that, when taxpayers paid for educational programs, parents could send their children to local schools and then youngsters would learn enough to assist them in having happy and successful lives in the future. For the most part, this type of understanding served as the basis for public education in the United States. About 25 years ago, however, there started to be an increasing skepticism on the part of taxpayers and parents regarding the extent to which American public schools were, in fact, meeting expectations to ensure that their children were actually receiving quality education.

Like many observations about service in a huge country the size of the United States, there are obvious problems in trying to paint accurate pictures of "reality" across the country. Without any question, there were (and no doubt still are) many communities in the United States where public education is not meeting the challenge of serving students effectively. On the other hand, there are also many places where public schools excel in their efforts to provide quality educational experiences to all learners.

It makes little or no sense to debate the general impressions held by many citizens regarding their perceptions of ineffective schools. As professional educators, we may debate the topic forever. But in the eyes of significant, influential groups such as political bodies, large corporations, and the news media, it is difficult to deny the view that American schools have been ineffective for many years. The results of this dissatisfaction, coupled with continued concern over the cost of taxes (and tax-based services like public schools) have been numerous efforts to find ways of either reducing taxes, or at least making certain that real value was received in the money spent for education.

It is because of this desire to ensure that education is really taking place in schools that state and the federal governments have been increasingly committed to enacting legislation that would hold public schools accountable for what they are doing in the name of public education. In short, politicians and others now promise that no more will schools waste limited dollars and allow children to graduate without demonstrating competence in core areas such as reading, writing, mathematics, science, and social studies. The *age of accountability* is truly a reality of American education.

Regardless of the reasons, the United States has witnessed an increase in interest in ensuring that schools are, indeed, providing adequate educational programs to all students, consistent with the terms found in the constitutions of each of the fifty states. Whether caused by parental concern, educator frustration, or even political posturing, steps have been enacted in all states and at the federal level to support the mandate of quality education across the United States. In general, educators have no problems with the intent of these measures. The challenge that faces you and all educational leaders appears in terms of enforcing and monitoring methods that have been mandated to assure that effective education is indeed taking place in your school and other schools across the nation.

The single most powerful model of the expectation that schools and school districts will be held accountable for student learning is found in federal legislation and policy. The federal reauthorization of the Elementary and Secondary Education Act of 1965 was presented and supported as law during the administration of President George W. Bush in 2003. This legislation, the *No Child Left Behind Act* (NCLB), has been either praised or cursed nationally as the source of most current measures associated with efforts to reform education in public schools across the nation. It includes many specific requirements for schools to ensure that all children, regardless of race, ethnicity, or economic level, are able to achieve adequate education at taxpayers' expense.

The NCLB legislation has its roots in the perceptions held by many concerning the overall adequacy of schooling in recent years. Among these beliefs are:

- In general, students are not sufficiently prepared academically;
- American students lag behind students in other countries in key curricular areas;
- The consequences of these inadequacies are likely to have a continuing negative impact on America's ability to compete economically with other industrialized nations; and
- Above all, practices and policies in America's public schools are less than fair to students from different ethnic, racial, gender, and socioeconomic groups.

In short, NCLB supporters take the stance that, while all children in the United States have access to free public education, the quality of that education has varied significantly from state to state, community to community, and societal subgroup to subgroup over the years. The goal of NCLB is to bring about equality of educational opportunity for all children.

✑ TERMS OF THE NO CHILD LEFT BEHIND ACT

No Child Left Behind legislation holds certain expectations for school performance and the ability to meet key objectives in the areas of accountability, average yearly progress, and the recruitment, selection, and retention of qualified teachers. In addition, there is a strong suggestion that meeting the demands of NCLB will also create a need for a critical review and likely improvement of curricula in schools and school districts.

Accountability

The first term that needs to be understood is the word *accountability* as it is used in the legislation. This is, after all, the cornerstone of everything that is promised in both the national policy of NCLB and parallel programs that have been initiated in individual states.

In its analysis of NCLB, the national principals' associations (i.e., National Association of Elementary School Principals and National Association of Secondary School Principals) collaborated with the Educational Research Service to produce the work, *The K–12 Principal's Guide to "No Child Left Behind"* (McLeod, D'Amico, & Protheroe, 2003). This book includes the following "characteristics of good accountability systems."

A good accountability system must:

1. set ambitious but realistic goals for improvement in student achievement;

2. measure improvement for students and schools against state-defined academic standards;

3. hold districts and schools responsible for raising student achievement, including the achievement of low-income and minority students, on a specific time line with benchmarks;

4. require continuous improvement for all schools and for all groups within schools to close the achievement gap;

5. be statewide, transparent, and understandable to parents and all other stakeholders;

6. minimize opportunities to "game" the system;

7. ensure that all students participate in assessments;

8. include as determinative indicators of school progress only quantifiable student outcomes;

9. be structurally sound to ensure true reform; and

10. reward success and ensure that students are provided with effective remedies; include public school options, in case of persistent failures.

These characteristics of accountability make it clear that a school leader will no longer allow beginning principals or experienced principals to carry on with "business as usual." Following are issues that you will need to address:

- Principals need to become directly involved with the business of overseeing teachers who may no longer "teach what we have always taught, the way we've always taught it" in a school. There can be little "down time" in a school. Teaching time is precious, limited, and finite. It must be focused on ensuring that students learn. The principal must be out and about the school, literally and figuratively, as a way to monitor instruction.

- More than ever, principals need to spend quality time with parents to let them know about their students' progress and the progress of the school as a total organization. Parents must be seen as active partners in the education of their children and not simply as factors that need to be "dealt with" on occasion. Student progress (or lack of it) toward educational achievement goals cannot be a surprise that parents hear about at the end of the school year, after the grading period, or just "after the test scores come out."

- The principal must ensure that teachers understand their responsibilities to communicate with parents and students.

- Principals are now called upon increasingly to be public spokespersons for their schools.

- Principals must appreciate that they are accountable in the performance of their assigned duties as leaders of student learning in their schools. They may no longer pass responsibility to others if students or groups of students have problems.

Adequate Yearly Progress

A significant cornerstone in efforts to reform educational practices in states across the nation may be found in the NCLB stipulation that schools must ensure that all of their students can be shown to making reasonable progress toward achievement of important educational goals. This insistence is referred to frequently as the requirement for *adequate yearly progress* (AYP) by all students enrolled in all public schools. According to the Education Commission of the States (ECS, 2002), there are several critical issues that serve as a way to gauge whether AYP is being achieved in schools across the United States:

1. AYP is measured primarily by gains in student achievement. However, individual states must make use of at least two additional indicators, such as retention rates or high school graduation rates.

2. Each state must develop publicly known starting points or thresholds as a way to begin the process of verifying student progress. (These starting points were to be derived from achievement data collected during the 2001–2002 school year.)

3. Time lines must be developed to guide implementation. (NCLB requires all students in each state to be performing at or above proficient levels in reading and mathematics by the end of the 2013–2014 school year.)

4. Performance objectives should continually increase over time, or an annual minimum percentage of students and subgroups of students should meet or exceed proficiency in mathematics, reading, and language arts.

As an example of the ways in which individual states can "translate" the expectation of AYP into terms that are relevant to local needs, consider the following criteria of a school district in the state of Texas. In order to meet AYP, schools must meet these criteria as a whole and in several socioeconomic subgroups:

- A passing rate of at least 53% in reading and 42% on the Texas Assessment of Knowledge and Skills (TAKS) and other local assessments;
- A participation rate of at least 95% in any of the tests being used to measure performance;
- A graduation rate of 70% or higher; and
- An attendance rate of 90% or higher.

Ensuring Staff Quality

The terms of NCLB realize that no long-term improvement effort will ever take place without schools being staffed by teachers who are well-prepared and qualified to teach the subjects in which students are expected to attain certain achievement goals. NCLB defines *highly qualified teachers* as those who have obtained full state certification, and this includes those who have received what many term "alternative teacher certification" credentials. As part of this process, there is a requirement that states make use of a teacher certification or licensure examination as the final determinant of a person's ability to be certified and, therefore, highly qualified. Quite clearly, traditional paths to service as a teacher through formal preservice preparation programs at universities are now discounted in an effort to attract many who have not gone through conventional training routes.

According to NCLB, all new elementary school teachers must hold at least a bachelor's degree and must also have passed a state test demonstrating content knowledge and teaching skills in reading, writing, mathematics, and other elementary curricular areas. New middle school and high school teachers are expected to hold at least a bachelor's degree and also be able to demonstrate content mastery in the subject they are teaching through success on a state licensing or certification examination. They must also demonstrate successful completion of either graduate work or undergraduate academic majors in their selected teaching fields, or receive advanced certification and credentialing. Absent from these minimum requirements is an expectation that any teacher engage in specialized training in such traditional teacher education subjects as child psychology, classroom management, instructional design, or many other fields. Quality teaching is defined largely as expertise in subject matter.

Elementary, middle, or secondary school teachers not newly hired must hold at least a bachelor's degree and must also demonstrate academic content area knowledge. This demonstration may be subject to an exam but also must be based on multiple measures of teacher competency and be made available to the public upon request.

Required preservice learning for "highly qualified teachers" requires only a bachelor's degree in an unspecified area (and in some cases, some additional graduate training, although not necessarily in educational fields). There is no demand that any teacher would have gone through a formal undergraduate teacher education program. There is clearly an assumption by politicians that teachers need only very strong content area backgrounds in order to be successful and contribute to student learning. No need is seen for specialized training in education is such areas as pedagogy, instructional design, psychological theories of learning, classroom management, and many other areas that normally serve as traditional foundations for teacher preparation. To put it bluntly, there is a strong belief that "as long as you know the content of *what* you teach, you will be able to learn *how* to teach soon enough after you're on the job."

Curriculum Reform

NCLB makes it clear that attention must be directed to curriculum refinement activities in each school and school district. Based on the results of standardized achievement testing during each year, school leaders should be prepared to lead local efforts to modify and improve curriculum, particularly in the basic skill areas of reading, writing, and mathematics. In the case of elementary schools, particular attention needs to be directed toward the development of reading skills in primary grades. This is meant as a foundation for all student learning in all school curricular areas.

❧ LIMITATIONS OF NCLB

The adoption of the reform programs and practices mandated by NCLB is, of course, not without criticism as well. While few would dispute the goals of enhancing overall quality and the effort to equalize the quality of education by making certain that basic standards of educational achievement can be realized by all children, there are, nonetheless, arguments that question the current movement to define educational accountability. Some of the issues frequently raised by critics are based on the following observations:

1. *The status of poor programs of public education in America has been greatly overstated by many.* While problems certainly do exist, most in this country are and have long been focused on providing quality education to all students for many years.

2. *Frequent efforts to discredit American schools because they are not comparable to schools in Germany, Japan, and many other countries of the world are distortions of reality,* in large measure because the goals and social expectations of schools around the world differ so greatly. For example, Americans want their children to learn how to read, write, and engage in problem solving in math. But we also value students who are well-adjusted to social expectations and well-rounded in terms of involvement in athletics and other activities. We also want our children to participate in after-school work experiences, sports, and social events. All of these issues are rarely a part of the schooling experience in other nations of the world.

3. *Assuming that children are not learning because test scores are low is an inaccurate and simplistic assumption* that overlooks the limitations of standardized testing to gauge much more than test-taking ability.

4. *Current legislation at both the state and national levels places too much emphasis on the testing of children,* a practice that defines learning in very narrow terms because the curricula of schools, districts, and states becomes defined in terms of "what is needed to score well on tests." As a result, we "teach to the test" so much that we ignore the opportunity for children to learn by "thinking outside the box" and develop creativity (Henson, 2006).

5. *From a practical point of view, NCLB legislation is yet another example of an "unfunded mandate" of government*—that is, it makes costly requirements of school districts across the nation without providing sufficient financial support for schools to implement what is required. For example, if pupils are unable to pass tests at grade levels, and they are retained for one (or more) years at their current grades, school districts could face the need to build more facilities and hire a large number of new teachers to serve the influx of retained students. In a school system with 5,000 students at grade 3, for example, 90 percent of the pupils might pass, but 10 percent (500 pupils) would be retained, thus potentially creating the need for a school that could house 500 students. If that type of result is projected over several grade levels in a school district, the obvious implications would result in colossal expenditures for new school facilities.

6. *The definitions of accountability and achievement are too narrowly focused.* If students do not perform well on standardized tests each year, the implication of current policy is that educators (teachers, principals, counselors, superintendents, and so forth) are somehow incompetent and deserving of all blame. Totally absent from the legislation is any emphasis on parental responsibility and individual student account-ability for their personal learning.

7. *Terms in NCLB are often vague and apparently insensitive to social realities at times.* Perhaps the best example of vagueness is found in the expecta-tion for adequate yearly progress to be demonstrated by all students. While the notion that all children in a school should learn a reason-able amount of content knowledge and acquire sufficient skills each year makes sense, the terms of NCLB are not that simple. Instead, an often confusing array of indicators and expectations, as noted earlier in this chapter, sometimes obscure what this relatively simple and important concept may involve. School administrators often complain that AYP is used to punish schools rather than as a means of measur-ing student progress from year to year.

8. *Some NCLB standards appear contradictory to reality.* For example, there is the expectation that schools insist on finding teachers who know their subject areas and demonstrate a commitment to serving children. However, the unfortunate reality is that teaching is no longer a profes-sion that seems to be very attractive to many in this country. Low sal-ary levels, few opportunities for career advancement, more demanding working conditions (which may relate to the expectations of NCLB itself), lack of fringe benefits, and other factors are now identified as strong disincentives to individuals who might otherwise follow careers as highly qualified teachers. In response to this reality, many states have initiated programs to enable individuals who appear "highly qualified" in terms of subject-matter expertise to move quickly into teaching roles through alternative teacher certification programs. While this strategy may enable greater numbers of people who know subject matter (e.g., in science and math because they used to work in fields where these skills were needed by employees) to suddenly achieve instant "highly qualified teacher" status, these individuals are often drawn from the ranks of unemployed workers in other fields who see teaching as a "backup job," without strong commitment to serving children as a major focus of their work. Principals often report significant concerns with alternative certification program (ACP) teachers who have a lack of understanding and appreciation of student needs, interests, and other conditions that promote true learning.

9. *The tone of NCLB is largely punitive.* In the name of making public educa-tion more accountable to taxpayers who assume that children entrusted to local schools would learn basic skills each year, provisions

of NCLB suggest that if its standards are not met, drastic measures will be taken against schools for failing to meet public expectations. These include the threat of losing large numbers of students who would be permitted and encouraged to transfer to "better" schools, the loss of financial support, and ultimately, closure. Critics point to the fact that, in many cases, schools with "failing grades" serve communities with low expectations for educational success and parents and children who have no interest in achieving success in the first place. Rather than operating under the suggestion that "the school is bad and should be closed," some schools should be provided with additional resources to enable the development of more effective programs and practices to reach out to populations of children who need stronger intervention, not simply "market choice" to "take their business elsewhere."

☙ REALITIES FACING SUPERVISORS AND OTHER LEADERS

It is critical that all school leaders across the nation continue to pay attention to the expectations found in NCLB. Whether you personally agree or disagree with specific features of this legislation, a great percentage of the American public is convinced that this type of action is warranted to ensure that students in our public schools are learning and that taxpayers are getting a reasonable return for their investment of dollars. As an educational leader, your job is often one of seeing that "the job gets done," not promoting philosophical discussions of relative worth and value.

Contrary to what many current school principals and other administrators and supervisors may believe, the expectation that schools will provide evidence to the public of the value of their accomplishments is not a fad that will soon disappear. The belief that "this too shall pass" is not an idea that has much merit these days. Whether educators like it or not, public schools in the United States are now being viewed by critics as failed organizations. This will continue to mean that a primary duty of anyone in an educational leadership will be to continue to provide evidence that students are learning and that teachers are teaching. It may be argued by many administrators that teachers and administrators have always felt themselves to be accountable to students, parents, taxpayers, and political bodies. That may be true, but what has changed is the fact that "success" is now defined in legally mandated ways. One can argue the value or shortcoming of No Child Left Behind, but such arguments are not likely to change public opinion and political intervention.

☙ SUMMARY

This chapter addressed the important issue of how school supervisors and administrators will be held increasingly accountable for their efforts to lead effective schools. While individual states may have been involved with efforts to ensure that tax money was being spent on quality educational programs, the most powerful mandate for focusing on educational accountability was clearly the passage of the No Child Left Behind Legislation in 2002. Since that time, the life and duties of school administrators and supervisors has changed drastically. It has become necessary to provide evidence that students are learning, attending school, and moving toward academic goals each year. Teachers must be qualified to teach their assigned subject areas, and school personnel must communicate openly and honestly to parents and other community members.

Nothing described here in the way of measuring school effectiveness is necessarily wrong. But the demand for accountability in public education in the United States has clearly increased stress among teachers and administrators. In and of itself, that is not necessarily bad. After all, lawyers, doctors, architects, and all other professionals are asked to provide evidence of their effectiveness. But the great difference that continues to frustrate professional educators is that often, despite the best efforts of teachers, supervisors, and school administrators, the most unpredictable variable will always be the willingness of individual students to learn. No one can mandate that to occur in any school.

Despite the limitations on definitions of school accountability, the movement is well underway. The future does not suggest that expectations now present in public schools will be decreased at any time soon.

Suggested Activities

1. Contact your state department of education to learn what the local definitions of "school success" are. Note specifically the state standards for such issues as "annual yearly progress" and definitions of "highly qualified teachers."

2. Carry out an analysis of the ways in which teachers may be made ready for service as "highly qualified teachers" in your district or across your state. How many alternative certification teachers now work in your school? Interview a sample of these individuals who have at least two years of experience as full-time teachers to learn what additional training might be needed for future alternative certification teachers.

3. Review the test scores and other indicators of student success in your present school or any other school in your district. (By law, these data should be readily available to any citizen in your state). If you were the principal of the school you have reviewed, what would data from last year suggest as needed areas for further development and improvement in the future?

Cases to Consider

Read each case and consider the following:

- What are the critical issues raised in each case, as they relate to the discussion of educational accountability presented in this chapter?
- How does each case relate to the development of proactive leadership?
- In what ways might you suggest a resolution to the issues raised?

Case 8.1   The "Three A's of Effective Schools"

Lionel Crawford had been the principal of Sanchez High School for 17 years. During that time, he had been proud to serve as the leader of one of the most successful schools in the southwestern United States. "Success" at Sanchez was defined largely in terms of the accomplishment of the boys' football and basketball teams. Each team had been the state champions more frequently than any other school in the entire state, and several of the former players had gone on to achieve success at major universities. Even more impressive was the fact that the school had 12 graduates who went on to earn places on professional football and basketball teams, a fact proudly demonstrated in a special "Ring of Fame" trophy case found in the front lobby of the school.

Mr. Crawford—a former all-conference player on State University's National Championship basketball team—was proud to say that Sanchez was truly a great school built on what he usually called the "Three A's of Excellence—Athletics, Activities, and Academics." The only problem with Mr. Crawford's model for success was the fact that many Sanchez athletes who went on to play for major university athletics programs did not complete their university degree programs after their sports careers were over—a fact frequently reported in newspaper stories over the years. In fact, six of the 12 "Ring of Fame" players left college to accept pro contracts after only one or two years. One of the more distressing stories came from the *State Journal* three years ago when it was discovered that three ex-footballers from Sanchez had failed an extremely low-level math test administered to applicants for state highway construction jobs.

Despite the periodic criticisms of Sanchez, Lionel continued to extol the virtues of "the finest high school in the greatest state" when he went out on speaking engagements across his state and in the region. He felt that such activity was important for a principal who really wanted to see his students succeed through receiving university scholarships. Unfortunately, the *State Journal* article was the beginning of a series of investigations into the football and basketball programs at the high school. Stories began to appear in national newspapers. The *Chicago Tribune* carried a three-part story on the decline of educational quality in high schools, as exemplified by the "Sanchez Story" in the Southwest.

In the state legislature, speeches were frequently made concerning the need to "straighten up schools" to counteract the national reputation for running "jock factories" instead of schools. Not surprisingly, several candidates for political office ran on and won elections based on the promise to "improve public education in the state." What this clearly meant was that schools would be held accountable for more than basketball and football victories. Evidence would be needed to show that all students were actually learning, not just getting recruited to play sports. The "accountability movement" had reached the state.

Upon passage of statewide comprehensive school reform by the state legislature, the media began what seemed like a planned assault on the activity of Sanchez and the leadership of Lionel Crawford. Whether deservedly or not, the school had become a lightning rod for critics who wanted to show how public schools were failing in their responsibility to educate children. Lionel's "Three A's" became a statewide punch line for pundits who noted that the order of the "A's" always listed academics *after* athletics and activities.

Finally, at a local school board meeting, as Mr. Crawford was again being drilled by board members and the public to learn more about the deficiencies at Sanchez High School, the principal concluded his comments by making a rather emotional statement concerning the fact that he and the coaches and teachers at his school had always put the education of children as the highest priority on their list:

> Education has always come first in this great school. But education in our school community must be based on pride, and pride comes from accomplishment. And our success on the athletic fields and gyms has allowed us to have the pride we need to succeed. Simply waving the "magic wand" of the legislature will not fix test scores and help the schools. It will only bring about more criticism and destruction of the great things we have done for our students over the years.

Case 8.2   "Let's Find Out What Happened"

Paddington Elementary School was built in the early 1930s to serve the children of an affluent neighborhood located on the edge of the downtown of the largest city in the state. It is a beautiful, well-preserved structure that clearly indicates a community's commitment to "only the best accommodations for the children of the movers and shakers of the city." Doris Euston has been the principal of Paddington for the past seven years. She taught in the school, served as a counselor there, and even attended the school when she was a child.

The Paddington community has changed over the years. When it served the gentry of the community, it was located in the heart of a neighborhood of wealthy people who lived in well-kept, three-story brownstone houses. New cars and well-dressed professionals were seen on the streets, and children who attended the school were all well-mannered and provided with a great deal of parental support. However, as the upper middle-class and wealthy residents of the neighborhood moved outward from the city's center, the community changed. More African Americans moved into the old brownstones. Next, advertisements on buildings gave evidence of another community shift as signs were now mostly in Spanish. The nature of old Paddington School began to change. Gone were the well-dressed young people of the "good old days." Now, children came from single-parent homes, and there were often signs of physical abuse. Parents no longer were engaged in school activities. Violence on the streets around Paddington seemed to be a part of the school's landscape.

Suddenly, about five years ago, the "white flight" to the suburbs began to decrease. Wealthier families seemed to collectively understand that driving two hours each day to and from work in downtown was no longer sensible. The Paddington neighborhood brownstones that were falling apart a few years ago were now starting to go on the market for nearly a million dollars. Change had taken place almost overnight within the community. Yet, inside the school, the children continued to reflect the immediate past reality of the community. The students were predominantly African American and Latino; the "returnees" to the community either sent their children to private schools, or the families now being able to afford housing near downtown could not afford children. The enrollment at Paddington was in a steep decline. Most children came from public housing units that remained on the edge of the old neighborhood.

Another interesting change had taken place, and this one had a direct impact on the life of Doris Euston. For years, the lack of parental support, the instability and poverty of the community in general, and the decline of morale among the teachers at Paddington had all been a part of a school that was in ruin. Attendance rates were very low. Students transferred in and out of the school each day. The dropout rates at Paddington and also at nearby Kings Cross High School were extremely high. And when the state began a mandated program of regular achievement testing, the Kings Cross/Paddington schools were generally the lowest performers.

For the most part, Paddington seemed to be ignored even with its low performance rates. Now, with the "gentrification" of the Paddington community well underway, the quality of the local elementary school was suddenly on the front burner again. Even though many of the new residents did not send their children to the school, there were numerous public statements being made to the effect that "the revitalized Paddington community cannot return to its full glory with poor schools." Doris was receiving phone calls every day from the media, community groups, the local alderman, and even the mayor's office to inquire what was going to be done to "get test scores up to where they were supposed to be."

Applying the Concepts

The following brief quiz is designed to improve your skills in applying some of the concepts discussed in this chapter. Read the brief introductory case and then respond to the multiple-choice questions. You will find the answers in the Appendix.

Dr. Herman Gerber, the new superintendent of the Gray Manor Schools, had taken on quite a challenge. The district had recently received word that the majority of its 19 schools would be classified as "Low Performing" next year due to their test results this past year. In most cases, the schools with low scores had been identified as unacceptable for at least two

years in a row. While the official announcement of Dr. Harriet Willis's res-
ignation as the previous superintendent noted that she was leaving the district "to pursue other professional opportunities" in the state capital, it was
also clear to most that she had been in a difficult spot with the Gray Manor
Board of Education because of the declining state scores. The word across
the state was that Gray Manor was one of those districts that would likely
continue to decline. After all, most students in the schools were either Latino or African American and came from very low-income homes. Parental
support and involvement were virtually nonexistent, and there were no
resources available in the community to support special programs in the
schools. In short, the word on the street was that the district was very close
to being taken over by the state department of education, and that all of the
district schools were very close to being reconstituted.

It was a surprise to hear that Dr. Gerber even applied for the position
as superintendent. This would be his first CEO position of a school district,
but he had many years of experience as the associate superintendent for
instruction at Monte Vista, another property-poor district with a largely
minority student population in the western part of the state. Contrary to
Gray Manor, however, Monte Vista had been quite successful in its performance on state tests for the past several years. In fact, many of the schools
in Monte Vista had received the rating of "superior" from the state board of
education. Herman Gerber was said to be the architect of that success.
While people were surprised that he was changing jobs, the principals and
teachers at Gray Manor were delighted to think that the demise of their
district (and jobs) might actually be averted.

The Gray Manor principals were the first group called by the new
superintendent to attend an organizational meeting at the beginning of the
school year. It was a "closed door" session that was not open to anyone
from the media, community associations, site councils, or any other group
but the building leaders of the district. In fact, not even assistant principals
were invited to this first session. Dr. Gerber said that it was critical to have
a chance for the "prime movers" of the district to get together to develop a
strategy, a "battle plan" for turning the district into a winning system, as
soon as possible.

The session began calmly enough, with Dr. Gerber asking each of the
19 principals to introduce him- or herself and make a brief statement about
what he or she believed to be the main challenges that the district would
face in terms of making a turnaround this next year. Not surprisingly,
nearly every individual commented on issues such as language problems
for many students, lack of parental involvement, poverty, and teachers who
had just "given up." Dr. Gerber sat quietly and listened for what turned out
to be nearly an hour of introductions. Then he stood in front of the group
and began his long-awaited self-introduction.

"Ladies and gentlemen, most of you already know about much of my
background as an educator. I met many of you when I was in town for some
of the community interviews that were held for candidates, and I know all
of you looked at my resume pretty carefully. You know I spent several years
in Monte Vista, and before that, I was a teacher in New Hampshire. Now let
me tell you a few additional things that may suggest the ways we are going

to go about saving this school district. I grew up on the streets of a tough neighborhood in Boston called "Southie." I learned how to fight a lot of battles as a kid, and I've continued to win tough battles through my career as an educator. I don't like losing, and to win I stretch the rules as far as I can without breaking them. The situation at Monte Vista a few years ago was the same one you all described to me here in Gray Manor a few minutes ago. But in less than three years, we were getting national recognition for our work. I can't necessarily promise you that our situation here will end up a feature story in *Education Week*, but I can assure you that we're going to turn around the public perception that our schools are no good. We're going to win the accountability game here, or I won't be here in two years."

The principals were happy to hear the words, but the reality of the current situation seemed well beyond the control of the new magician from the East. They then sat quietly as the new leader indicated that his past experience showed that there were plenty of ways to beat the numbers game of the state accountability system, and he was going to use them here. For one thing, principals were expected to step up their special-ed placements as soon as possible. As everyone knew, special-education students were exempt from the state test, at least for the next three years. "I want you to comb the special-ed rules and regulations and find out how some of your students who don't do well on tests are better served as special needs students." The same advice was given to those students identified as limited English learners. As Dr. Gerber noted, "At Monte Vista, we discovered that by exempting both the non-English-speaking students and special-education students, our tests scores were raised overnight and all of our low-performing schools got off the state Watch List overnight."

The remaining time for the principals' meeting included several more strategies that Dr. Gerber shared with the campus administrators. Matters such as the ways in which attendance figures were recorded and dropout rates reported, and the ways in which teacher certification matters were handled were all part of the message that was shared with the group "behind closed doors."

1. Of the following responsibilities that principals will need to address in the current climate of accountability in schools, the one that is most clearly side-stepped by the superintendent's suggestions is:

   a. Principals need to oversee teachers who may no longer "teach what they have always taught by teaching the way they've always taught."

   b. Principals will be called upon to be researchers.

   c. Principals must appreciate that they are accountable in the performance of their assigned duties as leaders for student learning in their schools.

   d. Principals must ensure that teachers understand their responsibilities to communicate with parents and students.

2. The principle of accountability that is being ignored most directly by Dr. Gerber is to:

a. require continuous improvement for all schools and for all groups within schools to close achievement gaps.

b. minimize opportunities to "game" the system.

c. be structurally sound to ensure true reform.

d. include as determinative indicators of school progress only quantifiable student outcomes.

Additional Reading

Daresh, J. (2007). *Beginning the principalship* (3rd ed.) Thousand Oaks, CA: Corwin Press.

Darling-Hammond, Linda (2000). Teacher quality and student achievement: A review of state policy evidence. *Education Policy and Analysis Archives, 8* (1).

Glanz, J. (1998). *Action research: An educational leader's guide to school improvement.* Norwood, MA: Christopher-Gordon.

Hamilton, L. S., & Koretz, D. M. (2002). Tests and their use in test-based accountability systems. In. S. P. Klein (ed.), *Making sense of test-based accountability in education.* Santa Monica, CA: RAND.

Joftus, S., & Maddox-Dolan, B. (2003). *Left out and left behind: NCLB and the American high school.* Washington, DC: Alliance for Excellent Education.

Kimmelman, Paul L. (2006). *Implementing NCLB: Creating a knowledge framework to support school improvement.* Thousand Oaks, CA: Corwin Press.

Orfield, G., & Kornhaber, M. L. (eds.) (2001). *Raising standards or raising barriers?* New York: Century Foundation Press.

Sunderman, Gail L., Kim, James S., & Orfield, Gary (2005). *NCLB meets school realities: Lessons from the field.* Thousand Oaks, CA: Corwin Press.

Wayne, A. J., & Youngs, P. (2003). Teacher characteristics and student achievement gains: A review. *Review of Educational Research, 73,* 89–122.

❦ 9 ❧

Managing Change

As Lipham (1965) pointed out, the fundamental essence of leadership must be conceived as the process of bringing about needed change. Implicit within any leadership role—whether director of a private corporation or educational administrator or supervisor—is a responsibility to foster the type of change that will stimulate continuous growth and development in an organization. Administration, on the other hand, deals with maintaining the status quo in an organization. This distinction confronts us directly with a perplexing problem that school leaders must face: Administrators and supervisors who wish to be effective must generally engage in administrative behaviors and duties on occasion. As a result, the supervisor who is charged with the responsibility of providing leadership (i.e., organizational change) must also take care to guard the status quo when that is the most appropriate route for the school to follow. Is effective educational supervision an impossibility, then? Or at best a case of trying to walk a narrow line between the competing demands of "changing" and "maintaining?" No change can mean organizational stagnation; change for the sake of change can result in organizational dysfunction. Being effective in this paradox of leadership and administration is like Goldilocks trying to find the right bowl of porridge: We need to be careful not to select something either "too hot" or "too cold"; it must be "just right." The educational leader has to know just the right times to push for change, and also when to hold the line.

This chapter explores organizational change processes as they relate to the practice of proactive educational leadership. A number of conceptualizations of change that have appeared in the literature are reviewed, and then some of the most consistent barriers to promoting needed organizational change are described. While change is a necessary condition for the improvement of organizations, it is not an easy condition to

179

either promote or sustain. As a result, this chapter concludes with a consideration of some strategies that may be followed to reduce typical constraints that inhibit needed organizational change.

❧ ALTERNATIVE CONCEPTUAL MODELS OF CHANGE

Douglas Paul (1977) categorized the major descriptions of change in four broad theoretical models: problem solving, social interaction, research-development-diffusion (RD&D), and linkage. In the sections that follow, brief descriptions are included of the underlying assumptions and most salient characteristics of each of the four principal models of change.

Problem-Solving Model

This model suggests that change is a logical effort to provide solutions to problematic states perceived by the organization. The basic view in this model is that, if something is wrong, change must occur. The role of the supervisor is to first determine as much as possible concerning the precise nature of the problem faced by the organization, then suggest modifications in policy and practice that might serve to solve the identified problems.

A rich tradition of support for this conceptualization of change can be found in the work of, among others, Warren Bennis, Kenneth Benne, and Robert Chin (1969), Ronald Lippitt, James Watson, and Benjamin Westley (1958), and Michael Fullan (1973). A major assumption underlying this view is that organizational problems, even when complex and threatening, can be identified with sufficient clarity to enable rational solutions to be formulated and applied. This led to the development of analytical schemes that suggest that organizational dilemmas may be tracked along a predictable continuum, to the extent that the leader can know when to initiate change in the same way that a physician might have a clear idea of when to introduce a new treatment for an ill patient.

The *concerns-based adoption model* (CBAM) for staff development devised by Gene Hall and Susan Loucks (1976) is an effective application of this change process. It may be noted that it serves as an excellent example of a practice founded on the problem-solving approach to change. The CBAM suggests that organizations demonstrate clearly identifiable *levels of use* of certain activities, and members of organizations experience certain key *levels of concern* regarding activities being introduced into their world. Because these two factors are rational, the supervisor (or any other leader) can consciously affect matches between levels of use and levels of concern, thereby resolving organizational problems and increasing the satisfaction and sense of efficacy felt by the people in the organization.

Gordon Lippitt (1969) identified six basic elements of the problem-solving model of change: (1) identifying the problem, (2) diagnosing the problem, (3) retrieving related knowledge and discussing its implications for overcoming the problem, (4) forming alternatives to action, (5) testing the feasibility of alternatives, and (6) adopting and implementing the selected alternative. These steps call attention once again to the most obvious characteristic of the model: It makes use of linear and rational thinking as the foundation for change.

Another outcome of the problem-solving perspective is a belief that networking among different organizations is a commendable practice. If we believe that organizational problems are basically rational, then we may assume that many schools, districts, or other organizations face roughly the same problems from time to time. Potentially creative solutions to these recurring problems can come from many systems working together, rather than facing each problem in isolation.

Perhaps the greatest drawback to the problem-solving approach to analyzing organizational change is found in this same absolute faith in the rationality of organizations. The approach firmly suggests that solutions can be identified for all problems and that change can be controlled so as to reduce the negative impact of the problems. The model tends to ignore the fact that solving organizational problems does not always involve selecting the "best" response, but rather finding a path that is less imperfect than any others available.

Social Interaction

Change often occurs in organizations solely because people in those organizations talk to other people who convince them to try something a little different. This is the basic assumption found in *social interaction*, a model for change analysis that has its roots in the field of agriculture. Benjamin Ryan and Neal Gross (1943), Everett Rogers (1962), and Everett Rogers and Fred Shoemaker (1971) were among the early proponents of this view, which was first recognized as a process followed by farmers who shared information concerning the development of new hybrid corn seeds. (The process is sometimes called the "agricultural model of change," and change agents are spoken of in the same terms used to describe county extension agents in farming communities.) Douglas Paul (1977) noted three important characteristics of this model that distinguish it from other conceptualizations of change:

- It strongly emphasizes communication channels and messages to be utilized for diffusing innovations.
- It recognizes interpersonal influence patterns leading to the adoption of innovations as legitimate features of organizational life.
- It focuses on stimuli for adoption of innovative practices that originate outside of the adopting system.

In addition, the social interaction model implies strongly that potential users of an innovation will subject both the innovator and the innovation to a good deal of scrutiny before accepting it, and that this scrutiny will be based to a large extent on the ways in which the potential users of the innovation within the adopting organization "feel" about the possible change.

This explains, at least in part, why the social interaction model is also occasionally referred to as the *organization development* (OD) *model* of change. This model places a great deal of emphasis not only on the nature of interaction that occurs between the user organization and the external environment that initially introduces the innovation, but perhaps more importantly on the nature of the population within the adopting organization. Richard Schmuck and Matthew Miles (1971), for example, argue in *Organizational Development in Schools* that the user-group population is never a passive body. Instead, innovations are always institutionalized in a school or any other setting because of the workings of the social interaction network within the school. As a result, the supervisor whose notion of change was founded on a belief in social interaction would probably invest considerable time and energy in working with a school staff to increase internal receptivity to desired outcomes.

The application of the social interaction model as a way to stimulate change in an organization normally follows a rather consistent pattern. First, people hear about a new and innovative practice, normally through face-to-face contact with direct users of the innovation or others assumed to have direct information concerning the practice. Next, proponents of the new process engage in a period of attempted persuasion, the goal being to mold the opinion of potential users in a positive and supportive way about the benefits of the new product or practice. Third, potential users make a conscious decision either to use or not to use the suggested innovation. Finally, if the new practice is adopted, efforts are made to determine whether the decision made was a good one.

A number of theorists in the field of change, including Ronald Havelock (1969) and Milbrey McLaughlin (1976) have raised serious questions regarding the extent to which the social interaction model may be applied realistically to educational settings. The greatest objection is that innovation in schools, unlike new breeds of corn, are generally intangible and therefore difficult to assess and evaluate.

Although this observation may seem to limit the use of the social interaction model as an approach to planned change in schools, the model nevertheless deserves our attention, particularly in its emphasis on personal contact and interpersonal relations. The educational leader needs to realize the power associated within school systems and others outside those systems whose ideas or products might have great value regarding what goes on in schools. Encouraging others to visit other schools, attending meetings of professional associations, and inviting outside consultants and guests to visit schools serve to increase social interaction between the school and its external environment which, in turn, might provide opportunities for introducing new and effective educational practices from outside. A leader mindful of the need to cultivate patterns of positive interaction within the school would probably encourage faculty retreats, staff discussions, school-wide decision-making processes, and many other approaches to enhancing the quality of interaction outside the school as well.

Research-Development-Diffusion Model

David Clark and Egon Guba (1975) and Ernest House (1974) are most directly associated with what has become known as the research-development-diffusion model (RD&D) of change. The fundamental assumption here is that processes of change based on structured research are begun in order to produce new ideas, practices, or products, which are then disseminated to possible users through a conscientious effort toward diffusion. Ronald Havelock (1973) noted that five basic assumptions underlie the RD&D model of change:

1. Both the development and the application of an innovation are assumed to take place in an orderly sequence that includes research, development, and packaging prior to a mass distribution procedure.

2. The management of this sequence requires extensive planning over a long period of time.

3. A division and coordination of labor are necessary among elements in the RD&D system.

4. A rational consumer is assumed to be one who will adopt an innovation on the basis of a mass dissemination program.

5. High initial development costs are balanced by the long-term benefits which come from an efficient, high-quality innovation that can be used by a mass audience.

In practice, what normally happens is that new users of an innovation are assisted by the initial researchers and developers to make certain that the innovation is successfully installed. This approach to understanding change was particularly influential in national educational policy in the 1960s and 1970s. Beginning with the Johnson administration, the federal government initiated an effort designed to increase the amount of research-validated information available to school practitioners interested in improving practice. One of the tangible results of this initiative was the creation of a network of federally funded research and development centers at major universities across the country, at which faculty served as basic researchers, and another network of regional educational laboratories supported jointly by federal funds and by the sale of contract service to state and local educational agencies. Although subtle differences existed between the labs and centers regarding the ways in which they would function and be governed, they both were created and commissioned to support a strategy for bringing about change in schools that is research-based, rational, and generally in line with the model suggested by Robert Owens (1987), which is shown in figure 9.1.

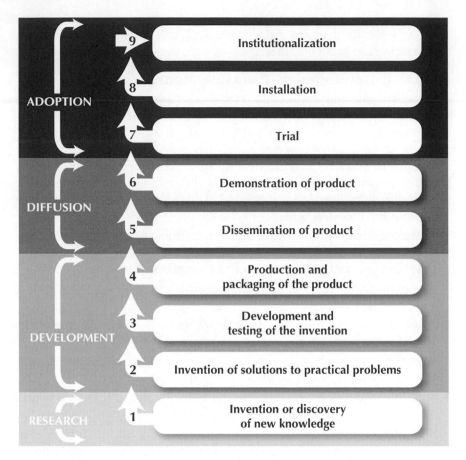

Source: Robert G. Owens & Thomas Valesky, *Organizational Behavior in Education* (9th ed.), © 2007, p. 238. Reprinted by permission of Allyn & Bacon.

Figure 9.1.   Robert Owens's concept of the research, development, and diffusion, and adoption model of change

The RD&D model of change, not surprisingly, holds a considerable attraction for the academic community, which so often assumes that change without data validated through research in the social sciences is not worth the effort. University faculty tend to place great stock in the linear concepts of research, development, and diffusion because the findings of basic research serve as the starting point for all future progress. Unfortunately, this stance, highly satisfying to many researchers, does not always fit with the reality of schools systems, where practitioners need immediate responses to their concerns and have little time for what they see as the time-consuming work of basic research. Proactive leaders are likely to be caught in some conflict over this issue. They will want to seek validated information to serve as the basis of their work with schools, thus promoting more thoughtful and less crisis-oriented behaviors. On the other hand, crises do arise, and practitioners seek answers even before the last bit of data is collected, the final statistical analysis completed, or the peer review panel accepts a piece of research for publication.

No matter what its limitations, the RD&D model of change must still be recognized as a potentially power conceptualization of how organizations adopt innovative practices. Over time, this model has been modified considerably by proponents like Havelock (1972), who suggested that in the initiation of organizational change there should be a rational sequence in the evaluation and application of an innovation; research, development, and packaging of a program change should occur before the dissemination of the program change; there should be planning on a massive scale; there should be a rational division of labor and coordination of jobs; and proponents of the innovation should be willing to accept high initial development costs prior to any dissemination activity.

This brief overview of the research-development diffusion model of change suggests that there are some clear potential strengths and weaknesses concerning the possible uses of this conceptual framework for installing organizational change. We need also to recognize at least one more assumption inherent in the RD&D model, regardless of whether it serves as a plus or a minus: Tremendous emphasis is placed on the adopting organization's ability to implement an innovative practice in line with the stated expectations for "proper" use of the research-based model. As Douglas Paul (1977, p. 27) noted, "The . . . model . . . places responsibility for accurate replication of RD&D products in the user organizations." As a result, the leader who approaches change from this perspective must be knowledgeable about the research and development carried out to support a particular innovation. In practice, many innovations are not "allowed" to be disseminated to a new setting unless someone from that setting has received substantial training in the proper presentation and use of the innovation.

Linkage Model

Henry Bhola (1965) and Ronald Havelock (1973) are most often associated with the final model of organizational change reviewed here, namely, the *linkage model*. Linkage borrows some characteristics from each of the other models reviewed, and it assumes that change proceeds through four distinct levels (Lipham & Hoeh, 1974):

1. In a fashion similar to what takes place in the problem-solving model, new knowledge relevant to an identified problem is searched for and retrieved;

2. Educational researchers (as in the RD&D model) carry on the research, development, and diffusion of research findings to a particular school where a problem exists;

3. Attention is focused on the relationship and communication systems among the researcher, practitioner, and consumer, as is true of the social interaction model; and

4. The linkage process model is enacted. In this phase, each organizational participant is helped to see what other members of the organization are doing in their respective parts of the process of changing.

It is in the fourth step of the model that linkage relationships are formed and supported to serve as a catalyst to innovation being accepted within the user organization. This is also the point in the model that calls for the greatest leadership skill and supervisory involvement. Someone must facilitate the linkage process required for staff within the school, as well as for those from agencies external to the school who provide information about the innovation. The supervisor is a likely candidate for the role of facilitator, or what the literature often refers to as a "linker" or "linkage change agent."

The linkage model synthesizes some of the best features of the other three models we reviewed, and as a result it has considerable value for use by supervisors in school settings. It does have some limitations, however, not the least of which is that it makes tremendous demands on the abilities of individual leaders who must be directly attuned to the activities taking place in the school in order to determine the need for changes. They must also understand the nature of intraorganizational communication that may serve to support desired changes. Leaders must also be aware of opportunities afforded for change and improvement from agencies in the external environment. Finally, leaders must possess the communication and interpersonal skills required of anyone who consistently attempts to bridge different groups. In short, the linkage model of organizational change is a powerful one, but it makes heavy and perhaps unrealistic demands on educational leaders.

❧ CHARACTERISTICS OF CHANGE

Each model of change reviewed here offers a unique view of how innovation is introduced into a system. There are some common characteristics of organizational change, however, on which all models agree. Gene Hall (1987) suggested the following summary of what is known about the phenomenon of change:

- Change is a process, not an event.
- Change is accomplished by individuals.
- Change is a highly personalized process.
- Change involves developmental growth.
- Change is best understood in operational terms.
- The focus of facilitation should be on individuals, innovation, and the content.

Each of these observations also implies important responsibilities to the educational leader, who must become actively involved in fostering change and not be content merely to sit on the sidelines and wait for things to happen.

✑ BARRIERS TO ORGANIZATIONAL CHANGE

The proactive educational leader must address one overriding concern about change. Because of several possible barriers, change can be difficult to initiate, implement, and maintain in an organization such as a school.

John Lovell and Kimball Wiles (1983) recognized the importance of the educational supervisor's role in stimulating change and identified the following typical barriers to organizational change in schools. For each barrier, suggestions are made as to ways in which the issue is often played out in schools.

1. *Lack of commitment to system goals.* If teachers or other school staff neither understand nor accept the school's goals, they will not endorse a change to ensure that those goals are being met. This often occurs in settings where the administrative team assumes total control over the establishment of goals. Teachers typically will do little to support an agenda mandated by others, particularly if substantive change is required.

2. *Inadequate feedback.* Teachers frequently lack concrete information and evaluative feedback concerning their performance. This problem has significant implications for change processes in schools. Teachers' feelings of being left to drift lead to tension, anxiety, and the type of low morale that causes people to withdraw into their roles and avoid any risks required for change.

3. *Inadequate knowledge about the conditions of teaching and learning.* Change implies that some ideal way of behaving is fixed in people's minds as a goal. A high percentage of classroom teachers and others in schools, while serving quite successfully, are nevertheless lacking in the kind of knowledge base that would suggest desirable goals for improved performance and change.

4. *Attitudes toward or values about the proposed change.* If people start out with negative views about an innovation, that attitude will be hard to change. When the concept of team teaching was introduced as an innovation to teachers several years ago, it did not take root in many settings because teachers started with negative assumptions even before the practice was formally introduced.

5. *Satisfaction with status quo.* Teachers demonstrate the same reluctance to change their behaviors that others do. The old saying, "If it ain't broke, don't fix it" applies equally to educators who are not always convinced of the need to change the way they have done things in the

past. This phenomenon is likely to be strongest in schools where there is a stable and maturing teaching staff.

6. *Inadequate skill development.* If people lack the skills needed to carry out a new program, they will resist change. A teacher who has little ability to work with groups of gifted students, for example, will resist being required to do just that as part of a new thinking skills program.

7. *Strong vested interests in the status quo.* People may believe that they will lose something for which they have worked if changes are made in the system around them. Consider, for example, a case where a teacher foresees losing leadership status as the head of a department in a junior high school under a new organizational pattern for a middle school that proposes to dissolve departments.

8. *Lack of organizational support.* People will resist supporting a change if they believe that the larger system will not reward or endorse the change. Teachers often express resentment toward engaging in practices that they believe the central office will not wholeheartedly endorse.

9. *Closedness rather than openness in the system.* Teachers who work in schools in what Andrew Halpin (1967) called an "open" organizational climate will be more likely to accept change. "Closed" climate schools offer fewer opportunities for social interaction that might, in turn, spark greater interest in and support for change.

10. *Lack of compatibility between the change proposal and other dimensions of the organization.* When a change is introduced to one grade-level team of teachers, for example, other teams may be affected by the change. If the reports from the first team are not positive, resistance will follow. On the other hand, when a small group gets "turned on" by an idea, others may follow readily.

11. *Threat to individuals.* The issue here is simple yet powerful: People fear new situations. Even a seemingly minor innovation introduced into school practices represents a new situation, and some resistance can be anticipated.

12. *Inadequate knowledge about restraints and possibilities in a situation.* People sometimes avoid participating in a change process because they assume that some unknown conditions will necessarily prohibit the change from being successfully implemented.

13. *Static organizational role structure.* Organizations do not always enjoy the kind of leadership that supports needed change. The majority of a teaching staff may push for some type of curricular or program change, but the principal may prohibit the change from taking place.

14. *Inadequate expertise for solving problems.* Change often brings with it certain problems related to transition. For the most part, people lack expertise in working with ambiguity and other problems that often accompany organizational change. In schools, teachers are generally well prepared

to serve in their assigned instructional roles, but they have had little or no preparation in handling the acceptance of innovation.

15. *Threat to officials in the organization.* The implementation of change in an organization implies significant modifications in existing power structures. Traditional leadership roles and the agendas held by those who inhabit these roles may need complete revision. Such modifications, or even the possibility of such a change, often carries with it great threats to those who have been "in charge" in the past. This potential "changing of the guard" causes the old guard to dig in its heels and resist. In schools, we often see resistance when principals or other administrators who have held their leadership positions for a long time are suddenly confronted with a change that they believe will erode their control of the schools. Teacher union activities in recent years have caused a considerable amount of negative reaction among some administrators who believed that teachers wanted to change things "too fast and too much." Recent suggestions by educational reformers that the role of the principal as now defined is obsolete are, of course, not winning many administrative supporters.

16. *Inadequate rewards for change efforts.* People are often aware of the need for some type of organizational change and have the competence to bring the change about, but they do nothing simply because they decide that the rewards of the change effort will not be sufficient. Teachers might be asked to adopt a new language arts curriculum, for example, but decide that the costs for doing so, in terms of extra meetings, lack of additional pay, and so forth, far outweigh possible rewards.

These identified barriers to organizational change are useful to us in more accurately understanding the nature of organizational behavior. Simply stated, people generally have a tendency to remain constant in their behaviors. Change requires effort; it is easier not to move. Fortunately, people sometimes do engage in innovative practices. To encourage them in that process, proactive leaders may find recent research on the phases of planned change useful.

❧ UNDERSTANDING THE PHASES OF CHANGE

Hall's (1987) definition notwithstanding, organizational change has been described for the most part as if it were a singular event, introduced in sum into the lives of people in an organization. In reality, however, change usually occurs slowly and in clearly defined, deliberate steps. Understanding the nature of these steps may prove helpful to the educational leader interesting in reducing some typical barriers (described later in the chapter).

Many conceptual frameworks have been developed to analyze the sequential patterns through which change occurs. Everett Rogers (1962) suggests that planned change and innovation efforts proceed through five identifiable and discrete steps: awareness, interest, evaluation, trial, and adoption. Gerald Hage and Michael Aiken (1970) modified this view to suggest that four steps—evaluation, initiation, implementation, and routinization—were in fact present in the introduction of innovation. Gerald Zaltman, Robert Duncan, and Jonny Holbeck (1973) proposed two major stages and five substages of change, as the following list shows:

Initiation Stage

- *Knowledge-awareness substage.* Potential adopters of an innovation must be aware that the innovation exists and that there is an opportunity to utilize it in the organization.

- *Formation of attitudes toward the innovation substage.* Organizational members form attitudes toward the innovation. Once the initial consideration of a new practice has taken place, the attitudes taken by organizational members are important.

- *Decision substage.* The information concerning the potential innovation is evaluated.

Implementation Stage

- *Initial implementation substage.* The organization makes the first attempt to utilize a particular innovation.

- *Continued sustained implementation substage.* If the implementation has been successful because organizational members understand it and have information about implementation, the innovation will continue to be important.

Table 9.1 compares the stages of change in these three conceptual frameworks (Rogers, Hage and Aiken, and Zaltman et al.). In addition, there has been some effort to examine the links between a given substage and the typical barriers to innovation through each of those substages.

Table 9.1. Comparisons of the various stages of change as defined and conceptualized in three different theoretical models

Rogers (1962)	Hage and Aiken (1970)	Zaltman, Duncan, and Holbeck (1973)
1. Awareness	1. Evaluation	*Initiation Stage*
2. Interest	2. Initiation	1. Knowledge awareness
3. Evaluation	3. Implementation	2. Formation of attitudes
4. Trial	4. Routinization	3. Decision
5. Adoption		*Implementation Stage*
		4. Initial implementation
		5. Continued sustained implementation

At Zaltman's "knowledge-awareness" substage, for example, Ronald Havelock (1969) noted not only the strong tendency that organizations show toward trying to maintain stability but also the constant personal threat that change suggests to organization members: people wonder, "What is this going to do to *me?*" Barriers at the "attitude formation" and "decision" substages often stem from organizational tendencies to modify the nature of messages so that the meaning of those messages might be ignored. Because they feel unprepared, organizations often do whatever they can to subvert any effort toward change.

When an innovation reaches the "initial implementation" substage, it interacts with organizational equilibrium at its highest point; members find it hard to know what they have really gotten themselves into. In other words, people at this point may not be absolutely clear as to the precise reasons why they ever began the change process in the first place. Finally, the greatest barrier to change at the "continued-sustained implementation" substage is undoubtedly the fact that people often lose interest quickly in any innovation.

❧ OVERCOMING THE BARRIERS

Despite the most effective of supervisory efforts, change is difficult to initiate, implement, and maintain in any organization for a multitude of reasons. There are many different barriers to change in general, as well as particular inhibitors that are characteristic of each identifiable stage in the process of adopting innovations. Although it is unlikely that all barriers can be completely overcome, Goodwin Watson (1966, pp. 145–146) identified twelve different ways in which people in leadership roles might be able to minimize the resistance to change found in their organizations.

1. Resistance will be less if administrators and managers feel that the project is their own—not one devised and operated by outsiders.

2. Resistance will be less if the . . . innovation clearly has wholehearted support from top officials in the system.

3. Resistance will be less if the [organizational] participants see the change as reducing rather than increasing their present burdens.

4. Resistance will be less if the [innovative] project is in accord with values already acknowledged by participants.

5. Resistance will be less if the program offers the kind of new experience that interests participants.

6. Resistance will be less if participants feel their autonomy and security are not threatened.

7. Resistance will be less if participants have joined in diagnostic efforts leading them to agree on what the basic problems are and their importance.

8. Resistance will be less if the project is adopted by consensual group decision.

9. Resistance will be reduced if proponents are able to empathize with opponents, to recognize valid objections, and to take steps to relieve unnecessary fears.

10. Resistance will be reduced if it is recognized that innovations are likely to be misunderstood and misinterpreted, and if provision is made for feedback of perceptions of the project and the further clarification of need.

11. Resistance will be reduced if participants experience acceptance, trust, and confidence in their relations with one another.

12. Resistance will be reduced if the project is kept open to revision and reconsideration, and if experience indicates that changes will be desirable.

On theme is apparent in all of Watson's recommendations: Overcoming resistance to change requires sensitivity by the educational leader to the personal concerns of people in the organization. In terms of proactive leadership, this reemphasizes the importance of knowing not only one's own priorities, values, philosophy, and action plan, but also those of the people who work in the organization. While such awareness will not conquer all resistance to change, the more that people know about and are sensitive to the concerns of individuals, the less those individuals will resist change.

❧ THE LEADER'S ROLE IN MANAGING CHANGE

The "bottom line" in this consideration of issues and problems associated with the management of change in schools and organizations is that change cannot be avoided. Change is an inevitable reality. As such, anyone who serves in a leadership role of a school, district, or any other organization must be ready to accommodate the changes that will occur, whether one wants them or not. In 1980, for example, few school leaders would pay much attention to discussions about computers, except for some business education students who might get involved with data-processing jobs in the future. In the year 2000, leaving discussions of computers and technology off the table brings about accusations of school people being ill-prepared to deal with modern life. And there is little doubt that the next several years will witness changes that will modify the nature of many people's lives and their practices in society. Change is going to happen, whether we create it or it is created for us.

Effective educational leaders are not clairvoyants who can predict the precise nature of the next stream of change that will befall the schools around the world. However, they have a major responsibility of ensuring that the proper climate is created within their schools and district so that, when inevitable change arrives, teachers, staffs, students, parents, and community members will not view it as some fundamental threat to the way things "should be" in schools. The way in which the leader can move her or his school in that direction involves the creation of an ongoing climate where discussions of new ideas and practices are the rule, not the exception.

What is known about the role of leader today—whether it is in a Fortune 500 corporation or in a local elementary school in a small town—is that the leader is increasingly responsible for understanding change processes. This results in two distinct duties for all leaders. First, the leader must promote needed change, using strategies such as those described earlier in this chapter. Second, the leader is responsible for managing the aftermath of change. Too often, the assumption is made that, after an organization has adopted an innovation, people embrace that practice and move forward with the effort to fine tune the change and, perhaps, look forward to the next adoption of a new practice. That is clearly not the case in most circumstances. After a new practice has been added to the pattern in a school, for example, someone must be around to help people adopt the innovation more completely. Furthermore, the leader must be able to assure adopters that the change will be something that improves the quality of life in the organization. That task may be even more difficult to address than simply getting people to "buy into" a new practice in the first place.

Change Facilitation Models

Gene Hall and Shirley Hord (2001) looked at the issue of leadership and its relationship to the process of facilitating needed change in schools and identified three distinct models of leadership styles in initiating and maintaining change (p. 132). These include

- *Initiators* who have clear goals and policies that include but transcend implementation of current innovations. They have very strong beliefs about what good schools and effective teaching should look like, and they work intensely to attain their vision.
- *Managers* who represent a broad range of behaviors, including both responsive behaviors and actions that are directed toward supporting change.
- *Responders*, or leaders who place heavy emphasis on allowing teachers the opportunity to take the lead in promoting change. They tend to spend their time as leaders in carrying out assigned administrative tasks while others promote change.

It is quite likely that principals and other school leaders will come from all three categories of change facilitation. The approach that individuals take in their careers as leaders is also influenced by such factors as the nature of the change, the context of a particular school, and even the level of experience of an individual supervisor or administrator. For example, a novice principal is probably more inclined to act as a responder than as an initiator. With time, this may change. And the needs of a particular school may also dictate the appropriateness of one pattern of behavior or another.

ℰℕ SUMMARY

This chapter assumes that change for the sake of change should not be promoted. On the other hand, innovation and change are inevitable and necessary for the continuing growth of any organization. Without periodic improvements, organizations will stagnate.

In the first part of this chapter, four conceptual models of change were reviewed: problem-solving, social interaction, research-development-diffusion, and linkage. All four models have strengths and limitations in terms of their potential to describe ideal strategies for implementing organizational change. However, linkage offers particular advantages because it incorporates elements from each of the other models.

A number of typical inhibitors to change were also examined, including general satisfaction with the status quo and lack of adequate rewards for participating in change. It was noted that educational leaders might find particularly helpful the recent efforts to define stages in the change process. In addition, educational leaders are likely to take on different styles as change facilitators, according to their own needs and also the needs of the school and staff with whom the leaders must work.

The chapter concludes by suggesting a number of strategies that might be employed by supervisors who are intent on reducing, if not eliminating, resistance to change efforts in schools.

Suggested Activities

1. Talk with a group of teachers within a school who have experienced some type of change in their school—for example, a new reading curriculum. The actual change itself is not important, but try to ascertain the strategies that were used by supervisors, administrators, other teachers, or whomever was responsible for introducing the innovation to the school. Compare the strategy with the various change processes described in this chapter.

2. Visit three different schools and make an assessment, after interviewing the principal and two or three teachers in each school, as to whether the schools might be classified as belonging to any of the change phases or stages described in this chapter. Remember that a school does not necessarily have had to go through a very dramatic change recently to qualify as having undergone change.

Cases to Consider

Read each of the cases below and consider the following:

- What are the critical issues raised in each case, as they relate to the analysis of change processes?
- How does each case relate to the development of proactive leadership?
- In what ways might you suggest a resolution to the issues raised?

Case 9.1   I Thought I'd Make the Place Nicer!

Mary Cochran was furious. She had just come back from the faculty room and found the new tablecloth she had purchased—with her own money—folded up and hidden in a drawer in the old cabinet next to the kitchen table where the teachers ate their lunch every day. The nerve of that group of ungrateful. . . .

It all started six weeks ago, the day Mary took over Woodson Avenue Elementary School as the new principal. Woodson, a small, old building in a blue-collar district, did not exactly look like the Taj Mahal, but it was a beautiful sight to Mary in her first job as a school administrator. It was a building with a lot of potential for improvement. The walls around the building seemed to be painted a shade of "perpetually institutionally gray and dull," and the bulletin boards seemed not to have been changed for almost a year. Her office looked quite functional, but it really resembled a locker room more than it did the place where she would be spending much of her life. She was the "new kid on the block" and, like most new principals, was likely to enjoy a brief honeymoon period with the central office when she could ask for a special favor now and then. She worked hard to get some new paint for the halls, new coverings for the bulletin boards, and even a few pieces of furniture in her office to brighten things up. As she looked around the building a week before the teachers came back, she began to see a little hope in the old place. She had one last challenge to address, namely improving the appearance of the faculty room.

Mary really wanted to do something special for the teachers in her new school. She knew that, as a rookie principal, a lot of her success on the job would be derived from her ability to have a good relationship with the teachers. In addition, she had heard that the staff at Woodson was a particularly tough group. They had made it clear to the central office that they were tired of being treated as "a training ground for new principals." As the smallest building in the district where principals were paid based on building size, Woodson had not had the same principal for more than three years in quite some time. Mary was determined to win over the teachers by showing that she really did care for them and that, with her as principal, things would be a lot better.

The faculty room was a place where she decided to invest her energy to provide people with a clear indication of where her heart was. She discovered when she took the job that the room was a mess. The paint was dull, cracked, and chipped. The windows (one of which was broken) had no drapes or shades. As a result, the old furniture lying around the room was faded. Year-old announcements filled the bulletin board. Perhaps most noticeable, however, was the kitchen table in the middle of the room. It was covered by an old plastic tablecloth that was worn and torn, seemingly ready to disintegrate at any moment. Mary decided that, as a subtle indication of her commitment to her teachers, she would make the improvement of the faculty room her personal project. She didn't have a lot of extra money due to the fact that she had just finished her doctorate at a local university, but she had a lot of energy and willpower. She and a friend spent an entire weekend painting, scrubbing, and cleaning the faculty room. She convinced her custodian to postpone some other jobs and replace the broken glass in the window, which she decorated with an old set of curtains from home. She couldn't afford any new furniture, but she could at least do something about the ugly tablecloth so painfully visible in the middle of the room. After everything else in the room was completed, she went to a local store and bought a new covering to place on the kitchen table. To finish the job, she made a mental note to bring in some fresh flowers from home to place in the center of the table for the first day, when all teachers were to report back to work. She believed that the appearance of the faculty room would be a subtle but important statement to let the faculty know that she would be a different, caring principal who believed that they were important.

The first day with the entire faculty was, of course, a busy day for Mary. It wasn't until Tuesday of the first week, long after most teachers had gone home, that she decided to walk down to admire her work in the staff room one more time. She walked into the room and immediately noticed the old tablecloth. She hadn't taken the time on Saturday to throw it out. Instead, she had left it folded on a shelf in the little cabinet where teachers often left their lesson books and other paraphernalia while they ate their lunch. The old cloth was back on the kitchen table, and her purchase was now on the shelf. She was so upset that she nearly ripped down the curtains. Although she resisted the temptation, she was still angry and hurt.

Case 9.2   Now We'll Get the Truth!

The Spencer Mountain Schools were known around the state as a good school district, but not necessarily one of the cutting-edge systems. When Irwin Frye became the superintendent, he vowed that would soon change. After all, Dr. Frye had just come from Golden Arch Local, a district in the northern part of the state with a long-standing reputation as one of the premier school systems, not only in the state but also in the entire region. Dr. Frye had told the school board that he would never be satisfied with being simply "good." His goal was to be excellent.

The new superintendent met the principals of the district at a group session during the summer, and he reiterated his belief that the school district was ready to assume a position as an elite school system in the state. While the principals were naturally reluctant to say much openly during the meeting, Irwin soon heard that the general consensus among his building administrators was that the "new guy" talked a good game but offered no clues as to how Spencer Mountain would assume its new status. Instead of being angry at the gossip, Frye set forth to develop a plan to increase the achievement of the students in the school district so that it could become a true model system.

Dr. Frye brought in a team of well-known educational researchers from the state university to provide a full-day inservice session to principals and select teachers. Each researcher had a strong reputation for being involved with some aspect of teaching or learning that would certainly stimulate the staff at Spencer Mountain to get working. Dr. Harriet Krusmeyer, a nationally known scholar in the area of mathematics, was particularly of interest. Spencer Mountain had a long history of students doing well in the state achievement tests, but never really going "over the top" in math. Frye was convinced Krusmeyer would be "just the ticket" to get this situation changed.

Irwin stared in disbelief, then, when he reviewed the evaluative comments made at the end of the day. In general, people seemed quite guarded in their statements, but one that really seemed to capture what the superintendent believed to be what he was seeing during the day was simple, yet disheartening: "Lots of talk, no action. Old wine in new bottles."

Applying the Concepts

The following brief quiz is designed to improve your skills in applying some of the concepts discussed in this chapter. Read the brief introductory case and then respond to the multiple-choice questions. You will find the answers in the Appendix.

Dr. Neil Collins was excited about his new job as the director of curriculum for the Spencer Local School District. As a former teacher and principal in the district, he had always wanted a position that enabled him to have a direct impact on the instructional practices used in classrooms. He knew last spring that he would be stepping into his new job this summer as the result of the retirement of Rita Valdez, a fine administrator who had been the director for nine years. Rita was a great person and an outstanding manager, but Neil believed that she was not particularly creative and sensitive to the curriculum processes in the district and across the state.

Throughout the last few months, Neil spent as much time as he could reading, viewing videotapes, talking to faculty at the local university, and attending workshops dealing with new instructional techniques. He was going to be ready to serve as a true resource person for the teachers and administrators in the district when he came on board in August. He wanted to know as much as he could, and with as much authority as he could, to answer questions about new practices adopted in the district. He read recent research on a variety of issues so that he could be ready to speak with authority.

It is now early October. Neil is sitting in his office, thoroughly discouraged. Earlier today, he had provided one of his weekly inservice sessions for interested principals. During the session, he presented some data recently collected by researchers at Mountain State University to show how the use of portfolios had a relationship to pupil achievement and parent satisfaction. He believed it was the kind of information that would convince a lot of skeptics that the portfolio presentation and review process was worth it. After his presentation, however, there was not a single question or comment regarding the research findings. Instead, the principals wanted to know how they were supposed to get the money they would need from the central office to pay the duplicating costs for the portfolios. They also wanted to know if they would be paid for the extra time they would spend reviewing portfolios. There were also a few principals who wondered aloud why Neil was coming down hard on them now. Weren't they the same competent colleagues with whom Neil had worked for several years? Or did they suddenly become ineffective?

1. Neil began to wonder if he would ever achieve his goals in this job. If you were to give some advice to Neil at this point, you might tell him _____

   a. to not get discouraged. He has to find some new topics to share with the principals.

   b. to go back to the principalship because he would never be effective in his new job.

   c. to not get discouraged with his efforts to lead change because it is a lengthy process.

   d. to enlist the superintendent to come forth with a strong statement demanding that the principals get more serious and listen to Neil.

2. The barrier to change that appears to be most related to Neil's problem at this point is _____.

   a. lack of commitment to system goals—diffusion.

   b. threat to individuals.

   c. inadequate skill development.

   d. inadequate knowledge about the conditions of teaching and learning.

3. If Neil wants his recommended changes to take root, he needs to work closely with the district principals and keep in mind that _____.

   a. change is always something that occurs "top-down"

   b. change is accomplished by individuals

   c. change is best understood in symbolic terms

   d. change must be described by people in the central office

4. Neil appears to be a strong believer in the model of planned change known as _____.

   a. problem-solving

   b. social interaction

   c. research-development

   d. linkage

5. When the principals raised the question about costs for duplicating, Neil should not have been surprised if he understood planned change because _____.

   a. there are often a lot of disconnected complaints voiced in any change effort

   b. principals never want to spend their campus money

   c. change efforts typically require high initial development costs

   d. people often raise a lot of objections simply to block change efforts

6. If you had to advise Neil about a more effective approach to introducing the use of portfolios to principals, you might note that _____.

   a. it is more effective to convince each principal personally that there is some merit to the changes

   b. occasional threats can be effective

   c. everyone must support the proposed change completely before initiating any innovation

   d. resistance will be less if administrators feel as if the project is their own

Additional Reading

Beitler, Michael (2003). *Strategic organizational change*. Greensboro, NC: Practitioner Press International.

Duke, Daniel L. (1978, March). Toward responsible innovation. *The Educational Forum, 42* (3): 358–359.

Hall, Gene E., & Hord, Shirley (1988). *Change in schools: Facilitating the process*. Albany: SUNY Press.

Kezar, Adrianna, & Kezar, Adrianna J. (2001). *Understanding and facilitating change in higher education in the 21st century*. San Francisco: Jossey-Bass.

Kotter, John P. (1996). *Leading change*. Boston: Harvard Business School Press.

Kotter, John P., & Cohen, Dan S. (2002). *The heart of change: Real-life stories of how people change their organizations*. Boston: Harvard Business School Press.

Sarason, Seymour (1971). *The culture of the school and the problem of change*. Boston: Allyn & Bacon.

Smith, Louis M., & Keith, P. M. (1981). *Anatomy of educational innovation*. New York: Wiley.

❧ 10 ❧

Exercising Power and Authority

Although supervisory activities in schools promote needed change, the concepts of power and authority inherent in supervision and leadership frequently evoke negative reactions. Classroom teachers intent upon exploring alternative career options in the field of education seem particularly concerned about the need for educational leaders to exercise power and authority, perhaps because of a long-standing reluctance among educators to think in terms of trying to control others.

This chapter explores the concepts of organizational power and authority in more descriptive and, hopefully, less threatening ways. A formal leadership role, such as that of school supervisor or administrator, carries with it responsibility of authority, and that authority brings a degree of power, whether earned or delegated. In short, anyone who finds it unpleasant to think in these terms should probably eschew a career in administration or supervision.

Regarding the dual issues of power and authority, it is suggested that the judicious use of these concepts by leaders may bring about more effective organizations. First, alternative definitions of power and authority are considered, followed by a description of the characteristics of each concept in greater detail. The chapter concludes with a consideration of some of the immediate, practical applications of these concepts for the individual interested in engaging in more effective and proactive leadership.

❧ ALTERNATIVE DEFINITIONS

Power and authority are terms that occur often in discussions of organizational leadership, but they are used with a surprising lack of precision. Many people, classroom teachers frequently among them, express distrust of those who appear to possess either characteristic. However, any fundamental understanding of the nature of supervision, whether in schools or other organizations, must include an understanding of power and authority.

In simple terms, Max Weber (1947) defined power as "the probability that one actor within a social relationship will be in a position to carry out his own will despite resistance" (p. 52). *Power*, then, is the fundamental ability of one person to command some degree of compliance on the part of another person. By contrast, *authority* suggests a much less general concept. Clayton Resser (1973) defined authority as "a right granted to a manager to make decisions, within limitations, to assign duties to subordinates, and to require subordinates' conformance to expected behavior" (p. 311). Based on the distinctions suggested in these definitions, we can make some important generalizations about these distinctions between power and authority.

Everyone has power, or at least the *potential* for exercising power. Each of us potentially has the ability to encourage another person to behave in some particular way. Even a person whose role in society seems most unimportant may effect some change in others or in society in general.

When we speak of power we tend to think in terms of its use. We think first of those whose rules automatically provide a potential for influencing others. Everyone has power, but not everyone makes use of it or develops the know-how required to exercise power effectively from a position that does not appear to be strong. This observation is true regardless of the way in which power was acquired in the first place, whether by assuming a position where formal authority is normally delegated or by demonstrating competence in a typical "nonpower" role.

Not everyone, on the other hand, has access to authority, which is a condition possessed by a relatively small percentage of people. According to Herbert Simon (1945), a person with authority has and "uses the formal criterion of the receipt of a command . . . as his basis of choice" (pp. 108–109). Authority is a legitimized statement of one (or more) person's formal designation to control the behaviors in an organization, and it derives from certain societal sources.

Another perspective on the nature of power comes from the writings of community activist Saul Alinsky (1971), who noted the social and political foundations of power:

> Power is the reason for being of organizations. When people agree on certain religious ideas and want the power to propagate their faith, they organize and call it church. When people agree on certain political ideas and want the power to put them into practice, they organize and call it a political party. The same reason holds across the board. Power and organization are one and the same. (p. 113)

Alinsky, then, affirms the notion that power is not in itself a negative characteristic of organizational life. Rather, it is a cornerstone of an organization and, as a result, cannot be understood solely as a negative feature.

The primary distinctions between power and authority are relatively straightforward. *Power* is the *ability* to make others behave in certain ways and is available to most people in society, regardless of whether or not they have formal authority. *Authority* is the *right* to make others behave in certain ways and is not available to everyone but rather is formally conferred on some. Interestingly, however, the fact that people have authority does not necessarily guarantee that they will exercise power.

In the next two sections, some specific features of these characteristics of organizational life are considered, beginning with the unique properties of power.

⟡ CHARACTERISTICS OF POWER

This section examines the broader concept of power by looking at its traditional sources. French and Raven (1961) have suggested five sources of social power, and each of these may be related to the role of an educational leader.

French and Raven: Sources of Social Power

Reward power is the capacity to provide rewards to others in an organization as a way to influence their behavior. In a school setting, for example, a school board might offer bonus pay to teachers who perform at a level consistent with established district goals. Merit pay proposals are fairly clear examples of attempts to exercise reward power in schools. Supervisory personnel are traditionally thought to have very limited access to the use of reward power in organizations. They do not necessarily serve as "line" officers with the right to make decisions and hold others accountable for the implementation of those decisions. Administrators, on the other hand, do possess the right to enforce their decrees. This perspective is delimiting, however, because the concepts of "rewards" can mean things other than the financial incentives usually controlled by school administrators or boards of education. Supervisors often exercise reward power in more subtle ways, such as assigning some teachers to more attractive communities or newer school buildings, or by distributing newer, more attractive curricular materials as a "reward" to some. Richard Gorton (198) identified the following assumptions inherent in the use of reward power:

- The strength of the reward power will increase with the magnitude of the rewards which one person perceives that another can obtain for him or her.

- The strength of the reward power will depend on the actual rewards that a person can produce, not on what she or he hopes or would like to produce.
- Unsuccessful attempts to exert reward power will tend to decrease the perceived strengths of that power in the future.

Coercive power is the capacity of one person to provide punishment or negative consequences to another in a deliberate attempt to control the other person's behavior. Again, this form of power is usually associated with administrators, not supervisors. However, supervisory personnel make use of coercive strategies when they do such things as write negative evaluations of teacher performance or reject new curricular programs that may be desired by some teachers. Gorton noted the following assumptions related to the use of coercive power:

- The strength of coercive power will increase with the magnitude of the punishments or costs which the other person perceives that the exercising person may apply.
- The strength of the coercive power will depend on the *actual* sanctions or punishments that are applied, not only on what one hopes to apply.
- Unsuccessful attempts to exert coercive power will tend to decrease the perceived strength of that power in the future.

Legitimate power is most similar to what shall later be described as formal authority. Control of one person by another is based on the assumption that the person exercising the power has a legitimate right to do so and is supported by a statement of policy, law, or even historical precedent and tradition.

Referent power is the tendency of other individuals to be attracted by and to identify closely with the person who exercises the power. A certain emphasis is therefore placed on the charismatic qualities of the supervisor, administrator, or other person who is making use of the power. Simply stated, this is power derived largely from the extent to which people like or respect the person in charge. Gorton's assumptions related to this source of power include:

- The greater the perceived attractiveness of the person exercising power by another person or group, the more likely that there will be identification with the leader.
- The stronger the identification with the leader by another person, the greater will be the likelihood that referent power can be successfully utilized by the leader.

Finally, *expert power* is the ability to influence others' behavior based on special knowledge. This is the power source most often linked to the supervisor's role. Because supervisors do not enjoy formal authority, the belief is that they must rely on public perceptions of their expertise and competence as a way to influence others. Teachers yield to the power of the supervisor of language arts, for instance, because they believe that the supervisor has special knowledge in the field of language arts. Gorton's assumptions concerning the application of expert power follow:

- The strength of the expert power of a person will vary with the actual knowledge and skill that he or she might possess, along with others' perceptions of her or his expertise.
- The stronger the perception by others that the leader possesses expert power, the higher will be their satisfaction and evaluation of him or her as a leader.

French and Raven's five sources of social power can be understood from both a descriptive and a normative perspective. They provide certain insights into how power may be classified for further analysis, and they can also provide the supervisor with a way of understanding the implications to be derived from reliance on one source or another. Understanding the differences that exist between referent power and reward power, for example, and the likely effect that each may have on people who work in organizations is a powerful guide to behavior. Consider the probable response to a supervisor who works at increasing her or his expert power by learning more about a particular topic as contrasted with the probable response to a supervisor who tries to "pull rank" by using threats, punishment, or other efforts associated with coercive power strategies.

Compliance Theory

Amitai Etzioni (1975) analyzed power relationships in organizations through the concept of *compliance theory*, which suggests that power sources should be matched with organizational types for more efficient use. Etzioni identified three major types of organizations, defined by their fundamental goal as "economic," "order," or "cultural." If the primary goal of an organization is to preserve order (political, moral, financial, or any other type), for example, the most appropriate source of power would be coercive. To understand this, one can look at how police use coercive power (or implied coercive power) in their work, which is primarily directed toward fostering order and control. In the case of schools, people make use of the value of learning and the goal is often cultural; power might be most often seen as expert power. However, we can see where an assistant principal in charge of student discipline for a high school would make much greater use of coercive power than of any other type, according to Etzioni's theory.

⚛ CHARACTERISTICS OF AUTHORITY

The legitimized and sanctioned use of power normally referred to as authority may also be understood according to certain characteristics.

Authority Types

German sociologist Max Weber suggested that there are three major types of authority utilized in different organizations:

1. *Traditional authority.* People accept the control of others because it is assumed that those "others" have some sort of traditionally legitimate, absolute right to exercise that authority with no challenge. In school settings, for instance, a parent may tell a child to obey a teacher for the simple reason that the person is a teacher, and a teacher always deserves respect. Although his may not hold true in all classrooms on a daily basis, many such forms of reliance on traditional authority types may still be seen.

2. *Charismatic authority.* Authority based on the assumption that the leader has some special gift, or even supernatural powers. Examples of this type of authority are religious leaders and some televangelists who, despite apparent inconsistencies in their private lives, continue to attract millions of followers (and their money) because the leaders have successfully established in the minds of their adherents that they possess special gifts from God.

3. *Legal authority.* Authority derived from laws, policies, or statutes. Military officers have authority because such authority is decreed by regulation. As many enlisted personnel recognize, superior officers may lack identifiable skills or charisma; they are, however, in charge simply because they *are* officers.

Educators can use these descriptions of different types of authority in understanding why we defer to certain individuals. In addition to determining type of authority, however, we also need to determine whether it is formal or functional.

Formal versus Functional Authority

Robert Peabody (1962) defined *formal authority* as authority derived from such sources as the organizational hierarchy, laws, a person's position in an organization, or office. *Functional authority* comes from such things as a person's professional expertise and competence, interpersonal skills, and suggestion of great experience in handling a particular situation. The tendency to assume that functional authority is "softer" or "better" is really not warranted. People who exercise authority make use of both approaches. On the other hand, a person may deliberately select one particular strategy in order to effect a desired goal. A school superintendent, for example, who might normally rely on her or his formal authority to bring about changes in the behavior of the teaching staff might choose instead to seek a more indirect way to influence changes in behavior. The superintendent, in other words, might consciously seek to exercise functional rather than—or in addition to—formal authority.

An effective leader should not necessarily shift between formal and functional authority patterns. Such inconsistency is unwise, if not impossible. Deliberate switches from a formal to a functional approach are often perceived by staff members as manipulative, just as the game of "good cop–bad cop" is a staged strategy used to manipulate criminal suspects. Selecting one pattern rather than the other might be impossible for those leaders who have no, or at best limited, access to formal authority strategies. The critical issues for the proactive educational leader is always to recognize the strengths and limitations of both formal and functional authority patterns.

✑ WHY DO WE SHY AWAY FROM THE WORDS?

Regardless of the explanations of different types and sources of power and authority, it remains one of the realities of discussion about leadership and supervision: People do not like to think of themselves as people who control others, exercise power, or exert authority. Teachers are particularly sensitive to the notion that it is improper to attempt to command others' attention and action. Perhaps it is an inherent sense of egalitarianism, or simply a wish not to be controlled by others, but there is a strong sense that *power* and *authority* are somehow obscene terms which should be avoided.

As it has been shown throughout this chapter, however, it is perfectly reasonable to assume that in any organization someone will eventually assume greater control and direct the activities of the group. Even in settings that proclaim to be "flat hierarchies," or "leaderless groups," someone still assumes some degree of ultimate responsibility for the actions of a group. Or, at times, groups equally share power and authority in a completely equitable fashion. The realities of power and control and authority simply do not disappear because people find them to be distasteful or laden with negative values and images.

The proactive educational leader is certainly not a person who assumes the role he or she does simply to be able to manipulate and control other people. As noted in the earlier discussion of values and leadership, such a personal agenda would likely never be consistent with shared visions and missions in any school setting. Instead, the effective leader must learn to reconcile personal beliefs that are opposed to controlling others and make a clear personal and professional choice as to when the control may be warranted. In other words, each person in a position of formal authority must make a determination of how she or he will engage in the judicious, moral, and sensitive use of the real administrative features of authority and control. Not to do so will ultimately create more dysfunctional practice in schools.

One last thought concerning the fact that power and authority are valid considerations for educational administrators and supervisors. The reason that a person is given the role of leader in any organization is because those who select leaders expect the goals and objectives of their organizations to be achieved in a timely fashion. While it may seem uncomfortable to some that they are given power over others, the fact is that they are ultimately held accountable, as leaders, for moving toward the desired goals. And often, that must be accomplished through the use of power and authority.

Implications for Educational Leaders

Power and authority are central issues in understanding the field of educational leadership. Supervisors often have some special limits placed on their formal authority, and so a reflection on the ways in which they can be effective in moving their organizations toward important objectives often becomes one of thinking about power and authority. Ultimately, a critical concern in assessing a supervisor's potential power rests in the appreciation of how much a supervisor can motivate others to do something.

Supervisors, as educational leaders, can be very effective, and they can be effective without any formal authority. Effectiveness can rest in functional authority and power. If the supervisor or administrator learns to engage primarily in behaviors that influence others, then he or she will bring about change. In school settings, the adoption of techniques designed to have an impact based on expertise, competence, and interpersonal skills will probably result in longer-lasting change on the part of teachers and other staff who are well educated, sophisticated, and accustomed to performing in settings where they must think for themselves. A supervisor or administrator who relies solely on formal authority and "pulls rank" to try to make others perform in a particular way will rarely be effective and, with professional employees, will actually do more harm than good. Teachers who are "told" what to do will often rebel against what they perceive as an effort to manipulate their behavior.

Proactive leadership assumes that a practitioner will carefully weigh the outcomes that are likely to result from the use of different types of power and authority. Proactive leadership is an effective approach because it leads toward finding ways of influencing as many people as possible within an organization. Power and authority are central to the questions of motivation or influence, and anyone who is uncomfortable with analyzing these topics in a school might well be advised to look at alternative professional roles.

Summary

This chapter considered some definitions of two inescapable concerns of supervisory and administrative personnel—power and authority.

The supervisor's need to understand and appreciate the most appropriate and judicious ways to exercise power and authority in school settings was emphasized.

Also reviewed were the salient characteristics of power, including the sources of power defined by French and Raven and compliance theory as developed by Etzioni. The section dealing with authority included a brief review of Weber's definitions of three types of authority—traditional, charismatic, and legal—and a discussion concerning the distinction between formal and functional authority. Finally, the chapter concluded by noting how the concepts of power and authority are germane to the development of understanding educational leadership, particularly proactive leadership.

Suggested Activities

1. Interview a group of supervisors and a group of administrators and ask them to describe the strategies and techniques that they would follow when trying to encourage teachers to comply with a new school district policy. As each group describes its practices, make an assessment of the types of power (according to French and Raven's conceptualization) that are being used. Are there differences between what the supervisors do, as contrasted with the administrative group?

2. Talk with four or five teachers and present brief descriptions of the different authority types presented in this chapter. Ask each person to identify situations in which they would expect supervisors or administrators to rely on or another type of authority.

Cases to Consider

Read each of the cases below and consider the following:

- What are the critical issues raised in the cases as they relate to the concepts of power and authority in educational supervision and leadership?

- How does each case relate to the development of proactive leadership?

- In what ways might you suggest a resolution to the issues raised?

Case 10.1   It Was Supposed to be Easier!

When the superintendent called Malcolm Fredericks and offered him the job as Apple View's new district coordinator of curriculum, it was a happy moment for Malcolm. Although he had been an elementary principal in the system for the past three years, he was never very comfortable in that job. He liked the children in the school and found satisfaction in the work related to curriculum development. However, Malcolm hated the times when he had to act like the boss and confront teachers or other staff members. It was really difficult for him to "pull rank" and order others around.

It was because of this overall discomfort with being in the too-powerful role of principal that Malcolm looked forward to his new position, where he could get involved with improving the district's curriculum and instructional practices. "No more hassles, and no more need to push anyone around," thought the new district administrator.

It was three weeks into the new school year, and Malcolm sat in his office wondering why he still didn't seem to be as happy with his new job as he thought he should be by now. Two weeks ago, at the request of the superintendent, he initiated a district-wide review of the mathematics curriculum. He then received several complaint calls from teachers across the district who stated that they saw no need to "waste a lot of time going over the math program again." They had been involved with a comprehensive review only five years ago. Yet the school board had made it clear to the superintendent that something had to be done with the math program in the school district. Now, Malcolm was in the "hot seat" and had to push the agenda along.

Malcolm believed that the curriculum review process was warranted, and he really did not object to leading the effort. Still, he was less than happy over the fact that he had to "get tough" with teachers again.

Case 10.2 "But I Had to Make My Point!"

Maria Rodriguez was a genuine star all through school. She finished high school at the age of 16 and went on to finish her bachelor's degree in art history at State University in only three years. Although many people tried to persuade her to take some time and go off to Europe for a year with the State Arts Fund Scholarship she had received, she persisted with her dream of going into education. At 19 she was too young to get a teaching job, so she worked as a teachers' aide in an inner-city school where she thought that she could offer a lot to the neighborhood kids. She was a huge success, and she continued with her career in education by pursuing a master's degree in Art Education at State U. By the age of 21, she had completed graduate school, received a prestigious honor from the state, worked with kids in a local school (and received front-page coverage in the *State Journal*), and was now being recognized as a bright young teaching talent. She had it all!

Soon after joining the art department faculty at Liberty High School, she was asked by the superintendent to participate in a newly formed task force that was asked to look into arts program funding in secondary schools. In accepting the invitation, she neglected to realize that she was taking the place of Caroline Vanezky, another art teacher at Liberty who had just completed 21 years in the district. Caroline was a good sport and said nothing, but the other teachers in her department and around the district were getting a bit tired of the "Whiz Kid."

In March of that year, the district arts study committee was asked to make its recommendations to the school board at a special meeting. Teachers from across the district came to the meeting because there was a chance that the outcome of the meeting could result in some additional funding for next year's instructional budget across the district. Each member of the committee was invited to make a few comments about their views of the committee's recommendation. When Maria's turn arrived, she received numerous positive comments from the board and superintendent. Few noticed that teachers in the boardroom took that opportunity to walk out as a group.

Applying the Concepts

The following brief quiz is designed to improve your skills in applying some of the concepts discussed in this chapter. Read the brief introductory case and then respond to the multiple-choice questions. You will find the answers in the Appendix.

The teachers at Hooten Hollow Middle School had been frustrated over the past few years. They were generally recognized as some of the most competent teachers in the school district, but they had recently worked with two experienced principals who rarely sought their opinions about issues that teachers viewed as important. They felt that the past two administrators did not show any respect; they apparently did not appreciate the teachers' hard work and dedication to the job.

Cheryl Gomez was the latest principal at Hooten Hollow. She was walking into the job with her eyes wide open to the problem of staff morale. She knew that her predecessors, Walter Fitzsimmons and Grace Flores-Whitley, had experienced a lot of problems. She had heard stories about how the teachers expressed their frustration with not being involved in decisions. Nevertheless, Hooten Hollow was recognized as one of the highest achieving middle schools in the state, and Cheryl wanted to come on board and do an outstanding job. She wanted to maintain the school's excellent academic performance and reputation while also making the teachers happy.

It was now the night before Cheryl's first appearance in front of her new staff. She was considering a number of alternative approaches that she might follow when she faced her new colleagues. She was not normally a harsh person, but she knew that she could be stern and she also recalled the way that she had been able to elicit positive results in the past when she portrayed herself as a no-nonsense administrator. She really did not want to foul up a good thing at the school; but she wanted to be herself with her new colleagues. How could she resolve this dilemma?

1. If Cheryl were to make certain that she spent a good deal of time at first by allowing her staff to get to know her on a personal basis, and also appreciate that their new principal was a good colleague who really wanted to work with the teachers as professionals, she would be using _____.

    a. coercive power

    b. legitimate power

    c. referent power

    d. reward power

2. Cheryl's predecessors apparently had problems with the staff because they may have relied too heavily on _____.

    a. reward power

    b. referent power

    c. charismatic authority

    d. traditional authority

3. If Cheryl were to somehow indicate that she would be very unhappy and begin to enforce the school's rules related to teacher behavior very narrowly if the staff did not "buy into" her vision for Hooten Hollow, she might be making use of _____.

    a. coercive power

    b. legitimate power

    c. referent power

    d. reward power

Additional Reading

Blase, Joseph, & Kirby, Peggy (1992). *Bringing out the best in teachers: What effective principals do.* Newbury Park, CA: Corwin Press.

Cohen, Allan R., & Bradford, David L. (2005). *Influence without authority.* New York: Wiley.

Kouzes, James M., & Posner, Barry Z. (1993). *Credibility: How leaders gain and lose it, why people demand it.* San Francisco: Jossey-Bass.

McClelland, David C. (1975). *Power: The inner experience.* New York: Irvington.

11

Dealing with Conflict

A great deal of "pop" management literature features self-improvement prescriptions for leaders and would-be leaders to follow, and among the most frequently stated is the notion that effective managers must learn to reduce, or even eliminate, conflict from their personal and professional lives. These books suggest simple steps, similar to time-management techniques, which may be followed to clean up conflict-riddled lives.

These "sure cures" for managerial blues are always amusing. It is, simply put, impossible to take on a leadership role without confronting conflict. In fact, the more successful a manager or supervisor becomes, the more likely it is that she or he will experience more intense, frequent, and visible forms of conflict. Even for those not in formal organizational leadership positions, conflict is an unavoidable fact of life.

Some organizational theorists argue that conflict is not only an inevitable feature of organizational life but it also is a desirable ingredient in effective, functioning organizations. Life without periodic change is stagnant, and the development of conflict is one way to force necessary change. Leaders are legitimately held responsible not for reducing or eliminating organizational conflict, but rather for using it to promote institutional improvement and growth.

The issue addressed in this chapter is not how to avoid conflict, but rather the ways in which an educational leader can minimize the negative consequences of conflict. The chapter begins with an exploration of what conflict is, in conceptual terms, followed by a presentation of four different types of conflict. The second half of the chapter focuses on a model designed to help leaders understand how to handle conflict in their lives.

❧ WHAT IS CONFLICT?

Morton Deutsch (1973; cited in Owens, 1998) noted that "a conflict exists whenever incompatible activities occur" (p. 231). For Deutsch, then, conflict is little more than a state of disagreement between two parties. The word can describe a range of phenomena all the way from a simple difference of opinion to a war. Kenneth Boulding (1962) suggested that the factor that distinguishes between types of conflict is the amount of hostility present in the disagreement. Conflict between two people who want to drive their cars in the same space on an expressway may range in potency from simple annoyance (low hostility) to absolute road rage, the violent and destructive behavior seen recently across the nation where drivers have even shot at one another (extremely high hostility). This kind of hostility cannot be avoided entirely, unless a person decides never to drive. Most people who live in cities such as Chicago, New York, or Atlanta must drive on freeways in order to just get around and go to work. Therefore, most people are occasionally "at risk" to encounter highway conflict. The key is to remain at the annoyance or low hostility end of the continuum.

Owens (1987) further distinguished among low- and high-hostility events by noting that the major difference

> . . . lies in the motivation behind them, often not easily discernible. Although considerable (and often vigorous) conflict may erupt over such issues as improving school performance, ways of desegregating a school system, or how to group children for instruction, the parties to the conflict may well be motivated by essentially constructive goals. The key is whether or not the parties involved want to work with the system or are motivated by a wish to destroy it. (p. 246)

If conflict is an inevitable organizational reality, what effects will it have? Obviously there may be good or bad consequences of any institutional characteristic, including conflict. When disagreements (marked by either high hostility or low hostility) occur, two things may happen. The lack of consensus may lead to improvement in the organization because communication takes place, and compromise or further appreciation of conflict may be described as "good." On the other hand, disagreement may result in polarization of viewpoints, the end of communication, and personal animosity among members in the organization. In such a case, the results of the conflict are clearly "bad." The responsibility of the leader, particularly a proactive educational leader, is to guide the conflicts that will always be present toward a lower level of hostility and therefore toward a higher probability of serving as positive forces for the organization.

To try to avoid or eliminate conflict is, simply put, to avoid a legitimate leadership responsibility, and the results of such an activity will almost always be negative. For instance, think of the school principal who wants to avoid conflict and therefore simply sits in an office all day with the door closed, shutting out the potential disagreements taking place in the corridors and classrooms. This behavior may be satisfying for the principal whose blood pressure does not rise in response to the events taking place outside the office, but its consequences to the organization, which consists of both children and teachers, are ultimately negative; opportunities for growth through resolution of conflicts are lost. In short, schools where the principal's door is always closed are rarely exciting schools. This is not to suggest that leaders ought to deliberately stir up conflict. But when conflict occurs, no effective leader should run from it.

⚂ SOURCES AND TYPES OF CONFLICT

Proactive leaders need to understand two additional dimensions of organizational conflict: the sources of conflict and types of conflict most frequently faced by educational supervisors and administrators.

Sources of Conflict

Educational leaders typically face conflict from three sources: within the organization, outside the organization, and within one's self. Robert Owens (1998) defined the sources of conflict in this way:

> Conflict can occur *within* persons or social units; it is *interpersonal* or *intrapersonal* (or, of course, *intranational*). Conflict can also be experienced between two or more people or social units: so-called *interpersonal, intergroup,* or *international* conflict. (p. 92)

The only conflict described above that does not appear almost daily in the school leader's life is international, although this is not always the case in school districts along the U.S.-Mexican border. All categories of conflict may be felt on a regular basis by educational leaders.

In the context of the overall goal of identifying ways to reduce the negative consequences of conflict, strategies for educational leaders will be explored. Fundamentally, the effective leader is one who develops the capacity to remain aware of what is occurring within an organization so that potential conflicts may be identified in advance whenever possible. Developing a *sensitivity* to potential conflicts both inside and outside the organization does not guarantee the prevention of future conflict, but it does increase the likelihood that the supervisor will not be surprised (or frustrated) when something does happen. There will never be, for example, a school in which every teacher gets along with every other teacher or is totally satisfied with every supervisory or administrative decision. Whenever a leader makes a decision, it is likely that someone will disagree. Poor leadership practice is anticipating neither the likely source nor the potency of the conflict that a decision will engender. Proactive leaders have a sense of where the "land mines" are located, not in order to defuse them all in advance, but rather to find a path among them which will cause the least damage.

Analyzing conflict that arises from within one's self necessarily grows from an individual's ability to "know thyself." As indicated in chapter 2, many important values may be defined in the process of developing and reviewing an individual philosophy of education. One of the greatest benefits of such continuous self-assessment is that it can alert a person to individual values and also to likely sources of personal conflict.

Types of Conflict

In the discussion of Getzels's social systems model in chapter 4, it was indicated that organizations are best understood as the products of an ongoing and dynamic interactive process involving individual (idiographic) and institutional (nomothetic) dimensions. Getzels defined effectiveness as the extent to which congruence (or lack of disagreement or conflict) was present in the interactions between the component elements of the theoretical model. From this view of effectiveness we can identify four major types of organizational conflict: interrole, intrareference group, interreference group, and role-personality.

Interrole conflict is the "disagreement between two or more roles simultaneously fulfilled by one person" (Lipham & Hoeh, 1974, p. 133). The supervisor feels the effects of trying to "wear too many hats."

High school subject department chairpersons often suffer from interrole conflict. Some released time from teaching is normally provided as compensation for chairpersons to engage in supervisory and administrative duties, but chairpersons are usually expected to teach classes, advise students, serve on assorted governance and planning committees in the school or district, and, in many cases, do a duty assignment each day, coach a sport, or moderate some student activity. These assignments and expectations are only those encountered during the workday; personal and professional commitments—family, graduate education, community activities, and so forth—add fuel to feelings of conflict and stress. Naturally, the many competing demands cannot always be kept separate from one another. At some point, for example, the department chair may find it impossible to grade student papers before the next class and also fill out a purchase order to get materials requested by the department faculty before the deadline imposed by the district business office. These professional pressures are often accompanied by the additional demands of personal activities and responsibilities. The department chairperson may also owe a paper for a university course, have two children who need attention, and be a soloist for the church choir.

Such situations, where people are trying to "juggle several balls at once," are by no means infrequent. Most of us occasionally find that we have more commitments than time, and we sense some degree of interrole conflict. The more competent we are at what we do, the more likely we are to feel this type of pressure; the conflict serves almost as recognition of ability. Nevertheless, the consequences can be negative. Important jobs are not completed, psychological stress intensifies, and our ability to fulfill our responsibilities is greatly impaired. We can take steps to reduce this type of conflict as well as its negative consequences.

People facing interrole conflict need to take stock of their various competing personal and professional commitments, set priorities, and decide which activities may be removed from their personal agendas. Must we sing in the church choir while we take graduate courses, or can we look forward to solos *after* completing the degree? Sometimes activities that are important must be dropped, at least temporarily, to provide time for activities of greater personal or professional value.

Another way to reduce interrole conflict is to engage in time management activities. Many schemes exist to help people control their personal uses of time. Larry Hughes (1984) provides a plan that we find particularly useful:

1. *Analyze your job* to clarify precisely what it is you are supposed to do in a particular setting. Formal job descriptions should be viewed as starting points in determining what is really expected in a school or district.
2. *Determine the difference between managing and doing.* Remember that efficiency (doing things well) must be consciously combined with effectiveness (getting the right things done well).
3. *Set personal goals and objectives* and develop strategies for achieving them. Define the goals precisely enough so that they may serve to guide continuing behavior.
4. *Conduct a personal time audit* as a way to see how you have really been using your time.
5. *Avoid interruptions on the job.* Watch out for "drop-in visitors" and unwanted telephone calls that divert you from your focus on effective use of available time.
6. *Delegate.* Organize yourself, your subordinates, colleagues, and bosses to accomplish necessary work most effectively.
7. *Plan and conduct effective meetings.* Meetings should serve the needs of the organization and the people who work in it, not be roadblocks to effective use of time. Consider how meetings might be arranged to reduce interrole conflict.
8. *Organize productive committees and task forces.* A primary cause of interrole conflict is that one person tries to do too many things. Increase effectiveness not only by delegating particular responsibilities to others but also by assigning tasks and projects to well-organized committees. Consider how others in the organization might be enlisted to reduce competing demands.

No matter how efficient your use of time management techniques may be, ultimately you can gain control over your commitments and the dysfunction caused by interrole conflict only through reviewing and assessing the personal principles that guide your choices. No one can do everything. At some point you need to decide which involvements are most important and which ones may be ignored.

Intrareference group conflict is "conflict or disagreement within a reference group in their expectations for the role of the supervisor" (Lipham & Hoeh, 1974, p. 133). The supervisor is "caught in a crossfire." Once again, the focus might be on the chairperson of a high school subject department. There may be a dozen or more teachers in the department, some of whom believe the chair is simply "one of the teachers" who happens to hold a title, and others who may look at the department head as a stock clerk, responsible for doing nothing more than securing materials and equipment for the teachers. Yet another group of teachers may expect direct instructional monitoring from the chair, such as observing teachers in their classrooms. No clear, common vision of the role of the department chair exists, and intrareference group conflict may well be the result.

Interreference group conflict is the "disagreement in two or more (different) reference groups in their expectations" for the role of the supervisor (Lipham & Hoeh, 1974, p. 101). Here, the supervisor is "caught in the middle." A central office supervisor, for example, who visits teachers in schools may be seen by these teachers as a trusted colleague who can help them address their instructional concerns. The same supervisor may be viewed by administrators in the central office as a perfect person to get out into the schools and "get the dirt" on teachers. The supervisor is thus viewed as a potential "snoopervisor" by one group, and a "human relations specialist" by another group. This is a precise example of interreference group conflict.

Conflicts that arise from a supervisor's relationships with different groups can be particularly frustrating and damaging to supervisory effectiveness. When groups have differing expectations about how a job will or should be carried out, the conflict is rooted in the perceptions of others; it is beyond the supervisor's immediate control. Nevertheless, some techniques can help reduce the potentially negative consequences of conflicts involving groups.

Many group conflicts can be headed off if jobs are precisely defined before they are begun. What are the formal, stated expectations listed as part of a high school subject department chairperson's position? Is there any suggestion that it is appropriate to be a "gofer?" An instructional leader? Is the job defined so vaguely that such wildly divergent expectations might exist? If so, try to clarify those expectations—and your own—at the outset. For the central office supervisor mentioned above, find out how teachers have traditionally viewed the responsibilities of central office supervisors and ask central office administrators directly about their views concerning proper performance by supervisors.

Group conflict can also be reduced if the individual supervisor has a well-developed concept of what it means to be a supervisor. Again, there is no real substitute for a well-articulated personal platform or philosophy. We can rarely be forced to juggle many competing expectations for a job if we have clearly defined our own role. This personal clarity may have the immediate consequence of angering some people in the organization who do not appreciate the supervisor's self-definition of role. This anger will typically be relatively short-lived, however, and considerably less dysfunctional over time than chronic uncertainty over what is proper behavior in a job.

Role-personality conflict is the "disagreement between the expectations for the role of the . . . [supervisor] and his [or her] personality need-dispositions" (Lipham & Hoeh, 1974, p. 133). Here, recalling the characteristics of Getzels's social systems model is particularly helpful. Figure 11.1 indicates that considerable incongruence can exist between the two elements of role and personality: The job may not fit the person.

Role-personality conflict may be the most frustrating of all because it suggests that a person has made an error in judgment by selecting the wrong career path. A teacher, for example, decides to leave the classroom for a supervisory or administrative position, based on the assumption of what the role responsibilities of the position will be, only to discover that the assumption was incorrect. It might be argued, of course, that the new supervisor can simply return to being a teacher, but going back may be extremely difficult. A teacher who goes into a supervisory position has typically invested a lot of time and money in additional university courses and has moved into a position with greater financial rewards. Turning away from the new status and prestige of a leadership role may be next to impossible—achievable, certainly for some, but hard for most.

Again, there are ways in which the negative impact of this kind of conflict can be reduced. It is most important to pay serious attention to the nature of a position *before* assuming it. We need to question the per-

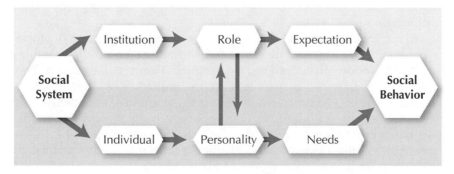

Figure 11.1.   Role-personality conflict in the social systems model of Getzels

sonal assumptions and review the motivation which underlie a choice of a new job. Are our expectations realistic? Do our assumptions match the actual tasks performed?

Those who are responsible for training people for new roles also have an opportunity—and a responsibility—to acquaint applicants with the realities of their intended positions well in advance of a move. Apprenticeships, training in clinical settings, and numerous other forms of field-based situations help people understand their roles before assuming their new jobs on a full-time basis. Lawyers go through clerkships, and physicians do residencies and clinical internships. In professional education, aspiring teachers must take part in student teaching, and future administrators and supervisors increasingly engage in internships, planned field experiences, and numerous other activities which allow them to "taste" the new job before coming on board permanently. The primary purpose of these activities is to teach people how to use certain practical skills that are associated with effective performance of their jobs. There is also a second, equally important purpose to be fulfilled by a preservice practicum. It allows people to experience a job in a low-risk setting, where no "loss of face" is attached to a decision not to pursue a career—a decision which has been based on actual experience rather than on false expectations. Preservice "tryouts" provide opportunities for people to drop out before experiencing the type of role-personality conflict that damages not only the organization but also the future educational leader. Those responsible for such programs must emphasize and safeguard their low-risk status and must condone in nonjudgmental ways the decisions that some participants may make not to continue.

✑ CONFLICT-HANDLING STYLES

Techniques for reducing personal conflict and for decreasing potential negative impact on the overall organization have been reviewed. In addition, the destructive power of conflict can be reduced by further analysis of the nature of conflict and the ways in which people address conflict situations in their lives.

A frequently employed diagnostic procedure for analyzing organizational conflict is a model that assesses the nature of conflict-handling styles. The model, first designed by Kenneth Thomas (Jamison & Thomas, 1974), suggests that people react to conflicting settings in one of two basic ways: (1) assertively, by becoming aggressive about their own needs above those of others; or (2) cooperatively, by playing down their own needs and trying to satisfy the concerns of others. Figure 11.2 illustrates how conflicts may be handled along a continuum, from addressing one's own needs to addressing the needs of others.

As the Thomas model suggests, people may engage in behavior of five different types: avoiding, competing, collaborating, accommodating,

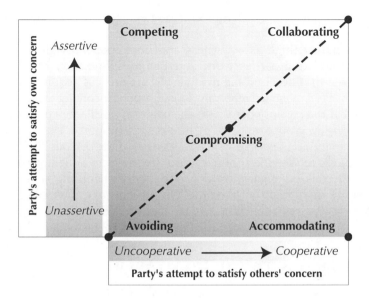

Source: D. W. Jamison and K. W. Thomas, Power and conflict in the student-teacher relationships, *Journal of Applied Behavioral Science,* Vol. 10, No. 3, p. 326, copyright 1974 by Sage Publications. Reprinted by permission of Sage Publications.

Figure 11.2. Types of behavior used in handling conflicts

or compromising. The three points at which there is a balance between equal efforts toward assertiveness and cooperation are represented by points along the dotted line in figure 11.2: avoidance, compromise, and collaboration. Robert Owens (1998) describes these points in the following ways:

Avoidance (low assertiveness and low cooperativeness) suggests withdrawal, peaceful coexistence, and indifference. Avoidance is useful when (a) the latent conflict probably cannot really be resolved ("live with it"), or (b) the issues are not so important to the parties as to justify the time, effort, and resources to work them out. As Blake and Mouton (1964) pointed out, avoidance can serve as a form of "cease fire." Ultimately, however, this is not a valid way to deal with unresolved conflict: it only serves to suppress conflict momentarily.

Compromise (medium assertiveness and medium cooperativeness) suggests "splitting the difference." Compromise has some elements in common with collaborative problem solving: (a) the parties must be willing to engage in the process, (b) there is some move toward collaboration, and (c) the process is basically conciliatory and not in flagrant conflict with the organization's well-being. Compromising behavior is useful because it does represent an effort to find a set of long-term behaviors that will reduce conflict, but it essentially looks at the parties in conflict as adversaries. Compromising behavior does not move toward resolution; it tries to "keep a lid" on the problem.

Collaboration (high assertiveness and high cooperativeness) suggests that the conflicting parties work together to define their problems and then engage in mutual problem solving. This process requires, first, that parties involved must actively want to use problem-solving techniques and second, that the parties possess (a) the necessary skills for communicating and working in groups, and (b) attitudes that support a climate of openness, trust, and frankness in which to identify and work out problems.

Thomas's model does not provide a prescription to deal with conflict. Indeed, there is no suggestion that one conflict-handling style is necessarily better than others all the time. On the contrary, the model suggests that a wide range of behaviors may be needed to deal effectively and positively with whatever conflicts arise in the life of the educational leader.

✑ DEALING WITH THE INEVITABLE

"You can't make everyone happy all the time." If there is one motto that probably should be posted in front of every administrator, manager, supervisor, or executive on the face of the earth, that might be the one. Not many people—if anyone—seriously looks forward to and relishes the idea that he or she will need to engage in conflict. Few, if any, people want to tell someone that they are fired, or did not get a desired job, or need to do something that they do not want to do. In fact, it may be argued that conflict is irrational behavior, and human beings strive to achieve rationality most of the time.

Having said this, the fact remains that leaders are often people who serve at the crossroads of several competing agendas, value systems, or points of view. Leaders receive directions—from boards of directors, organizational superiors, voters, and many others—that they must implement. At the same time, they work with others—as colleagues, students, employees, and so forth—who must also receive directions. At times, those who receive disagree with those who send. And conflict arises.

As noted throughout this chapter, the existence of conflict is ultimately avoidable only through total withdrawal from reality. It has even been said that death is the only absolute escape mechanism for conflict. That is not a reasonable choice, even if it enabled a person to escape conflict. Besides that, it would be a boring way to resolve conflict. Seriously, though, our best course of action is not to dream of an impossible reality where no conflict ever faces us. Rather, administrators, managers, and supervisors need to accept conflict and realize that the only thing to really fear may be allowing conflict to totally rule our lives. So, the message here is clear: Learn to live with it, but don't let the conflict control your behavior.

❧ SUMMARY

Conflict is a very real—and unavoidable—part of organizational life. Because it is inevitable, leaders need to know how to *work with* or *reduce* conflict, not how to eliminate it totally from their lives.

Conflict is defined simply as a disagreement between two parties. Conflict becomes more intense with the introduction of additional emotional commitment and hostility, so an important leadership skill is the ability to review the *emotional level* in all conflicts. This chapter reviewed typical sources and types of conflict and suggested how each type of conflict might be rendered less harmful. Throughout this discussion it was suggested that a key element is the leader's ability to know her or his personal educational values and philosophy. Next, there was an explanation of Thomas's theoretical model, which was designed to help the diagnosis of the nature of conflict. Finally, the chapter concludes with a restatement of the inevitability of conflict as part of a leader's life, and a recommendation to aspiring administrators and supervisors that it is an important skill to learn how to cope with that reality.

Suggested Activities

1. Using the list of time management techniques proposed by Hughes, compile a survey questionnaire and distribute it to a number of administrators in your district. Ask people to indicate which items that they find exceptionally useful in practice and also which items that they do not follow. See if any patterns exist in the responses.

2. Find examples of conflict in the local newspaper over the span of a few days. Classify these conflicts according to the typologies found in this chapter.

3. Using the concepts found in Thomas's model of conflict-handling styles, ask a group of teachers, supervisors, and administrators to estimate the predominant strategies that they use when faced with conflict in their professional lives. Do the same regarding personal conflicts. Are there differences in how people believe they handle conflict "at work" as contrasted with "at home?"

Cases to Consider

Read each of the cases below and consider the following issues:

• What are the critical issues raised in each case, as they relate to organizational conflict?

• How does each case relate to the development of proactive leadership?

• In what ways might you suggest a resolution to the issues raised?

Case 11.1   But That's Not What Greg Did!

Allison Binder stepped into her new office and was pleased to realize her ambition of several years. She was now an elementary principal. This represented a dream come true for a woman who had spent sixteen years as a classroom teacher and had nearly killed herself by working night and day to complete a graduate degree in educational administration at the local university. She had given up many hours with her three children and husband to finish her graduate studies and complete the requirements for a state administrative certificate. Now she was actually going to be a principal!

She knew that her job at Hawthorne Elementary School would be challenging. After all, Hawthorne was a relatively poor school in a blue-collar district that had clearly seen better days. Fortunately, she was following in the footsteps of Greg Spencer, a man who had spent the last five years effecting a strong sense of pride at Hawthorne. Now, Hawthorne was no longer viewed as a school with no sense of purpose and dignity. Mr. Spencer had made the school orderly; student discipline was the most visible characteristic.

As Allison moved into her office, she noticed that many of Greg's belongings were still there. The bookshelf still contained all of his books. Allison noted that every item on the shelf dealt with some aspect of student discipline and behavior management. She was annoyed that in the middle of her office remained two carrels that had been used to provide space for in-school discipline suspensions. Since Greg had taken on the job of primary disciplinarian for the past five years, it was not a surprise that part of his work environment contained the carrels. However, Allison needed the space and besides, she did not want to begin her new life as a person who only worked with "bad boys and girls." The books were sent to Greg at his new school, and the carrels were sent into storage.

The school year started calmly. After all, the kids at Hawthorne were still used to a setting where no nonsense was allowed, and the teachers were happy to start another year. The teachers barely realized that Greg had gone and that they had a new administrator in the building.

During the last week of September, a few changes became apparent. Mrs. Quincy, a fourth grade teacher with more than twenty years of experience in the classroom, suddenly charged into Allison's office to demand that something be done with "that awful Charlie Fenster." Allison quickly determined that Charlie was a boy who had spent a good part of the last two years as a fixture in Greg's office. He was off and running, trying for a third straight year. Mrs. Quincy made it quite clear that the principal was supposed to do something about Charlie—right now. After she had listened to Mrs. Quincy, Allison simply looked at her and asked her what she proposed to do with this student in her class. Allison's question was not what Mrs. Quincy expected. As she turned to go back to her class, she looked the novice principal in the eye and said coldly, "Greg would have taken care of this right now. The other teachers will be very disappointed to know that you're not really one of us. Thanks for nothing, Mrs. Binder."

Case 11.2 "No Matter What You Do . . ."

By the end of the first week of the new school year, the teachers at Gridley Locks Middle School were starting to wonder if they had missed some important information during the past summer. Two days before the students reported, all the teachers in the district were brought together at the Civic Center to hear a "Welcome Back" speech from Dr. Caesar Delgado, the new superintendent of schools. During his presentation, he noted the work recently completed by the Argyle Trust, an educational research foundation in the state capital, in which a study of the 25 best school districts in the state all featured teachers who expressed the belief that they felt able to take risks and did not feel threatened by administrative pressures in their classrooms. Dr. Delgado proudly proclaimed this as a model that he expected in his new school system.

The next day, however, a different message came to the staff. Two years ago, Gridley Locks had received a commendation for how well its students did on the math and reading portions of the statewide achievement test. It was able to fly a flag all year that said, "We're recognized as a great school!" However, during the summer, the state department of education released the achievement test scores for last year. Gridley had gone down, slightly, but enough to lose the status of a "recognized" campus. Gina Tortelli, the principal for the past three years, was called into the office of the superintendent who told her that she had only one course of action now. Her job was to "get on those teachers at Gridley and get those scores back up in time for the next round of tests in the spring!" Gina had no choice but to call her faculty together yesterday and let them know that they were going to have to knuckle down and focus on the minimum-competency testing process. That meant no more experimental programs, new teaching techniques, or anything that was not tried and tested. Scores would now go up or heads would roll. Ms. Tortelli did not fancy the idea of losing her job.

What the teachers did not really understand was how the message on one day had so quickly changed the next day. Gina was their friend. She was one of them, and she always fought to make sure that teachers could act like professionals. All had changed in a few days—and with a few points on a test that everyone but state legislators hated.

Applying the Concepts

The following brief quiz is designed to improve your skills in applying some of the concepts discussed in this chapter. Read the brief introductory case and then respond to the multiple-choice questions. You will find the answers in the Appendix.

David Carson was eager to begin his new job as the supervisor of mathematics for the Forest Glen City Schools. He had spent 19 years as a teacher in the district, and as a result, he believed he had a handle on what the school system needed to do to bring about change in the curriculum.

He was looking forward to next Monday, when he would walk into the central office and assume his new role.

The only thing bothering David was a certain feeling he was now experiencing. He wanted the job as a supervisor, but he knew that once he accepted that title, many of his teacher friends would start to shy away from him and become aloof. He had seen this pattern before: One of the "troops" went into the administration building but never came back to live with the rank and file. He was afraid that this new job would make him an outcast and outsider forever.

David was also concerned about other aspects of his new job and life. As a classroom teacher, he knew that he would always be home from work at about the same time every day. This was rather important because he enjoyed playing with his four daughters, puttering around the house, and in general being a good family man. However, his new job would require many evening meetings with curriculum committees, appearances before the school board, and so forth. It also meant that David would have little time to devote to his work at his church on weekends and to graduate studies at State University. In short, David achieved a most important milestone in his professional life—prestige and a greatly enhanced salary, but he also started to feel the pressure that would surely accompany his new world. Was it going to be doable? More importantly, would it all be worth the price?

1. The fact that David was conflicted over his ability to commit adequate time to family, job, church, and other activities is a classic example of a person experiencing _____.

   a. interrole conflict

   b. intrareference group conflict

   c. interreference group conflict

   d. role-personality conflict

2. Perhaps the most effective strategy that David might follow in attempting to reconcile his sense of conflict would be to _____.

   a. avoid interruptions on the job

   b. determine the difference between managing and doing

   c. analyze his job to clarify precisely what he is supposed to do in a particular setting

   d. set personal goals and objectives, and develop strategies for achieving them

3. If you were to advise David of a way to help him deal with his feelings of conflict, you might suggest that he _____.

   a. return to the classroom as soon as possible

   b. not invest so much time in his job

   c. take a vacation

   d. read over his platform to determine personal priorities and professional goals; then act upon these standards

Additional Reading

Blake, Robert R., Shepard, Herbert A., & Mouton, Jane S. (1964). *Managing intergroup conflict in industry*. Houston, TX: Gulf Publishing.

Gerzon, Mark (2006). *Leading through conflict: How successful leaders transform differences into opportunities*. Boston: Harvard Business School Press.

Katz, Neil H., & Lawyer, John W. (1992). *Communication and conflict resolution skills*. Dubuque, IA: Kendall Hunt Publishing.

Likert, Rensis, & Likert, Jane Gibson (1976). *New ways of managing conflict*. New York: McGraw-Hill.

Thomas, John M., & Bennis, Warren G. (1972). *Management of change and conflict*. Baltimore: Penguin Books.

PART IV

Working with People
Process, Program, and Evaluation

Much of what educational leaders do involves organizing, motivating, understanding, evaluating, and planning for instruction. All of these processes imply great understanding of the people with whom the leader must work. Part IV discuss strategies for working with teachers, staff, and others who are engaged in or around school settings in order to improve the educational climate and, ultimately, to provide a better education for children.

❧ 12 ❧

Working with Groups

We often think of the educational supervisor as working almost exclusively with one-to-one contacts. Up to now in this book, emphasis has been on the individualistic dimensions of supervision—the personal educational platform and action plan, leadership, the need to deal with conflict as an ingredient of individual effectiveness, and so forth. Proactive leadership places great emphasis on the actions of a single person engaged in shaping a more effective organization. We need to remember, however, that a large proportion of the supervisor's or administrator's professional life is spent working with, through, and for groups. This reality tends to complicate organizational life—after all, it is easier for most people to work on a one-to-one basis—but there is a compelling need to develop insights into the nature of groups, both as components of larger organizations and as organisms unto themselves.

The purpose of this chapter is to explore the nature of groups, which are the building blocks of organizations. The chapter will examine some alternative definitions of groups and then explore group characteristics and some of the ways in which they can be classified, along with some of the roles and responsibilities within them. That will be followed by a discussion of teams and how the proactive leader can be involved with using this approach to organizational focus that can make significant changes in the quality of life in a school. Next, characteristics of group effectiveness are considered. The chapter concludes with some specific suggestions about how the analysis of groups may apply to the process of proactive leadership.

❧ DEFINITION OF A GROUP

There are many "bunches" of people in society. Not every one may accurately be called a group, however. For the purposes of the discussion

231

presented here, a group is defined quite simply as *a condition wherein two or more people join together in the pursuit of a common, shared purpose*. The definition is similar to a classic view offered by Michael Olmstead and Paul Hare (1978) in their oft-cited work on the nature of small groups: "A group . . . may be defined as a plurality of individuals who are in contact with one another, who take one another into account, and who are aware of some significant commonality" (p. 51).

The "commonality" that must knowingly be shared by all members of a group is an overriding sense of purpose. Further, the more strongly the purpose is established and accepted by all, the stronger a group will be; it is relatively simple to tear apart a group when its members are uncertain why they have been brought together in the first place.

Groups exist throughout schools and school systems, some strong and some weak. Consequently, educational leaders need to develop sensitivity to various kinds of groups. The definition of groups here is sufficiently simple and general to include groups currently in place. On the other hand, it provides a distinction between what may legitimately be called a "group" and what are simply "bunches of people," or what sociologists commonly refer to as "collectivities." The key difference is the extent to which there is a clearly identified emphasis on a common purpose. Collectivities can become groups; a number of people who happen to be in the same place at the same time may quickly form a shared identity and purpose. Consider the way in which airline passengers who receive repeated notice that their flight will be delayed begin to form a common purpose of complaining to the airline.

By contrast, groups can also become collectivities as once-shared common visions and purposes diminish. This occurs all too frequently in school settings; a faculty that has existed as a strong and cohesive group for a long time eventually loses its identity and sense of purpose, and finally it becomes nothing more than a collection of teachers "doing their own thing." This might be caused by some event such as a teachers' strike, where half of the staff stays in the classrooms while their colleagues (and former group members) walk the picket line for several days.

❧ BASIC CONSIDERATIONS OF GROUPS

Now that there has been a definition of what groups are, there are some specific typical characteristics of these bodies. In the following section, some commonly accepted classifications of groups are reviewed, along with special properties of groups and the behaviors of people who belong to them.

Classification of Groups

Researchers have tried to develop classifications for groups as a way to understand some of their essential features. One of the most famous of these efforts is the work of Charles H. Cooley (1909), who noted the existence of *primary* and *secondary* groups.

> By primary groups I mean those characterized by intimate face-to-face association and cooperation. They are primary in several senses, but chiefly in that they are fundamental in forming the social structure and ideals of the individual. . . . Primary groups are primary in the sense that they give the individual his earliest and complete experience of social unity, and also in the sense that they do not change in the same degree as more elaborate relations, but form a comparatively permanent source out of which the latter are ever springing. . . . (p. 212)

Olmstead and Hare (1978) suggest that primary group members tend to have warm, intimate, and personal ties with one another; family, for instance, is a clear and immediate example of a primary group. However, other primary groups are formed in society when individuals are drawn together in highly personalized settings. What does the effective supervisor need to know about primary groups? First, primary groups are never created artificially; the supervisor cannot create a primary group, regardless of whatever sincere desire exists to knit strong bonds among individuals. Second, primary groups are rarely found in school settings, but leaders still need to understand how primary groups work because when they do exist, they represent powerful forces that supervisors may use in order to channel organizational energy toward attainment of organizational objectives. Some school faculties have worked together for so long and so well that they have truly become a "family unit," in Cooley's terms. Supervisors who are not sensitive to such a group's strength will soon learn how it may subvert or support their agendas.

The secondary group complements the primary group. Olmstead and Hare (1978) noted:

> Relations among (secondary group) members are "cool," impersonal, rational, contractual, and formal. People participate not as whole personalities but only in delimited and special capacities; the group is not an end in itself but a means to other ends. (p. 94)

Most groups are best classified as secondary groups. They gather to achieve some identified objective, and then they dissolve. They are not necessarily unfriendly, but members do not serve together as a matter of personal survival or fulfillment. People drift in and out according to highly personalized agendas. Most school faculties form secondary groups. Cordial and professional relations exist among group members, but the absence or presence of the group has little long-term effect on the satisfaction of the needs of its individual members. What are the implications for supervisory practice? When working with most school staffs, supervisors need to recognize that, while teachers may show commitment to the goals of the group, they probably have stronger allegiances to other groups outside the school.

Groups may also be classified as formal or informal. Formal groups tend to be sanctioned by a particular organization to carry out one or more of the functions and responsibilities associated with that organization. In a school setting, examples of such formal groups might be the school board, the district administrative team, the local teachers' association, the PTA, a subject department in a high school, or the National Honor Society chapter. Membership requirements to such groups tend to be firmly established and identified, and it is relatively simple to determine who is and who is not a member. English teachers are not members of the math department; building principals are not members of the school board. In addition, the practices and behaviors of these groups tend to be well defined and openly shared with members. Formal groups, then, display generally clear standards of both membership and behavior.

Informal groups tend to rise out of the immediate needs or interests of individuals. Such groups may or may not have titles. They are fairly constant in their lack of precision concerning membership; people tend to drop in and out of informal groups in somewhat erratic and unpredictable fashion. Finally, informal groups tend to have short lives due to the frequency with which their memberships and purposes fluctuate. Some informal groups do last for several years, but typically "here today, gone tomorrow" is an appropriate description of their fundamental character.

For the researcher, formal groups are easier to identify, name, track, and analyze than are informal groups; as a result, we know a considerable amount about the nature of formal groups but little about the precise nature of informal groups as organizational components. This lack of knowledge could be disastrous for the educational leader, of course. Imagine a situation where the leader assumes that a formal, recognized group (e.g., a subject department in a high school) is the only group with an interest or stake in the subject area it represents. Unhappily, such assumptions are frequently made, rarely correct, and the source of almost inevitable conflict. The effective proactive leader is aware of who really has control of and interest in such issues, not merely what responsibilities are listed on a formal organizational chart.

W. J. Reddin (1967) classified groups and suggested that the following eight types might appear at any time in any organization:

1. *Problem-solving group.* All members demonstrate deep commitment to each other and to finding best solutions for whatever problems they face. This group, generally viewed as the most desirable, is high in both *interaction* effectiveness and *task* effectiveness.

2. *Production group.* This group is focused on accomplishing the task, with little or no emphasis on the needs of group members as people.

3. *Creative group.* The purpose of this group is the development of group members and their ideas. It is generally seen as a direct reverse of the

production group, because little emphasis is placed on the completion of identified tasks.

4. *Procedural group.* Group members are more interested in complying with stated guidelines and procedures established for group behavior than in successfully completing a task, promoting individual growth and development, or keeping the group together in a harmonious fashion. Meeting the letter of the law and following regulations are critical goals for the group.

5. *Mixed group.* This group's behavior is typified by compromise and vacillation between hurting the feelings of group members and getting a particular job done. As a consequence, such a group achieves very little in terms of either interactions or task effectiveness.

6. *Fight group.* This group exhibits almost constant conflict, argument, and disagreement, usually based on the personalities and values of individual group members rather than the substantive issues being considered by the group. Virtually nothing of substance is accomplished.

7. *Dependent group.* Similar to the creative group, this group focuses almost exclusively on achieving interaction effectiveness. The critical difference here is that discussion regarding even slightly controversial substantive issues is altogether avoided. Only issues on which the group is likely to achieve immediate and absolute agreement are ever introduced. This lack of risk taking can quickly lead to group stagnation.

8. *Group in flight.* This group barely qualifies for the title of group in the first place. Members are not committed to any common purposes, and there is a general corresponding avoidance of participation.

Two observations are important concerning Reddin's group types. First, despite the images evoked by the descriptions of the eight classifications, it does not follow that under *all* conditions in *all* organizations one group is necessarily and absolutely "better" than another. The problem-solving group may appear more efficient, and being a member of such a group may seem more appealing than participating in a fight group, but there are times when disagreement might actually be more appropriate.

Second, these descriptions are not absolutes. Any grouping of people, formal or informal, goes through a periodic metamorphosis from one classification to another. For example, a board of education might be characterized as a fight group because its members frequently engage in much conflict and petty bickering. That same group of five or seven people, however, might quickly close ranks and become a productive group or a problem-solving group when forced to deal with a commonly felt challenge. Personal feuds might cease when the district needs to develop a policy concerning AIDS, for example. By contrast, a subject department might normally appear to be a creative group, devoting most of its attention to providing for the continuing professional development of faculty, but the introduction of certain issues that require absolute adherence to district policy might turn the department into a procedural group. Any group, regardless of its long-standing tradition of behavior, will become an in-flight group if it loses its common purpose and shared vision.

Properties of Groups

Regardless of classification, any group tends over time to take on *characteristics* similar to those of individual human beings. We can talk about "mature" groups, for example, in the same way we discuss mature people. A mature group might be one that has been in existence for a long time, or one that demonstrates particularly well-reasoned patterns of behaviors, or both. An "immature" group, by contrast, might be a newly formed or particularly unpredictable one. As in the case with a person, of course, a group may become increasingly mature over time.

Groups also possess certain identifiable value orientations, defined as *norms*. In some groups it is acceptable for members to be argumentative; in others, members tend to nod and agree with everyone else—at least in public. All members of some groups are expected to go to lunch together every day and behave as a unit at all times in public; other group members allow members to act independently and expect them to come together only on rare occasions. At some universities, for example, professors come to the office every day and keep consistent and predictable hours for student contact. In other institutions, the norm calls for faculty to stay at home and write and rarely come to the office at all. A leader's ability or inability to identify accurately the existing norms of a particular group may be particularly relevant to successful interaction. If the leader assumes that a particular group is loosely knit and that one person speaks for everyone, the implications he or she draws from a conversation with that person may be absolutely false.

Group value patterns may shift rapidly at times, or they may not move for many years. The introduction of new members to a particular group may or may not have an immediate and observable impact on established beliefs and practices. As Dorian Cartwright and Alvin Zander (1960) explained in their classic analysis, *Group Dynamics*, group norms or standards must be understood both by members of the group and also by outsiders (such as educational leaders) who work with the group for at least three reasons:

1. Norms are consciously utilized by the group to help accomplish its goals;

2. The norms are part of an ongoing self-maintenance process used by groups; and

3. Norms help group members develop validity or "reality" for their opinions.

In addition to human characteristics and norms, groups possess a third common property: They always have leaders or at least exhibit the pretense of something called leadership. Herbert Thelen (1954) considered leadership as the ultimate focusing agent of groups: "Leadership is a set of functions through which the group coordinates the efforts of individuals" (p. 6). The implication is that groups would fail to exist if no evidence of leadership toward goals achievement were present.

Although formal leaders may be designated to serve groups, informal leaders may emerge in these same groups. This phenomenon begs the attention of the practitioner of proactive leadership. Consider, for example, a high school foreign language department with a formally named chair, but one or more teachers who wield such influence over their colleagues' behavior that they also enjoy group leadership status. In fact, these individuals may have considerably more power than does the formal leader. An outsider must then be extremely sensitive to the nuances of leadership—to the fact that the formal leader may not really be in charge, or that multiple sources of leadership may exist in the group. Determining who really is in charge is a critical task in any organization, whether it is a huge city school system or a four-member teaching team in an elementary school. Assuming that the person at the top of an organizational chart is always in fact in charge could be an embarrassing error that makes effective contact and working relations with a group nearly impossible to achieve.

Group Functions

Groups as total organizations carry out special roles in institutions. These are generally defined as either *task functions* or *group maintenance functions*. Marleen Pugach and Lawrence Johnson (1995, pp. 115–116) have further defined these two broad areas and noted specific skills associated with each broad area.

Task functions are ways in which the group is enabled to move forward toward its assigned goals and objectives. Specific skills within this functional domain are:

- *Initiating.* Initiation is a skill involved in beginning a group. It includes things such as imposing an agenda and defining the group goals.

- *Seeking information.* In seeking information, one requests facts, ideas, beliefs, and suggestions to expand upon the information provided or to ensure accurate representation of the group members.

- *Providing information.* In providing information, one offers facts, ideas, and new information related to the group's task.

- *Clarifying.* When seeking clarification, one requests elaboration or new information from group members.

- *Consensus testing.* Group members are checked to determine whether they are ready to reach a decision or if a unified position—consensus—is being established.

- *Summarizing*. Restating ideas or information generated in the group should produce a concise summary of what the group has accomplished.

The following maintenance functions become critical as efforts are made to keep the group moving toward the accomplishment of its tasks:

- *Gate keeping*. Gate keeping is a process that ensures the participation of all group members. If one or more individuals are dominating group discussion, they are called upon to curtail their discussion so other group members can participate more fully.

- *Encouraging*. Comments and information of group members are accepted and, when appropriate, praised. Encouraging facilitates full participation by all group members.

- *Harmonizing*. In harmonizing, differences among group members are arbitrated or mediated. The intent is to reduce tensions among group members and to create an atmosphere in which all members feel supported.

- *Standard setting*. Standard setting means reinforcing the group's intent. It includes reminders of group goals and progress toward reaching the goals (Hames & Joseph, 1986).

Properties of People in Groups

As groups demonstrate certain functions, people within those groups tend to play identifiable corresponding roles as well. Kenneth Benne and Paul Sheats (1948) noted three major classifications for group roles:

1. *Group task roles*. Individuals primarily concerned with "getting the job done" usually take on one of the following roles: initiator-contributor—developing or contributing new ideas or in some way stimulating the group to undertake new directions; information seeker; information-giver; coordinator; energizer; procedural technician; or recorder.

2. *Group maintenance roles*. People particularly attentive to the business of "keeping the group together" take on the following specific roles: gatekeeper—helping to keep the group "on track" and move forward toward the achievement of group objectives; or clarifier—helping group members understand what is being said or what is happening in the group.

3. *Individual roles*. People interested almost exclusively in their own self-interests take on these roles, including that of blocker (preventing the group from making progress toward its goals).

People in groups often play different roles in different groups or even shift roles over time in the same group. Most people belong to many different groups in society. Teachers may also be members of church congregations, parent associations, bridge clubs, community councils, and other formal and informal groups, some of which may have been around for years, and others that have popped up overnight to accomplish a specific task. The same person may serve one group as a compromiser (group maintenance role), trying to help others achieve agreement and harmony, and another as an information-giver (group task role), committed to helping the group become productive. That same person may leave a meeting of either group and move directly to a third setting where he or she is so "tuned out" from the proceedings that personal recognition-seeking (individual role) is the only identifiable activity. Everyone serves as members of many groups, performing different functions at different times. This complex shifting of roles occurs for many reasons, including the extent to which a person feels personal affiliation with other group members, the level of acceptance demonstrated by the group members toward the individual, and external issues such as the amount of time available to participate in group activities.

The fact that people serve different roles in different groups has certain serious implications for the educational leader. A teacher, for example, might be perceived as "out of it" and uninvolved in the larger group of the school faculty, and the leader might make assumptions about how that teacher might be treated (or ignored) based on those assumptions. This same teacher might play an entirely different, more positive (and more powerful) role as a member of a curriculum committee, however. A leader who is unaware of the frequency with which such shifts occur runs the risk of ignoring a very important contributor to the goals of the organization.

◈ GROUP EFFECTIVENESS

As noted throughout this chapter, an important responsibility for the effective leader is to analyze the ways in which groups function. Educational leaders also play a critical role in assisting newly created groups to find ways to attain their goals. According to Marion (2002):

> Leaders foster the development of effective group personalities by discouraging the evolution of behaviors that hinder effectiveness, such as interpersonal conflicts, mediocre work habits, or boring work. This is a tricky task, for . . . interactive dynamics are highly complex and idiosyncratic; they resist top-down control and at times seem to have a mind of their own. (p. 315)

For Bernard Bass (1960), group effectiveness consists of two characteristics: *interaction effectiveness* and *task effectiveness*. Interaction effectiveness, as noted earlier, measures the extent to which group activities reduce conflict and enhance harmony within the membership of the group. A group is "good" or effective to the degree that positive, open, and friendly interaction occurs among its members. Task effectiveness measures the extent to which group activities promote, define, clarify, pursue and accomplish the group's goals. Groups high in task effectiveness focus on "getting the job done," at almost any cost.

The balance between these two dimensions of group effectiveness determines a group's success. A *creative* or even *dependent* group may result from too high an emphasis on interaction effectiveness; while these designations are acceptable for brief periods and may even be highly desirable under specific conditions, groups generally cannot exist merely to satisfy members' personal needs for affiliation with others. On the other hand, a group too high in task orientation might be cold and impersonal and ultimately might become an absolute, productive group or even a fight group, with members so caught up in doing a job that they ignore the needs of others. Effective groups balance an appropriate amount of both interaction and task effectiveness.

The relevance of this is important for the educational leader. Educational personnel and classroom teachers, in particular, tend to look at the quality of interaction patterns as a primary indicator of the effectiveness of a particular group. If things are going smoothly and no one is angry with anyone else, then the group is likely to be judged "good," and no further effort is made to analyze the group. Whenever complacency sets in, whenever a school staff, task force committee, subject department, or any other group is satisfied with positive interaction as an outcome, the effective leader prods the group by demanding to see outcomes and concrete results from the group effort. The operating theme needs to be "So you like each other, but what have you *done?*"

On the other hand, leaders must be willing and able to introduce strategies for more positive interactions among group members when the group becomes so blindly focused on accomplishing a given task that all concern for other group members is ignored. The danger in totally ignoring interpersonal needs is that, once a given task is completed, group members will rarely want to work together again toward achieving another goal. Such situations often occur in fields such as engineering, where a high premium is place, perhaps stereotypically, on purely technological skills. Engineers may join forces to design a new product and focus so intensely on the project that no one associated with the effort gets to know anyone else. When the job is done, which may take months, the group immediately dissolves, although maintenance of the group might be useful for the organization to deal with future tasks. This phenomenon was witnessed many times in the aerospace industry during the early 1970s, where engineers who worked side by side to send the first astronauts to the moon found that they knew little about their co-workers when the mission was accomplished. Great isolation and, frequently, personal depression resulted. The educational leader facing such a situation must encourage group members to look at each other as people from time to time so that task accomplishment does not block communication.

⚘ TEAM BUILDING

To this point, the discussion in this chapter has centered almost exclusively on the development of leadership skills associated with being able to identify characteristics of groups. The emphasis has been on analytic skill rather than implementation skill. Few words have been directed to another important responsibility of effective proactive leaders, namely, the creation of successful work groups and teams. At the beginning of this chapter, it was noted that not every collection of people may be properly called a group. Instead, people who are together but who share no common goal form collectivities. In the same vein, when groups form they may or may not have any benefit to the organization. In fact, the opposite may be the case when a group is formed out of common purpose or goal to simply disrupt and even destroy an organization.

In a sense, then, the goal of a leader is to work with groups, but also to direct the energy that is present among these individuals into the creation of a better overall organization. This is generally referred to as the leadership responsibility of creating teams. In order to appreciate the differences that exist between groups and teams, think of the new school administrator who walks into her or his school for the first time. The first thing that is recognized is that there are already many people who work in the school as the faculty and staff. So, in a sense, the administrator typically "inherits" several groups. Groups, however, are not always functioning in ways that enable the school to achieve its goals; they are not necessarily teams. It becomes a critical responsibility to forge the kind of positive relationships that allow collectivities to become groups and groups to become teams.

Chuck Kormanski (1999), in describing the differences between groups and teams, notes that other analysts (Reilly & Jones, 1974) have identified certain criteria which enable a group to be called a "team." First, team members must share goals. This in itself does not distinguish a group from a team. In a team, however, there must be strong commitment to the goals. Group members often say they hold beliefs and goals in common with others, but they are not necessarily committed to the same degree as others. Third, team members must be able to work independently toward achieving the goals. Teams do not consist of friends who espouse common goals but work as a bunch of "lone rangers." Finally, teams submit themselves to the needs of the organization; they are willing to be held accountable for the achievement of certain common goals. By implication, then, the members of a team function in a positive way to enable the organization to be better. Teams are not teams if they work in ways that make them opponents of the good of the overall institution.

The educational leader who is committed to the proactive development of effective teams must recognize that the creation of a team is not likely to be an "overnight" event. One of the most recognized descriptions of how teams are formed comes from the work of Bruce Tuckman and Michael Jensen (1977), who reviewed more than 70 studies of how groups are formed and noted that teams proceed through five discernible stages as they are developed. Peter Fay and A. G. Doyle (1982) later added specific characteristics of team building under each of the Tuckman and Jensen stages. These characteristics may guide the work of the educational leader intent on creating effective teams in his or her school.

Stage 1: Forming

- Members get to know each other and identify behaviors that are acceptable to others in the group.
- People begin to identify themselves as group members, not individuals who must belong to a group.
- Members begin to show reliance on group norms and leaders.
- Members remain hesitant to "plunge into" group work.
- Members retain suspicion of others.
- Minimal work is accomplished.

Stage 2: Storming

- Members continue to express individuality.
- Members begin to recognize the complexity of prescribed tasks.
- Polarization of group members occurs.
- The group appears to be dissolving in disharmony as people strive to retain independence.
- Pecking orders are established.
- Minimal work is accomplished.

Stage 3: Norming

- Members begin to accept the others as team members and express trust in others' roles.
- Emotional conflict begins to abate.
- Members begin to feel comfortable in expressing honest emotions openly.
- A sense of cohesiveness becomes apparent.
- Moderate work is accomplished.

Stage 4: Performing

- The team begins to function as a problem-identifying and problem-solving body.
- Members trust each other, and open communication is the norm.
- A great deal of work is accomplished.

Stage 5: Adjourning

- Members express need and desire for renewal.
- The team celebrates its accomplishments.
- The team wants to stay together, even when its purposes are long met.

A remarkable feature of team development is found in the last "adjourning" stage. The work of forming the team is a challenging task for the leader throughout the first four stages. However, the last stage requires the leader to intervene directly to dissolve the team if it has no further function. Team building is critical, but even more important is the need to recognize when teams have served their purpose. The leader then must encourage all to move on.

⚛ APPLICATIONS TO EDUCATIONAL LEADERSHIP

School supervisors and administrators need to understand how groups function, for they will spend a considerable part of their professional lives working with people in this social pattern. Effective, proactive educational leaders are able to do a number of things regarding groups:

1. *Educational leaders know how to "read" groups.* Administrative and supervisory personnel often work with the teaching staffs of many different schools or even school districts, with frequent shifting from one setting to another and many brief encounters with different groups. The luxury of spending a lot of time getting to know groups is frequently not available. Leaders need to be able to determine quickly whether a group is truly a group, or an existing team, or merely a collectivity. They also need to determine who is really in charge, whether a group is too high in task orientation or interaction orientation, and who is playing what role for what purpose in the group.

2. *Educational leaders need to create groups and teams.* Supervisors and administrators often need to pull people together momentarily to engage in a particular task—an ad hoc committee to review the math curriculum for the district, for example. The first responsibility in creating a group is to establish as firmly as possible the purpose for convening it. If members don't understand the group's purpose from the outset, little further progress toward group formation will be possible. Extending this to the concept of team building, it will be absolutely impossible for a team to be created around unclear goals and visions.

3. *Educational leaders need to keep groups going.* Once a group has been fashioned from a collectivity or a team has been created out of a group, the leader needs to keep it going toward its shared purpose. As noted earlier, groups will periodically shift from problem solving to groups in flight. When this happens, and group members lose their focus on the team's goals, the leader must intervene to reestablish the structure

and purpose of the group. As a result, knowledge of group process skills and group developmental activities is extremely useful for effective school administration and supervision.

SUMMARY

This chapter emphasized the vital need for educational leaders to understand groups. The reason for this emphasis is that groups are found everywhere in the administrator's and supervisor's environment— in administrative and teaching teams, subject departments, school boards, parent associations, student councils, or local school advisory committees. Dozens of formal and informal staff groups are constantly forming and reforming. Leaders must recognize the powerful potential that groups have for contributing to the school environment and the quality of organizational life in schools. Supervisors and administrators who do not recognize this potential will rarely be entirely effective.

The chapter began with a consideration of some definitions of groups and settled on one that defines a group as two or more people assembled for a common, shared purpose. We reviewed some basic features of groups and of the people who form their memberships, along with a review of concepts inherent in group effectiveness. Next, we provided a brief overview of the leader's responsibilities in working toward the development of teams. Finally, the chapter concluded with a listing of some essential skills needed by any educational leader who wishes to build and maintain groups and teams that will effectively aid in reaching the stated goals and objectives of the school in which the groups operate.

Suggested Activities

1. Analyze any group (at a school or in your personal life) in which you are a member to determine if it conforms to the characteristics of groups described throughout this chapter.

2. Interview a practicing administrator or supervisor to determine the numbers and types of groups with which he or she interacts during a typical work week. To what extent are the various types of groups listed by Reddin present in this listing?

Cases to Consider

Read each of the following cases and consider these issues:

- What are the critical issues raised in each case, as they relate to the need to understand the nature and behavior of groups?

- How does each case relate to the development of the concept of proactive leadership?

- In what ways might you suggest a resolution to the issues raised?

Case 12.1   We've Got a Winning Team . . .?

One of the things that Grant Edwards heard over and over about the teachers over at New Horizon Elementary School was that they were one of the most difficult groups of teachers to work with in the entire district. In his own mind, Grant figured that was one of the main reasons why he had been placed there as the new principal. He had just finished his fifth year as the campus administrator at Philbrock Primary, another school that had a less than great reputation when he first went there. Philbrock had also been known as a place where teachers simply did not get along, but Grant was able to get people going in the same direction within about four years. Now he was going to do the same thing at New Horizon. At least he hoped that he could pull off the same change that worked before.

The change process at Philbrock seemed to take forever, and Grant was determined to use what he had learned in the past and move his new school toward teamwork a lot faster. At his last school, for instance, when he first launched his effort to create a sense of teamwork, he seemed to have a lot of support. However, he lived through a horrible second year where all the teachers seemed to be fighting over the most ridiculous matters. As the principal, he thought that he was going to lose his patience as people always seemed to be jockeying for position. That year was really bad, but then everything came into place in the third year.

At New Horizon, Grant started his work to build a new social climate with stronger teamwork as soon as he walked in—almost literally. From the first faculty meeting on, he constantly focused his teaching staff on the notion that they would soon become a better school because they worked together toward a common vision. Rather than repeating the mistake he believed he made at Philbrock, this time Grant decided not to let people wander. He moved people into their instructional teams as soon as the year started. Next, he spent a lot of time each week during the first half of the school year visiting with teams, attending meetings, and generally making certain that the groups did not get off track and begin the type of sniping among themselves that he had seen in his last setting.

Now, it was nearing the beginning of the final six-week marking period for the school year and Grant was really frustrated. He had worked like crazy to make sure that the teams spent time on track, looking at the things that were going to have a positive effect on the New Horizon students. These were ideas and plans that came from the teachers who, in turn, had seemed very enthusiastic earlier in the year. Now, however, all that Grant could see was the same kind of carping and moaning that he had seen at his last school after he had initiated an emphasis on team building.

As the school year was ready to wrap up, Grant considered the very distinct possibility that he was about to admit defeat and go to the superintendent with a request for a transfer to another school where he could be more successful in setting up a true team.

Case 12.2   That's Not What They Told Me a Few Weeks Ago!

Nick Kelly was happy about his new job as the supervisor of science in the Marytown Independent School District. He had been recognized as very effective high school teacher and science department chair in the neighboring Frankton Schools. He was excited about the opportunity to work in the well-respected Marytown school district and about the considerable raise in his salary. In addition, he didn't even have to move. His office in the Marytown central administration building would be closer to his house than the Frankton Senior High was.

The first few months on the job were extremely pleasant. Nick's main duty consisted of meeting the building principals, teachers, and department chairs at all the secondary schools in the district. He also found that he enjoyed the lifestyle of the central office. No bells and no set time schedule meant that he could actually control his daily work life. He even had the luxury of making needed phone calls during the day and going to the restroom whenever he needed!

Nick knew that one of the reasons he was hired was to assist the Marytown Schools in the implementation of a new biology program as part of the high school science curriculum. In general, Marytown did very well in terms of statewide achievement tests each year, but the state biology exam was always a problem. Nick recalled that the same thing had happened in Frankton, and he knew that the implementation of a new program was a painful process. The new program involved a lot of team teaching, and teachers were not always extremely happy about what that would mean for them. Fortunately, he had heard that the same frustration was not likely to occur in Marytown. After all, this new approach to biology might just be the answer that the teachers were looking for in terms of raising their test scores. Besides that, the department chairs from the three Marytown high schools had already met with Nick to assure him that they were highly supportive of the new program and curriculum.

Nick was therefore extremely confident on the morning of the day he was to have an extensive discussion with the teachers in all of the high schools regarding the new biology program. After all, he was still "one of them," because he had just left the classroom a few months ago. He also knew the department chairs were on his side. He had positive feelings as he stepped into the meeting with the teachers from Eastside High School, but he felt a sudden chill in the air shortly after being introduced to the teachers. This was going to be a long meeting, a long day, and an even longer year.

Applying the Concepts

Take the following brief quiz to see how well you can apply some of the concepts in this chapter to an actual administrative or supervisory problem. Answers are found in Appendix I.

"You'll think you've died and gone to heaven. They're like one big happy family here at Wood Valley Elementary." Those were the words that Emily Schaeffer, the assistant superintendent, shared with Mark Richards, the new principal. Mark was an experienced classroom teacher who was taking on his first principalship after 15 years in the classroom and five years as an assistant principal. He was glad to hear Emily's description, but he was a bit skeptical based on his past experiences.

The year began quietly enough. Despite being the "new kid on the block," Mark did not feel as if the teachers had any resentment toward him. All encounters were cordial. Nevertheless, he didn't feel the kind of enthusiasm and "family atmosphere" described by Emily during the job interview.

Wood Valley was a small school, with only 30 teachers. In one sense, it was a great place to begin a career as a principal. But Mark quickly realized that the smallness could also be a restriction. Everyone knew everything about everyone else in the school. Every time Mark walked into a teachers' meeting, he felt as if were intruding on a set of private conversations. He began to understand that each teacher played a certain role, too. Bobbi Wilcox, for example, would always challenge Mark at some point during the meeting. It didn't seem to matter if the issue was a weather report or the new district policy on reporting the immigration status of students—Bobbi would object. And Chuck Starr, a third grade teacher for many years, would always agree with whatever Mark said. Anne Forsyth would say nothing, but her first grade teaching partner, Sylvia Martinez, would always explain what Anne's silence meant on every issue. It was truly an amazing set of behaviors that reminded Mark of the family dinners he had attended after he moved out of his parents' home, when the best part of the meal was not the dessert, but rather the opportunity to head back home to his own place.

1. Mark discovered that the faculty of his new school could easily be classified as a _____.

   a. primary group

   b. secondary group

   c. family group

   d. subversive group

2. In Reddin's terms, the faculty at Wood Valley is most closely aligned with the description of a _____.

   a. production group

   b. creative group

   c. mixed group

   d. group in flight

3. Another way to classify the teachers at the school would be to note that they are a(n) _____.

   a. mature group

   b. dysfunctional group

   c. happy group

   d. immature group

4. The leadership action that Mark must take with his faculty is to
   _____.
   a. stop the teachers from meeting
   b. ensure that the teachers at his school focus more on group mainte-
      nance rather than task functions
   c. ensure that his teachers focus more on task functioning rather than
      group maintenance
   d. disperse many people to different schools in the district
5. The behaviors of Bobbi Wilcox, Chuck Starr, Anne Forsyth, and Sylvia
   Martinez could be classified as examples of _____.
   a. group task roles
   b. group maintenance roles
   c. individual roles
   d. necessary roles

Additional Reading

Delbecq, Andre L., Van de Ven, Andrew H., & Gustafson, David H. (1975). *Group techniques for group planning: A guide to nominal group and delphi processes*. Glenview, IL: Scott, Foresman and Company.

Harris, Thomas E., & Sherblom, John C. (2004). *Small group and team communication* (3rd ed.). Boston: Allyn & Bacon.

Harshman, Carl L., & Phillips, Steven L. (1994). *Teaming up: Achieving organizational transformation*. San Diego: Pfeiffer and Company.

Little, Judith W. (1982). Norms of collegiality and experimentation: Workplace conditions of school success. *American Educational Research Journal, 19* (3): 325–340.

Lumsden, Gay, & Donald Lumsden (2003). *Communicating in groups and teams: Sharing leadership* (4th ed.). Belmont, CA: Wadsworth.

Reddy, W. B. (1988). *Team building blueprints for productivity and satisfaction*. San Diego: Pfeiffer and Company.

Rees, Fran (1991). *How to lead work teams: Facilitation skills*. San Diego: Pfeiffer and Company.

Wellings, R. S., Byham, W. C., & Wilson, J. M. (1991). *Empowered teams*. San Francisco: Jossey-Bass.

⚔ 13 ⚔

The World of Teachers

In 1974, Arthur Blumberg published his analysis of the nature of working relationships between teachers and supervisors. The title of his book, *Supervisors and Teachers: A Private Cold War* is a straightforward description of a truly unfortunate reality in the area of supervisory practice. The relationships that have existed historically between teachers and supervisors in schools have tended to be negative or, at best, typified by uneasy tolerance. There are many probable explanations for this. The earliest historical image of supervision as a form of inspection has provided a powerful continuing image of how supervisors view teachers (i.e., mostly as incompetent and untrustworthy employees). More recently, the lack of friendly relations between supervisors and teachers has been reinforced by collective bargaining agreements outlining clear distinctions between "labor" and "management."

General societal factors also play a role. For example, recent financial constraints and enrollment declines in several districts have raised anxieties for many teachers, creating automatic adversarial relationships in many school systems. Demands for greater accountability placed on social institutions, including schools, have further widened the gulf between teachers and supervisors. However, we must recognize that whatever the unique emphasis on the differences between teachers and formal school leaders is, this emphasis cannot ultimately be allowed to prevent cooperation. Supervisors must develop strategies that permit teachers, supervisors, administrators, and other school staff members to work together as colleagues. Collaboration is clearly an essential ingredient in proactive educational leadership.

This chapter looks at the world of teachers and teaching to provide some insights into the professional life of the people who work in our schools each day. Virtually everyone who serves as a supervisor or school administrator has spent some time as a classroom teacher. Living the life of a teacher, however, does not necessarily provide the kind of understanding required by a *leader*, who must appreciate those subtle features of the world of teaching that will affect the relationships between supervisors and teachers. This chapter does not deal with the analyses of the activity of teaching per se; the emphasis here is on who teachers and supervisors *are*, not *what* teachers do.

To begin, we examine some characteristics of teachers identified by numerous demographic studies, with particular emphasis on those factors identified as having attracted people to the field of teaching in the first place. The chapter concludes with a discussion of the professional environment in which teachers work each day, along with an examination of strategies that may be employed by supervisors who are interested in finding more effective ways to work with teachers as colleagues. The goal in each section is to provide insights into the nature of the life of teachers—the people who ultimately "make things happen" for children in schools.

❧ WHO ARE TEACHERS?

Researchers have tried to answer this question many times over the years. In *The Sociology of Teaching*, Willard Waller (1932) undertook a classic, frequently cited review of the characteristics of teachers. Blanche Geer (1965) and Dan Lortie (1975) carried out similar investigations. These reviews and many others have yielded remarkably similar observations, all of which are relevant for those who invest a large amount of time and energy in working with teachers.

First, research has shown that teachers have often come from humble backgrounds. Historically, teachers have been depicted as representatives of the middle class or even lower-middle class, but these designations are generally meaningless in present-day society; what is clear is that the majority of teachers today do not come from wealthy families.

Unsurprisingly, then, a large number of teachers have traditionally represented the first generation of college graduates in their families. Some evidence suggests that this is changing, as more people in society are able to pursue university studies. Nevertheless, while physicians and attorneys often come from families with a long tradition of access to higher education, the same cannot generally be said of teachers. Lortie (1975) suggested that controlled access to a college education is an important characteristic of teaching. Socioeconomic constraints typically reduce the range of career choices available to those who eventually become teachers.

> Few occupations are in as good a position [as teaching] to take advantage of socioeconomic constraints which limit access to college education. The system of colleges for teacher training turns out to be

more than an institution of socialization—it also recruits. One finds a
kind of "entrapment" as such colleges draw in students of limited
opportunity whose initial interest in teaching is low. (p. 48)

Lortie's observation suggests not only that teachers often come from
families who cannot be selective when it comes to choosing a college, but
also that this characteristic serves to entice people into teaching in the
first place. People from humble family backgrounds who can barely pay
for post-secondary education are still able to look at teaching as a realistic professional goal. The extent of the financial outlay required for medical school or law school prevents most people from pursuing those
careers. Professional preparation for teachers, however, is widely (and
relatively inexpensively) available at public universities; any student can
aspire to a teaching career.

Not surprisingly, this observation has come into play in the controversies surrounding recent reports such as that of The Holmes Group
(1986), which recommended an increase in status and professionalism
for teachers, often including postbaccalaureate education. Critics of such
proposals have suggested that forcing prospective teachers to undergo
significantly greater formal preservice preparation at the university level
will automatically limit access to teaching to those who are able to afford
such advanced training. An old saying suggests that the only career
options available to inner-city residents are those of "teacher, preacher,
or social worker." Clearly this situation may be changing, but the fact
remains that teaching is more easily accessible to more people than most
other professional roles.

Research also suggests that teachers select the classroom as a career
goal fairly early in their lives. Women tend to identify teaching as a likely
career while still in elementary school, and men at least tentatively
choose teaching by the time they leave high school. More recent surveys
suggest that current teachers made these choices at a slightly later point
in their lives, in part no doubt because women now have more options
available than they once did. Evidence continues to suggest, however,
that people who select teaching as a career tend to stay with it, even if
that choice is made slightly later in their lives than it once was.

Profiles of the teaching field in the United States, which have been
developed by state departments of education and professional organizations, substantiate several other enduring characteristics:

1. *Racial characteristics.* Overwhelmingly, teachers in the United States are
   white, although the 10 percent of the teachers who are African Americans come closer to proportionately equaling the nearly 12 percent of
   the general population that is also African American. Of black teachers, more are female than male. Further, members of nonwhite or non-
   black racial groups make up even smaller percentages of the
   classroom-teacher population in this country.

2. *Sex distributions.* Nearly 60 percent of American teachers are female. In addition, there is an historic tendency for the percentage of male teachers to increase at the more advanced levels of schooling (i.e., as one moves from elementary to middle schools).

3. *Age levels and teaching experience.* Recent shortages of teachers in some areas of the country and in some subject specialties are beginning to have an impact on the average ages and years of experience of teachers in the United States. In 1911, the average age of teachers was twenty-four, and the typical teacher had five years' experience in the classroom (Rodgers, 1976). Today, the typical teacher is slightly more than thirty-five years old, with approximately eleven years' experience. These figures are higher in larger school systems where there is traditionally less turnover among teachers.

These assorted characteristics provide us with an interesting snapshot of the people who work in America's classrooms. Teachers do not generally come from wealthy backgrounds, and they often work hard to pay for the education that will enable them to reach their goal—a goal that they have typically established early in life. The "typical" teacher is white, female, in her mid-thirties, and married. For the most part, teachers come from a relatively homogeneous pool of people; they tend to be more similar to, rather than dissimilar from, one another. Research also suggests that most are politically conservative but are probably registered Democrats and are regular churchgoing Protestants. Obviously, these "typical" traits go only a short way toward providing valid and usable data to educational leaders; they tend to obscure the huge numbers of teachers who are liberal Republicans (or even unaffiliated anarchists), who are Jewish, Catholic, or atheist, or who are unmarried—in other words, those who deviate from the statistical norm. To some extent, however, such research-based information can inform supervisory "hunches" or guesses about how teachers may react in different situations.

❧ WHY DO PEOPLE BECOME TEACHERS?

Once again, we can identify patterns in response to this question, but the differences that exist are as wide-ranging as the number of people who are teaching. Still, supervisors can gain some insights into the nature of teachers from the research available.

An extremely important study of why people become teachers was carried out by Dan Lortie during the 1960s and reported in his work, *Schoolteacher*, published in 1975. In this work, five major attractors to teaching were identified:

1. *The interpersonal theme.* Perhaps the response most frequently given by teachers to questions about their selection of teaching as a career is based on their desire for continuing contact with young people. Other

professions also enable people to maintain steady interactions with the young, but as Lortie (1975) noted, "Unlike other major middle-class occupations involving children, such as pediatric nursing and some kinds of social work, teaching provides the opportunity to work with children who are neither ill nor especially disadvantaged" (p. 27).

2. *The service theme.* Some people select careers in teaching because they believe that, by devoting their lives to this work, they can fulfill some special mission in society. The aspiring teacher is taking on a responsibility to provide service by engaging in what many societies in the world view as an honored (if not well compensated) vocation.

3. *The continuation theme.* Some individuals become teachers because they were comfortable as students sheltered in the world of schools. As they grew, they continued to be so attached to life in schools that they could not bear to leave that environment. Lortie summarized this phenomenon by observing, "Some [teachers] said they 'liked school' and wanted to work in that setting; others mentioned school-linked pursuits and the difficulty in engaging in outside educational institutions" (Lortie, 1975, p. 29). Supervisors should recognize that those who choose to teach because they wish to stay where they are comfortable are unlikely to engage in activities that will change the status quo of schools.

4. *Material benefits.* Surprisingly (especially to many teachers!), Lortie discovered that some people selected teaching for reasons of prestige, money, and employment security. This seems to contradict the general perception that teachers suffer anxiety because they lack these amenities, and this anxiety may be a feature in the attitudes of teachers now in the classroom. We can understand how "material benefits" can motivate some people to become teachers if we recall the reviews of background characteristics which show that teachers traditionally come from relatively modest socioeconomic groups and are often among the first members of their families to attend college. The opportunity for a steady, relatively secure job that offers a beginning salary of at least $30,000 in most parts of the country for ten months of work might indeed be appealing. For many, an entry-level teaching job may be considerably more lucrative than a job that was held by a parent for many years. In short, new teachers may sometimes look at their chosen profession not as one that "pays well" but rather as one that "pays better." The more time spent as a teacher, however, the less powerful this motivation becomes; teachers see neighbors and friends in their middle-class worlds who are able to move toward financial rewards at a rate and level far beyond that available to a classroom teacher.

5. *Time compatibility theme.* An old saying suggests that the three best reasons for teaching are "June, July, and August." Lortie and many others have found considerable truth in this notion: People find teaching appealing because it does, when compared to most professions, offer

more time for the pursuit of other interests and responsibilities. Although teachers may not always admit it, teaching appeals to many because one can go to work each day before most people get on the freeways, arrive home or go shopping before others, and enjoy protracted vacation periods throughout the year. Teaching has traditionally been recognized as a job that allows women to raise children while working full time: They can put their own kids on a school bus in the morning, go to work, and return home at about the same time their children do.

Lortie's study of the reasons why people enter teaching remains a milestone for those interested in learning more about the realities of life in the classroom. Other motivating factors have been identified in other studies. David Armstrong, Kenneth Henson, and Thomas Savage (1993) suggested the following ideas:

1. *Nice working conditions.* Many teachers comment on their favorable impressions of both the physical environments in which they work and the kinds of people with whom they work. In addition, teaching is perceived as a job that allows for considerable personal autonomy, which many people find appealing.

2. *Lack of routine.* Teachers who have had to depend on other jobs at other points in their lives, often jobs with great monotony attached, find teaching refreshingly unpredictable. Students are diverse, and as a result, each day in the classroom is to some extent different. In addition, teachers control some of what they do in the classroom and can "program in" variety. Finally, the typical school-year "life cycle" contains many natural peaks and valleys, sometimes predictable and sometimes not.

3. *Importance of teaching.* As Lortie's "service" theme suggests, some teachers do what they do because they view their work as a way to transmit culture to new generations, provide information to youngsters, serve as positive role models, and achieve scores of other important goals that will ultimately serve as part of the design for a more positive society.

4. *Excitement of learning.* Many teachers were eager learners when they were in school, and they continue to believe in the fundamental value of learning. Many recall their own sense of excitement as they acquired new knowledge and assume that, as teachers, they will stimulate the same learning and bring about similar challenges for new generations of students.

What other answers can we provide to the question, "Why do people teach?" In addition to this list of attractors, Lortie also identified other factors that tend to direct people toward teaching. He noted, for example, that people become teachers because they have identified with a single teacher at some point in their schooling, because someone in their family had been a teacher, through "labeling" by significant others, or because aspirations to some other field (e.g., medicine or engineering) have been blocked by socioeconomic or other factors. What is remarkable in most reviews of the reasons people become teachers is the virtual absence of what might be called "negative influences." For example, virtually no teachers suggested that their own early experience with poor teachers had compelled them to try to "do something better" than they had seen in their classrooms. This contrasts, incidentally, with reasons often cited by teachers who move into administration and supervision (that they can do better than what they see others do).

⊘ WHAT DO TEACHERS DO?

Teachers instruct students. In addition, they learn how to function in an environment with some very special characteristics—characteristics that need to be appreciated by educational leaders who wish to find strategies for enhancing the effectiveness of school staff.

The General Nature of Teaching

Anne Lieberman and Lynne Miller (1984) carried out an extensive analysis of what teachers' lives are like, and they considered the implications of these "social realities" of teaching for those who wish to improve the quality of educational practice. Lieberman and Miller noted that to understand teaching we must appreciate the nature of teaching. Thus, they identified the following features:

1. *Teaching style is highly personalized.* Because teachers must constantly work with large groups of students (often twenty-five or more at a time) but must do so in as individualized a fashion as possible, teachers often develop highly personalized and idiosyncratic strategies. When teachers settle upon their own ways of dealing with the contradictions between group and individual, they become quite defensive and even militant regarding their strategies. What they do often becomes "the right way" to do things.

2. *Teachers' rewards are derived primarily from students.* Lieberman and Miller (1984) noted that "the greatest satisfaction for a teacher is the feeling of being rewarded by one's students" (p. 2), and these rewards tend to be found in the affirmation by students that a teacher is doing his or her job properly. Students show support for teachers by participating in class discussions, studying more diligently for exams, or volunteering for special projects. Teachers recognize these behaviors and perceive them as signs that what they are doing is "good." Importantly, teachers usually do not perceive this type of approval as a regular part of their contact with peers, superiors or other colleagues in their schools.

3. *Teachers are uncertain of the link between their teaching and student learning.* Teaching is much like "shooting an arrow into the air, never knowing where it may fall." Most teachers are continually frustrated by their inability to see the ultimate effects of their work. Not knowing the "final product" has for years been one of the most often discussed limitations on teaching as a profession. Teachers never did really know whether what they did in the past, or what they are doing now, will serve any truly positive purposes. According to Lieberman and Miller (1984),

> A teacher does his or her best, develops curricula, tries new approaches, works with individuals and groups, an yet never knows for sure what are the effects. One hopes the children will get it, but one is never sure. A teachers operates out of a kind of blind faith. (p. 3)

This characteristic of the workaday life of teachers was also recognized by Joseph McDonald (1992) and Alan Tom (1984), who developed the metaphor of "teaching as a moral craft" and made the following observation:

> This . . . [relationship of] teacher behavior to student learning . . . is what I call the billiard ball hypothesis. The pool player [teacher] aims the cue ball [his or her behavior] so that it will strike the target billiard ball [the student] at exactly the right angle to cause the billiard ball to go into the pocket [the achievement of what the student is supposed to learn]. (p. 55)

This analogy is flawed only in its failure to recognize the teachers' traditional perspective that, just as they strike the cue ball, they are forced to turn their backs to the table and never see if they have met their targets.

4. *The knowledge base of teaching is weak.* Teaching, unlike medicine, law, engineering, and other professions, possesses no unified and highly codified body of knowledge that provides clear direction to those who wish to "cover what is important." Educators agree neither on what should be taught nor what methods should be used to teach. Is Louis Rubin (1985) correct in emphasizing the "artistry of teaching?" Are the "scientific" approaches to the analysis of teaching more appropriate? This general lack of consensus concerning the content and techniques of "good" teaching provides a weak knowledge base that in turn impacts negatively on the sense of commitment felt by many classroom teachers. Often, this perception by teachers that they do not have the requisite knowledge needed to have a positive effect on learners must be overturned by a belief in themselves. As McDonald (1992) noted, "Whenever they teach, teachers must to some extent swallow the uncertainty they feel, believe wholeheartedly in their goals and efforts, even though riddled by doubt" (p. 6).

5. *The goals of teaching are vague and often conflicting.* What are teachers "supposed" to do? Disseminate a fixed body of knowledge? Entertain?

Babysit? The lack of clarity about a teacher's role leaves teachers with no true understanding of a single purpose. "When all goals are addressed, no goals are met" (p. 5). Lieberman and Miller noted that, because of this vagueness and corresponding conflict concerning purpose, "individual teachers make their own translations of [educational] policy and this contributes directly to the lack of consensus often found in schools" (pp. 5–6).

6. *Control norms are seen as necessary features of schools.* Educational goals are not always clear, but the end result usually is: Schools are expected to exercise strong control over young people to guarantee that social order is maintained. This educational "fact of life" is demonstrated almost daily in schools where parents, other teachers, supervisors, administrators, and often students hold in high esteem those teachers who "hold the kids in line." By contrast, the inability to "control" students is typically viewed as a serious flaw in a teacher's professional performance, and is in fact often seen as grounds for dismissal.

7. *Professional support is lacking.* Paradoxically, although contact between people (i.e., teacher-to-student, student-to-teacher) is a primary feature of teaching, teachers are remarkably isolated as workers, particularly from colleagues and other adults. This lack of collegiality usually begins with the first classroom assignment where "rookie" teachers who have just completed their student teaching are thrown into the same setting—with the same expectations for professional performance—as considerably more experienced teachers.

Stuart Palonsky left his position as a university professor to spend two years teaching social studies in a suburban high school. In his analysis of that experience, *900 Shows a Year: Looking at Teaching from a Teacher's Side of the Desk* (1986), Palonsky provides a poignant description of the loneliness of teaching:

> Lou was one of the teachers who had retreated from the mainstream of the faculty, and he defined teaching personally and in isolation from other teachers. At one time he had played tennis with Sal, and he considered one of the French teachers to be his friend, but these teachers were now married, and Lou was divorced. He claimed he no longer maintained social relationships with his colleagues, and he rarely went to faculty parties. From our conversations, it did not appear that he liked most of the other teachers, but he enjoyed teaching. (p. 7)

Examples such as this are not unique in the world of schools. It is not uncommon to meet teachers with many years of professional experience who have little contact with colleagues. It is not unusual to hear of cases where no one other than administrators or supervisors have ever seen other teachers teach, and even more remarkable and equally lamentable are cases where teachers have never had the opportunity to ever seen another teacher teach.

8. *Teaching is an art*. Lieberman and Miller concluded their analysis by suggesting that the efforts to turn teaching into a precise science are wrong. "... in the long haul, more artistry... is practical as teachers struggle to adjust and readjust, to make routines, and establish patterns, only to recast what has been done in a new form to meet a new need or a new vision. Teachers are best viewed as craftspeople; the reality of teaching is of a craft learned on the job" (p. 94). Efforts to make teachers conform to behavioral patterns that represent "good teaching" are usually futile because artists struggle to express their uniqueness and resist conformity.

Louis Rubin (1985) provided the following list of features normally associated with "artistic teaching." Artistic teachers:

- Focus on the subtleties of teaching—how to motivate, pace, and control students—which invigorate basic instructional methods and subject matter;

- Improvise tactics for reaching objectives and overcoming difficulties that are creative, inventive, and know how to "go with the flow";

- Take advantage of unexpected opportunities to clarify ideas and reinforce concepts;

- Make use of their intuition and hunches to guide the modification of routine practices and have a special sense of when to throw away the lesson plan;

- Set high expectations for themselves and their students;

- Find the most efficient and expedient ways of getting things done;

- Are good storytellers and are sensitive enough to know how to use temporary digressions on related topics to enrich lessons, stimulate interest, and increase student involvement;

- Base their control of learning activities on the nature of student behavior;

- Take great pride in what they do and in the achievements of their students;

- Concentrate on a few dominant goals that they believe to be central to their purposes as teachers;

- Respect their own convictions; and

- Devote as much time as possible to whatever they enjoy most in teaching.

In addition to the issues noted above, it is clear from discussions with many teachers now working in the field that there is an increasing sense of pressure derived from the belief that public expectations for more accountable schools are actually evaluations of teacher performance. Emphasis on standardized testing is often viewed by teachers as a disrespect for professional judgment. The mandate that, as a result of

NCLB, all school teachers might now be "highly qualified" implies that prior to 2002, most U.S. teachers were, in fact, *not* qualified to do the jobs for which they continue to be largely underpaid.

The "Dailiness" of Teaching

Supervisors and others who wish to understand the teacher's world must appreciate, according to Lieberman and Miller (1984), not only its general nature but also its dailiness.

Predictability

The life of a teacher follows certain predictable cycles and rhythms—as anyone who has spent time around schools will agree. Teachers begin each day at the same time, drink coffee at the same time, even go to the bathroom at the same time each day; all of these activities are regulated by the need to provide "coverage" for students. "For the majority of them they are bound in space and time. In most instances, teachers need the permission of the principal to leave the building during school hours" (Lieberman & Miller, 1984, p. 5). The predictable rhythms of each school day occur in the context of the larger rhythms of each school year. Every day, the excitement of September slows until the holiday season begins at the end of October and continues through early January. Winter doldrums set in, and days are dull until March or April when spring break occurs. The weeks after that vacation are almost always marked by the increasing fatigue of teachers who are trying to cope with the decreasing interest of students, who are already anticipating summer vacation. The same cycle is found in virtually every school—public and private, elementary or secondary—across the nation each year, and significant change in its peaks and valleys are highly unlikely.

Interestingly, the observable and predictable nature of the normal teaching day and year contradicts the perception of many entering teachers that the classroom represents a way of life free from routine and predictability. Teacher-student relationships within individual classrooms may indeed be unpredictable, but that spontaneity is not characteristic of the large number of teachers' lives. Palonsky provides a noteworthy portrait of the "grind" of daily school life:

> For the most part, one day blended with the next, with little to distinguish one from another. I saw the same teachers at the same time every day, said hello to the same people as often as a dozen times a day, but rarely engaged any of them in more substantive conversation. I arrived at school at the same time; I ate lunch at the same time; and I left at the same time every day. (1986, pp. 81–82)

Regulation

The daily world of teachers is also a highly regulated one. Some of these rules are the official policies and procedures specified by the local board of education. In this sense, teaching differs little from other occupations where employees are told when to start work, how many sick days are available, how to complete certain forms, or what to do when dealing with emergencies or crises.

Other "rules" associated with teaching, as Lieberman and Miller point out, are not formal policies but rather informal norms that serve to govern the behavior of classroom instructors. Two important norms are the expectations that teachers will always be practical and private.

Teachers are expected to be *practical* and to find immediately applicable solutions to whatever problems they encounter in the classroom; perhaps the worst thing that can be said about an educator's ideas is that they are "theoretical." As noted in chapter 2, most educators have a strong antitheoretical bias, which both results from and reinforces the practicality norms found in schools. More research on how this norm has developed over time might help in determining if teachers tend to be people who view the world in concrete and nonabstract terms in the first place, or if the nature of teaching forces its practitioners to look for practical solutions rather than theoretical concepts.

Privacy in teaching "means not sharing experiences about teaching, about classes, about students, about perceptions" (Lieberman & Miller, 1984, p. 8). Unfortunately, and contrary to Shirley Heck's and Ray Williams's (1984) description of teachers as colleagues, the norm of collegiality has traditionally been absent from most schools; teachers, of course, lose a great deal by not having the opportunity to share their work with co-workers. The strong pull toward privacy derives at least in part from the fact that unobserved people cannot be judged as incompetent. Do teachers believe that they have had inadequate preservice preparation for their roles and consequently spend a large percentage of their professional lives trying to disguise what they fear are inadequacies in their performance? Or do teachers close their classroom doors to others because they have learned, either through personal experience or via oral tradition, that anyone who sees you teach will inevitably find fault? In short, is retreat to privacy one of the strategies employed as part of Arthur Blumberg's (1974) "cold war"?

Limitation of Contact

Interactions among teachers are typically quite limited. The vast majority of interpersonal contact experienced by classroom teachers is with children, not with coworkers. The average time teachers spend with adults each day is usually less than half an hour. If teachers are asked to indicate the amount of time spent in "meaningful talk" with adults (i.e., not lounge chitchat concerning yesterday's football game, upcoming television shows, or momentary gossip, for example), the average amount of time is generally reduced. Teachers live in a world surrounded by people, but with little opportunity for discussion with peers. A serious consequence of this lack of contact is that teachers assigned to classes with difficult students live daily lives filled to overflowing with negative human contacts. No wonder that at the end of the school day, many teachers have trouble being animated in discussions about new approaches to math instruction, team learning, or performance-based education. As Lieberman and Miller (1984) suggest:

> For most teachers in most schools, teaching is indeed a lonely enter-
> prise. With so many people engaged in so common a mission in so
> compact a space and time, it is perhaps the greatest irony—and the
> greatest tragedy of teaching—that so much is carried on in self-
> imposed and professionally sanctioned isolation. (p. 11)

⚘ WHAT DO TEACHERS EXPECT OF LEADERS?

Teachers work in close proximity with those who hold leadership positions in their schools each day. One would assume that this type of contact would result in clear understanding of what it is that principals, assistant principals, and other supervisors and administrators do. However, teachers spend most of their time in their classes, working with students. They simply do not have that much time to engage in direct observation and analysis of another professional role.

Despite this limitation, teachers do have strong feelings about what they wish their leaders would do. Joseph Blase and Peggy Kirby (1992) engaged in one of the most comprehensive reviews of this topic and noted that, contrary to popular opinion which states that teachers often view the best administrators as those with whom they have no contact, there are some clear expectations for leadership behavior. They note eight specific areas in which teachers have indicated that they look positively toward the involvement of principals:

1. *Teachers seek principals who use praise honestly, openly, and sincerely.* This is not to suggest that teachers want to hear nothing but positive statements coming from the mouths of their principals and assistant principals. To the contrary, they want people who are honest and straightforward with comments, and who provide praise when it is warranted.

2. *Teachers look to their principals for high expectations regarding professional performance.* Teachers do not want to "get away with" not doing their work. Instead, they respect most those administrators who have a clear vision of what they want to see accomplished in their schools, and then hold themselves and teachers accountable for achieving that vision.

3. *Teachers want to be involved.* While it may seem contradictory to what was noted earlier about teachers often being aloof and disengaged from others in school settings, teachers want to feel as if they are a part of the activities in a school. This is particularly true when decisions are being made that have a direct effect on the world of teachers. In these cases, they want to be able to make their opinions heard.

4. *Teachers seek professional autonomy.* Those who work in classrooms perceive themselves as professionals, even when the public does not hold the same opinion. Teachers believe that they have expertise in what they teach and how they teach it. Therefore, they value greatly those educational leaders who demonstrate respect to their colleagues by not interfering with and micromanaging the teaching process.

5. *Teachers want administrators to support them.* Blase and Kirby refer to this as "leading by standing behind" (1992, pp. 64–76). In general, it means that teachers want leaders who provide opportunities for professional development, necessary instructional materials, and support in such matters as student discipline and parent confrontations.

6. *Teachers do not wish to be told how to do their jobs.* At the same time, they know that they can often improve their performance in certain areas, and they know that leaders can help them. What they respect most are those situations where their principals tactfully show them how, or "nudge them" toward different practices.

7. *Teachers respect principals who act in a way that earns respect.* Teachers do not respond favorably to those who tell them, either directly or indirectly, that they must comply with rules and commands simply because the principal has the formal authority to command this form of followership. Instead, they will follow and respect those who engage in a different form of authority based on expertise and ability.

8. *Perhaps, above all, teachers want principals to be "mirrors to the possible."* Again, perhaps in contrast with common opinion, teachers want to do a good job; they want to be challenged to do great things on behalf of their students. Such efforts must come about in a climate where everyone is challenged to achieve success. Principals must be clear advocates of a vision for their schools. Even when teachers do not necessarily fall in line with every element of the vision, they will respect leaders who have a vision that goes beyond simple daily survival in their buildings.

❧ So What Can Leaders Do?

This chapter has painted a picture of the lives of teachers and the business of teaching which, while accurate, is also quite depressing. Other brush strokes could be added to this picture, including "the poor public image and inadequate public appreciation" (Geer, 1965, p. 6) faced by teachers and the general lack of esteem, low pay, and social status afforded them. These latter characteristics clearly have a serious impact on the daily lives of educators, but we do not dwell on them because a leader, proactive or otherwise, can do little to modify societal perceptions that have emerged over time. A leader alone cannot make the public value teachers and pay them more money. A leader can, however, modify some of the daily conditions faced by teachers. Even if changes are not always possible, the leader who wants to make a difference will be more effective and more readily accepted by teachers if he or she appreciates the characteristics of teachers' lives.

Daniel Duke's thoughtful analysis, entitled *Teaching: An Imperiled Profession* (1984), found many of the same conditions discussed above not only to be present but also to be likely to cause paralysis in both teachers and schools. In Duke's view, the greatest constraints to teacher effectiveness are rooted in *ambiguity* (teachers must cope completely with the lack of rationality and consensus surrounding goals and purposes) and *insecurity* (teachers face instability in jobs, social status, assignments, and finance). In response to these issues, Duke proposed a reconceptualization of teaching as a profession, guided by the following "What if . . ." considerations:

1. *What if we stopped acting as if there were one best type of teacher and began valuing diversity?* If educators believe firmly that schools must deal with the uniqueness of individual children as learners, why do many of these same educators assume comparability and similarity among all teachers? Particular teachers might best be matched with particular students who possess the same values and perspectives on learning. Policy makers and other educational leaders need to acknowledge the true value of individual differences among teachers. Some leaders spend as much time learning about the individual qualities of the teachers with whom they work as they do watching those same teachers perform in classrooms and thus more completely appreciate the differences and richness of their teaching staff.

2. *What if teaching were reconceptualized as a set of complex technical skills, including problem solving, hypothesis testing, decision making, information processing, logical analysis, and resource allocation?* We need to define teaching as an activity that requires as much skill as it does pure emotional commitment to children. The latter is clearly important, but society values skills and knowledge as well as commitment. Some leaders work with their teaching staffs to design and implement action-research projects that not only increase the knowledge base regarding local school issues but also promote thinking and acting by teachers that go beyond traditional patterns and limitations.

3. *What if teachers would be regarded as discipline-based scholars as well as instructors?* Would the consequence of this reconceptualization of teaching further enhance the strength and positive image of the profession? As Duke noted, "Such action might also help bridge the gulf now separating public school teachers from professors" (Duke, 1984, p. 139). In this way, too, teachers may become more actively involved as researchers in their professional fields.

4. *What if part of a teacher's time was spent teaching adults?* One of the traditional limitations on the teaching profession is that teachers work

only with children. Could we redefine schools as total learning communities, where adults and younger people come together on occasion to partake in mutual learning experiences? Such a setting would be consistent with the desirable behaviors of effective organizations described by Peter Senge in his book, *The Fifth Discipline* (1990). Further, teachers might then be seen not only as true specialists with important bodies of knowledge, but also as possessors of special skills for disseminating that knowledge.

5. *What if students came to school with questions and teachers helped them find answers?* Would such a turnaround in traditional student-teacher roles decrease the familiar patterns of passive learning now found in most schools? Can teachers be viewed increasingly as facilitators of the learning process for students, rather than providers of all knowledge to students? Such a pattern might be an important step toward the goal of making students control their own learning.

6. *What if teachers at age fifty-five did not have to perform the same functions that teachers perform at age twenty-two?* Is it not reasonable to assume that some teachers do some tasks better when they are younger, and others have different insights when they are older? In most schools, a beginning teacher is just as likely as a thirty-year veteran to be assigned an Algebra I class. Interchangeability of teaching assignments (and teachers) is a time-honored tradition in school administration growing out of the Scientific Management era in the early 1900s, but some creative placement of teachers might benefit the quality of interactions between students and teachers and might also serve to make teachers more satisfied with their professional status. Increasingly, supervisors are aware of the particular needs of adults as learners at different times during their lives and realize that beginning teachers and inexperienced teachers are not the same.

❧ How Can Leaders Attract and Support Good Teachers?

Duke's suggestions are a good way to begin the process of thinking about ways in which the teaching profession might be changed over time. If that type of fundamental change does not begin to occur, it will be increasingly difficult to attract bright and energetic individuals to move toward careers in the teaching profession. Even more important is the fact that ways need to be identified to keep qualified and high-quality teachers in the classroom. There are some very concrete and immediate things that supervisors and administrators might do on a daily basis to enhance the quality of teachers' work life in schools, thereby making the choice of teaching a more desirable career path for individuals to follow.

First, educational leaders must find ways of restructuring teachers' daily schedules so that more prolonged, if not more frequent, contact is possible among adults on the school staff. At present, teaching assignments are almost universally constructed in ways that make contact impossible; teachers see colleagues only during the mad dash that usually represents a daily "duty-free lunch period." Prep times, when provided, are rarely arranged so teams of teachers can get together. In many schools, duty assignments appear more highly valued than opportunities for communication and professional dialogue among peers.

Second, supervisors should examine those factors that attract teachers to the field and use that information in promoting a more effective learning environment. What is suggested here is that leaders can structure some elements of the teacher's world so that the factors that attracted teachers to the field in the first place are more evident. As noted earlier in this chapter, one of the strongest drawing points to teaching for many people is the opportunity to have contact with students. In reality, however, a teacher's life is often filled with so many administrative responsibilities that the ability to spend much meaningful time with young people is severely constrained. Leaders who can find ways of cleaning administrative tasks off teachers' desks would go far toward encouraging those teachers to feel much happier about their jobs; the long-term result of this satisfaction would be improved teaching and enhanced student learning. This same strategy may not work for all teachers, but the same basic premise—that leaders need to become aware of teachers' real characteristics and concerns—is always an effective way for supervisory and administrative personnel to work with staff.

Educational leaders who are intent upon getting performance from teachers need to spend time analyzing any conflict with teachers that is linked only to the nature of the roles rather than to the people who fulfill these roles. At many times in the life of an organization, people will not get along, but these times should not be based solely or even largely on job titles. Supervisors, administrators, and teachers do not have to live in a state of constant war, cold or otherwise.

Finally, the terms of recent efforts to increase public education accountability are changing the landscape of teaching. Leaders need to recognize that, in light of the terms of NCLB, the world of teachers is beginning to shift from careers that were driven by the traditional images described in this chapter to many new images of teaching. In these days of "fully qualified teachers" being defined only in terms of teachers who meet requirements for state certification and licensure, the profiles of dedicated teachers who have looked forward to careers in classrooms since they were students have changed drastically. The result in many cases is the increasing presence of teachers in our classrooms who tend to view teaching as a "job" that was available when other careers changed. Former engineers now teach math, insurance salespersons teach third grade, and recent army officers are high school English teachers as the result of expedited programs that offer certification, but not always sufficient preparation. The net result is a world of teachers where the traditional "attractors" noted here are no longer valid. Principals and supervisors will likely find fewer career teachers in their schools.

⚜ SUMMARY

This chapter reviewed the world of teaching and teachers as it relates to the responsibilities of the proactive leader. We began by looking at who teachers are and noted that, for the most part, those of us who have spent time in the classroom are far more similar than not, in terms of our socioeconomic backgrounds, value orientations, and stated reasons for having gone into teaching in the first place. Next, there was a review of the general characteristics of the life of a teacher, including isolation from one's colleagues and other adults and the expectation that teachers will enforce certain norms not always supported in their own minds. Finally, there were some suggestions as to ways in which supervisors or administrators can increase their sensitivity toward the realities of teaching in order to enhance the quality of the teaching-learning process in their schools.

Suggested Activities

1. Conduct a series of brief interviews with a group of teachers to determine such information as their backgrounds, reasons for becoming teachers, and reasons for continuing in the classroom. Compare your findings to those presented in this chapter concerning the characteristics of teachers. What generalizations can you make from the similarities and differences found?

2. Using the features of the lives of teachers described by Lieberman and Miller, conduct a survey instrument and ask a group of teachers in your school or district to respond in terms of their agreement or disagreement with the views of the authors. Are teachers, for example, as lonely in their work as suggested? If some of these perceptions have changed, what do you perceive as the cause(s) of these changes?

3. Review the propositions for improvement listed by Daniel Duke with two or three practicing administrators or supervisors to determine if they have any concrete suggestions for ways in which those strategies for improvement might be implemented in their schools or district.

4. Interview several high school seniors or beginning university students to ask them if they have ever considered careers in teaching. If they have, ask them what attracts them to that choice of career. If they indicate no interest, ask them to explain what they consider to be disincentives to teaching.

5. Interview one or two teachers who have gone through "alternative teacher certification programs" to determine the reasons why they have decided to pursue careers in education. Compare the findings of your interview research with the traditional descriptions of why people go into teaching that were noted in this chapter.

Cases to Consider

Read each of the cases below and consider the following:

- What are the critical issues raised in each case as they relate to an analysis of teachers and their work environment?
- How does each group relate to the development of the concept of proactive leadership?
- In what ways might you suggest a resolution to the issues raised?

Case 13.1   Welcome to the World of Technology

A regular part of every school board agenda for the Weebanks Falls Schools is a report to the board by the superintendent, Janice Jamieson. Normally, Janice has relatively little exciting news to present. After all, Weebanks Falls is a small district, and nothing too remarkable ever seems to happen in town. Tonight would be different, however. Janice had just gotten word that the grant that she and Tom Dawkins, principal at Weebanks primary, had written had just been funded. The State Department of Education was awarding their district over $100,000 to support the implementation of a new computerized curriculum management system. It would be one of three pilot projects funded in the state.

The proposal was quite simple. It required teachers to input daily grades from quizzes, homework, tests, or whatever they might require of each student on a daily basis. In addition, teachers would be expected to define curricular objectives at the beginning of each week. Next, the teachers would be expected to develop individual student profiles based on progress in their classes to that date, and additional information found in the cumulative files kept in the main office. There would be no mistaking the fact that this would be a very innovative approach to meeting the new accountability standards required by the state legislature for school districts to implement within the next three years. The teachers, no doubt, would be very happy to hear of the grant. After all, each of the three schools in the district would now get enough new laptop computers that teachers could regularly check them out, take them home, and enter all the required data for the new system. Janice was certain that the teachers would be really thrilled to get a chance to make use of some really state-of-the-art technology. Further, the project would also provide Internet connections for every teacher at no cost, provided that they made use of the information taken from the Net and documented its use in their daily classes.

When Homer Fredericks, president of the board, invited Janice to offer her monthly report, she happily told the school board and all others assembled for the meeting about the grant. She went into great detail about all the things that teachers would now be able to do, and how the grant would truly bring Weebanks Falls into the high-tech world! She was a bit puzzled, however, during her presentation. As she got to various points in the description of the project, she noted that teachers in the room seemed to become somewhat agitated. In fact, by the end of her presentation, she noticed that the dozen or so teachers who were in attendance had all drifted out to the lobby of the board offices. She could see through the windows on the boardroom's doors that they seemed to be having their own meeting.

Case 13.2 Why Aren't They Interested?

Jack Charles had just taken the principalship at Halsted Middle School, one of three middle schools in the Georgetown Schools. This was to be his second principalship. He had spent five very successful years as the administrator of the Daley Intermediate School on the other side of Georgetown.

While at Daley, Jack had developed a positive reputation as a very effective manager. He had taken a school with high student absentee rates and teachers with low morale to a point where it had become apparent that things had been totally reversed. Jack's former school was now recognized as a model of positive change. When it was clear that Daley was well on its way to success, Jack decided it was time to move on and seek new challenges. He applied for the opening at Halsted. Because of his previous work at Daley, Jack Charles was an easy choice as the new principal. The school board and superintendent were confident that, if Jack Charles was able to improve a school with the past bad reputation of Daley, he would do an even better job with the highly experienced child-centered teachers at Halsted.

One of the reasons for such a significant change at Daley, Jack believed, was that he was successful in promoting a lot of involvement and participation from the teaching staff, a group that had been described by many to be totally disconnected from their students and the school over the past several years. At Halsted, Jack was looking forward to the immediate implementation of many new instructional practices, such as team teaching and cooperative learning. Although he had heard stories about how committed the teachers at Halsted were, he felt that a successful change would be possible only if he could get his teachers involved with the new practices that he was promoting. As he planned for the next school year, teacher involvement was the last thing that Jack worried about. He assumed that, while it was critical, it would be simple to achieve. After all, Jack's predecessor had missed a great opportunity for years; he had rarely asked his staff for input on major issues, despite the fact that the teachers were recognized across the district as outstanding educators. Clarence Stevens, the previous Halsted principal, was a nice person who firmly believed that he was most effective in making certain that "teachers teach and administrators administer."

Jack was really excited about how this year would progress. He was now about to lead his first full faculty meeting, where the topic would be how to encourage all teachers to become leaders and seize every moment for true empowerment.

As Jack made his plans for sharing his vision with the teachers, he shared his agenda with his assistant principal, Sarah Lowe. She had fifteen years of experience at Halsted, both as an administrator and as a teacher. "Jack," she said, "I like your idea of promoting greater involvement by teachers, but get ready for a room full of silence when you start talking that way. It just won't work here at Halsted."

Applying the Concepts

The following brief quiz is designed to improve your skills in applying some of the concepts discussed in this chapter. Read the brief introductory case and then respond to the multiple-choice questions. You will find the answers in the Appendix.

As the new principal of a school in your school district, you begin the year by making your teachers understand that you expect them to do their share with regard to required attendance reporting, preparing very detailed lesson plans each week, keeping track of supplies, and many other similar matters. You believe that this is a reasonable approach to delegating responsibilities. After all, you know that not all of the important work in an effective school must be done by administrators or clerks.

1. By taking this approach to working with staff, you run the risk of violating which of the following traditional attractors to teaching that Lortie identified through his research?

    a. the interpersonal theme

    b. the continuation theme

    c. the material benefits theme

    d. the time compatibility theme

2. Another thing that you do is to make certain that teachers engage in firm, fair, and consistent behavioral management of students in their classes at all times. This is an example of which of the following "social realities of teaching" identified by Lieberman and Miller?

    a. Professional support is lacking.

    b. The goals of teaching are vague and often conflicting.

    c. Control norms are seen as necessary features of schools.

    d. The knowledge base of teaching is often weak.

3. Because your teachers are starting to display a great deal of disagreement with your actions as the principal, you decide to start sending a daily memo to them indicating that they are doing a "great job," or similar kinds of statements. These now come from your office two or three times each week. However, the apparent conflict persists, possibly because _____.

a. teachers seek principals who use praise honestly, openly, and sincerely

b. teachers look to their principals for high expectations regarding professional performance

c. teachers want to be involved

d. teachers want administrators to support them

Additional Reading

Ashton-Warner, Sylvia (1963). *Teacher*. New York: Simon and Schuster.

Cherniss, C. (1980). *Professional burnout in human service organizations*. New York: Praeger.

Glickman, Carl C. (2002). *Leadership for learning: How to help teachers succeed*. Alexandria, VA: Association for Supervision & Curriculum Development.

Goodlad, John (1984). *A place called school*. New York: McGraw-Hill.

Jackson, Philip W. (1968). *Life in classrooms*. New York: Holt, Rinehart, and Winston.

Kidder, Tracy (1989). *Among schoolchildren*. Boston: Houghton Mifflin.

Lieberman, Ann (ed.) (1990). *Building a professional culture in schools*. New York: Teachers College Press.

Lightfoot, Sarah L. (1983). *The good high school: Portraits of character and culture*. New York: Basic Books.

McCourt, Frank (2005). *Teacher man*. New York: Scribner.

McPherson, G. (1972). *Small town teacher*. Cambridge: Harvard University Press.

Rosenholtz, Susan J. (1989). *Teachers' workplace: The social organization of schools*. White Plains, NY: Longman.

Sarason, Seymour (1982). *The culture of the school and the problem of change* (2nd ed.) Boston: Allyn & Bacon.

✂ 14 ✂

Curriculum Leadership

In the earlier chapters of this book, ways were described for educational leaders to improve overall organizational performance by becoming involved in many aspects of organizational life. For example, there was a discussion of the nature of leadership, motivation, and the structure of organizations. Each case highlighted the fact that, contrary to traditional images of educational administration and supervision, an effective and proactive leader is involved with a wide variety of issues in a school or school district.

This chapter returns to a discussion of educational leadership practice in more conventional terms by discussing how supervisors and administrators might be active in the development and oversight of the school's curriculum. The chapter begins with alternative definitions of the term *curriculum* to guide you in formulating your own definition. An individual's personal definition of this term will shape his or her involvement with curriculum development and evaluation. Next, three stages of curriculum development are discussed because, when each is properly carried out, the stage will yield effective results. Particular attention is directed toward the ways in which the proactive educational leader works to involve everyone who will be involved in the initial planning and implementation stages of curriculum development. Finally, there is a review of some of the key issues and problems associated with the evaluation and assessment of the curriculum after it has been established.

✂ ALTERNATIVE DEFINITIONS OF CURRICULUM

The purpose here is not to engage in lengthy philosophical treatments of the nature of curriculum. It is therefore not proposed that the effective educational leader would possess a strong foundation in numerous alternative curriculum theories. Nevertheless, proactive leaders must come to grips with some critical issues that may serve to shape their behavioral patterns as they appropriately assess whether teachers have taught effectively or whether students have learned any worthwhile body of knowledge. Too often, there is an assumption that the curricular role of the educational leader is simply to oversee that what others (i.e., the local school board, the state department of education, etc.) have determined to be the substance of instruction for local school districts and schools—which is, in fact, the curriculum.

Curriculum is defined here in very simple terms: "what" schools and individual teachers choose to do in their encounters with children. Although the definition sounds simple enough, it implies an important delimitation on curriculum development. By specifying that curriculum involves a choice by schools and teachers, there is an implicit statement that curriculum represents experiences that should be acquired by learners. Further, a stance is taken that suggests educational curriculum is somehow bounded by the planned activities provided specifically by "teachers" or "teaching institutions."

By contrast, it would also be possible to take a much more inclusive view of curriculum. For example, curriculum might be viewed as everything that learners acquire, whether through planned or unplanned events. In this view, students learn not only the content of courses in schools and the products of teachers' lesson planning, but from all they experience on a daily basis—their encounters to and from school each day, the content of television programs and newspapers, and interactions with peers. There is no denial that such events and materials are powerful determinants of the total formation of young people. In fact, it is likely that almost every child is influenced considerably by after-school television—perhaps more than by what his or her teachers have tried to share for six or seven hours during that same day. Home life is also a critical influence on the development of a child; what is absorbed in life events is a form of curriculum, whether planned or not.

Every individual serving as an educational leader must address alternative perspectives of curriculum. Each person must make a conscious decision about incorporating appropriate definitions and must determine the purpose of the curriculum, its scope, and perhaps, its ideal sequence. These issues will not be settled here in absolute terms, any more than they have been settled since the publication of Franklin Bobbitt's classic work, *The Curriculum* (1918) or with other works such as John Dewey's *The Sources of a Science of Education* (1929) and Ralph Tyler's *Basic Principles of Curriculum and Instruction* (1950). Before an individual can be expected to become involved with the responsibility of planning, implementing, and evaluating a school's curriculum, she or he must think about what that means in personal terms. If the curriculum is viewed in narrow terms (i.e., incorporating only a few learning orientations), the supervisor or administrator takes on curriculum development duties which might be very narrowly determined. An inclusive perspective of curriculum would call for educational leaders to assume greater responsibility for all the things that student might learn in and away from school by designing the curriculum to incorporate everyday experiences. Neither stance is correct or incorrect. However, those who aspire to hold roles of leadership in school settings need to be attentive to these issues. It is a critical "plan" in a strong educational platform.

While the intent here is not to provide any single definition of curriculum which would be appropriate for all practitioners, a conceptual framework might be helpful as people go about deciding what to teach, to whom, and for what purposes. Elliot Eisner (1985), for example, offers the following five alternative orientations to curriculum:

1. *Development of cognitive processes.* "In this view, the major functions of the school are (1) to help children learn how to learn and (2) to provide them with the opportunities to use and strengthen the variety of intellectual facilities that they possess" (Eisner, 1985, p. 62).

2. *Academic rationalism.* The orientation of the school must be to foster intellectual growth through the rigorous study of challenging issues.

3. *Personal relevance.* The curriculum is a personal quest for individual meaning. The school makes a wide variety of stimuli possible so that learners can select a relevant path.

4. *Social adaptation and social reconstruction.* The content of schooling is derived from an analysis of issues that are to be faced in "real life" by each learner.

5. *Curriculum as technology.* ". . . conceives of curriculum planning as being essentially a technical undertaking, a question of relating means to ends once the ends have been formulated. The central problem of the technological orientation to curriculum is not to question ends but rather to operationalize them through statements that are references to observable behavior" (Eisner, 1985, p. 79).

William Schubert (1986) offers three differing perspectives on alternative visions of curriculum:

- *Intellectual traditionalist*—subject-oriented, disciplined approaches to what is to be taught—consistent, perhaps, with Eisner's first two orientations noted earlier.

- *Experientialist*—promotes the learner's constant acquisition of knowledge through a variety of planned and unplanned events and appears most related to Eisner's concept of the curriculum as a form of finding personal relevance.

- *Social behaviorist*—holds that it is legitimate to construct patterns of desirable behavior on the part of learners, consistent with Eisner's social adaptation and reconstructionist views

Other perspectives and frameworks are found in abundance in the literature associated with curriculum theory and curriculum development. Perhaps the classic framework which has guided so much thinking in this field over the past half century is the work of Ralph Tyler (1950), who proposed that three data sources must be consulted in making decisions about curriculum development: society, the student, and the nature of the subject matter. Whatever framework might be reviewed, however, the primary work of the educational leader is not to engage in philosophical discussions of what factors should be considered, but how to enact a plan which exposes students in some meaningful way to a body of knowledge that will promote personal growth and development. You must determine which perspectives and orientations to use as you proceed through the development of your personal platform statement.

❧ MAKING THE CURRICULUM HAPPEN IN SCHOOLS

The educational leader must, above all, be a practitioner of curriculum. That is, it is not sufficient for the administrator or supervisor to ponder theoretical perspectives. Once the decision has been made to identify one or another orientation to what should be learned, the real work of putting that "what" into place must be carried out. In this section, a strategy is offered to assist the proactive leader as he or she proceeds with the business of moving forward with curriculum development at the local school level. In very simple terms, this process is divided into three phases: planning, implementation, and evaluation. The focus here is not on theoretical or philosophical issues, but rather on practical issues that might guide local school leaders in their work.

Initial Planning

To the extent that it may be possible for the educational leader to become involved with the broad, creative process of planning a curriculum (a starting point where ideas are generated, assimilated, and assessed), the following steps may be consulted:

1. *Scan the nature of the environment for curriculum development.* Here, the role of the leader might be to review the three possible sources of the curriculum—the nature of society, the nature of students, and the nature of the subject matter itself—identified by Tyler (1950). It is the role of the educational leader not to change any of these variables but rather to appreciate the realities found in each one and to lead the curriculum in the proper direction. For example, efforts to develop a high-powered college prep curriculum will not likely lead to a high degree of success in communities where students' and parents' prevailing goals and objectives are not necessarily directed toward the completion of a college or university degree. Devising a curriculum

with a strong emphasis on the study of classics, therefore, might be a less-than-productive activity.

The same concerns might also be voiced with regard to the need for effective leaders to take stock of the *nature of learners* served by their schools or school districts. We are not suggesting that effective curriculum development must be based on simply maintaining the status quo with regard to learning activities.

Finally, school supervisors or administrators ought to examine the *nature of the subject matter* to be included in the planned curriculum. For example, there are some subjects that need to be learned in a relatively tight-sequenced fashion. Mathematics and foreign languages might be in this category. On the other hand, social studies, for the most part, can be learned in a variety of sequences. During the initial planning of curriculum, the effective supervisor or administrator includes the input of experts from the fields of study that are being reviewed to achieve the maximum benefits from the curriculum.

2. *Develop a strategy to include interested parties.* One of the surest ways to make certain that a curriculum development project will ultimately fail is to avoid including in the initial planning process those who might have a stake in the delivery of the curriculum. As a result, effective curriculum leadership necessarily involves making certain that teachers, parents, board members, other citizens, and students themselves be able to voice their opinions regarding the potential value (or lack of value) that might be derived from including certain elements and issues in the established curriculum. Recent cases where local citizens have formed groups to "bring back the basics" to schools are often examples of situations where people felt disenfranchised from curriculum planning in the past, to the extent that great dissatisfaction was the final result.

3. *Clarify the relationship between the learning objectives and the curriculum.* This step has two implications. First, it suggests that there has been a determination of what learning outcomes are to be—for example, teachers might work with parents to identify desired cognitive, affective, or psychomotor outcomes for students at different points in the educational program. On the other hand, learning outcomes can be the result of standards that are identified and mandated by agencies external to the school. Such groups might include the state department of education or even the state legislature. For our purposes, it makes little difference as to who identifies what students should learn in school. The simple but critical fact is that, as part of an effective planning process, a conscious decision must be made to find ways of linking those desired outcomes for learners and the ways in which the content will be delivered. How does the curriculum match objectives? If, for example, it is decided that an appropriate and important out-

come is for learners to demonstrate proficiency in fundamental arithmetic processes, it is likely that corresponding curriculum will include addition, subtraction, multiplication, and division skills.

It is not the purpose here to promote any specific learner outcomes, or even the "best" way to specify those outcomes. For example, no one wants to take sides in ongoing controversies regarding "outcomes-based education" versus "standards-based education" versus "basic education." Instead, what should be noted is that it is absolutely essential to include a clear indication of learning objectives as part of the planning phase for effective curriculum development.

4. *Anticipate political consequences.* Traditionally, educators have insisted that they are involved in a profession that is apolitical. Yet, it is not uncommon to hear teachers lamenting the fact that they could be much more effective if they could only avoid "playing politics." Such a view of the world of schools is unrealistic. "Politics" and political behavior means being able to anticipate and deal with those who may have different opinions or negative feedback and who may apply pressure to apply their goals.

Whether politics should be a part of education is not an issue. Politics is related to what goes on in schools each day, and those who are involved with curriculum development need to be aware of this fact. If there is an assumption that curriculum can be developed in a type of sterile environment that deals only with lofty educational ideals, this assumption will soon lead to frustration and disenchantment. If there is any doubt about this statement, one need only look at virtually any daily newspaper to note how local community action groups have been successful in intervening in educational reforms because there was a sense that the school had a different agenda than the community.

Proactive leaders may not be able to change the agendas of community interest groups. However, if during the initial planning phase educators are sensitive to the kinds of pressure they are likely to face during the implementation of new educational practices and curricula, they may be able to divert potential criticism and achieve their ultimate goals smoothly and successfully.

Implementation

During this stage, the curriculum is fined-tuned and molded to fit within the specific parameters dictated by the many factors affecting its actual delivery. The steps that need to be followed during this phase of a curriculum process are quite similar to the activities that we suggested as part of initial planning.

1. *Identify relevant parties.* If a new curriculum is to be implemented, either in an individual school or across an entire school district, the

first thing that must be done is to identify accurately all those who will likely have a part in or be affected by that implementation process. Who will make use of the new curriculum? In response to this question, it is wise to think more inclusively than exclusively. In other words, changes in the mathematics curriculum of a high school (or for the secondary schools of a district) will not only involve mathematics teachers in the secondary schools, but also have a potential impact on the math teachers in the elementary schools of that district. Also, how changes in the curriculum will affect other subject specializations, such as science, must be examined.

Identifying those who will have a legitimate role in the implementation of any part of a new curriculum is critical and will have an important impact on whether implementation efforts are ultimately successful.

2. *Consider resource issues and potential limitations.* The central purpose of the initial planning phase of curriculum development is meant to be very creative and devoid of the type of bounded thinking that takes into account the practical issues of "how much will it cost for our students to learn X?" During the implementation phase, such realistic concerns must be brought back into full view, because ignoring the potential costs associated with curricular change (in terms of financial costs as well as human resource expenses) is a certain way of ensuring that change will not occur. Before moving forward with an ambitious agenda related to technology in the curriculum, is it likely that a school system can afford to make a huge investment in new computers, video equipment, and so forth? Or will it be necessary to develop linkages with agencies outside of the district as a way to provide opportunities for students to have access to the latest technical equipment and expertise needed to develop a new curriculum? Such questions must be addressed as part of the implementation phase.

3. *Identify staff development support that may be needed, and provide it.* The previous step noted that implementation efforts must be guided by a review of resources needed to enhance the likelihood of a new curriculum being adopted. One of the central resources in any school is the staff who will be responsible for carrying out the changes on a daily basis. Consider, for example, cases where new programs have been initiated in the area computer technology, perhaps at the insistence of local community groups who fear that their students will fall behind other children if new computer courses are not added to a district's curriculum. Or the state department of education, pushed by the state legislature which in turn was listening to business interests, now mandates that "all students will have access to the Internet" because that will boost the state's economy in the future.

The bulk of costs associated with the implementation of these new courses and programs typically involves massive investments in hardware and software, perhaps even capital investments in remodeling large portions of school buildings in order to accommodate additional computers and printers. In addition, planning must take place to ensure that, as current technology quickly becomes obsolete, provisions are made for replacement technology. After such expenses are incurred, little is left in the budget to pay for what may be the single most critical factor associated with effective curriculum adoption, namely, the training of teachers and other staff. In short, it makes no sense to invest time and money in new programs if teachers are not prepared to deal with the changes. An effective and ongoing support system and staff development programs must be a major part of any effort to implement new curricular practices in schools.

4. *Maintain effective communications.* There are many unfortunate examples of school districts where parents, pupils, staff members, and the community at large are promised that certain outcomes will occur "if only" the district is allowed to engage in one program refinement or another. Often, these ambitious promises for improvement not likely to produce immediate results. After all, test scores do not leap to appreciably higher levels overnight, and high school dropout rates are not suddenly eliminated simply because a school system has adopted a new reading program in the elementary schools or has taken steps to implement a new program in computer technology. Thus, if overstated claims are made by district administrators, it is understandable that the public will quickly become disenchanted with educational practices.

While it is certainly not an absolute guarantee to widespread and enduring public support for curricular change, a critical part of any program development process must be the creation of effective, accurate, and realistic communication designed to maintain linkages between schools and the public.

5. *Make certain that accepted practices related to curriculum development are reflected in the implementation plan.* Here, the focus is on the actual delivery of curriculum, defining what needs to satisfy and the best way to meet those needs. Among the most critical issues that must be incorporated are the following:

   • Traditional curriculum perspectives and foci (e.g., information processing, cognitive development, human development, and constructivism) are addressed.

   • Concepts of curricular scope (How much materials should be included, and in what time frame?); sequence (In what order should content be presented?); balance (How much subject content should be presented, as compared with other areas?); alignment (How does identified content fit with broader educational goals?); and integration (How does everything fit together?).

- Matching occurs between curriculum objectives and teaching styles on an ongoing basis.

Evaluation

The final stage in the curriculum development process is to design an evaluation procedure to answer the critical question, "Did what we plan actually work?" Again, a number of important steps are suggested to assist a person in becoming an effective and proactive educational leader.

1. *Return to stated objectives.* The first step in designing an effective assessment or evaluation tool involves a consideration of what the initial goals of the curriculum were to be. For this reason it is suggested that during the initial planning phase, the learning objectives and goals to be achieved as a result of changes in the curriculum be stated as clearly as possible. The important question to be answered here is simply, did what we want to happen actually take place? In order to respond, it is essential that "what we wanted to achieve" is fixed and clear in everyone's mind.

2. *Identify the audience for the evaluation.* Will evaluative data regarding a newly implemented curriculum be used to inform teachers and administrators (and other professional staff) who work in the schools on a full-time basis? Or is the primary audience for the curriculum evaluation to be the school board, a group with an interest in overseeing program efficiency? Perhaps the real audience for the evaluation will be the general public with an interest in knowing "how the schools are doing" in very general terms.

   Clearly, the audience for the evaluation is a critical issue to be determined by educational leaders. If data is to be available to professional staff, then it might be assumed that the nature of data could be a bit more technical in nature. School boards, on the other hand, may be filled with very intelligent people, yet they may not be ready to appreciate what is meant by stanines and percentiles on criterion-reference tests. There are too many examples of well-intentioned presentations of curriculum evaluation projects being presented by district officials to bored board members. It is strongly advised that considerable thought be given toward the most effective strategy for communicating results with policy makers. Finally, the larger public in the community will likely respond more favorably if they can appreciate how a local district initiative appears to compare with results in other similar districts.

   The critical issue, then, is not changing an evaluation process to get the "right" results, but rather looking at who will be listening to evaluative data and deciding how to use the data to inform those who will be affected by the outcomes of curriculum renewal.

3. *Decide appropriate time lines.* This involves determining what information will be necessary, and when. A common error in many evaluation schemes is to assume that assessment results are needed sooner than when they are actually required. The consequence of such an error may be collecting and analyzing data prematurely, a practice which may have serious negative consequences. An example might be a rush to provide data relative to the "success" or "failure" of a new reading program before the next school year so that an adoption decision might be made across all schools in the district. There are numerous unfortunate examples where this type of rush to find an answer has led to school systems making costly errors based on too few cases of new programs being tried for too little time.

4. *Settle on appropriate techniques for obtaining information.* A common public perception is that all that must be done to validate a new program is to "try it out" and then "take a look at test scores to see if the kids have learned any better." While this approach appears logical, reliance on gains in student achievement scores is generally an overly simplistic approach to evaluating new programs, particularly if a new program is not meant to be directed toward the improvement of student cognitive achievement alone.

   Depending on the nature of the curriculum development project, a wide array of strategies and techniques may be selected as part of the evaluation process. Test scores can be examined, of course, but so can results of locally developed surveys administered to teachers and others who were involved with implementing a new curriculum. Parents and students themselves might also be surveyed to determine their perceptions regarding new programs and practices. In addition, if long-term data (for example, showing academic trends over a several-year period) is desired by evaluators of new curricula, longitudinal evaluations might be developed.

5. *Decide what next steps will be followed after the evaluation.* The ultimate purpose of an evaluation is to provide data to people for the purpose of making further decisions about what was evaluated. After evaluating any aspect of a planned curriculum, the issue that needs to be addressed is not simply whether new practices appeared to "work," but what to do as a consequence of a practice "working" or "not working." For example, if a new mathematics curriculum is effective in one school for one year, the decision might be made to implement the same program district-wide. By contrast, even if a program does not appear to have achieved its goals and objectives, evaluative data might prompt decision makers to refine the new program, or to try it as designed but with a different group of users, or totally reject it for future use.

☙ THE ROLE OF THE EDUCATIONAL LEADER

The final issue considered here might be the most important one for you to consider as an educational administrator or supervisor. Specifically, it is critical to think about the specific actions that you will need to take as a school leader in order to provide direction to your staff concerning the issue of "what shall be taught," and ultimately, "how it shall be taught." Allan Glatthorn (2006) addressed this central leadership responsibility and noted that six areas must concern the administrator or supervisor who would serve as a curriculum leader:

1. *Developing vision or goals.* The leader must work with her or his staff in defining what the curriculum shall be for the individual school. Clearly, this curriculum must be related to and address broader curricular issues presented in state and district visions of curriculum. But the leadership in an individual school must still carve out a curriculum that is consistent with campus goals and objectives.

2. *Rethinking the program of studies.* Here, the leader continues to work with staff in identifying a knowledge base that is relevant to the needs of learners in a particular school. Necessary resources must be secured to ensure that the desired knowledge base, or program of studies, may be delivered effectively and efficiently. In addition, the staff of the individual school must develop a comprehensive plan for evaluating the effectiveness of the newly articulated program of studies.

3. *Committing to a learning-centered schedule.* The timetable of school classes is arranged in a way that is consistent with the value that students should be the central focus of all that takes place within a school.

4. *Integrating the Curriculum.* The curriculum leader must find a way to ensure that the sum of all courses and learning experiences in a school are greater than individual parts. This suggests that an important feature of the curriculum of any school is that there would be a sense of a program offered in a school, not simply a collection of random and disconnected courses. A critical skill for any leader must be to collaborate with staff in determining if it is more appropriate to work at curriculum integration while maintaining clear identities for each individual subject (a task more consistent with the departmentalization of most traditional high schools), or if integration should focus on blending content found in two or more subjects. In this second case, practices such as multi-age grouping (a concept more related to elementary and middle school practice) and team teaching become more compatible with desired curricular structure.

5. *Aligning the curriculum.* As noted in table 14.1, there are six types of curricula needing attention by the curriculum leader. A critical task of any leader is to work with staff in ensuring that these various types of curricula are aligned with and congruent with each other so that student achievement is improved.

Table 14.1.   Six types of curricula needing attention by the principal

• *Recommended curriculum*	That which is recommended by scholars, professional organizations, and state departments of education.
• *Written curriculum*	Appears in locally produced documents, such as district scope and sequence charts, district curriculum guides, teachers' planning guides, and curriculum units.
• *Taught curriculum*	That which teachers actually deliver day by day.
• *Supported curriculum*	Includes those resources that support the curriculum—textbooks, software, and other media.
• *Assessed curriculum*	That which appears in tests and performance measures: state tests, standardized tests, district tests, and teacher-made tests.
• *Learned curriculum*	The bottom-line curriculum—the curriculum that students actually learn.

Source: Glatthorn, 1997, pp. 77–78.

6. *Monitoring the implementation process.* According to Glatthorn (1997), "[t]he monitoring of the curriculum involves the use of processes to determine to what extent the approved curriculum has been implemented" (p. 84). Here, the administrator or supervisor who plays the role of curriculum leader must work with staff in considering, among other things, whether the curriculum first planned really must be implemented in the way in which it may have first been conceptualized, and if so, how strictly it must be evaluated according to that initial vision. A critical responsibility of an educational leader must be to reconsider decisions made earlier to determine whether they were truly in the best interests of students, or whether the curricular objectives are now realistic and feasible. If the answer to either of these questions is "No," it is incumbent upon the leader to work with staff in identifying objectives which are more clear, viable, and related to the needs of the school's learners.

❧ SUMMARY

This chapter considered some fundamental issues associated with the analysis of curriculum. Included were some of the competing philosophical perspectives and definitions which have tended to surround (and often confine) conversations related to curriculum for many years. The remainder of the chapter consisted of looking at a number of specific steps that might be followed by educational leaders who would go about the business of planning, implementing, and evaluating programs.

Although the curriculum development process and the role of educational administrators and supervisors are issues that deserve considerably more attention than may be given in these few pages, certain principles can be consulted on a continuing basis to guide the overall curriculum development process. One of these principles involves making certain that clarity is achieved between purposes and processes. In other words, it is essential that links be established and maintained between the objectives of new programs and the programs themselves. Second, the development of curricula cannot be done effectively in isolation by professional administrators. All those who have a stake in a new curriculum for a school or district should be involved in its planning and shaping. Finally, decisions made about the adoption of programs, changes in practices, or the rejection of programs cannot be done quickly and without serious thought regarding practical, financial, social, or political consequences. In short, when appropriate time and effort is spent on curriculum development, the results will be enduring.

Suggested Activities

1. Attend a school board meeting and keep track of the number of decisions that are made concerning the curriculum of the school district. Review minutes and agendas from several recent past meetings of the board and document curricular decisions. Is there any pattern concerning the kinds of issues that are best classified as "curricular" in nature? What percentage of a school board's time is devoted to a review of curriculum?

2. Review any recent adoption of new curriculum in a school or district and assess the extent to which the steps discussed in this chapter (initial planning, implementation, and evaluation) appeared to have been followed.

3. Interview some teachers and administrators in your school district and ask them to define what they mean by "curriculum." Do most definitions suggest one or another fundamental philosophy of the inclusiveness of a curriculum? If these various definitions were represented among teachers in a school in which you were a supervisor or administrator, what types of problems might emerge as a result of this diversity of views?

Cases to Consider

Read the two cases presented and consider the following:

- What are the critical issues raised in the cases, as they relate to the supervisor or administrator's role in curriculum development?
- How does each case relate to the development of proactive supervision?
- In what ways might you suggest a resolution to the issues raised?

Case 14.1   I Thought Everybody Bought the Vision

When Jim Snow was recruited to the Graystone Local Schools as the new superintendent, the promise was made by the board to support his vision of a more effective instructional program for the children of the district. The way in which Jim wanted to improve education was to initiate a system that focused on students demonstrating the adequacy of learning through the attainment of desired outcomes. In this way, promoting students through the educational program of the system automatically would be a thing of the past. Jim Snow was going to make a difference by instituting a system of outcomes-based education (OBE) in the Graystone Schools. In short, this would improve the quality of education available to students, and it would make Graystone a national model. Some critics immediately noted that Jim Snow would also become considerably more visible as well, and that would enable him to find an even better superintendency in a few years.

The first two years of the new OBE program in Graystone appeared to work pretty well. Teachers modified traditional instructional practices so that greater attention could be placed on individual students and their ability to master learning objectives at their own pace. However, the truth is that many teachers were unhappy with the amount of work they now had to do as students tended to become increasingly "spread out." It was harder to plan and carry out instruction when, at any time, within a group of twenty students, there might be ten to fifteen subgroupings of students, each with a different learning objective.

At first, parents also seemed to like Jim's vision of focusing the program on individual student learning rather than traditional lock-step learning. After about two years, however, disenchantment began to appear as many parents were confused about what certain indicators of student progress really meant. Traditional letter grades were no longer being used, and periodic reports sent home contained what many mothers and fathers believed to be very confusing statements regarding how well children had apparently mastered individual learning goals and outcomes. The general view of many was summarized by the statements of one elementary school parent who commented to her principal, "But I really don't know how well my daughter is doing in fourth grade this year if I can't see her progress compared with the rest of her peers."

Outcomes-based education in the Graystone Schools was in trouble. In addition to the criticism it had been receiving from parents and from a growing number of teachers, it was now appearing on the agendas of many right-wing conservative groups as an example of how schools were no longer reflecting traditional family values. Even religious fundamentalist groups were pointing to the new OBE program as positive proof that public schools were somehow bastions of secularism and immorality.

Jim Snow grew increasingly depressed and now contemplated leaving the superintendency in Graystone. He recently had been contacted about an opening at a nearby educational research center. He truly had a dream and vision concerning how a school district could be restructured—how the curriculum and instructional practices could be made more responsive to the real learning needs of students. Jim had worked so hard to share his vision with the board, administrative team, and teachers. Now, it was all starting to fall apart.

Case 14.2   But It Works!

Larry Hooks sat at his desk in the principal's office at Piedmont Middle School, wondering if anything could be done to fix the mess that he now realized existed in his school. This second principalship in his career as a school administrator was in its third year, but things were unraveling a lot faster than they did when he served as a principal of a junior high school in same district for 10 years. At first, everything here at Piedmont had seemed to be going so well. Dr. Alfonso Ramirez, the superintendent of the Vista Del Sol Schools, had hired him to be a stabilizing influence in a school where the faculty had "run wild" in the past. That was largely due to the previous principal having spent a good deal of time trying to implement a middle school program where students would work together in multi-age teams, and where teachers would serve as advisors to each child. The young faculty in the school balked at this notion because they were afraid that they would have to spend an inordinate amount of their professional time engaged in "hand holding" with problem students. Their jobs were to teach science, math, and language arts in ways that would adequately prepare the students for a rigorous college prep curriculum at Vista Del Sol High School. Numerous complaints from the teaching staff convinced Dr. Ramirez that it was time for a change of leaders, and Larry was transferred to Piedmont to return order to the school and improve the morale of the teaching staff.

The first thing that the new principal did was to notify all teachers that there would now be a new focus on the traditional curriculum of the school, not on any new student-centered instructional programs that had not been tried in the past. Teachers were extremely supportive of this statement; they could now get on with the business of teaching what they had to teach within their classrooms. No more time would be wasted with endless meetings to consider cross-disciplinary instruction, team teaching, or anything else that they believed was a waste of time. Larry was quite satisfied with his ability to be a strong administrator. The school was now operating like clockwork!

That was two years ago. This past year, however, things at Piedmont began to change. When the visiting team from the Regional Accreditation Agency left after spending two days in the middle school, they left Larry and Dr. Ramirez with what could only be described as a scathing attack of what they saw in the school. The most damaging line in their report noted, "It is apparent that recent changes at Piedmont Middle School have had the net effect of taking a school from the brink of being a reasonably effective middle school with a commitment to the needs of learners to a model of a junior high school that one might have seen 25 to 30 years ago, when the needs of students were outweighed by the vanities of teachers."

Larry Hooks was horrified at the report. His first reaction was to condemn the visiting team. He even began a rebuttal letter in which he noted the many accomplishments of the past two years. Piedmont was now more efficient; every class was filled to the state maximum. In fact, he was able to save the district a substantial amount of money by not filling the positions left by two retirements. Hooks had been able to prepare a schedule in which every teacher was now working with a full load of students in each class in every period of the day. And the curriculum of the school was a perfect model of the state-mandated program in terms of required courses, number of minutes of instruction per week, and supervision by fully certified teachers. The teachers were happy, and Dr. Ramirez seemed pleased that no more complaints were coming to him from the staff at Piedmont. What more could Larry have possibly done as an effective school administrator? This report was simply unfair. No doubt that was why he was being asked to report to the superintendent's office the next day.

Applying the Concepts

The following brief quiz is designed to improve your skills in applying some of the concepts discussed in this chapter. Read the brief introductory case and then respond to the multiple-choice questions. You will find the answers in the Appendix.

Amy Hartley was really enthusiastic about her new job as the coordinator for elementary schools in the Pine Grove Independent School District. She had enjoyed her last ten years as a classroom teacher, but she was ready for a change. Becoming a coordinator would enable her to move out of her classroom into a new leadership role, while at the same time she could also "keep her hands busy" with the instructional program of the district.

Although her new job would include a wide array of assigned duties (including "those duties not specifically identified in the job description" but assigned to her by the director of curriculum), she knew that her main job would be to lead the district in a review of the reading curriculum with an eye toward how it might be improved in the future. Amy would be responsible for going out to all of the elementary schools in the district to determine the kinds of changes that teachers wanted to see in the reading curriculum.

She was not quite ready for her first encounter with the teachers in the district. Last Thursday, she met with the staff at Bloomington School. After about twenty minutes, she was truly concerned that she had made a terrible mistake by leaving the classroom for her new role. As soon as she announced to the teachers that she was going to lead a review of the district's reading curriculum, she was met by a series of objections. There was quite a bit of hostility among the teachers, about half of whom wanted to know why the district wanted to "disrupt" a very effective program that had worked quite well for many years. The other half of the teachers immediately reminded Amy that there was no sense in trying to change the district curriculum. After all, what was now required of students was consistent with the objectives and material required by the "state curriculum." Why bother to change what was already there?

1. When the teachers noted that there was already an acceptable curriculum because what was done in the district was consistent with the state's expectations, it was a reference to the fact that there was already a _____ .

   a. taught curriculum

   b. supported curriculum

   c. learned curriculum

   d. recommended curriculum

2. If you were to advise Amy, you might suggest that she _____ .

   a. tell the teachers that they had to change their attitudes soon

   b. bring in an expert from the university to talk about the new reading program

   c. begin by asking teachers what they believed might be addressed beyond the state curriculum

   d. return to the classroom as soon as he could

3. A big problem that Amy might be facing with the teachers at Bloomington is that they _____ .

   a. resented not being involved in the evaluation of the current reading curriculum

   b. wanted to enforce the state curriculum standards more rigidly

   c. were more in tune with a curriculum that was more directed toward social adaptation than the new curriculum would allow

   d. wanted to engage in curricular practices that were more aligned with an intellectual traditionalist view of curriculum

Additional Reading

Ellis, A. K., Mackey, J. A., & Glenn, A. D. (1988). *The school curriculum*. Needham Heights, MA: Allyn & Bacon.

Glatthorn, Allan A. (1997). *The principal as curriculum leader: Shaping what is taught and tested*. Thousand Oaks, CA: Corwin.

Glatthorn, Allan A., Whitehead, Bruce M., & Boschee, Floyd (2005). *Curriculum leadership: Development and implementation*. Thousand Oaks, CA: Sage Publications.

Griffin, Gary A. (1988). Leadership for curriculum improvement: The school administrator's role. In L. N. Tanner (ed.) *Critical issues in curriculum*. Chicago: University of Chicago Press.

Henson, Kenneth T. (2006). *Curriculum planning: Integrating multiculturalism, constructivism, and education reform* (3rd ed.). Long Grove, IL: Waveland Press.

Spady, William G., & Marshall, Kit J. (1991). Beyond traditional outcome-based education. *Educational Leadership, 48* (2), 67–72.

✑ 15 ✑

Evaluation

Educators often assume that educational supervision is virtually synonymous with evaluation—that supervisors do little more than evaluate teachers and curricular programs, and when we talk about an administrator's supervisory responsibility, we often mean how that administrator goes about evaluating teachers. As we have seen throughout this book, supervision in schools is in fact much more than evaluation. To be sure, a strong relationship exists between supervision and evaluation. Supervisors do have a responsibility to carry out evaluation. However, this chapter establishes a context for the evaluation duties of the proactive educational leader. Evaluation is simply one important aspect of the effort to match individual human abilities with organizational goals, objectives, and priorities, and the chapter will try to defuse the notion that educational evaluation automatically and necessarily involves evaluation of the teaching staff for the purpose of making employment decisions.

How does the proactive educational leader carry out evaluation responsibilities? To answer that question, the chapter begins with an overview of three different types of evaluation matched to common educational objectives, followed by a review of the most prevalent problems in the area of staff evaluation. The chapter concludes with suggestions to leaders on how to deal with the common problems.

Evaluation is simply the process of determining the worth—the goodness or badness—of something. Blaine Worthen and James Sanders (1987) provided further explanations of the basic concepts of educational evaluation by noting:

> . . . in education, [evaluation] is the formal determination of the quality, effectiveness, or value of a program, product, process, objective, or curriculum. Evaluation uses inquiry and judgment issues, including: (1) determining standards for judging quality and deciding whether

289

those standards should be relative or absolute; (2) collecting relevant information; and (3) applying the standards to determine quality. Evaluation can apply to either current or proposed enterprises. (p. 22)

Evaluation implies the necessary existence and use of a criterion or standard to which the "something" being evaluated may be compared to determine relative worth. Evaluation thus differs from another term with which it is often confused—assessment, which describes a process of judging something with or without an external standard or guide. All evaluation, therefore, is a form of assessment, but not all forms of assessment are examples of evaluation. Both organizational evaluation and assessment have basically the same purpose, which is to collect data that people in the organization may use to make decisions. In educational evaluation, the purpose is to enable decision makers to determine the value of certain activities and processes used in educating children.

❧ TYPES OF EVALUATION

The three basic types of evaluation are diagnostic, formative, and summative.

Diagnostic Evaluation

Diagnostic evaluation is normally used to determine the beginning status or condition of something. It is carried out prior to the application or intervention or treatment in order (1) to determine what intervention or treatment may be necessary (as a physician diagnoses an illness to establish needed medical treatment), or (2) to determine the nature of an object or person prior to taking an action that affects the object or person so that after the intervention is completed, its effectiveness can be assessed (as physical scientists note the nature of an environment before they conduct an experiment so they know what effect their experiment has had at its conclusion). Social scientists make use of this same research strategy that, in turn, increases the overall importance of precision in the conduct of diagnostic evaluation.

The educational leader frequently uses diagnostic evaluation procedures for both purposes. Supervisors and administrators are often called upon to suggest treatments, remedies, or approaches to "fixing" things that are going wrong in schools. In the same way that a physician uses diagnostic data to determine treatment, the educational leader is expected to prescribe solutions on the basis of a diagnosis. Diagnostic evaluation also provides a picture of conditions before anything is done, so the effect of an intervention can later be determined. In both cases, care and precision in the diagnosis are vital, or the treatment and/or its results will be in error. To return to the medical analogy, a physician must have precise data concerning a patient's weight, heartbeat, blood pressure, and so forth before the patient undergoes any medical procedure.

Only in this way can the attending physician ascertain if critical aspects of a patient's condition have changed over time. Observed changes provide the diagnostician with a place to look for the cause of the malady.

Similarly, in a school setting the educational leader can profit considerably from a careful and precise analysis of changes that occur in, for instance, student achievement on some evaluation instrument after a period of instruction. The whole concept of pretest and posttest measurement is based on the logic of using preliminary diagnostic evaluation information as a baseline to examine the net effect of instructional intervention.

Formative Evaluation

Michael Scriven (1967) first distinguished between *formative* and *summative* evaluation, and Worthen and Sanders (1987) noted the importance of keeping these two evaluative forms, which often appear similar in practice, apart.

Worthen and Sanders (1987) point out that "formative evaluation is conducted during the operation of a program to provide program directors evaluative information useful in improving the program" (p. 34). Formative evaluation is used to gain intermittent feedback concerning the nature of some activity or practice while it is in progress. Activities can be evaluated many times, and feedback from this kind of evaluation is usually supplied to whoever is in control of the activity being evaluated. Unfortunately, formative evaluation is the least frequently employed of the three forms of evaluation reviewed, and when educational supervisors do employ it, they rarely follow through with appropriate feedback to their teaching staffs. Supervisory and administrative personnel have not traditionally worked with teachers in formative ways.

Formative evaluation implies that the project or activity being reviewed could be improved if properly analyzed and assessed. Business and industry have long used the concept of formative evaluation, particularly in assembly lines. Consider, for example, the supervisor who oversees the production of automobiles. It is this person's responsibility to note minor flaws in the assembly process before the car proceeds too far down the assembly lines, and major revision is necessary, or a flawed total product results. "Mid-course correction" does not always occur on assembly lines, and evaluative feedback is not always acted upon, but the value of periodic formative evaluation is clear. For the most part, this conscious effort to employ continuous evaluation has not been implemented in the field of education.

Educational administrators and supervisors would do well to find more opportunities for formative evaluation procedures. Leaders need to become "sensors" or monitors of work in progress. They also need to develop the skills and strategies necessary to feed information gained in this way back to the teaching staff. In most schools such practices have not traditionally existed.

Summative Evaluation

"Summative evaluation is conducted at the end of a program to provide potential consumers with judgments about the program's worth or merit" (Worthen & Sanders, 1987, p. 34). Summative evaluation is the process of collecting data in order to make final decisions about the future status of whatever is being evaluated. It is the "last chance," the final point where an ultimate disposition regarding a person or thing is made. Data collected as part of summative evaluation is directed exclusively toward the goal of final judgment.

In both private corporations and public organizations such as school systems, newly hired employees are generally given a standard probationary period during which the new person can decide if the organization is the kind of place in which he or she wants to work, and the organization can look at the performance of the new person and decide if, over time, he or she can "fit in" and be successful in the organization. Some type of formative evaluation is probably carried out from time to time to let the new employee know how well his or her work has generally met the expectations of the company. Finally, at the conclusion of the agreed-upon probation period, the organization takes one last look at the employee's work. That summative evaluation is a final, "go–no go" decision point. Virtually every summative evaluation we undergo in our lives represents a major milestone, because of the final nature of the decision that is made.

Summative evaluation differs from diagnostic and formative evaluation precisely in its emphasis on finality. Because it represents and absolute endpoint or a final decision, summative evaluation typically carries with it a sense of anxiety and seriousness, whether or not these feelings are warranted.

OBJECTIVES OF EVALUATION

The four major educational areas most frequently evaluated are students, curricular programs, curricular materials (which are often evaluated with programs), and staff. Each of these objectives is examined below, and examples are provided of each of the evaluation types matched with these objectives.

Student Evaluation

Students are evaluated almost continuously in most schools, and all three processes are employed. *Diagnostic* student evaluation might involve a simple pretest administered by a classroom teacher at the outset of a chapter or unit to determine the level of students' awareness of central concepts to be taught; this pretest might then guide the teacher in selecting appropriate instructional strategies. Special education teachers use multiple techniques to diagnose the nature of individual learning needs so that future instruction can be directed more precisely, and standardized achievement test scores serve as a baseline to plan instruction.

Formative student evaluation is an ongoing practice in most schools. Teachers give "pop quizzes" precisely because they want to get some sense of how well students are learning during the course of instruction and also to give students some hints concerning the teacher's expectations for student mastery of course content. Formative evaluation need not necessarily be confined to written tests or other evaluative instruments. Good teachers use formative evaluation techniques constantly; they watch student behavior patterns, and they invite particular students to participate in class discussion to assess their progress. Teachers can then adjust instruction accordingly.

A typical example of *summative* student evaluation is the traditional final exam that concludes a marking period, the results of which are used to make a summary "pass/fail" decision for a student. Similar judgments are made at the end of instructional units in subject areas and at the end of the entire school year, when most schools use comprehensive examinations to evaluate student success across all subjects. Standardized achievement tests are frequently used to make summative judgments about student learning—an undesirable and perhaps invalid form of evaluation, but one that must be recognized as widespread practice in schools.

Curricular Programs and Materials

Schools frequently assess the quality of their overall curriculum as well as the materials available to assist students in attaining the stated goals of the curriculum. As noted in chapter 14, committees of teachers, administrators, and others may work together to review the adequacy of the curriculum and the books that fit it. These activities are all basically *diagnostic* in nature.

A school or department might also review a new textbook midway through the year in which it is initially used. The results of that review would not be used to decide whether to continue using the text, but rather used to determine if it could be used more effectively. Do students need supplementary readings? Would a workbook be helpful? Should the speed with which teachers cover the material be varied? This "mid-course" evaluation is *formative*.

At the end of the school year, teachers and administrators who have suggested new curricular programs or products earlier in the year might reconvene to decide if their recommendations were effective. *Summative* evaluation would provide data to assist the committee in making its final decisions and recommendations.

Staff Evaluation

Many educators believe that making decisions about staff is the supervisor's sole evaluative responsibility. Staff evaluation is clearly a critical area and one that may cause considerable anxiety for both the supervisor and the people supervised. However, as seen in the previous sections of this chapter, it is far from being the only area of evaluative responsibility for educational leaders.

The traditional employment interview carried out before an individual is hired by a school district is an example of *diagnostic* evaluation. Other methods frequently used to determine if an individual is suited for a particular job include employment exams to determine basic competency, psychological profiles or, in recent years for teachers in some states, statewide teacher competency tests. Districts also review letters of recommendation submitted on behalf of candidates for staff positions, academic records, and employment files from other positions. Most of these forms of diagnostic evaluation provide information for the employing school system about potential staff members before they are hired. In addition, such evaluation also allows the candidate to learn more about a particular school system.

Formative evaluation of staff is one of the most poorly developed features of the entire range of supervisory responsibilities. Periodic evaluation designed to provide teachers and other school staff members with feedback to encourage better performance sounds like a simple thing to do. In practice, however, few schools provide constructive criticism to their staffs in an open, nonthreatening fashion. Several explanations account for this. First, a high percentage of supervisors and administrators are untrained in how to provide feedback to staffs that would encourage "mid-course correction" and improvement. For supervisors and administrators, undertaking an "improvement" responsibility is foreign to the traditional image of the supervisor as an authority figure who makes final judgment about job performance. Second, when administrators and supervisors do provide formative assistance, they are generally expected to make final judgments concerning staff competence at the same time. This dual responsibility means that, when supervisors offer feedback, ask teachers to share problems, or urge them to "take risks" to improve their performance, supervisors are expected at the same time to be "filing away" information on which to base future decisions on adequacy or inadequacy of performance. It is virtually impossible for the same practitioner of supervision to engage in both formative and summative evaluation responsibilities with equal effectiveness, yet school systems tend to hold supervisors and administrators accountable for making the difficult decisions associated with summative evaluation. Finally, formative evaluation is a time-consuming process that emphasizes interpersonal skills and communication between the supervisor and the persons being supervised. In many cases, supervisors do not have— are not willing to invest—enough time or interpersonal skills to make formative techniques effective. Whatever difficulties formative evaluation may engender for supervisors, it is important and well worth doing frequently and regularly in schools. Various models have been developed to help supervisors increase opportunities for this type of evaluation.

As noted above, educational leaders are often perceived as engaging in summative evaluation of teachers and others. Principals, for example, regularly make class observations for teachers being considered for tenure or a continuing contract. Because tenure decisions are normally made only once in a teacher's professional life, the evaluation process carried out in this case is clearly *summative* in nature. In reality, it is generally administrators with formal personnel responsibilities who make summative career decisions about members of their staffs. There is no doubt that summative evaluation is important in the traditional job descriptions of supervisors, but it is typically a rarely employed skill for a person classified as a supervisor.

Figure 15.1 suggests the potential relationships between types and objectives in school evaluation.

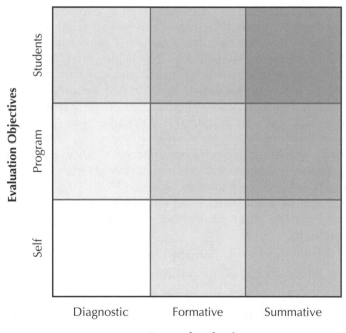

Figure 15.1.   Types of evaluation in relation to typical objectives of educational evaluation

❧ CURRENT PROBLEMS AND ISSUES IN EVALUATION

The area of staff evaluation presents some very tangible and special concerns to the practitioner of proactive leaders. We generally accept that, to improve practice, we need to determine the worth and effectiveness of that practice. On the other hand, we are all aware of the trauma that frequently surrounds discussions of evaluation. This paradox will probably never be resolved. The educational leader may, however, reduce the negative stigma associated with evaluation of educational personnel by remaining aware of significant current problems in the area, as well as suggested ways of avoiding these problems.

Mixing Purposes

Evaluation effectiveness often suffers because the objectives of evaluation are mixed. This is particularly true of formative and summative staff evaluation. Formative evaluation suggests a climate of openness and trust between leader and staff member, to the extent that staff members can admit their deficiencies openly and request feedback that might lead to improved performance. If staff members suspect that information collected as part of the formative evaluation will come back to haunt them during a summative, personnel decision-making part of the evaluation cycle, trust and openness will be either destroyed or damaged to the point where open communication is no longer possible. Consequently, administrators and supervisors should strive to separate formative and summative evaluation as completely as possible, even to the extent of involving different people at each stage.

For staff evaluation to be truly an effective activity, and one that conforms to proactive leadership, one must first clearly understand what evaluation is supposed to do. Gary Borich (1977) suggested five legitimate functions of evaluation, the first two of which are formative in nature, and the last three summative. According to Borich, evaluation may be useful to:

1. Guide self-improvement efforts by teachers;

2. Assist a supervisor in the process of improving someone else's teaching;

3. Advise potential "consumers" of teaching, particularly students;

4. Guide personnel decisions by present or potential employers or supervisors; and

5. Provide data to external audiences interested in self-effectiveness, accountability considerations, or the success of a particular project.

With regard to the last item on Borich's list, there is undoubtedly some considerable organizational value to be obtained by looking at the findings of evaluation activities to determine whether responsible professional activity is taking place in a school or district. However, recent movements in some states across the nation have added yet another dimension to the confusion and mixed purposes that cause problems in evaluation in schools. In Texas, for example, the statewide student achievement test is now combined with state-mandated and standardized teaching evaluation in a way that produces a somewhat unclear picture of what is truly talking place in the schools and classrooms there. In short, a part of teacher performance is based on how well students in each school perform on standardized tests in math, science, reading, and social studies. Efforts to link student achievement directly with teacher activity have been seen for years as a simple way to "kill two birds with one" test. But the danger is still present that this practice contributes to the mixing of purposes, which is problematic in developing more focused and usable evaluation results to assist school leaders.

Lack of Teacher Involvement

Teachers often report that they feel they have not had significant involvement in the development of district staff evaluation programs. This problem is on the wane in many school systems where teachers have become more and more involved with committees and task forces convened to review evaluation practices. It is increasingly recognized that, as primary consumers of the evaluation process, teachers have a legitimate stake in the design of procedures.

Lack of Self-Evaluation

Traditionally, little emphasis has consistently been given to the concept of staff self-evaluation. The predominant view suggests that evaluation is "done to" staff by administrators and supervisors. In fact, evaluation conducted by a person regarding his or her own performance is a much more powerful activity than evaluation conducted by an external source. Supervisors designing formal staff evaluation programs need to emphasize self-evaluation as well as the review and evaluation carried out by supervisors and administrators. Teachers are willing to engage in and even welcome self-evaluation as long as it is conducted in an appropriate manner, they participate in the planning stages, and they have some assurance of how the results will be used (Good & Brophy, 2002).

Inadequate Evaluation Criteria

Criteria used for staff evaluation often vary according to the supervisor or administrator's personal preferences. Some leadership personnel, for example, tend to judge the effectiveness of teaching performance according to the extent to which the teacher's activities resemble how the leader would have taught the same material. An example of reliance on personal preference criteria, or at least on criteria that are extremely subjective, is illustrated in the teacher evaluation checklist shown in figure 15.2. Note the number of items that are to be interpreted solely by the supervisor or administrator.

In fact, staff evaluation criteria and instruments should be based primarily on teacher effectiveness research rather than on personal preference. David Berliner and William Tikunoff (1976) proposed the following list of effective teacher behaviors:

1. The teacher reacts constructively (in overt, verbal, or nonverbal ways) to students' feelings and attitudes.

CLASSROOM OBSERVATION

Always	Frequently	Seldom	Hardly Ever	
				Teacher _____ Subject _____ Date _____
❑	❑	❑	❑	1. Shows specific interests in students as they enter and leave the classroom.
❑	❑	❑	❑	2. Calls students by name.
❑	❑	❑	❑	3. Looks at class when in discussion with them.
❑	❑	❑	❑	4. Makes an effort to involve all students.
❑	❑	❑	❑	5. Provides a variety of classroom activities and experiences.
❑	❑	❑	❑	6. Provides a comfortable and attractive environment for the students.
❑	❑	❑	❑	7. Uses room arrangements appropriate to the teaching-learning techniques employed.
❑	❑	❑	❑	8. Displays disturbing mannerisms and expressions.
❑	❑	❑	❑	9. Directions are clear and understandable.
❑	❑	❑	❑	10. Learning materials are readily available.
❑	❑	❑	❑	11. Responds appropriately to unplanned occurrences.
❑	❑	❑	❑	12. Goals for activities are clearly communicated.
❑	❑	❑	❑	13. Teacher is enthusiastic.
❑	❑	❑	❑	14. Contacts students individually to observe, answer questions, etc.
❑	❑	❑	❑	15. Maintains adequate supervision for activities.
❑	❑	❑	❑	16. Encourages and develops each student's point of view.
❑	❑	❑	❑	17. Demonstrates interest in activities of students (curricular and co-curricular).
❑	❑	❑	❑	18. Displays an appropriate sense of humor.
❑	❑	❑	❑	19. Handles classroom management efficiently.
❑	❑	❑	❑	20. Maintains order and discipline within the class.

Figure 15.2.   A typical checklist designed to guide teacher observation and evaluation

2. The teacher actively listens to what a student is saying, reading, or reciting.

3. The teacher gives a direction or makes a threat and follows through with it.

4. The teacher seems confident in teaching a given subject and demonstrates a grasp of it.

5. The teacher checks a student's progress regularly and adjusts his or her instruction accordingly.

6. The teacher expresses positive, pleasant, and optimistic feelings and attitudes.

7. The teacher seems to perceive the learning rate of students and adjusts his or her teaching pace accordingly.

8. The teacher encourages students to take responsibility for their own class work.

9. The teacher capitalizes instructionally on unexpected incidents that might arise during class time.

10. The teacher prepares students for a lesson by reviewing, outlining, explaining objectives, and summarizing.

Research has shown that all of these behaviors have a high relationship with student outcomes, as measured by performance on standardized achievement tests in mathematics and reading. This is certainly not intended as a "perfect" listing of all characteristics shown by effective teachers, but these behaviors may be observed in a more objective fashion than the items presented in the checklist in figure 15.2.

Effective teaching has been conceptualized as something other than specific in-class instructional behaviors that produce improved student outcomes on standardized achievement tests. Instead, researchers have emphasized a more subtle, "holistic" pattern. Elliot Eisner (1982) described *artistic supervision* as an approach to evaluation that requires the following:

1. Attention to the muted or expressive character of events, not simply to their incidence or literal meaning.

2. High levels of educational connoisseurship; that is, the ability to see what is significant yet subtle.

3. Appreciation of the unique contributions the teacher makes to the educational development of the young, as well as those contributions a teacher may have in common with others.

4. Attention to the process of classroom life and observations of this process over extended periods of time so that the significance of events can be placed in a temporal context.

5. Establishment of rapport between the supervisor and those being supervised so that dialogue and a sense of trust can be established between the two.

6. An ability to use language, to exploit its potential so as to make public the expressive character of what has been seen.

7. An ability to interpret the meaning of events so that their educational importance may be fully appreciated.

8. Recognition of the fact that the individual supervisor with his or her strengths, sensitivities, and experience is the major "instrument" through which the educational situation is perceived.

These basic principles of artistic evaluation are further developed by Louis Rubin (1985), who defined a series of behaviors that suggest artistic teaching. In Rubin's view, artistic teachers are those who

1. Focus on the subtleties of teaching (i.e., motivation of student, pacing, control) which invigorate basic instructional methods and subject matter;

2. Improvise tactics for reaching objectives and overcoming difficulties;

3. Take advantage of opportunities to clarify ideas and reinforce concepts;

4. Make use of intention and hunch in modifying routine practice;

5. Set high expectations for themselves and their students;

6. Find the most efficient and expedient ways of getting things done;

7. Use temporary digressions on related topics to enrich lessons, stimulate interest, and increase pace;

8. Base their control of learning activities on student behavior;

9. Take pride in what they do and in the achievement of their students;

10. Concentrate on a few dominant goals that are central to their purpose;

11. Respect their convictions; and

12. Devote as much time as possible to whatever they enjoy most in teaching.

Whatever perspective the educational leader values—artistic or more scientific—the point here is that a consistent, research-based, and objective set of standards should serve as the basis for evaluation of staff.

Evaluation Procedures Not Communicated

In many schools, the purposes, criteria, and processes of staff evaluation are not adequately communicated to staff members. School systems often take great pains to improve the quality of their evaluation procedures. In Texas, Colorado, and other states, for example, state law requires school districts to form committees of teachers, administrators, supervisory personnel, and community representatives to oversee effective evaluation programs for staff. Efforts are made to find objective evaluation criteria that reflect local educational priorities and values. Often, such staff evaluation programs are excellently "packaged." Yet many of these attempts fail, simply because once the new evaluation programs are designed, they are not sufficiently communicated to the entire staff of the district. Districts frequently develop new evaluation procedures one year and then fail to "reeducate" staff about these procedures in following years, assuming that "we all know about those practices around here." Unfortunately, that assumption is often incorrect. Supervisors should ensure that the purposes, criteria, and procedures of any staff evaluation program are clearly communicated periodically to all staff. Such practice increases the likelihood that staff will "buy into" evaluation practices and, more importantly, will raise suggestions for improving the status quo from time to time.

Insufficient Expertise

Staff evaluation procedures often experience difficulties because the administrative or supervisory personnel called upon to implement these procedures lack sufficient technical expertise in the area of evaluation. For years, school administrators were trained to serve as managers of their buildings. The expectation that supervisors and administrators will engage in behaviors more reflective of instructional leadership is relatively recent. Thus, few educational leaders have had extensive training in evaluation practices. Those who do have a background in this area tend to have had specific training primarily in summative staff evaluation procedures. Aspiring administrative and supervisory personnel currently in training must receive additional specialized training and preparation in all types of evaluation and for all objectives. Present administrators and supervisors who feel that they lack sufficient knowledge about how to evaluate or what to evaluate must utilize the expertise of others in evaluating staff. In secondary schools, for instance, a principal with a teaching background in math may need to observe and evaluate a teacher of German. The obvious solution here is to ask help from someone with great subject area expertise—a department chairperson, subject supervisor, or senior teacher—in providing both criteria for the evaluation and specific feedback regarding mastery of the instructional content.

This issue becomes even more significant in the current climate that describes teaching effectiveness almost exclusively as mastery of subject matter. In the past, teachers could be evaluated in areas such as content knowledge and expertise of delivery. Now, the emphasis across the country is increasingly directed in ways where "how" one is taught is not viewed as important as "what" one is taught. Therefore, involvement of others in the evaluation process becomes even more important than it was in the past.

Due Process Issues

Considerable evidence suggests that, with the advent of negotiated teacher contracts and other more sophisticated efforts to take into account the rights of teachers as employees, the concern that due process is not always observed in staff evaluation has been alleviated. The concern is particularly powerful, understandably, in the area of summative evaluation, from which final decisions concerning employment may result. Effective supervisors ensure that due process is always observed in staff evaluation by following these recommended procedures:

1. Whenever a teacher is evaluated, provide that teacher with a written identification of strengths as well as a diagnosis of weaknesses. In addition, provide specific recommendations for the ways in which weaknesses might be improved.

2. Offer intensive follow-up to the teacher so that he or she can, in fact, implement the specific recommendations provided by the supervisor or administrator. The supervisor or administrator is responsible for documenting this follow-up.

3. If the results of the evaluation and improvement plan still warrant an unfavorable or adverse personnel decision, communicate advance notice of this decision in writing to the staff member. Also provide notice of the staff member's rights to a hearing with the supervisor or administrator responsible for making the adverse recommendation.

4. Specify appeal procedures should the staff member be dissatisfied with the outcome of the hearing.

5. Communicate all these procedures in writing, as well as any additional information unique to the local setting, to all staff members.

   In addition to following the specific procedures listed above, adherence to a few general principles will alleviate much of the anxiety supervisors and administrators may feel about the issue of due process and legal responsibilities in general.

1. Evaluation of teaching must be based on a sense of equal respect between supervisor and teacher. Teachers and other staff members are human beings who possess certain rights. All evaluation procedures must respect the simple human dignity of school staff members.

2. Evaluation of teaching must be reasonable. Evaluation procedures must be neither arbitrary nor capricious. Decisions based on information gathered for evaluation must be warranted by that information.

3. The purpose of evaluation must be clearly identified with educational effectiveness. Evaluation procedures must promote good education. Evaluation should assure that the aims of the school are being met in an effective manner.

Inadequate Follow-Up

Throughout this discussion we have assumed that the ultimate purpose of any educational evaluation (staff, student, or curricular; diagnostic, formative, or summative) is to enhance the quality of education available to children. To ensure that such enhancement actually occurs, sufficient follow-up about instructional improvement must be provided to teachers, after they have been evaluated by administrators or supervisors. Unfortunately, current evaluation practice is often marked by a decided lack of feedback.

As will be seen in the next chapter, the *clinical supervision model* is designed largely as a formative evaluation technique that stresses direct feedback from supervisors to teachers. Keith Acheson and Meredith Gall (1987) note that effective feedback in postevaluation conferences requires three kinds of activities. The first of these must take place before and during the observation or evaluation session itself; the second and third must take place during the post-evaluation conference.

The following activities, according to Acheson and Gall, must occur before and during the evaluation session:

1. In a preevaluation planning conference, the teacher and supervisor must set goals for the year, identify concerns, establish a rationale for working together, consider strategies the teacher has been using and intends to use, and translate abstract concerns into observable behaviors that the supervisor can record.

2. Before the observation session, the teacher and supervisor must identify the nature of the lesson to be observed, make the objectives explicit, discuss what the teacher will be doing, predict what the students will be doing, consider specific problems or concerns that the teacher anticipates during the lesson, and select appropriate observation techniques and recording systems.

3. During the observational visit, the supervisor must employ one or more devices for the specific situation as related to the goals and concerns, and record data unobtrusively and without disruption of the class.

The above activities are normally included in the first two stages of the clinical supervision model, and they represent what should occur in order for an effective conference to take place.

For Acheson and Gall, the second set of activities that represent part of effective follow-up to evaluation are the following, which form the general, conceptual basis for post-evaluation feedback:

1. The supervisor must provide the teacher with feedback using objective informational data.

2. The supervisor must elicit the teacher's opinions, feelings, and inferences about the observational data.

3. The supervisor must encourage the teacher to consider alternative lesson objectives, methods, and reasons.

4. The supervisor must provide the teacher with opportunities for practice and comparison.

Finally, Acheson and Gall (1987) suggest five specific activities that should occur at the post-observational conference.

5. The observer displays the data recorded at the observation. This is done without evaluative comments.

6. The teacher analyzes what was happening during the lesson as evidenced by the data. The supervisor simply helps to clarify what behaviors the recorded data represent.

7. The teacher, with the help of the supervisor, interprets the behaviors of the teacher and students as represented by the observational data. At this stage the teacher becomes more evaluative because causes and consequences must be discussed as desirable or undesirable.

8. The teacher, with assistance from the supervisor, decides on alternative approaches for the future in order to attend to the dissatisfaction with the observed teaching or to emphasize those aspects that were satisfying.

9. The supervisor reinforces the teacher's announced intentions for change when the supervisor agrees with them or helps the teacher modify the intentions if there is some disagreement.

Such detail does not have to be included in every case of post-evaluation follow-up; indeed, effective conferences can consist of an informal chat in the hallway after an observation. There is a critical need, however, for adequate feedback to be made available to staff members as soon as possible after evaluation has been carried out.

Although Acheson and Gall use a clinical model that employs in-class teacher observation as the sole data-gathering technique, observation certainly is not the only way in which evaluative data may be collected. Self-evaluations by teachers (probably the most potent form of evaluation), student evaluations of teaching, and even informal discussions with staff members outside of their normal teaching responsibilities also represent ways in which information can be gathered and structured as part of staff evaluation.

Evaluation of Evaluation

Evaluation programs themselves are rarely evaluated. Procedures often are followed primarily because "we've always done it that way around here," rather than because a solid history of effectiveness argues for the continuation of existing practices.

Richard Kunkel and Susan Tucker (1977) suggested five criteria by which supervisors and administrators might evaluate the quality of their own evaluation activities. These are suggested as an appropriate and natural starting point for the development of a strategy for periodic review of existing evaluation practices.

1. *Holism.* Does the evaluation activity look at the total picture without an undue emphasis on quantification, or only on a few variables?

2. *Helpfulness toward program improvement.* Does the evaluation program promote growth, improvement, increased effectiveness, and other

similar types of positive benefits, rather than serving only as a ranking, judging, or criticizing technique?

3. *Acceptance of hard and soft data.* Does the evaluation process emphasize both empirical and intuitive methodologies?

4. *Evaluation vulnerability.* Is the person responsible for conducting the evaluation able to grow as much as the persons being evaluated?

5. *Vision of the future.* Does the evaluation activity have a future orientation, directed toward helping improve things later rather than "fixing" things now?

Regardless of the criteria selected, evaluation practices must be reviewed periodically to determine if they are continuing to serve the same purposes that they were originally designed to serve.

✑ A Last Word on Evaluation

For many years, evaluation in schools has been equated by many educators as simply "one more ritual that needs to be carried out each year." Student achievement testing and evaluation, for example, is certainly not a new idea. Schools have been administering such instruments as the Iowa Test of Educational Development or the Metropolitan Test for many years before the current emphasis on testing and accountability came along. Teachers have been evaluated periodically, and in recent years many states have "tightened up" the process requiring that every teacher in every school must be evaluated every year. Instructional materials have been reviewed in schools and districts for many years as part of adoption processes.

Practices continue to appear the same now as they have always appeared. But in the era of accountability, the stakes associated with conducting serious evaluation in schools are much higher than they have been in the past. As a result, school leaders must now do much more than simply carry out the rituals of evaluation and assessment. As a supervisor or administrator, it is important to note that the public expects that the outcomes of evaluation must be used as data to guide future decision making. In terms of student achievement, it is no longer acceptable simply to note that, for instance, African American girls do not demonstrate high achievement scores in third-grade writing skills, or that Latino students score lower than Anglo student in seventh-grade mathematics. Leaders are now expected to act to address these findings. The term *data-based decision making* is gradually becoming a cliché that is lost in the volume of new expectations for principals and supervisors. But it is a reality that is long overdue as part of the responsibilities to be addressed by school leaders, and it is a duty that will continue into the future. Simply evaluating because it is time to evaluate (teachers, students, materials) is no longer enough.

⅏ SUMMARY

Evaluation is a critical responsibility for the educational leader. Although evaluation is far from being the only duty for a supervisor, it is clearly one of the most important. Only through effective evaluation can data be obtained to assist the leader in making appropriate educational decisions; only through evaluation can the quality of instruction—and of education overall—be improved. Quality education demands continuing efforts at improvement, and improvement often implies changing existing practices. To make correct and effective changes, accurate evaluative information is vitally important.

This chapter began with a definition of evaluation, namely, a process for determining the basic worth of something by measuring that "something" against established standards or criteria. Three types of evaluation were described: *diagnostic*, which determines the nature of something prior to an intervention; *formative*, which determines how well something is working in progress; and *summative*, which determines whether or not something has ultimately succeeded. All three types or stages are vital activities for improving schools—although, as noted, too much attention is typically directed toward summative activities and too little toward formative activities.

Primarily, educational evaluation assesses students, curricular programs and activities, and staff. We provided examples in this chapter of evaluative activities directed at each of these three areas. The chapter concluded with a review of some typical problems associated with evaluation in schools, including confusion over the purpose of evaluation, lack of objective criteria, and lack of strategies to evaluate the evaluation activities themselves.

The most important point made in this chapter is this: We need to work to improve evaluation processes in education because effective educational evaluation will ultimately result in better teachers—and better education—for our children.

Suggested Activities

1. Collect descriptions of the teacher-evaluation procedures used in at least four school systems. Analyze these descriptions in terms of the criteria for determining the effectiveness of evaluation practices specified by Kunkel and Tucker.

2. Interview a sample of teachers from your school to determine what they believe are the areas that need improvement in staff evaluation practices for your district. Engage in the same activity with a group of principals and other administrators in your school district. Make sure to ask people for suggestions regarding the ways in which improvement may be carried out.

3. Ask a number of administrators to estimate the percentage of their weekly time that is devoted to the different types and objects of evaluation described in this chapter. If they had more time to spend on evaluation, which types would they do more and why?

Cases to Consider

Read each of these cases and consider the following issues:

- What are the critical issues raised in each case, as they relate to the understanding of evaluation practices of the proactive leader?
- How does each case relate to the development of the concept of proactive leadership?
- In what ways might you suggest a resolution to the issues raised?

Case 15.1   It Seems to Work . . . So Far

The administrators in the Buena Vista School District were quite pleased with the work they had done over the past five years. Under the direction of their superintendent, Dr. Sylvia Moreno, the district had been able to implement what many across the country were now referring to as one of the most extensive programs of outcomes-based education (OBE) in any public school system. Traditional grading systems and lock-step promotions of children from one grade to the next, regardless of whether any true learning had occurred, were a thing of the past. This was truly a remarkable accomplishment in a school system where there had always been a history of ultra-conservative practice. Dr. Moreno had come to the district with a vision, and that vision had included OBE.

Little by little, however, rumblings were being heard in the community. Letters to the editor of the local newspaper began to question the wisdom of discarding all the time-honored traditions of the past. "How will we really know if our kids learned anything now that grades are gone?" "This outcomes-based stuff is for the birds. What outcomes are being taught?" "What was so wrong with the way we learned in the past?" "Why are schools out there teaching those values as outcomes? Where are the basics?" These are only a few of the many questions that were being asked in the district by a wider and wider segment of the community.

Criticisms of the outcomes-based education program in Buena Vista were now being given greater credibility by the school board, particularly since the district was facing a critical bond election for capital improvements in only six weeks. Dr. Moreno, therefore, was not surprised to be summoned to a special executive session of the board. During that meeting, she was asked to explain how important the OBE program was, in her professional judgment.

"The OBE effort here in Buena Vista is central to a long-term vision of more effective schooling. We cannot turn around how, just because some in the community don't like what we're doing," she said. "We are now a national model."

Tom Gresham, the board president, responded to Dr. Moreno by stating, "Sylvia, we are not using this as a referendum on your performance as a
superintendent. All we are asking now is the same question that a lot of
voters are also asking. Do you have any evidence to show that this innovation has made any real difference in what's going on in our schools? I'm
assuming that you have some data, so please be prepared to make a public
presentation within the next month. I'm sure that we'll all be relieved when
you can start to answer some of the objections in a more objective fashion."

Sylvia Moreno walked out of the board meeting knowing that she had
a lot of work to do in the next few days.

Case 15.2   It's All in the Numbers—And Don't Forget It

The principals came out of the meeting without saying a word. What
could they say after hearing a two-hour lecture by Amos Cartwright, the
brash young associate superintendent for instruction who was clearly the
"right-hand man" of the superintendent, criticize the work of the principals
in terms of the statewide achievement testing program. The results just
came back to the district from the state department of education. Only
three of the 22 elementary districts had achievement scores by their third
and fifth graders that would merit the receipt of a state "Outstanding
Achievement" award. One middle school out of nine received the commendation, and none of the five high schools in the district were recognized.
What this meant was that the school system would not be able to receive
another banner from the state superintendent to proclaim itself as one of
the "top urban systems in the state." That award was bestowed on the district two years ago, and Amos, the superintendent, and other district officials were all invited to serve as members of the Governor's Task Force on
Educational Reform. In turn, they had also been invited to a luncheon in
Washington where they met with the president and the secretary of education to receive awards for "leadership in an age of reform."

Amos was on his way to greater things, both personally and professionally. First, there would be opportunities to consult with other districts
around the state. Next, he would get a doctorate at the local university
largely by convincing the faculty that his expertise in the field made him a
"sure thing" candidate for their graduate program. Next, he would move on
to a superintendency in a wealthy district near the state capital, and with
any luck, look forward to a future role as the state superintendent.

The presentation to the principals started off quite calmly, given the
nature of the subject being presented. About 15 minutes into the session,
however, Howard Rossi, the principal of Golden Meadows High School and
most experienced administrator in the district, raised his hand during one
of Amos's numerous reviews of data from two years ago contrasted with
current scores. "Cartwright, what you're explaining to us is something we
all knew would happen this year. For the past five years, the state has
explicitly exempted students from taking the test if they were classified as
special-ed kids, or if they demonstrated limited English proficiency. You
and your staff did a great job of making sure that those kids were excused
from the testing program. Now, we have to serve all our students. Frankly,

I think we've got a lot of serious work to do here besides listening to you tell us how incompetent we are." Howard drew the smiles of every other principal in the room with his speech who envied the fact that he would likely be retiring from Golden Meadows in another three months.

Predictably, the public challenge from one principal prompted Amos to fly into a rage. He had little patience with principals anyway; he had never been one himself, and he was suspicious of their tendency to always try to come to the support of their teachers and other staff in the buildings. Amos knew that this testing program was important for the district, and so he exploded with a fist-pounding denial of "hiding" special-education students. "Look, all of you. You know that the reality we face is one of proving ourselves as a good district. That's how we will get things from the state legislature and from the state education agency. It's all in the numbers, and you know that as well as I do. I want you to get back to your schools and start lighting some fires under your teachers who aren't producing. I want to see some of the people who are dragging us down out of here next year. And for those of you who think I'm kidding and just throwing around threats, remember that the superintendent and I look very closely at your school's test scores before we recommend renewals of anyone's contracts. This sounds harsh, but it is the reality we all face."

Applying the Concepts

The following brief quiz is designed to improve your skills in applying some of the concepts discussed in this chapter. Read the brief introductory case and then respond to the multiple-choice questions. You will find the answers in the Appendix.

Carl Franklin had spent his first three years as a school administrator in Crawford Township, a blue-collar community about 45 miles from the city of Clarksville. While he enjoyed his experience, he was getting increasingly tired with the two hours he wasted each day while driving between his home in the suburbs of Clarksville and Crawford. He had taken the job three years ago because it was the only principalship available in a community where he would be able to maintain residence in the Clarksville area. This was important because he wanted to realize his ambition of a principalship, but he could not relocate because his wife was a resident physician at the Clarksville Regional Hospital; he did not expect her to drive long distances between their home and her place of work.

Carl had been keeping his eyes open for an administrative position in a community close to Clarksville for the past three years. Finally he saw an opening in the very prestigious Woodland Estates School District. It was a principalship of a medium-sized elementary school. It also would bring a considerable increase in pay. Even more important, Carl would be working considerably closer to home. He had begun to feel like a stranger in his own house recently. The Woodland Estates job would mean working closer to home, better money, and more time to spend with his wife.

Not surprisingly, Carl was called in for an interview. That was a clear indication that he was one of the finalists for the Woodland Estates job. He was extremely confident that he was exactly the person who would be a great choice for the district. The only thing that really bothered Carl after the first round of interviews were the kinds of questions that he seemed to be getting from the administrators on the interview committee.

Specifically, Carl was asked about his "philosophy of supervision." While he spent a considerable amount of time responding to that question by talking about the kinds of things that he had done at Crawford with the teachers, he didn't seem to be answering the questions in the ways people wanted. Carl talked about teacher empowerment, staff development, observing classes, inservice sessions, and so forth. But the interviewers kept returning to questions about his "supervision experience." In every instance, the main concern seemed to be whether or not Carl was truly the kind of principal who could "get rid of some very bad teachers."

Although he wanted to work closer to Clarksville, Carl was more than a bit uneasy as he drove back to his house following the interviews. He was afraid that he was going to tell his wife that he would be driving a lot again next year.

1. The interview team at Woodland Estates seemed to have the assumption that _____.
   a. all their teachers were bad
   b. Carl was unable to work effectively with teachers
   c. supervision was synonymous only with teacher evaluation
   d. Carl could be used in only one way in their district—terminating bad teachers

2. If Carl does not take the job, it will likely be because _____.
   a. his new school would still be too far from home
   b. there was a basic conflict between his values and the district's values
   c. he did not know anything about supervision
   d. his wife did not like the job

3. An implication of this scenario is that the Woodland Estates School District _____.
   a. wanted to emphasize diagnostic evaluation of programs only
   b. wanted to emphasize formative evaluation of teachers only
   c. wanted to emphasize summative evaluation of students only
   d. wanted to emphasize summative evaluation of teachers only

4. Of the following "mixed purposes" of evaluation noted in your reading, the one that appears to be the primary emphasis of the Woodland Estates School District is _____.
   a. guiding self-improvement efforts by teachers
   b. assisting supervisors in the process of improving teaching

c. guiding personnel decisions by employers

d. providing data to external audiences interested in self-effectiveness.

Additional Reading

Chockalingam Barker, Cornelius, & Searchwell, Claudette J. (2003). *Writing meaningful teacher evaluations—Right now! The principal's quick-start reference guide* (2nd ed.). Phoenix, AZ: Crown Press.

Danielson, Charlotte, & McGreal, Thomas L. (2000). *Teacher evaluation: To enhance professional practice.* Alexandria, VA: Association for Supervision and Curriculum Development.

Firth, Gerald, & Pajak, Edward (eds.) (1998). *Handbook of research on school supervision.* New York: Macmillan.

Nolan, James Jr., & Hoover, Linda A. (2004). *Teacher supervision and evaluation: Theory into practice* (2nd ed.). New York: Wiley/Jossey-Bass Education.

Tracy, Saundra J., & MacNaughton, Rober (1993). *Assisting and assessing educational personnel: The impact of clinical supervision.* Needham Heights, MA: Allyn & Bacon.

Tucker, Pamela D., & Stronge, James H. (2005). *Linking tacher ealuation and student learning.* Alexandria, VA: Association for Supervision and Curriculum Development.

PART V

Models for Supervision
Now and the Future

This section reviews clinical supervision as well as other models in the field, which some see as cure-alls for the ills of educational supervision. The section also includes a review of the important issue of staff development and inservice training. In conclusion, the book provides a glimpse of future trends and issues likely to affect the ability of educators to serve as proactive leaders.

16

Clinical Supervision and Other Models

As noted in the previous chapter, educators have rarely had a strong record in formative evaluative practices. Well-developed strategies guide diagnostic and summative staff evaluation. Even though researchers generally recognize that intervention to improve any activity is most effective if undertaken while that activity is in progress, formative evaluation of staff has not been given high priority in most school systems. This situation has begun to change during the last forty years or so. One reason for that change is the arrival of the kinds of alternative supervisory models that are presented in this chapter.

UNDERLYING ASSUMPTIONS OF ALTERNATIVE SUPERVISORY MODELS

Many educators endorse clinical supervision and other new models of supervisory practice as "the" perfect approaches to the supervision of teachers. In Ohio, Colorado, and Texas, for example, the most recent standards for the certification of educational administrators and supervisors require candidates seeking administrative or supervisory credentials to receive special, intensive training in the use of models which often resemble the standard clinical model. There is no reason to assume, however, that the adoption of a single model will correct all current ills. However, clinical supervision and recent developments such as developmental and differentiated supervision might be useful strategies to consider in efforts to improve supervisory practice. However, all models of supervision that offer promise must be understood in an appropriate context. In the case of clinical supervision, the most prominent of all models of formative evaluation, that context is defined largely by the assumptions and historical background upon which this model is based.

Clinical supervision, the most notable of all the models discussed in this chapter, is typically presented as the brainchild of Robert Goldhammer, Morris Cogan, and Robert Anderson, who worked together at Harvard University during the late 1950s and early 1960s. They were responsible for the development of curriculum and instructional practices for Harvard's experimental Master of Arts in Teaching (M.A.T.) Program, normally referred to as the Harvard-Newton Summer School Project (Cogan, 1961). Cogan, Goldhammer, and Anderson were charged specifically with the development of a practicum that would be a part of this new program. The Harvard-Newton Program was never designed for all teachers; it was a highly selective project intended to refine the teaching skills of some of the best teachers in the country. From its inception, the Harvard effort was directed toward the enhancement of excellence, never at "fixing" mediocre or poor teachers, and the practicum was an important way in which excellent, experienced teachers could become even better.

Cogan, Goldhammer, and Anderson were faced with a critical dilemma. How could they design a field-based learning program that was not established, like traditional student teaching arrangements, to provide basic hands-on learning in real, live classrooms? The participating teachers were master teachers in their own districts and were often called upon to work with weaker colleagues. How could anyone hope to provide feedback to people of this quality who were returning to student teaching?

The answer to this is what Cogan, Goldhammer, and Anderson— later joined by Robert Krajewski—called *clinical supervision*. Cogan (1973) defined their model as "supervision focused upon the improvement of the teacher's classroom instruction. The principal data of clinical supervision includes records of classroom events; what the teacher and student do in the classroom during the teaching-learning process" (p. 9). The notion of "clinical" as opposed to "general" supervision was selected to suggest and emphasis on supervision related specifically to classroom observation, analysis of events taking place within the classroom, and the in-class behavior of teachers and students. The primary goal of this model was to provide an opportunity for teachers to gain feedback that would allow them to improve already good teaching skills. Noreen Garman (1982) notes, "In the clinical approach to supervision, the supervisor provides the practitioner with a service that is concerned with the quality of his or her practice" (p. 35).

Weller (1977) identified the following elements of clinical supervision:

1. To improve instruction, teachers must learn specific intellectual and behavioral skills.

2. The supervisor should take responsibility for helping teachers to develop

  a. skills for analyzing the instructional process based on systematic data;

  b. skills for experimentation, adaptation, and modification of the curriculum; and

  c. a broader repertoire of teaching skills and techniques.

3. The supervisor should emphasize what and how teachers teach with the goal of improving instruction, not changing the teacher's personality.

4. Planning and analysis must center on making and testing instructional hypotheses based on observational data.

5. Conferences should deal with a few instructional issues that are important, relevant to the teacher, and amenable to change.

6. The feedback conference should concentrate on constructive analysis and the reinforcement of successful patterns rather than the condemnation of unsuccessful practice.

7. Feedback must be based on observational evidence, not on unsubstantiated value judgments.

8. The cycle of planning, observation, and analysis should be continuous and cumulative.

9. Supervision is a dynamic process of give and take, in which supervisors and teachers are colleagues in search of mutual educational understanding.

10. The supervision process is centered primarily on the analysis of instruction.

11. The individual teacher has both the freedom and the responsibility to initiate issues, analyze and improve his or her own teaching, and develop a personal teaching style.

12. Supervision can be perceived, analyzed, and improved in much the same manner as teaching can.

13. The supervisor has both the freedom and the responsibility to analyze his or her own supervision in a manner similar to a teacher's analysis and evaluation of his or her instruction.

Acheson and Gall (1987) noted five major goals implied by the clinical supervision model. Clinical supervision is designed to:

1. Provide teachers with objective feedback of the current focus of their instruction;

2. Diagnose and solve instructional problems;

3. Help teachers develop skill in using instructional strategies;

4. Evaluate teachers for promotion, tenure, and other decisions; and

5. Help teachers develop a positive attitude about continuous professional development.

All of these assumptions and goals accurately reflect the nature of supervisory practice that follows the clinical model. There are two additional considerations. First, clinical supervision is not for everyone; it is designed to support and provide feedback to experienced, reflective, and generally very good classroom teachers. Anne Lieberman and Lynne Miller (2001) note that "those teachers who have high self-esteem are more likely to accept objective feedback, see themselves as others see them, make desirable changes, and behave in a cooperative and collegial way" (quoted in Lunenburg & Ornstein, 2004, p. 562). Second, clinical supervision presumes that teachers should direct the supervisory process precisely because, as users, they are experienced and effective. This teacher-controlled model should not be used to judge teaching quality, but rather as a resource for good teachers to refine their instructional techniques. Effective supervisors should be capable of making these practices available to teachers at any time the teachers request them.

Clinical supervision is best viewed as a collegial practice—not as something that a superordinate (an administrator or supervisor, for example) does to a teacher, but as a peer-to-peer activity. Thus, some practitioners suggest that the clinical supervision model is best used between teachers, and that supervisors and administrators have no real ongoing role in it.

None of the above observations are meant to reduce the potential value of this model. Rather, the best use of clinical supervision must be based on its documented strengths, and not on inappropriate assumptions. The clinical model, for instance, cannot be used with a first-year teacher. Also, true clinical supervision is probably not an appropriate way to provide feedback to a teacher judged as incompetent. Because of these limitations, considerable caution must be used when weighing suggestions that clinical supervision should automatically be used with all teachers in all schools under all circumstances.

⚛ DEVELOPING AN APPROPRIATE CLIMATE

Before legitimately considering the structure of the clinical supervision model, certain conditions must exist in order to make this model effective. Just as clinical supervision is not appropriate for every teacher, it is also not appropriate for every school setting. Under certain conditions, clinical supervision may cause more harm than good.

Clinical supervision is collaborative, collegial, and teacher-centered. As a result, clinical supervision can only be effectively used if supervisors or administrators truly trust the teachers in the school, to the extent that they are willing to allow those teachers to define and control the analysis of their own instructional behavior. Moreover, teachers must feel comfortable enough in the school environment to "act naturally." Improvement can only take place among those who are willing to admit to their own imperfection.

If no climate of trust exists, then any clinical practices employed in supervision will be without substance. John Lovell and Kimball Wiles (1983) noted the importance of this condition in discussing potential pitfalls of clinical supervision:

> Sometimes supervisors are not willing to take the time, or do not have the ability, to establish a basis of mutual trust. Such a condition is essential. However, there is also a need for mutual respect for professional competence. Without these two conditions, it impossible to have effective clinical supervision. (p. 182)

Many supervisory schemes make use of structural steps of clinical supervision. Without the proper climate, however, true clinical supervision simply is not taking place. As Lovell and Wiles (1983) observed:

> Some organizations like the "sound" and the glamour of clinical supervision but do not have the conviction and/or ability to provide the human and material resources. To implement clinical supervision, it is essential that supervisors and teachers have time to participate in various kinds of activities on a continuing basis. Time is needed for pre-observation conferences, observations and analysis of teaching, and post-observation feedback and corrective procedures. Clinical supervision requires in-depth thinking and working together over an extended period of time. If it is going to work, the organization must provide the necessary personnel, arrangements, rewards, equipment, leadership, and support. (p. 211)

✑ STAGES OF THE CLINICAL SUPERVISION MODEL

Cogan's (1973) initial design of a clinical supervision model included eight steps:

1. Establishing the teacher-supervisor relationship
2. Planning with the teacher
3. Planning the strategy of observation
4. Observing instruction
5. Analyzing the teaching-learning process
6. Planning the strategy of the conference
7. The conference
8. Renewed planning

Acheson and Gall (1987) simplified the clinical model by suggesting only three stages:

1. Planning conference
2. Classroom observation
3. Feedback conference

Practitioners will undoubtedly continue to disagree over the "official" number of steps in the clinical supervision model. Goldhammer, Anderson, and Krajewski (1993) advocate a five-stage description:

1. Preobservation conference
2. Observation
3. Analysis and strategy
4. Supervision conference
5. Postconference analysis

Preobservation Conference

The first stage allows participants to form a mental framework in anticipation of the observation of teaching that is to follow. This stage has the following specific purposes:

1. Communication can be opened (or reopened) between supervisor and teacher. Goldhammer (1969) suggested that "it can be useful for [the] teacher and [the] supervisor to talk together . . . to renew their habits of communication, their familiarity with one another's intellectual style and expressive rhythms. . . ." (p. 57)

2. Supervisor and teacher may become familiar with each other's goals and intentions, as well as reasons, premises, doubts, motives, and ultimate expectations, and interpersonal communications may become more fluent.

3. Teacher and supervisor can rehearse what will take place during the actual episode of classroom observation.

4. Last-minute revisions of the teacher's goals, objectives, and lesson plan may be carried out.

5. The nature of specific practices to be followed in the observation can be determined and a "contract" can be agreed upon regarding the ground rules (i.e., how long the supervisor will observe, at what time during the school day, when the supervisor will enter the classroom, and so forth) made between the teacher and supervisor.

In short, during this first stage a teacher and supervisor plan the clinical supervision cycle. It is here that the teacher articulates (often in a vague and ill-defined way) his or her reasons for requesting someone to observe a class. During this step, supervisors should avoid a tendency to make demands and place restrictions on teachers in anticipation of the observation. Instead, the supervisor primarily listens to the teacher specify what is wanted. If it is not well-defined, the supervisor helps the teacher articulate concerns more completely. The following outline, developed by Goldhammer, Anderson, and Krajewski (1993, pp. 86–87), offers a sample agenda for a well-designed preobservation conference.

1. Establish a "contract" or "agreement" between the supervisor and the teacher to be observed, including:

    a. Objectives of the lesson

    b. Relationship of the lesson objectives to the overall learning program being implemented

    c. Activities to be observed

    d. Possible change of activity format, delivery system and other elements based on interactive agreement between supervisor and teacher.

    e. Specific description of items or problems on which the teacher desires feedback

    f. Assessment procedures of activities and problems

2. Establish the mechanics or ground rules of the observation, including:

    a. Time of the observation

    b. Length of the observation

    c. Place of the observation

3. Establish specific plans for carrying out the observation:

    a. Where shall the supervisor sit?

    b. Should the supervisor talk to students about the lesson? If so, when? Before or after the lesson?

    c. Will the supervisor look for a specific action?

    d. Should the supervisor interact with students?

    e. Will any special materials or preparations be necessary?

    f. How shall the supervisor leave the observation?

Observation

This step, so simple to describe (the supervisor observes the teacher) may be the most difficult and complicated for the supervisor to actually carry out. Observation is difficult and complicated because it requires the supervisor to make use of many different skills, which we can cluster into two basic categories: determining what to observe, and determining how to observe.

Deciding what to observe ought to be guided by the discussion between the supervisor and teacher at the preobservation conference. As Oliva and Pawlas (2004) note:

> If we follow through with this cycle of clinical supervision, the teacher and the supervisor in the preobservation conference have decided on the specific behaviors of teachers and students which the supervisor will observe. The supervisor concentrates on the presence or absence of the specific behaviors. (p. 519)

This is, at least in theory, the proper focus for classroom observation—but only if what the teacher indicated in advance is in fact an accurate description of the major issues that exist in the classroom. If the teacher suggested, for example, that a major problem is knowing whether or not she is using sufficiently demanding questions to elicit high-level thinking skills from students, and if the observers finds that this indeed is the major classroom issue, then the observation can be nondirective. If, however, the observer finds many other classroom problems that need to be addressed, then the observer needs to make an immediate decision: Will he or she observe the teacher's stated problem or instead note the true problems that were perceived in the classroom?

The issue of *how* to observe also deserves attention. The best intentions of supervisors will be pointless if their efforts at observation are not guided by the overriding realization that data must be gathered in an efficient and objective fashion. The ultimate goal of data gathering is to obtain information to share with the teacher after the observation has concluded, so that the teacher can analyze his or her own classroom activities. One recent development in refining classroom observation techniques is the research focus on analyzing classroom activities. Researchers with no particular interest in supervision have developed instruments that enable supervisors to engage in more sophisticated in-class observations. Acheson and Gall (1987) reviewed many of these techniques and suggested their potential application for clinical supervision:

1. *Selective verbatim.* The supervisor makes a written record of exactly what is said, in a verbatim transcript. Not all verbal events are recorded; the supervisor and teacher, as part of their preobservation conference, have decided what kinds of verbal events ought to be written down in a selective fashion. For example, if a teacher believes that he or she is not asking sufficiently difficult questions to challenge the very bright students in a class, the supervisor may spend the entire observation doing nothing but transcribing the questions used by the teacher. This transcription can take place while the class is in progress, or from a review of a taped recording of a class.

2. *Observational records based on seating charts.* The supervisor documents the behaviors of students as they interact with a teacher during a class session. A considerable amount of complex behavior and interaction can be described pictorially. An application of this approach might be in a case where, during a preobservation conference, a teacher expresses concern about the fact that some students are more involved in class discussions than others. Using a seating chart observation form, the observer may document graphically that the teacher is in fact interacting more frequently with a handful of students, suggesting that some students are not receiving much attention. This may serve as an explanation of why some students are not as involved as others are.

3. *Wide-lens techniques.* The observer makes brief notes of events in the classroom that answer, in a very broad fashion, the question, "What

happened?" Wide-lens notes are also called *anecdotal records*. The observer makes no effort to record precise, individual events, but rather writes down overall impressions and larger major events. This technique might be particularly appropriate when the teacher does not have a precisely defined concern or problem related to teaching. Often a teacher will simply recognize that "something just isn't going well in my class." The wide-lens technique might then be employed by the supervisor who wishes to collect data that reflect broad impressions of what is going on in the classroom. These broad impressions might then serve to assist the teacher in more precisely describing his or her concerns.

4. *Checklists and time line coding*. The supervisor observes and collects data about the teaching behavior being observed and categorizes these activities according to predefined classifications. A famous example of this procedure is the Flanders Interaction Analysis Scale (Flanders, 1970), which suggests that teaching behavior may be understood in terms of the extent to which classroom activities fit into three broad categories—teacher talk, student talk, and silence. Each of these categories is further divided in the illustration of the Flanders Interaction Analysis Categories Instrument (FIAC) in Table 16.1.

Another checklist used to guide classroom observation is the time line coding technique developed over the past forty years, principally as part of research designed to study teaching categories. Here, the observer notes certain predetermined behaviors of either teachers or students at particular times during a class. These techniques can provide data to teachers who are unable to articulate precisely what they feel should be observed in their classes. These widely validated instruments can guide supervisors in their observations and provide specific feedback within accepted classifications.

A wide variety of techniques may be used to direct the observation stage of clinical supervision. The effective supervisor should be aware of many approaches in order to choose one that fits the concern of the teacher. What is seen from time to time, unfortunately, is the reverse. In many settings, supervisors learn about one technique such as verbatim scripting or the Flanders Interaction Analysis Scale and become wedded to that approach. Techniques have clear strengths, but these strengths quickly disappear when a supervisor insists on using a single approach to guide every observation process, rather than allowing the teacher's instructional concerns to dictate the tool for observation.

Despite the limitations inherent in this stage, observation is absolutely critical for many reasons. As Goldhammer (1969) noted when he first described the purpose and rationale for observing teaching in classes:

> In the most general sense, observation should create opportunities for supervisors to help teachers to test reality, the reality of their own

Table 16.1   Flanders Interaction Analysis Categories

Teacher Talk	*Response*	1. *Accepts feeling.* Accepts and clarifies an attitude or the feeling tone of a student in a nonthreatening manner. Feelings may be positive or negative. Predicting and recalling feelings are included. 2. *Praises or encourages.* Praises or encourages students: says "um hum" or "go on"; makes jokes that release tension, but not at the expense of a student. 3. *Accepts or uses ideas of students.* Acknowledges student talk. Clarifies, builds on, or asks questions based on student ideas.
		4. *Asks questions.* Asks questions about content or procedure, based on teacher ideas, with the intent that a student will answer.
	Initiation	5. *Lectures.* Offers facts or opinions about content or procedures: expresses his or her own ideas, gives his or her own explanation or cites an authority other than a student. 6. *Gives directions.* Gives directions, commands, or orders with which a student is expected to comply. 7. *Criticizes student or justifies authority.* Makes statements intended to change student behavior from nonacceptable to acceptable patterns: arbitrarily corrects student answers; bawls someone out, or states why the teacher is doing what he or she is doing; uses extreme self-reference.
Student Talk	*Response*	8. *Student talk—response.* Student talk in response to a teacher contact that structures or limits the situation. Freedom to express own ideas is limited.
	Initiation	9. *Student talk—initiation.* Student initiates or expresses his or her own ideas, either spontaneously or in response to the teacher's solicitation. Freedom to develop opinions and a line of thought; going beyond existing structure.
Silence		10. *Silence or confusion.* Pauses, short periods of silence, and periods of confusion in which communication cannot be understood by the observer.

Source: Based on Flanders, Ned A. (1970), Analyzing teaching behavior, in Keith A. Acheson & Meredith Damien Gall (eds). (1987), *Techniques in the clinical supervision of teachers* (2nd ed.). White Plains, NY: Longman.

perceptions and judgments about their teaching. I have argued that supervision should result in heightened autonomy for [the] teacher and . . . particularly, in strengthened capacities for independent, objective self-analysis, and that supervision which increases [the] teacher's dependency upon supervision to know whether his teaching is good or bad, that is, supervision in which [the] supervisor's unexamined value judgments predominate, is bad supervision. But the supervisor's perceptions and evaluations, rather than counting for nothing, represent a potentially excellent source of data from which consensual validation can be obtained; given his own perceptions of what has taken place. Teachers can "test reality" by ascertaining whether [the] supervisor's observations (and later his value judgments) tend to confirm or to oppose his own. (p. 61)

This description of the potential value of observation suggests another issue: Is clinical supervision in fact primarily an activity of staff *development* rather than staff *evaluation*? One theme that permeates existing explanations of the model is that teachers may use clinical supervision to assume increasing control over their own professional development. Recent years have witnessed the creation of numerous programs across the nation that are built upon teachers' wishes to engage in positive collegial relationships on the job. These schemes have made use of the structure and assumptions of the classic clinical supervision model.

Analysis and Strategy

In the third stage of the clinical supervision model, the supervisor and the teacher independently reflect on the nature of what has just transpired and assess the extent to which the observation was related to the goals and objectives developed during preobservation. Goldhammer's initial description of this stage noted that there are two general purposes to be addressed. The first, *analysis*, involves making sense of the observational data. In the second, *strategy*, supervisor and teacher plan the agenda of the conference that will follow: "that is, what issues to treat, which data to cite, what goals to aim for, how to begin, where to end, and who should do what" (Goldhammer, 1969, p. 63).

Supervision Conference

As soon as possible after the actual observation, supervisor and teacher meet for a follow-up conference designed to permit the two actors in the clinical model to "debrief" about what has taken place to that point: Were the goals and concerns of the teacher identified during the preobservation conference accurate? What was seen during the observation? What do we now know as a result of the observation?

Lovell and Wiles (1983, p. 179) identified the following specific goals of the supervision conference:

1. Anticipated teacher and student behavior and actual teacher and student behavior are compared.

2. Discrepancies are identified between anticipated teacher and student behavior and actual teacher and student behavior.

3. Decisions are made about what should be done about discrepancies and incongruencies between anticipated and actual behavior.

4. Comparisons are made between projected use of subject content, materials, equipment, physical space, and social environment with their actual use, with emphasis on the identification of congruencies and discrepancies, and plans for their future use.

5. Comparisons are made regarding desired learning outcomes with actual learning outcomes within the context of other appropriate factors in the situation, as described by observation.

Goldhammer, Anderson, and Krajewski (1993) acknowledge that, in addition to providing feedback to the teacher and a basis for the improvement of future teaching, the conference can meet at least five additional goals:

1. Teachers can be provided with adult rewards and satisfactions. A supervisor might say to a teacher, in essence, "You are worth my time, and I value you as a colleague sufficiently that I am glad I work with you." Teachers rarely receive this kind of signal from others with whom they work.

2. Issues in teaching may be defined more precisely. The supervisor can affirm that what the teacher sensed as a problem is indeed something that needs attention.

3. If appropriate, the supervisor can offer to intervene directly with the teacher to provide didactic assistance and guidance. Depending on a number of circumstances (particularly the level of trust between the supervisor and the teacher), the supervisor may usefully suggest specific changes to be made by the teacher.

4. The teacher may be trained in techniques of self-supervision. The clinical supervision is, ultimately, to be replaced by the ability of the individual teacher to "do without" the supervisor. Good teachers, of course, will always value feedback from colleagues, but an effective clinical supervisor aims at making teachers increasingly responsible for their own improvement. The postobservation conference can be used to increase capability in this area.

5. Teachers can be provided with additional incentives for increasing future levels of professional self-analysis.

Postconference Analysis

Four basic objectives may be achieved in this final stage which is structurally part of the supervision conference. First, teacher and supervisor reconstruct the salient features of the conference so that they understand what took place and determine what agreements were made. Second, the participants assess the supervision conference to decide whether or to what extent the conference was of value to the teacher. Third, supervisor and teacher consider whether or not the entire process of clinical supervision has had any value to the overall professional development of the teacher. Finally, teacher and supervisor assess the quality of the supervisor's skill in carrying out each of the stages of the model. In short, this final stage in the clinical supervision model allows teacher and supervisor to relax, reflect, and consider the strengths and weaknesses of the process in which they have just been involved. Was it worth all the effort? Did it have any payoff? Should it be done again in the future? In what ways might the process be changed? These questions and others might be considered by teachers and supervisors during the postobservation analysis phase.

These five stages of clinical supervision are not absolute requirements. As noted earlier, different theorists have included more or fewer steps, but virtually all these descriptions can be logically structured into three stages: preobservation conferencing, observation, and postobservation conferencing. Adherence to every step in a model is not a critical issue; in fact, the specific steps are much less important than the precondition described earlier, namely, the establishment of a climate of mutual trust and open communication.

Conversely, then, we can point out that merely employing the five stages (or eight, or three, or whatever particular description is selected) does not produce clinical supervision. Many evaluative programs require supervisors or administrators to hold conferences after the observation has taken place. Unless this sequence occurs in a setting where the *basic assumptions* of clinical supervision are observed (i.e., that it is a formative activity, teacher directed, and carried out in an environment where collegial trust is present), the model has not been implemented.

❧ LIMITS OF CLINICAL SUPERVISION

As noted in the beginning of this chapter, the process of clinical supervision holds considerable promise as a technique for stimulating teachers to take more control of their own development and, as a result, improve the quality of their teaching behavior. However, clinical supervision is not a panacea to be applied to all teachers in all circumstances. Other limitations of the model also exist.

Ben Harris (1976) presented a precise review of the limitations inherent in the clinical supervision mode. He suggested restrictions in three broad categories: the settings in which the model is deployed, the personal abilities of those involved with the model, and the strategies that need to be followed to make clinical supervision work.

Limitations in Settings

The day-to-day realities of life in schools make clinical supervision exceedingly difficult. The model requires considerable time to implement—from two to five hours to carry it out in its entirety. If that amount of time is multiplied by the number of times any given teacher might wish to be clinically supervised (remember that the true model is "on demand"), little would go on in a school other than teacher conferencing and observations. This problem can be substantially reduced in situations where the role of the supervisor is broadly enough defined to include the possibility of teachers observing other teachers in peer programs. According to Lunenburg and Ornstein (2004), peer coaching "takes place when classroom teachers observe one another, provide feedback concerning their teaching, and together develop instructional plans (p. 556). Some educators suggest that most supervisory and administrative time in schools should be devoted to precisely the activities of the clinical model. Nevertheless, the fact is that time is limited in schools, and this restricts the unbridled use of clinical supervision.

Harris (1976) also suggests that, because of the press toward conformity felt by teachers at most schools, the highly individualistic nature of clinical supervision makes the model appealing to many who feel it sets them aside as "special" from their peers. From their initial preservice programs, teachers are trained to do what everyone else on the faculty does. Clinical supervision threatens to violate this norm by asking that teachers think of their own needs differently from those of their co-workers.

Personal Limitations

Not every teacher is motivated enough to make the intense time and energy commitment required of clinical supervision. Teachers can be quite talented, experienced, and generally fit the profile of those who may profit from the model, but they simply may not wish to go through all the bother.

Other teachers simply may not be, as Harris (1976) points out, "intelligent, creative, imaginative, open [or] uninhibited" (p. 87) enough to engage in the model. These teachers are not capable, for example, of reflecting on their teaching to the point of sophisticated analysis.

Personal limitations can also restrict the supervisor. Some supervisors are not sufficiently creative or reflective to use the clinical process. Also, the model implies a strong ability to be nondirective in encounters between supervisors and teachers; the fact is that many in supervisory positions have neither the patience nor the inclination to allow teachers to direct the supervisory process.

Strategic Limitations

The fundamental assumption of clinical supervision is that the quality of education in a school can be improved through intervention into the behaviors of teachers in classrooms. The model ignores the fact that other factors contribute to the quality of life in schools. More than observations and analysis of in-class phenomena must be taken into account in the strategies employed to supervise teachers.

Lovell and Wiles (1983, pp. 181–182) described other "pitfalls" inherent in the ways in which the clinical supervision model is carried out in many schools:

1. Some organizations have yielded to the temptation to use "clinical supervision" as a system for evaluating teachers for summative personnel decisions. Such a system precludes the use of privileged information, can be threatening, can limit willingness to share problems and concerns, can put teachers in a role of dependency and inferiority, and can limit the hoped-for outcome of teachers becoming better functioning and self-improving professionals.

2. Sometimes clinical supervision is delivered in a rigorous and inflexible series of steps, which may not take into consideration the needs and concerns of a teacher, or his or her readiness to participate in things like observation and analysis of his or her teaching, feedback, and corrective procedures. This practice could be a "turnoff" for some teachers and a downright shattering experience for others. Supervisors need to be sensitive to the individual differences among teachers.

3. Sometimes supervisors think that the way they observe a situation is the way it truly is. However, it is impossible ever to see things as they are. We can only see them the way we think they are. Thus, it is necessary for supervisors to share their observations with teachers and get teacher feedback, with the hope of reshaping data toward agreement. The teaching situation is too complex and filled with stimuli to see everything. We need to remember that observational data are rough and incomplete at best, and we need to keep working to improve it.

4. The possibility of tenseness and fear are present when teachers are getting feedback about their behavior. Supervisors must take appropriate steps to ease these situations by stressing the positive aspects of a teacher's performance before making any statement that could be perceived by the instructor to be negative feedback.

Other models of supervision have recently been developed which, like clinical supervision, hold promise in making the supervisory process an effective approach to teacher development rather than simply teacher evaluation. Included here is a discussion of Carl Glickman's view of developmental supervision and Allan Glatthorn's description of differential patterns of supervision.

⚜ DEVELOPMENTAL SUPERVISION

The basic assumption in the developmental supervision model is simple: Teachers are adults, and the supervision of adults must acknowledge the nature of their ongoing developmental process. This model suggests that a supervisor must recognize the individual differences among teachers in schools. This simple notion is powerful, and Glickman's contribution has been significant. His system is designed to take into account *human development* and *individual differences*.

The core of developmental supervision is that two basic factors have an impact on whether supervisors provide more or less effective treatment: the supervisor's basic beliefs about supervisory practice and the teacher's characteristics.

Supervisory Beliefs

The first factor that influences supervision consists of those basic beliefs that any given supervisor holds when working with teachers. Ten different behaviors are indicative of these beliefs, which in turn suggest three basic orientations toward supervision: *nondirective, collaborative,* and *directive*.

Nondirective

1 *Listening*. The supervisor says nothing when working with a teacher but might give slight nonverbal cues such as a nod of the head to indicate that the teacher should continue to speak without interruption.

2. *Clarifying*. The supervisor asks questions but only to the extent that these will draw the teacher into giving information that provides fuller understanding of his or her problems.

3. *Encouraging*. The supervisor encourages the teacher to talk about those factors that may be part of the problem.

4. *Presenting*. The supervisor offers a limited number of personal perceptions and thoughts about the difficulties that are expressed by the teacher.

Collaborative

5. *Problem solving*. The supervisor initiates discussions with the teacher by using statements that are aimed at exploring possible solutions to the teacher's problems.

6. *Negotiating*. The supervisor attempts quickly to get to the matter at hand by prodding the teacher to resolve his or her problem immediately.

7. *Demonstrating*. The supervisor physically shows a teacher how to act in similar circumstances, thus eliminating the teaching problem.

Directive

8. *Directing*. The supervisor details simply and exactly what the teacher must do in order to address a problem and improve performance.

9. *Standardizing.* The supervisor explains to the teacher what must be done in order to comply with the behaviors of all others in the school.

10. *Reinforcing.* The supervisor specifically delineates the conditions and consequences for the teacher's improvement.

The relationship between specific supervisory behaviors and general orientations to supervision is shown in figure 16.1. Note how behaviors signify a gradual shift of control over the supervisory encounter from the teacher to the supervisor. Those practicing supervision generally have a preferred approach to supervisory behavior, which is in line with some specific point on the continuum. Glickman refers to this as the *predominant supervisory belief.*

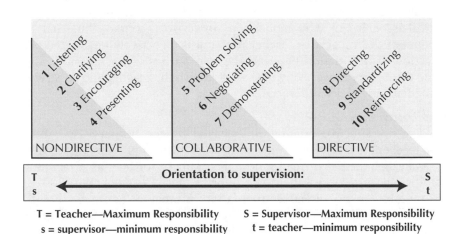

T = Teacher—Maximum Responsibility   S = Supervisor—Maximum Responsibility
s = supervisor—minimum responsibility   t = teacher—minimum responsibility

Adapted from Carl Glickman, *Developmental supervision: Alternative practices for helping teachers improve instruction*, p. 37. Alexandria, VA: Association for Supervision and Curriculum Development. Copyright 2007 by ASCD. Reprinted by permission. All rights reserved. The Association for Supervision and Curriculum Development is a worldwide community of educators advocating sound policies and sharing best practices to achieve the success of each learner. To learn more, visit ASCD at www.ascd.org.

Figure 16.1.   The supervisory behavior continuum in the developmental supervision model

Orientations to Supervision

In order to understand the developmental supervision model more thoroughly, one needs to look more closely at the three major orientations to supervision. These three orientations—directive, collaborative, and nondirective—have great impact on the ways in which an individual interacts with teachers in a school.

Directive supervision

In this orientation, the supervisor tends to exercise great control in the relationship with the teacher. This does not necessarily mean that the supervisor acts in an authoritarian or arbitrary fashion, but rather suggests that the supervisor sets very precise standards for teacher and then openly explains his or her expectations that those standards will be met. As Glickman (2007, p. 46) noted, "The approach presumes that the supervisor knows more about the context of teaching and learning than the teacher does. Therefore, the supervisor's decisions are more effective than if the teacher is left to his or her own devices."

Collaborative supervision

This approach suggests that either teacher or supervisor may appropriately take the initiative to require a meeting to discuss concerns. The critical issue is not who requests a supervisory contact, but that the product of the supervisor-teacher meeting is an actively negotiated plan of action. If negotiation between the two parties is not possible, then some third party must be invited to work with the teacher and supervisor to mediate any major difference.

Nondirective supervision

The nondirective orientation is based on the primary assumption that teachers are capable of initiating their own improvement activities by analyzing their own instruction. The supervisor acts as a facilitator helping teachers control their own improvement. As Glickman (2007, p. 157) notes, "a nondirective orientation ultimately assumes that the teacher makes the wisest and most responsible decisions for his or her own behavior; thus the final determination is still left with the teacher." The true clinical supervisory model with its emphasis on teacher control of the supervisory process fits well with the inherent assumptions of nondirective supervision.

Teacher Characteristics

In addition to supervisory beliefs, a second important factor concerns the characteristics of teachers being supervised. Glickman suggests that two features of teachers are critical in this analysis: level of commitment and level of abstraction.

Level of commitment

Based on research by Gould (1972), Loevinger (1976), and Levinson (1978), and observations by others such as Sheehy (1976), Fuller (1969), and Hall and Loucks (1978), we can identify a number of fairly specific stages through which teachers progress during their professional lives. Glickman has built his developmental model upon these recognized stages of teacher development and has indicated that identifiable characteristics parallel the increasing intensity of individual commitment to a teaching career. "Low commitment" is demonstrated by such things as little concern for other teachers, little time or energy expended toward the job, and great emphasis directed toward simply keeping one's job. These low commitment characteristics interestingly parallel lower-level needs on Maslow's hierarchy. At the other end of the continuum, those teachers "high" in professional commitment display high degrees of concerns students for and other teachers in the school, interest and willingness to spend more time and energy on job-related activities, and a primary concern with being able to do more for others.

Level of abstraction

A continuum also defines the range of teachers' abstract thinking ability, which Glickman (2007, p. 119) defines as "levels of cognitive development, where abstract/symbolic thinking predominates (as a way) to function with great flexibility in the classroom."

Teachers described as "low" in level of abstraction are easily confused by the professional problems they face, tend not to know what choices can be made to solve problems, need specific direction from others, and often have one or two habitual responses to problems, regardless of the complexity of issues involved. Teachers with a "moderate" level of abstract thinking ability are better at defining the problem at hand, can think of two or more possible responses to a professional problem, but have trouble developing a comprehensive plan for dealing with complex and multifaceted problems. These teachers can usually define a problem in their own terms and then develop a limited range of potential solutions. Finally, teachers with "high" levels of abstract thinking ability can look at a problem from many different perspectives; they can, for example, see things from the perspectives of other teachers, of students, and of parents. As a result, they are able to generate many alternatives and viable solutions to complex problems, to choose a plan of action, and to think through each step in that plan.

The continuums of abstraction and commitment combine to form four typical teacher profiles that generally describe the staff of virtually any school:

- *Teacher dropouts.* Low in both level of commitment and level of abstract thinking ability.
- *Unfocused workers.* High commitment, but low abstract thinking skills.
- *Analytical observers.* High thinking skills but low level of commitment.
- *Professionals.* High in both level of commitment and abstract thinking skills.

Figure 16.2 demonstrates the relationships between teacher characteristics and supervisory orientations.

The developmental supervision model has potential to help proactive leaders do their job better and be more sensitive to the needs of the teach-

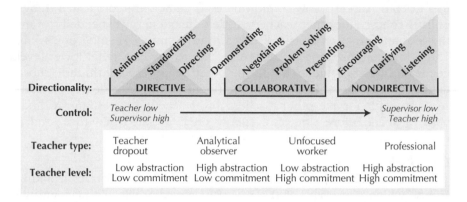

Directionality:	DIRECTIVE	COLLABORATIVE	NONDIRECTIVE
Control:	*Teacher low* *Supervisor high* →→→→→→→→→→→→→→→		*Supervisor low* *Teacher high*
Teacher type:	Teacher dropout	Analytical observer	Unfocused worker	Professional
Teacher level:	Low abstraction Low commitment	High abstraction Low commitment	Low abstraction High commitment	High abstraction High commitment

Adapted from Carl Glickman, *Developmental supervision: Alternative practices for helping teachers improve instruction,* p. 42. Alexandria, VA: Association for Supervision and Curriculum Development. Copyright 2007 by ASCD. Reprinted by permission. All rights reserved. The Association for Supervision and Curriculum Development is a worldwide community of educators advocating sound policies and sharing best practices to achieve the success of each learner. To learn more, visit ASCD at www.ascd.org.

Figure 16.2.   Developmental directionality of the supervisory behavior continuum

ers in the school. Many different conditions are likely to impact how a person engages in supervisory responsibility. A personal platform, for example, influences how one supervises and leads. Also, organizational and environmental features have an effect on supervisory orientations.

The value of Glickman's model is that it suggests that the best and most appropriate supervisory strategies are those which recognize that not everyone should receive the same treatment under all circumstances. Developmental supervision is not always an easy model to follow, but, perhaps because of that, it is a good one. It stresses the need to develop sensitivity to the backgrounds, abilities, needs, and characteristics of a heterogeneous teaching staff which possesses many special skills and talents and, when properly analyzed, will provide excellent learning opportunities for children.

⚘ DIFFERENTIATED SUPERVISION

Allan Glatthorn (1997) developed an approach to appropriate supervisory strategies in which the basic premise is quite simple: Different circumstances require different approaches. Research conducted by many such as Lovell and Phelps (1976), Young and Heichberger (1975), Cawelti and Reavis (1980), and Ritz and Cashell (1980) has made it clear that teachers have traditionally viewed supervisory activities in schools as rigid and inflexible. Options are needed that will address a variety of needs, interests, skills, and backgrounds.

In response to these assumptions, Glatthorn proposes four types of supervisory practice for schools: clinical supervision, cooperative professional development, self-directed development, and administrative monitoring. Glatthorn (1997, pp. 4–5) defines these approaches as follows:

- *Clinical supervision* is an intensive process designed to improve instruction by conferring with a teacher on lesson planning, observing the lesson, analyzing the observational data, and giving the teacher feedback about the observation.

- *Cooperative professional development* is a collegial process in which a small group of teachers agree to work together for their own professional growth.

- *Self-directed development* enables the individual teacher to work independently on professional growth concerns.

- *Administrative monitoring,* as the name implies, is a process by which an administrator monitors the work of the staff, making brief and unannounced visits simply to ensure that staff are carrying out assignments and responsibilities in a professional manner.

Certain situations arise in which each of these four models might effectively be used.

Clinical Supervision

In addition to the issues raised earlier in this chapter regarding this model, Glatthorn (1997) further divides this differentiated approach to teacher supervision into three additional categories: Scientific supervision, accountable supervision, and artistic supervision.

Scientific supervision has achieved considerable popularity in recent years because it appeals to our sense that there must be "right ways" to do certain things. It is reassuring to think that teaching can be assessed according to certain tenets that have been shown "by research" to be true. An example of this form of scientific clinical supervision is found in the work of Madeline Hunter (Russell & Hunter, 1980), who suggested that teaching might best be assessed according to the extent which a classroom teacher engages in nine specific activities:

1. *Diagnosis.* Identifying a general objective and assessing pupils' present attainment in relation to it.

2. *Specific objectives.* On the basis of the diagnosis, selecting a specific objective for the daily lesson.

3. *Anticipatory set.* Focusing student attention on what is to come.

4. *Perceived purpose.* Clarifying the objective for pupils and relating it to previous learning.

5. *Learning opportunities.* Choosing learning opportunities that will help learners achieve objectives.

6. *Modeling*. Providing both a verbal and a visual example of what is to be learned.

7. *Check for understanding*. Assessing the extent to which pupils are achieving objectives.

8. *Guided practice*. Guiding pupils' practice of learning and checking to see that they can perform successfully.

9. *Independent practice*. Giving pupils the opportunity to practice the new skill on their own.

Accountable supervision emphasizes a supervisory focus not on the teacher's behavior as much as on the apparent student outcomes derived from the instructional activity. This approach to teacher supervision is quite consistent with state and national trends that point to the need to hold teachers, administrators, and schools generally accountable based on the single criterion of whether or not students demonstrate that they have learned something as a result of instruction. Those who disapprove of this perspective suggest that it is a narrow view of what should take place in the teacher-student interaction. The notion that measurable student outcomes can serve as the criterion for whether or not a teacher is doing a good job is the basis of considerable criticism. Despite the objections, however, it is hard to argue with the argument that states that if students are not learning, something must be wrong with teaching.

Artistic supervision, the third perspective in Glatthorn's model, is compatible with clinical supervision. As Elliot Eisner (1982, p. 59) noted, "[Artistic supervision] . . . relies on sensitivity, perceptivity, and knowledge of the supervisor as a way of appreciating . . . subtleties occurring in the classroom. . . ." The value of this approach is that it defines teaching more holistically than other models do. Teaching is an art that changes according to a variety of conditions that do not always fit preconceived models of how teachers must teach. Critics of Eisner's perspective point to its almost total emphasis on subjective assessment and ask, "If the model does not say what is *right*, what can be *wrong*?"

The basic assumptions of scientific, accountable, and artistic supervision are all compatible with the overall assumptions and structure of the clinical supervision process as it was described in the opening to this chapter.

Cooperative Professional Development

Glatthorn (1997) defines cooperative professional development as a "moderately formalized process by which two or more teachers agree to work together for their own professional growth, usually by observing each other's classes, giving each other feedback about he observation, and discussing shared professional concerns. Often in the literature it is referred to as *peer supervision* or *collegial supervision*" (p. 39).

The approach to supervision inherent in this cooperative development model speaks to a very serious problem found in most schools, namely, the unfortunate isolation of teachers from their colleagues in most schools. Cooperative professional development offers several ways for teachers to work together to improve their performance, thus considerably reducing this kind of professional separation.

In this model, teachers, as professional peers, can serve as informal observers and consultants to their colleagues. Teachers may also serve as true clinical supervisors of their colleagues, an approach that has become increasingly popular as evidenced by recent peer supervision programs in many communities. Peer clinical supervision has become a highly formalized program, negotiated between district administrators and local teachers' associations, with the particular purpose of helping new teachers or teachers experiencing difficulty on the job.

Like most other models, cooperative professional development has considerable potential value, but not necessarily for all teachers in all schools. It provides another option for some situations in some settings, most notably in those schools where a demonstrated climate of openness and trust already exists among teachers.

Self-Directed Development

Glatthorn (1997, pp. 49–50) defines self-directed development as a process for professional growth characterized by four features:

1. The individual teacher works independently on a program of professional growth. Although a member of a leadership team acts as a resource for the teacher, the teacher is not supervised by others, in the conventional sense of the term, and the teacher does not work cooperatively with other members of a team.

2. The individual develops and follows a goal-oriented program of professional development. The goals of this program stem from the teacher's own assessment of professional need; there is no need for the teacher's goals to be derived from organizational goals. It is assumed that any professional growth will contribute at least indirectly to the school's goals.

3. The individual has access to a variety of resources in working toward those goals. Based on the nature of the goals set, the leader and the teacher may decide that one or more of the following resources and experiences might be appropriate: videotapes of the teacher's teaching; feedback from students; professional books and computerized information services; graduate courses and intensive workshops; support from school and district supervisors and administrators; intraschool visitations.

4. The results of the self-directed program are not used in evaluating teacher performance. The program is entirely divorced from evaluation; it is assumed that the teacher will be evaluated by whatever district program is in place.

As with Glatthorn's other supervisory approaches, self-directed development has both strengths and weaknesses. For example, critics cite research suggesting that teachers have not traditionally been very skillful in appraising their own teaching (Carroll, 1981). On the other hand, supporters stress the value in recognizing teachers as adult learners and of putting them in charge of their own learning and development. Further, teachers are individuals with distinct needs, and self-directed development allows for the highly individualized aspects of teacher development (Bents & Howey, 1981).

Administrative Monitoring

Glatthorn recognizes that some situations call for a more directive approach to supervision. He refers to this as administrative monitoring, or "drop-in supervision," the brief and informal observations of teachers made by principals or assistant principals. Glatthorn (1997, pp. 63–65) has identified four characteristics as part of this supervisory approach:

1. Administrative monitoring must be open. (The purpose of this approach is to see teachers at work under normal conditions, not to catch them doing something incompetent).

2. Administrative monitoring should be planned and scheduled, not done randomly and unsystematically.

3. Administrative monitoring should be learning centered.

4. Administrative monitoring is likely to be most effective when it is interactive across two dimensions: The administrator gives feedback to the teacher and uses the observational data as part of an ongoing assessment of the instructional program and the school climate.

Administrative monitoring is an essential activity in all schools, but not for all teachers under all circumstances. It may sound like a rather harsh concept—administrators wandering around in teachers' classrooms without any real warning. At the same time considerable evidence suggests that when supervisors and administrators know what is going on in an organization, everyone benefits.

◈ SUMMARY

In this chapter, several different models for carrying out the activity of supervising and evaluating teacher performance were identified. Some of these are focused exclusively on the observation of teaching, while others have as a target a wider range of professional development behaviors for teachers.

The chapter began with a review of the background, assumptions, and traditional practices associated with a model known as clinical supervision. It was noted that this model, while cited widely as a standard practice in schools, may not be actually carried out in all cases in the spirit in which it was first designed. Above all, it must be understood as a teacher-centered and directed approach to supervision that should be used exclusively as a formative evaluation strategy.

Two other supervisory models were also described in some detail. One was Glickman's model of developmental supervision, an approach calling for supervisors to look at key variables such as the nature of the teacher and the nature of the supervisor's belief system as conditions to guide the supervisory process. Glatthorn's differentiated supervision model suggests a multitude of approaches that may be used to evaluate teachers, or at least promote teachers' abilities to supervise their own practice. Both Glickman's and Glatthorn's models represent ways in which proactive leaders can work with teachers to achieve the goals of their schools.

The most important issue raised throughout this chapter is the fact that, in order to be effective, educational leaders must be able to employ a wide array of strategies and practices that can help teachers improve their own performance. In short, it is not possible to adopt a single "correct" way to be an effective, proactive leader.

Suggested Activities

1. Interview a group of practicing school principals to determine the extent to which they are familiar with the concepts and practices of clinical supervision. Are they using the model in their schools? Why or why not?

2. Role-play a preobservation conference with a teacher, and practice strategies for asking the teacher to articulate as clearly as possible the things that you might observe in his or her class.

3. Review Glickman's Supervisory Behavior Continuum. Ask several teachers to indicate the behavior that they prefer to receive from supervisors (i.e., "listening," "encouraging," etc.) and also the behaviors they believe they actually witness in supervisory relationships. Do the same with three or four supervisors by asking them to indicate the ways in which they believe they interact with teachers. What are the differences and similarities among these various perceptions?

4. Using the various alternative approaches to supervision provided by Glatthorn, conduct a survey of practices used in your district to determine the percentage of time individual schools spend in using each of the models reviewed.

Cases to Consider

Read each case and consider the following:

- What are the critical issues raised in each case, as they relate to the alternative supervisory models reviewed in this chapter?

- How does each case relate to the development of proactive leadership?
- In what ways might you suggest a resolution to the issues raised?

Case 16.1   Everyone's Different

Dr. Don Westphal has enjoyed an outstanding reputation as one of the most effective principals in the school district for several years, particularly in the area of teacher evaluation. As a consequence, it was not surprising to hear that he had been named as the new principal of Luther Hawkins High School, perhaps the most run-down school in the entire system. Although it was an old building in need of repair, it was also known as a good school because of an outstanding staff dedicated to helping the students in the surrounding inner city neighborhood. In short, Hawkins was a dump, but it was a school where people cared.

Dr. Westphal was looking forward to his new assignment. He had heard so many stories about the quality of the teaching staff at Hawkins, and he believed that this would be a great place for him to achieve many goals that he had never achieved earlier in his career. As he looked over the roster of nearly one hundred faculty members, he saw three individuals with backgrounds and descriptions that seemed to call out for special attention as soon as the year started. All three were experienced teachers who were due for periodic evaluation by the principal, and Don knew that each case would call for a different evaluation strategy.

Lucy Erlich was a science teacher with about five years experience in the classroom. She had several years of experience as a nurse before going into teaching after she lost her husband, a bright young surgeon, about eight years ago. Lucy was highly regarded as a teacher with considerable expertise in life sciences, but she had an equally strong reputation as a somewhat abrasive person who was often short-tempered and sarcastic with her co-workers.

Craig Marx was also due for intensive evaluation. Craig was clearly one of the brightest classroom teachers that Don Westphal had ever encountered. His work in the American history classroom was superb, and he had received many awards over the years pointing to his excellence as a great instructor. He was also known as one of the great egos in the school district. Other members of the history department respected Craig because of his intelligence and his work in the classroom, but he intimidated his colleagues to the point that he was often isolated from the majority of teachers in the school.

Finally, Don was due to evaluate Morris Jackson, the youngest of the three teachers on his list. Morris was a young man who seemed to lack any self-confidence. He was bright, cared about his students, and demonstrated considerable skill in the classroom each day. However, he simply did not appear to believe in himself.

What would Dr. Westphal do with this trio?

Case 16.2   Visiting Mr. Greeley's Class

Sara Gallagher, the principal of South Central High School, had always been impressed with clinical supervision as an effective approach to teacher evaluation. She was impressed that this was a most effective way to provide teachers with the kind of formative feedback that would help them increase their effectiveness in the classroom. She also subscribed to the notion that clinical supervision must be a process controlled by teachers. Because it is a non-directive approach, she always promoted the idea that she was a resource to teachers who were best prepared to identify their concerns.

Harry Greeley was new to the math department at South Central. Sara was really looking forward to observing his class for the first time. She did not know much about his past work at other schools in the district. He was a last-minute hire during the summer. Ordinarily, Sara spent a lot of time looking over the past teaching records of any instructors brought into her school. However, because of the need to locate a new math teacher just before the school year started, she had not looked too deeply at Harry's file. Besides, he was the only certified math teacher seeking a transfer within the district, and the district policy made it clear that a principal could not refuse such a request for a transfer unless there was clear evidence of past unsuccessful performance. Harry's personnel folder carried no such warning.

Now, Sara was about to see her new math teacher in his class. Her preobservation conference had gone extremely well with Mr. Greeley. He was articulate about the kinds of things he wanted Sara to observe. He indicated that he was concerned about the ways he was involving students in his class presentations. He was concerned that his examples were not clear enough for some of the less able students. After all, most of Harry's previous experience had been with more advanced math classes than the ones assigned to him at South Central.

Sara was prepared to go into Mr. Greeley's class to observe and record the illustrative examples used by the teacher so that Harry could assess the quality of his work during the postobservation conference. However, what she saw in the class was considerably different from what she expected to see. It was many years since Sara had taken a math class, and she did not consider herself an expert in algebra or geometry. However, what she saw in Mr. Greeley's class shocked her. For one thing, Mr. Greeley was clearly disorganized. He had no clear lesson plan in mind. Moreover, his explanations of math were wrong. He made mistake after mistake in explaining some of the principles of geometry that were covered in this class session. And the students knew it. They continually interrupted him with comments about "what it says in the book" and what Mr. Greeley was saying.

Sara had quite a headache as she sat in her office waiting for her postobservation conference with Harry Greeley. This was going to test her belief in clinical supervision!

Applying the Concepts

The following brief quiz is designed to improve your skills in applying some of the concepts discussed in this chapter. Read the brief introductory case and then respond to the multiple-choice questions. You will find the answers in the Appendix.

Carl Dorezas just learned that he was selected to be the new principal of Elm Street Elementary School. Since this was to be his first principalship, he was quite happy with the news. However, he had done quite a bit of research on the school by talking to former teachers, the retiring principal, and members of the community who also belonged to his church. He discovered that there were some issues regarding the faculty that would need his attention.

Sure enough, when Carl came on board in July, he sent out a letter to all returning faculty and invited each person to drop by his office during the summer and "have a cup of coffee." He made it clear that no one was obligated to do so, but he wanted to have a chance to get to know his staff informally, before things became so busy at the beginning of another school year. Several staff members took Carl up on the offer, and he began to get a few visitors almost every day after mid-July.

One of the first people to stop in was Jeremy Ormsby, a young man who introduced himself as a teacher about to begin his second year of teaching. He admitted that he had had a rough start last year, but he was really enthusiastic about getting a "fresh start." After he left the office, Carl checked his personnel folder and discovered that his predecessor had indicated a large number of deficiencies last year, from basic classroom management skills to knowledge of some content areas. He was coming back to Elm Street largely because he had demonstrated a positive attitude.

The next teacher who stopped in was Miriam Gonzalez, a fourth-grade teacher. She had seventeen years of experience at the school (and 31 years in education in general) and admitted that she had hoped to be retired by now, but her husband's illness prevented her from leaving the workforce. She seemed like a nice enough person, and it was clear that she knew her duties and the field of teaching, but there just wasn't much spark.

A day later, kindergarten teacher Bobbi Callahan stopped in. After a lengthy opening statement about all the problems that she had had with the previous principal, Bobbi then launched into a number of other complaints about the school, the district, and parents. After she left, Carl asked his secretary for some insights into Bobbi. "She's been a thorn in everybody's side. Gripe, gripe, gripe," said Margaret. "And the worst thing is that just about everyone here thinks she's a lousy teacher. I guess I shouldn't have said that to you before the year begins. But the previous principal had several serious discussions with her about getting her out of here. But he never seemed to be able to get her relocated."

Finally, an hour after Bobbi left the office, Timothy Shinkunas, a fifth-grade teacher, walked in and began to chat with Carl. He had only met Timothy that morning, but Carl felt as if he had known this young man for several years as they talked. He was enthusiastic, clearly cared about his students, respected the other teachers and staff, and knew his business as a teacher. Carl had taken a lot of courses in his years in the education business, and he thought that this teacher could have a career teaching teachers all he knew. And he had a great attitude.

1. According to Glickman's model of developmental supervision, Timothy Shinkunas would be classified as a _____.

   a. teacher dropout

   b. unfocused worker

   c. analytical observer

   d. professional

2. Bobbi Callahan would be a _____.

   a. teacher dropout

   b. unfocused worker

   c. analytical observer

   d. professional

3. Miriam Gonzalez appeared to be a _____.

   a. teacher dropout

   b. unfocused worker

   c. analytical observer

   d. professional

4. Jeremy Ormsby was clearly a _____.

   a. teacher dropout

   b. unfocused worker

   c. analytical observer

   d. professional

5. The most appropriate approach to differentiated supervision to be used by Bobbi would be _____.

   a. clinical supervision

   b. cooperative professional development

   c. self-directed development monitoring

   d. administrative monitoring

6. Clinical supervision would not be an appropriate approach for Jeremy because _____.

   a. he was too inexperienced

   b. he was too distracted with other personal issues

   c. he had a bad attitude and seemed to be an incompetent teacher

   d. he was simply too good, and he did not need any feedback

Additional Reading

Bellon, Jerry J., Eaker, Robert E., Huffman, James O., & Jones, Richard V. (1978). *Classroom supervision and instructional improvement: A synergistic process*. Dubuque, IA: Brown.

Bernard, Janine M., & Goodyear, Rodney K. (2003). *Fundamentals of clinical supervision* (3rd ed.). Boston: Allyn & Bacon.

Burke, Peter J., & Krey, Robert D. (2005). *Supervision: A guide to instructional leadership* (2nd ed.). Springfield, IL: Charles C. Thomas.

Campell, Jane M. (2005). *Essentials of clinical supervision*. New York: Wiley.

Clinical Supervision. (Theme Issue). *Journal of Research and Development in Education, 9* (4).

Cooper, James M. (ed.) *Developing skills for instructional supervision*. White Plains, NY: Longman.

Eisner, Elliott (1979). *The educational imagination*. New York: Macmillan.

Falender, Carol A., & Shafraske, Edward P. (2004). *Clinical supervision: A competency-based approach*. Washington, DC: American Psychological Association.

Glickman, Carl D., Gordon, Stephen P., & Ross-Gordon, Jovita M. (2007). *Supervision of instruction: A developmental approach* (7th ed.). Boston: Allyn & Bacon.

Gordon, Stephen P. (ed.) (2005). *Standards for instructional supervision: Enhancing teaching and learning*. Larchmont, NY: Eye on Education, Incorporated.

Gregory, Gayle H. (2003). *Differentiated instructional strategies in practice: Training, implementation, and supervision*. Thousand Oaks, CA: Corwin Press.

Rubin, Louis J. (1985). *Artistry in teaching*. New York: Random House.

Tracy, Saundra J., & MacNaughton, Robert (1993). *Assisting and assessing educational personnel: The fact of clinical supervision*. Needham Heights, MA: Allyn & Bacon.

Zepeda, Sally J. (2002). *Instructional supervision: Applying tools and concepts*. Larchmont, NY: Eye on Education, Incorporated.

❧ 17 ❧

Leadership for Professional Development

Educational reform requires that more attention be paid to discovering how classroom teachers increase the effectiveness of the learning process for children. For the past few years the relationship of specific practices and behaviors of teachers to student achievement, particularly in the basic skills areas of reading, language arts, and mathematics, has been the focus of considerable research. We are learning more about how teachers organize their classrooms, interact with students, and deliver instruction to elicit positive results. Still, many teachers are not aware of practices that may have the greatest potential for improving their schools. Staff development and inservice education—the traditional systems that support professional development for teachers and other educators—are typically viewed as relatively ineffective. The perception of ineffectiveness hinders judgment about an activity which can be a potentially valuable contribution to school improvement. As stressed throughout this text, the effective proactive leader always focuses on one ultimate goal: the enhancement of school effectiveness for the improvement of student learning.

One of the proactive leader's most important ongoing responsibilities is to improve the continuous professional growth and development of all those who are working toward achieving the goals and objectives of the school. In short, leaders need to be aware of effective practices associated with staff development and inservice education, both of which must be improved if schools are to improve. The responsibilities of educational leaders include staff development, but efforts to make staff development and inservice education more effective tend to be sporadic. Often, little attention is paid to the relationship between professional development for teachers and the improvement of instruction for students. Research on school effectiveness has shown that the ability of school supervisors and administrators to provide instructional leadership in their schools and districts is an important factor in the improvement of instruction. Yet few educators seem to recognize that positive change occurs when school leaders accept the responsibility of working with their staffs to plan, carry out, and ultimately evaluate inservice and staff development activities.

This chapter considers a number of issues related to the supervisor's ability to provide more effective professional development. It begins by defining educational development and examining some of the more positive trends in the design of more effective staff development and inservice education programs. Particular attention is paid to recent research findings that focus on the determination of desirable content and delivery in development programs. Finally, the chapter concludes by examining two issues associated with more effective staff development and inservice programs; adult learning theories and individual differences among learners. In this regard, the concept of mentoring is also examined as a form of professional development that addresses these two issues.

⚛ FINDING A DEFINITION

Staff development and inservice education have become hot topics of discussion for educators. Increased attention to an important topic is generally a good thing, but the downside of this phenomenon is that many people talk without always knowing what they are talking about. All sorts of schemes have appeared on the market, promising to increase the effectiveness of staff development overnight. These quick-fix packages for staff development cannot be eliminated immediately. However, educators can begin to take a giant step toward improving the quality of staff development and training by more clearly defining just what staff development is.

The distinctions between staff development and inservice education is normally based on whether an activity has been designed primarily to address a perceived deficit in professional knowledge or performance or to stimulate long-term improvement and on-the-job growth. An accepted view is that *inservice education* covers those activities directed toward remediating a perceived lack of skill or understanding; *staff development* refers to an ongoing process that promotes professional growth rather than remediation.

This distinction makes inservice education sound somehow "bad," and staff development "good." The fact is, in certain situations each activity may be effective and enhance the quality of education. Inservice education, generally perceived as something done "to" people "to fix them," is in fact necessary and appropriate in some settings and is an entirely positive process. There are times when people need special training to correct deficits in their skills. Consider, for example, the number of very good teachers who have recently taken part in inservice education programs designed to provide skills related to the implementation of instructional technology. Most teachers who graduated from college before the mid-1980s had little or no training in the use of computers; as a result, they were "deficient" in a very important area. Inservice education corrected that deficiency positively and appropriately. By contrast, developmental activities, designed to engage teachers in process experiences to provide personal and professional insights, are sometimes totally inappropriate. For example, engaging a beginning teacher who has few classroom survival skills in a developmentally focused consciousness-raising staff development exercise is both pointless and potentially harmful. The young teacher may indeed grow, but at the cost of not acquiring some basic mechanical skills absolutely vital to teaching.

There is a need to minimize the artificial distinctions that have been drawn between inservice education and staff development. Suggestions that one activity is better than the other are false. In the real world of schools, in any case, little difference is made in the use of the two terms. Practitioners face daily problems in implementing more effective inservice education and staff development; they are far more concerned with the quality of implementation than with subtle conceptual differences. If a distinction must be made, staff development may be seen as a broader term that includes inservice education as a subset. Whatever term is selected, it deals with a learning process designed to assist the professional staff of a school or district in carrying out their duties more effectively so that children are better able to learn.

❧ RESEARCH RELATED TO INSERVICE AND STAFF DEVELOPMENT

The complexities of current educational activities require teachers and other staff members to receive additional opportunities for learning. Simply stated, effective inservice and staff development are needed for effective schools; they may no longer be viewed as "extras" that are made available only if school systems have a few additional dollars to spend. Despite the critical need for effective approaches to staff development and inservice education, however, these activities remain part of a field with few theoretical or conceptual roots (McLaughlin & Berman, 1977; Henderson, 1979), little respect from practitioners (Brimm & Tollett, 1975), and a generally meager research base (Swenson, 1981). Theorists suggest that both staff development and inservice education lack sufficient intellectual rigor, whereas practitioners often complain that what has been written has little practical value for addressing problems faced in the "here and now."

A review of the research on staff development and inservice education (Daresh, 1987) found that from the many studies that have been conducted, two observations could be made. First, the research techniques used to study staff development and inservice education have been seriously limited. Second, and more relevant to the concerns in this text, most research has centered on only three targets: (1) the evaluation of specific inservice and staff development models, (2) the content of inservice and staff development activities, and (3) the delivery systems typically used.

Research on specific programs has consisted primarily of individual researchers studying the effectiveness of workshops, seminars, or other forms of inservice education that the researcher designed. Not surprisingly, a large number of these studies indicated that such efforts at providing inservice education were quite effective, but the studies added little to the goal of learning more about improving inservice education and staff development because of the difficulty of generalizing from a single setting to a larger sample. Studies that are focused on content and delivery aspects of staff development and inservice education are of greater interest because their conclusions are more clearly applicable in helping leadership personnel determine how they might improve these activities.

Content of Staff Development and Inservice Education

A review of studies on the nature of inservice education and staff development contents provides four major observations:

1. Staff development and inservice education are perceived as more effective when content is based on the self-reported needs of participants.

2. Desired staff development and inservice education content reflects topics of immediate concern to practitioners. Great interest was expressed in how to implement externally mandated programs—for example, competency-based instructional programs; less interest was expressed in programs or activities designed to deal with less concrete, more conceptual topics, such as building a more supportive organizational climate for student learning. At a mid-range of interest were topics concerning human-relations skills development, such as how to enhance communication skills in the classroom.

3. Few strong relationships appeared to exist between teachers' demographic background characteristics and staff development and inservice education interests. In fact, the only characteristic repeatedly linked to desired content was length of service, or experience, as an educator. Beginning teachers (usually defined as those with one to three years' experience) sought activities that helped them deal with feelings of insecurity, frequent uncertainty, and limited knowledge concerning their immediate teaching environment and the larger field of professional education. Experienced teachers (with more than ten years in the classroom), who were generally less favorable toward staff

development and inservice education, did express interest in topics that focused on student instructional needs. In other words, the length of teacher experience was an important and accurate predictor of staff-development and inservice education interests. Teachers' interests shifted gradually through their careers from teacher-centeredness to greater child-centeredness.

4. Teachers and other educators expressed a desire to be involved in planning their own staff development and inservice education programs and activities.

Delivery of Staff Development and Inservice Education

Many studies addressed methods for planning and carrying out staff development and inservice education activities. Many of these studies were designed to examine the issue of content as well. The review of these studies produced the following four generalizations:

1. There is a great dissatisfaction with, or at least a lack of interest in, existing procedures associated with most staff development and inservice education activities. Studies did not always pinpoint the exact nature of the procedures causing the dissatisfaction; instead, such evaluations concerned the general ways in which staff development and inservice education are "usually" provided.

2. Staff development and inservice education participants want to be involved with planning, implementing, and evaluating their learning experiences. The general finding expressed in many studies was that participants do not wish to have someone "do" staff development "to" them. This attitude correlates with research findings which conclude that adults want to play a primal role as the source of their own learning (Bredeson, 2003).

3. Staff development and inservice education participants prefer learning activities and programs that make them engage in a process. They do not wish to be mere passive observers of presentations by others. In addition, demonstrations were more highly valued than lecture presentations (Lindstrom & Speck, 2004).

4. Both staff development and inservice education are viewed as more effective when they are part of training that continues over an extended period of time. Short-term, one-shot sessions were viewed negatively (Lindstrom & Speck, 2004; Guskey, 2000; Killian, 2002).

Educational leaders need to recognize some general issues raised by recent research on staff development and inservice education. For example, skills most frequently sought by professional educators, as determined through the research, are knowledge-level skills. More often than not, those knowledge-level skills are related to issues of immediate interest and concern to practitioners.

Current research on staff development and inservice education seems focused on collecting information of apparently limited benefit to the improvement of school practices, the ability of educators to be more successful in their roles, or the condition of staff development and professional education. Despite these limitations, leaders may cull some important insights concerning the characteristics of effective staff development from the existing research. A number of researchers (Lawrence, 1974; Nicholson, Joyce, Parker, & Waterman, 1976; Paul, 1977; McLaughlin & Marsh, 1978; Hutson, 1981) have offered useful guidelines:

- Effective inservice and staff development programs are directed toward local school needs.

- Inservice and staff development participants are actively involved in effective programs.

- Effective programs are based on participant needs (Speck & Knipe, 2001).

- Effective local school inservice and staff development programs are supported by a commitment of resources from the central office.

- Effective programs provide evidence of quality control and are delivered by competent presenters.

- Programs that enable participants to share ideas and provide assistance to one another are viewed as successful (Guskey, 2000; Lindstrom & Speck, 2004).

- Rewards and incentives, both intrinsic and extrinsic, are evident to participants in programs that are viewed as successful.

- Inservice and staff development activities are viewed more positively when provided during school time.

- Effective inservice education and staff development activities are accompanied by ongoing evaluation.

The above guidelines are general, but they should prove useful to leaders charged with designing, developing, and implementing an effective inservice or staff development program. Other useful research includes that of Sprinthall and Thies-Sprinthall (1983), who also described effective practice for continuing professional development programs to improve educational practice:

Collaboration between participants and program sponsors. Building or district-wide professional development councils can foster collaboration and cooperation in planning effective inservice programs.

Learning needs identified by participants. Professional development programs responsive to the needs of participants will maximize the probability of success. A comprehensive assessment of needs should be undertaken before planning specific programs.

Programs offered at convenient locations. Sites are easily accessible. Intrinsic and extrinsic rewards provided. Intrinsic rewards are derived by gaining competence (self-esteem) or success (self-actualization). Extrinsic rewards could include certificates, enhanced promotional opportunities, or increments in pay.

Modeling by experts of skills and concepts. Demonstrations by skillful practitioners should be an integral part of professional development programs.

Utilization of participants' talents and abilities. Independent study, role-play exercises, or presentations by participants can be used to draw upon participants' talents and abilities.

Synthesis of content and adaptation to diverse situations. Case analyses, site visits, or guided group discussions may be employed to achieve synthesis of content and to explore its adaptation to diverse situations.

Individualized learning activities. Small group discussions, private counseling, or case studies written and analyzed by participants may be useful.

Significant and challenging role-playing experiences. Role playing can be an integral part of many professional development programs, particularly those dealing with interpersonal relationships or instructional procedures.

Opportunities for reflection. Time for reading and reflection is essential; programming must provide time for this to occur.

Opportunity and logical sequencing of activities. All presentations and activities should be carefully planned and coordinated to build on previous learning.

Both personal support and personal challenge. Participants grow through confrontation with challenges; they must have freedom to try, to fail, and to try again without fail.

Assessment of results. The program should be evaluated in terms of its objectives, which might be cognitive, affective, or psychomotor development, or combinations thereof.

Information about useful and effective practices regarding inservice education and staff development is clearly available. However, school districts and other agencies engaged in these activities too often tend to be unresponsive to the practices and guidelines noted here. Consequently, professional development efforts are not as effective as they might be. Attitudes are frequently quite negative. Those negative perceptions results in part from a lack of attention to two important features of staff development that have traditionally been ignored by school personnel.

৶ IMPORTANT MISSING INGREDIENTS

Two basic ingredients associated with "good" programs of professional development are often missing in practice: recognition that adults have specialized learning needs, and reflection of an understanding of individual differences among learners.

Characteristics of Adult Learning

Intuition has long suggested that adults have different learning needs or characteristics from those of children. Malcolm Knowles (1970), a major contributor to the field of adult education, is generally credited with coining the word *andragogy* (the art and science of teaching adults) as distinct from *pedagogy* (the art and science of teaching children). More important, Knowles identified four critical characteristics of adults and their patterns of learning:

1. As a person matures, his or her self-concept moves from one of dependency to one of self-direction.

2. The mature person tends to accumulate a growing reservoir of experience that provides a resource for learning.

3. The adult's readiness to learn becomes increasingly oriented toward the developmental tasks of his or her assigned social roles.

4. The adult's time perspective changes from postponed application of knowledge to immediate application, and accordingly his or her orientation toward learning shifts from subject-centeredness to problem-centeredness.

Predictably, Knowles's work encouraged others to research and write in the field of adult education, and some researchers' work is useful in guiding the improvement of staff development in schools. Fred Wood and Steven Thompson (1980), for example, reviewed some salient aspects of adult learning:

- Adults will learn when the goals and objectives of a learning activity are considered *by the learner* to be realistic, related, and important to a specific issue at hand.

- Adults will learn, retain, and use what they perceive as relevant to their immediate personal and professional needs.

- Adults need to see the results of their efforts and have frequent and accurate feedback about progress that is being made toward their goals.

- Adult learning is highly ego-involved. When a person is unsuccessful at a given learning task, it is likely that he or she will take it as an indication of personal incompetence and failure.

- Adults always come to any learning task with a wide range of previous experiences, knowledge, skills, and competencies.

- Adults want to be the originators of their own learning, and they wish to be directly involved in the selection of learning objectives, content, activities, and so forth.

- Adults will tend to resist any learning experience that they believe is either an open or implied attack on their personal or professional competence.

- Adults reject prescriptions by others for their own learning.
- Adult motivation comes from the learner and not any external source. While this may be generally true of motivation of all individuals, it is true that, as a person matures, efforts to motivate from outside the individual will decrease in probable effectiveness.

Taken together, these characteristics of adult learning should provide leaders who design and lead staff development experiences with some important insights into how such experiences should be planned and carried out. First, the fact that adults want (and learn best from) experiences that address immediate problems suggests that leaders should direct activities toward answering the perennial question, "What should I do on Monday morning?" Presentations of the latest research on teacher behavior and school effectiveness, no matter how carefully prepared, will be exercises in futility unless staff members clearly understand how research relates to their school's immediate needs. However, it can be dangerous to focus too directly on issues of immediate importance to a school or district if the offered solutions are merely prescriptions—quick fixes—to complex problems. Adults tend to reject prescriptions. Those planning staff development should understand what the real problems are in a school or district, avoid "band-aid" responses, and be careful not to ignore other serious issues.

The study of adult learning or andragogy also provides some important clues about adult self-concept needs. Teachers frequently complain that staff development and inservice education seem threatening—that participants are often made to feel incompetent. The implication here is that as people become more mature and fixed in their ways, they feel become increasingly self-conscious in situations where they believe they might experience failure (and perhaps ridicule) in front of others. Staff development and inservice education activities must therefore be planned so that teachers and other staff will not be put in situations where their performance might be compared publicly with that of their co-workers. Thus, one might question the wisdom of using activities, such as role playing, which require people to perform in front of others to demonstrate particular techniques, especially when people have clearly not volunteered to do so.

Finally, the literature on adult learning shows that as people mature, they tend to accumulate additional learning experiences. Leaders who work with staffs with a variety of adult learning experiences should recognize the potential and varied richness of this previous learning. Nothing is more frustrating to teachers than being asked to participate in activities designed to send everyone "back to square one." Practices that do this not only ignore an important resource for teaching adults but also violate a basic rule of effective staff development, namely, that individual differences among learners must be taken into account.

Individual Learning Differences

Although educators frequently affirm the belief that every learner is different, they seem to forget this principle when they plan staff development activities. A recurring message from critics of "bad" staff development is that teachers do not like to be treated as if they were a herd of sheep—a sort of amorphic blob known collectively as "the staff." Supervisors and others who plan development activities often seem to overlook the fact that, with the staff, many different needs, interests, learning styles, and abilities exist. Time and again, teachers report that staff development and inservice sessions are a waste of time because no effort was made to match learning activities with learning needs.

Fortunately, a considerable amount of information is now coming from researchers concerning differences among teachers. This information offers much to educational leaders as they plan staff development and inservice education. Unruh and Turner (1970) defined four stages of professional growth reflected within most school staffs. These categories should be useful to the leader in determining broad groupings of teachers who might be interested in different staff development activities and learning opportunities:

1. *The preservice period.* Within the school, this period is represented by student teachers and interns. Although this is not a period with great immediate implications for staff development, general interest is usually high because much of what happens in education is actually a supplement to what took place (or should have taken place) as part of college training.

2. *The initial training period.* Teachers in this period, who generally have between one and five years' experience, often have "beginner" problems such as discipline, routine organizational and administrative chores, and general class planning and curriculum development. The leader aware of the unique concerns of staff in this period might design activities to address these problems.

3. *The security-building period.* Teachers with five to fifteen years' service might be most interested in increasing their personal knowledge and skills. The supervisor needs to make certain that inservice and staff development experiences are appropriately designed to promote individual growth for teachers in this category.

4. *The maturing period.* "Master teachers" have an undefined number of years of experience but a clear depth of professional expertise. The leader would do well to tap into the knowledge and skills possessed by these teachers as additional resources in promoting professional growth.

Although these stages of professional growth suggest differentiated patterns for staff development and inservice education, their usefulness is somewhat limited by the fact that the majority of teachers in most schools belong to the "security-building" period. Finer definitions are needed to assist in devising more effective strategies.

Promising work has been done over the years by Gene Hall and his colleagues (Hall & Loucks, 1978). Building on earlier work by Frances Fuller (1969), Hall suggests that an important way to differentiate needs of staff members is according to their levels of concern about a particular educational practice. Hall indicates that teachers might be classified according to the following descending order of "Levels of Concern":

7. *Refocusing*. The teacher believes he or she has some ideas about making good practices even better.

6. *Collaboration*. The teacher is interested in combining her or his good ideas with the ideas of co-workers.

5. *Consequence*. The teacher is concerned with the extent to which there will be a positive impact on student learning.

4. *Management*. The teacher is concerned with getting materials ready for instruction.

3. *Personal*. The teacher is most interested in what personal effect a school practice will have on him or her.

2. *Informational*. The teacher is most concerned with finding out basic information about a practice.

1. *Awareness*. The teacher is not interested in a particular issue or practice.

This classification system is in no sense evaluative. In other words, we should assume that, at any given time, a school's staff will be distributed across all seven levels of concern, *depending on the issue at hand*. Teachers are not automatically better than their co-workers because they are at the "refocusing" level; conversely, virtually all teachers may be legitimately classified at the "awareness" level from time to time. In fact, shifting from one level to another depending on the issue may indicate a healthy professional environment, where staff members feel free to act in an honest and open fashion.

The implications of this work for staff development and inservice education should be fairly obvious. It makes it clear that not every staff member will be interested in every topic, and that a particular lack of interest does not constitute a negative evaluation of the school's total staff development plan. A second implication is that the design of any staff development of inservice education activity must be flexible enough so that staff members can approach an issue according to their own levels of concern, without feeling anxious or threatened if they are not interested in a particular issue at a particular time.

Gene Hall and Susan Loucks (1978) summarized the most crucial lessons to be learned in the area of staff development according to the "Levels of Concern" categories:

- The staff development leader must attend to the teachers' concerns as well as to the content to be covered.
- It is all right to have personal feelings.
- Change cannot be accomplished overnight.
- Teachers' concerns might not be the same as those of the staff developer.
- Within any group, there is a variety of concerns.

Finally, Gordon Lawrence (1982) has suggested the analysis of psychological types as a fruitful path for educational leaders to explore. Lawrence's work is based on the original premise of the Swiss psychologist, C. G. Jung (1923), who noted that people's behavior could best be explained through the extent to which they follow certain patterns, or "psychological types." Jung based these types on how people prefer to make and perceive judgments. Lawrence (1982) noted that in Jungian psychology, "all conscious mental activity can be classified into four mental processes—two perception processes (sensing and intuition) and two judgmental processes (thinking and feeling). What comes into consciousness, moment by moment, comes either through the sense or through intuition. To remain in consciousness, perceptions must be used. They are used—sorted, weighed, analyzed, evaluated—by the judgment processes, thinking and feeling" (p. 6).

Sixteen different psychological types have been identified, and measures such as the Myers-Briggs Type Indicator (MBTI) designed by Isabel Briggs Myers and Katherine Briggs (1962) help us determine the extent to which individuals fall into one or another of the different types by looking at relative strengths in four areas: extroversion (E) versus introversion (I); gathering information through sensing (S) versus intuition (N); making judgments as a product primarily of thinking (T) versus feeling (F); and a desire to live in a world defined mostly through judgment (J) versus perception (P). The possible combinations of these different descriptors, along with typical behaviors associated with each of the sixteen possible types are shown in table 17.1.

For our purposes, the value of the psychological types noted by Lawrence is that they provide important clues about the individualized concerns of teachers and enable us, once again, to avoid the trap of assuming that all teachers have the same needs and interests. "Staff" development, then, becomes increasingly involved with defining and meeting individual developmental needs and concerns of members of the staff.

This section included two concepts—adult learning characteristics and differentiation of individual needs—that are often ignored in current staff development programs. It is tempting to suggest that adding these two ingredients will improve all that ails staff development and inservice education in schools, but to do so would be to suggest a quick-fix solution to a complex problem. The comments of many teachers today reflect deeper concerns. However, designing professional development that recognizes both adult needs and differences among staff members will certainly address two major clusters of individual complaints.

Table 17.1. Brief descriptions of the 16 possible psychological types*

ENTJ—Intuitive, innovative *organizer*; aggressive, analytic, systematic, more tuned to new ideas and possibilities than to people's feelings

ESTJ— Fact-minded, practical *organizer*; aggressive, analytic, systematic, more interested in getting the job done than in people's feelings.

INTP—Inquisitive *analyzer*; reflective, independent, curious, more interested in organizing ideas than situations or people.

ISTP— Practical *analyzer*; reflective, independent, curious, more interested in organizing ideas than situations or people.

ESTP—*Realistic adapter* in the world of material things; good natured, tolerant, easygoing, oriented to practical, firsthand experience, highly observant of details of things.

ESFP— *Realistic adapter* in human relationships; friendly and easy with people, highly observant of their feelings and needs, oriented to practical, firsthand experience.

ISTJ— Analytical *manager of facts and details*; dependable, decisive, painstaking and systematic, concerned with systems and organization, stable and conservative.

ISFJ— Sympathetic *manager of facts and details*; concerned with people's welfare, dependable, painstaking and systematic, stable and conservative.

ISFP— Observant, loyal *helper*; reflective, realistic, empathic, patient with details, gentle and retiring, shuns disagreements, enjoys the moment.

INFP—Imaginative, independent *helper*; reflective, inquisitive, empathic, loyal to ideals, more interested in possibilities than practicalities.

ESFJ— Practical *harmonizer* and worker-with-people, sociable, orderly, opinioned, conscientious, realistic and well tuned to the here and now.

ENFJ—Imaginative *harmonizer* and worker-with-people, sociable, expressive, orderly, opinioned, conscientious, curious about new ideas and possibilities.

INFJ— People-oriented *innovator* of ideas; serious, quietly forceful and persevering, concerned with the common good, with helping others develop.

INTJ— Logical, critical, decisive *innovator* of ideas; serious, intent, highly independent, concerned with organization, determined and often stubborn.

ENFP—Warmly enthusiastic *planner of change*; imaginative, individualistic, pursues inspiration with impulsive energy, seeks to understand and inspire others.

ENTP—Inventive, analytical *planner of change*; enthusiastic and independent, pursues inspiration with impulsive energy, seeks to understand and inspire others.

*Derived from the Myers-Briggs Personality Type Indicator (MBTI).

✑ Promising Practices

Defining Goals

One promising development is not truly a new practice per se but is, nevertheless, an important improvement in the areas of inservice education and staff development—that is, the way in which this topic is defined. We do appear to be coming closer to developing a clear conceptualization of what both inservice and staff development are supposed to be and do—a goal that we noted as critical earlier in this chapter. Kenneth Howey (1985) suggested, for example, the following six critical functions to be served:

1. *Continuing pedagogical development.* Learning about more effective instructional techniques in the classroom, such as classroom management skills and teacher presentation skills;

2. *Continuing understanding and discovery of self.* Learning more about developmental needs, for example, in interpersonal skills;

3. *Continuing cognitive development.* Determining the level of cognitive ability and development of teachers so that future staff development and inservice schemes might be able to address potential differences more completely;

4. *Continuing theoretical development.* Contributing to the attainment of goals set forth in a selected educational theory;

5. *Continuing professional development.* Increasing the competence levels of teachers in a way that would enable these individuals to contribute to a knowledge base which would, in turn, also contribute to the development of teaching as a profession;

6. *Continuing career development.* Creating greater leadership skills and other competencies that might lead teachers eventually to greater development opportunities.

Other valid assessments of the purposes for staff development and inservice education are no doubt possible; Howey's ideas are offered primarily to indicate that this field has become increasingly sophisticated over the years. Staff development is no longer viewed as a "chore" that must be done periodically in schools or as a "frill" to be carried out only in wealthy districts. A look at the multiple purposes for staff development and inservice education suggests how critical a responsibility it is for those who provide leadership in schools. The effective leader must not only be well versed in the techniques for implementing staff development but must also settle upon a clear understanding of its purpose.

Program Evaluation

A second promising development in inservice education has appeared in an area often overlooked throughout most of professional education:

program evaluation. Bruce Joyce and Beverly Showers (1988, p. 118) suggest a useful conceptual framework for the evaluation of staff development, derived from a review of responses to questions in three categories:

- Questions related to the human resource development system as such. (The purpose of these questions is to determine generally how a system is doing. Is it in good health? Does it succeed in its purpose? How well does it provide for individuals, schools, and district initiatives?)

- Questions related to the major dimensions of the system and the health of those dimensions. (How well are individuals, schools, and system initiatives being served? What can be done to improve each identified dimension within a system?)

- Questions related to the study of specific programs and events within each dimension of a system. (A number of specific questions can be asked here, but only a few may be addressed in a formal evaluation system: Are programs that give teachers the opportunity to study teaching skills and strategies succeeding? Are school improvement programs being implemented and affecting the lives of students in a positive way? Are school district initiatives being implemented, and are they improving the performance of students?)

Once again, the suggestion here is not that this single analytic framework must be followed, but the work of Joyce and Showers is presented as one example of what is being done in one critical area. Staff development and inservice education programs must be evaluated intensively to determine if they are truly worth the effort of maintaining them. Past staff development programs have too often been attempts to provide simple answers to complex organizational problems, and they have not been adequately evaluated according to schemes such as the one presented here. This lack of evaluation contributes greatly to the perception of many teachers that programs are ineffective or at least that they are "snake oil remedies" that promise more than they deliver. Educational leaders need to direct their attention to ongoing evaluation if they truly want their efforts to be successful.

Mentoring

This chapter concludes by noting that there are some very promising practices associated with implementing more effective ongoing professional development opportunities for school personnel. One that is particularly noteworthy is mentoring, defined here as the forming of mutually supportive and learning relationships between two individuals who work together in the same or similar organization. Others have also called this type of relationship either *peer coaching* or simply *coaching*. Proactive leaders have an important part to play in designing and promoting mentoring in their school districts or within individual schools.

Many current mentoring programs have been established primarily to support beginning school teachers or, in a few cases, school administrators. In these instances, mentoring has been seen as a way to initiate newcomers to schools by pairing them with more experienced colleagues who can assist others in learning some "tricks of the trade" that are needed for survival and success in a new role.

Mentoring relationships can also serve as strategies to promote ongoing dialogue and collaboration between educators at all levels of their professional careers. Thus, teachers (or administrators) with several years of professional experience can learn from colleagues who might be willing to serve as "sounding boards" for their co-workers. The paradox of education is that, in spite of a world ostensibly filled with continuing needs for interpersonal contact, schools are indeed typically quite lonely places where teachers and others so often work in complete isolation from other adults. Mentoring programs may reduce this type of problem.

⚜ SUMMARY

Effective staff development and inservice education programs are critically important to the development of good schools. As a result, the planning, the implementation, and the eventual evaluation of formal professional development programs are particularly important responsibilities for the proactive leader, whose ultimate goal is always to make schools more effective.

This chapter considered the nature of recent research related to professional development. It also defined the characteristics typical of development programs that are considered effective, and noted that recent studies have tended to focus on the content and delivery of effective programs.

Two areas were explored where professional development programs experience their greatest problems: the extent to which adult learning and development principles are ignored and the lack of attention to individual learner differences. Following that were some suggestions of useful studies that leaders might consult to remedy persistent problems. The chapter ended with some promising recent trends in the areas of definition, evaluation, and mentoring that may lead to eventual refinement and improvement of professional development.

Suggested Activities

1. Interview a group of teachers to determine their perceptions of the strengths and weaknesses of staff development and inservice education programs in which they have recently been participated. Compare your findings with the issues related to individual differences and adult learning that were reviewed in this chapter.

2. Using the Levels of Concern description presented here, review how a group of five or more teachers react to the implementation of some new practice in their school. Chart the number of people found at each level as you carry out your interview.

Cases to Consider

Read each of the cases and consider the following:

- What are the critical issues related to each case, as they relate to the design of effective staff development and inservice education as a responsibility of the proactive leader?
- How does each case relate to the development of the concept of proactive leadership?
- In what ways might you suggest a resolution to the issues raised?

Case 17.1　But This Expert Was Highly Recommended!

Kathy Kleinschmidt sat in her office, staring out the window. The inservice session she sponsored yesterday for the teachers of Big Salmon High School was the biggest disaster she had seen in her five years as the staff development director of the Big Buckle School District.

Last year, when Kathy had attended a national conference on community involvement in local schools, she heard nothing but praise about Dr. Kyle Alexander, a former school superintendent now running his own consulting agency. Staff development directors whom Kathy had known for several years told her what a great job Dr. Alexander was reported to have done in school districts around the country. He was gaining a formidable reputation as a person who could motivate even the most resistant school staffs to get interested in site-based management and community involvement. He sounded like the kind of speaker who was needed at Big Buckle. Kathy made initial contacts with Dr. Alexander while at the conference and tentatively invited him to be the keynote speaker for the high school inservice day in the fall.

In the next few weeks, Kathy called the consultant to review the topics that should be addressed in his session. Dr. Alexander agreed to the plans and even sent the Big Buckle Schools a copy of his latest book, *Ten Steps to Community Involvement*, at no charge, along with a preview edition of his latest videotape. This was going to be a great inservice session—Big Buckle was finally going to play in the "big leagues" and get a big-time speaker for a change. This would be the typical day-long session where the teachers simply got together to work in teams to plan their strategies to deal with district goals.

When the day of the inservice session arrived, the high school auditorium was filled with teachers, central office staff, two board members, several professors from a local university, county office representatives, and some guests from other school systems. Dr. Alexander took the stage and began his session by sharing several brief jokes about his past experiences as a superintendent, as a teacher, as a parent, as a Rotary Club member, as a consultant, as a former high school student. The list of stories, many of which convulsed the audience with laughter, never seemed to end. Between each story, Dr. Alexander introduced one of his "Ten Steps" that appeared in his book. In fact, Kathy began to recognize whole sections of the book being presented almost verbatim to the crowd. Not once did Dr. Alexander make reference to any of the local concerns that Kathy shared with him before he arrived. For the first hour and a half, the crowd was attentive to the speaker. After the morning break, it was apparent that something was wrong. The laughter was not quite as loud, and people started to slip away for "urgent phone calls" or other matters outside the auditorium. It was clear that most people were not returning.

Luncheon was served in the cafeteria, and Kathy saw that teachers were speaking to each other in small groups around the room. As she circulated among the tables, she knew that the main topic of conversation was the morning session. At one o'clock the group reconvened in the auditorium to watch two of Dr. Alexander's tapes. The speaker seemed totally oblivious to the fact that, as he launched into yet another recollection of how his ten steps worked well in another community, the audience was less than half the size it had been at the opening session that morning. By three o'clock, when the audience was invited to question the speaker, the first ten rows of seats were barely full.

Kathy dreaded the thought of reading the evaluations for the day. She received a message to see the superintendent and knew that it was not going to be a pleasant meeting.

Case 17.2   Enough of These Frills!

Dr. Roberta Clark, superintendent of the Stone Hedge Independent Schools, was reflecting on the events of the last few weeks. In May, four members of the school board—the majority—were replaced by candidates who ran on a most appealing platform. They promised consistently that, if elected, they would do everything to "cut every cent of waste" from the district's operating budget. "Anything that can't be shown to have a direct impact on student learning goes." First on their "hit list" were the "deadbeat bureaucrats" working at the central office, or as one of the new board members consistently stated, "The Superintendent's Taj Mahal."

At last night's board meeting, the "hit list" was unrolled publicly for the first time. First, Dr. Clark was encouraged to look into ways to streamline administrative practices in the district. A strong suggestion was that she might think about phasing out the role of deputy superintendent, currently a job held by Ross McGinty. This would be a tough loss for Roberta because Ross did an awful lot of work behind the scenes to keep the budget for the district in line. On the other hand, he was identified by the new board members and one of their most prominent public supporters, a former district principal now turned talk-show host, as a drain on district finances. Roberta could only wonder if the fact that Ross had been the immediate supervisor of the former principal before he was dismissed from his last assignment had anything to do with his identification as a "waste of taxpayer money."

She was comfortable that she could eventually maneuver a compromise with the board over Ross. A bigger immediate concern was another focus of the "cost saving board." They had also begun to wonder publicly about the need to keep the director of staff development, Naomi Ramos, and her staff. One board member stated—in front of several television news reporters—that "money to send administrators and teachers off on vacation conferences and money to pay old friends as consultants to do inservice was money that could be used in classrooms." Roberta knew that it would be a matter of just a few days before the board "suggested" that she look into ways to get rid of that staff development "stuff."

Before the inevitable phone call would come from the board president, Roberta decided to develop a plan to safeguard staff development for the district. She called a meeting with the director and five principals for this afternoon. In that session, she would assign the task for the ad hoc committee to develop as strong a position paper as possible to identify the importance of maintaining a viable staff development and inservice initiative program for the district. This was to be a task that needed to be accomplished by "yesterday" so that it could be distributed to board members and key community members in advance of the next official board meeting. Having this kind of document out in the community might not prevent any further attacks, but it might provide a kind of "cooling-off period" so that a more effective long-term solution could be found.

As the five principals were called by Roberta and given a briefing on the issue and the desired report, each began to organize a few key points that needed to be included as part of this afternoon's discussion.

Applying the Concepts

Complete the following quiz to check your ability to apply concepts from this chapter to administrative and supervisory problems. Answers are found in Appendix I.

Greta Mahoney just became the assistant principal of Mountain Top Middle School. Her principal, David Koznofsky, had asked her what kinds of programs she believed that she could lead as an administrator, and her immediate response was, "Staff development. I'd love to lead the staff development program for the school." David was quite happy to turn over the assignment to his new assistant principal (along with all other duties she was expected to carry out this year). He personally did not really like the notion of running inservice sessions for teachers. If Greta wanted to do that kind of thing, she was welcome to it.

One of the first things that Greta faced was the design of the workshops and staff development activities that the teachers had to attend at the beginning of each new school year. She had a lot of freedom to determine what the topics for the training would be, for whom they would be designed, and the activities that would be used. Although she already knew many of the teachers at Mountain Top, she decided that, for the first activity as a new school administrator, this would be her show completely. This would be a way for her to introduce so many great ideas that she had wanted to share with her new colleagues.

Greta knew that one of the challenges that her new school would face this year would be the need to improve math scores on the state achievement test. So she decided that the two days of pre-school work sessions would be directed toward "Jolly Numbers: Moving Mountain Top to the Top of the Mountain in Math Skills." She lined up several different large-group sessions that would feature presentations by members of the district's Math Improvement Team, a few teachers at Mountain Top whose students did very well in math last year, and two professors from the local university who had once done a great deal of research on how to improve math instruction in middle schools. It would be a time filled with a lot of important content that teachers could use this next year.

The pre-school sessions came and went. Greta thought that things went very well—until she took a look at the evaluation forms that the teachers filled out after the two-day session. While many people thanked Greta for the hard work she had invested in setting up the workshop, the universal comment and feeling about the workshop was that the session was a disaster. Words like "irrelevant," "boring," "unrelated to my work," and other similar statements filled the forms. Greta now realized that she probably didn't know as much about staff development as she thought.

1. Of the following problems that have been identified with ineffective inservice programming, the one that might be most seriously affecting Greta's effort was that _____.

   a. the setting for the sessions was inappropriate

   b. presenters did not really know what they were talking about

   c. teachers felt as if they had no part in planning the program

   d. teachers were forced to attend the session

2. By requiring all teachers to attend all sessions, one of the following characteristics of well-planned adult learning activities that seems to have been ignored by Greta was that _____.

   a. adult learning is ego involved

   b. adults need to see the results of their efforts and have frequent and accurate feedback about progress being made toward their goals

   c. adults come to learning tasks with a wide range of diverse previous experience, knowledge, skills, and competencies

   d. adults reject prescriptions by others for their learning

3. In terms of Hall's "Levels of Concern" categories, the issue that seems to have been most clearly forgotten in this scenario of poor service was that _____.

   a. teachers' concerns might not be the same as those of the staff developer

   b. it is all right to have personal feelings

c. change cannot be accomplished overnight

d. within any group, there may be a variety of concerns

4. As Greta spoke with several teachers during the year, she began to appreciate that one of the problems that was not addressed in her inservice session was that the teachers in her school represented various experience groups of teachers. There were beginning teachers and several people who had just gotten through the first years of experience in classrooms. But the vast majority of teachers in the school had been there for many years. They had clear depth of professional expertise and experience. This group could be called people who were in the

_____.

a. preservice period

b. initial training period

c. security-building period

d. maturing period

5. Even though the first inservice of the year did not go well, after Greta spoke with many teachers and realized that her initial view that inservice should be directed toward math improvement was not off base. She would persist with the focus of inservice to improve math for more sessions during the year. In this case, she was committing her programs to which of the following functions that inservice can follow?

a. continuing understanding and discovery of self

b. continuing pedagogical development

c. continuing theoretical development

d. continuing professional development

Additional Reading

Avillion, Adrianne E. (2004). *A practical guide to staff development: Tools and techniques for effective* education. Marblehead, ME: HCPro, Inc.

Barth, Roland S. (1990). *Improving schools from within.* San Francisco: Jossey-Bass.

Daresh, John C. (2001). *Leaders helping leaders: A practical guide to administrative mentoring* (2nd ed.) Thousand Oaks, CA: Corwin Press.

Kagan, Stephen S. (2003). *30 reflective staff development exercises for educators.* Thousand Oaks, CA: Corwin Press.

Little, Judith W. (1981). *School success and staff development in urban desegregated schools: A summary of recently completed research.* Boulder, CO: Center for Action Research.

Loucks-Horsley, Susan, Harding, Catherine K., Arbuckle, Margaret A., Murray, Lynn B., Dubea, Cynthia, & Williams, Martha K. (1987). *Continuing to learn: A guidebook for teacher development.* Andover, MA: The Regional Laboratory for Educational Improvement of the Northeast and Islands.

Overly, Norman V. (1979). *Lifelong learning: A human agenda.* Alexandria, VA: Association for Supervision and Curriculum Development.

◆ 18 ◆

Future Trends in
Proactive Leadership

This final chapter explores some of the issues that serve as the basis for analyzing the field of educational leadership and that are believed to have an impact on the direction of future analysis.

◆ CONTINUING DEMANDS FOR ACCOUNTABILITY

This trend is, of course, tied directly to the increase in political activity in schools. As politicians seek greater favor with voters concerning their ability to demonstrate responsibility in the face of increased public demands for increased efficiency by public agencies, school leaders will also have to respond to this press. To date, this emphasis on increased accountability has resulted in more and more efforts to "prove" school effectiveness through such widely-used measures as statewide achievement tests and other similar indicators of whether or not schools are "doing the job." Although educators may carry on elaborate discussions to protest the use (or misuse or even abuse) of such approaches to determining the goodness of practice, it makes little difference when those who pay for schools are convinced that accountable practice in schools is a simple thing to determine. Educational leaders may note that "high numbers do not necessarily mean high levels of learning." But those who provide support for schools believe in this vision.

Educational leaders must be prepared to face ever-increasing demands for "higher test scores" and "lower dropout rates." There are likely to be more and more attempts to tie teacher and administrator salaries and even job evaluation directly to these types of indicators.

✑ GREATER RESPONSIVENESS TO DIVERSITY

As America has progressed in its development over the past century, there has been an increasing recognition of what it means to be a truly free and open, democratic society—in theory if not always in practice. The Civil Rights Movement of the 1960s moved this nation closer to an understanding and appreciation of its potential as society where racial, ethnic, gender, and religious differences among citizens can increasingly be viewed as an asset rather than a problem to be "solved."

For school leaders, this has enormous implications. A generation or so ago, the issues discussed in this vein often led to considerations on how to bring about desegregation of schools. Now, the educational leader is faced with the challenge of bringing about true unification with an eye toward maintenance and appreciation of diversity. In addition to the integration of racial and ethnic minority populations into the mainstream of American society, diversity now must include appreciation of linguistic differences, lifestyle differences, and differences in terms of learning abilities and needs. The challenges facing educators in the future will involve not only such issues as how to avoid discrimination against African American and Hispanic students and parents, but also how to work effectively with those populations, along with increasing numbers of Asian residents and immigrants from Eastern Europe, as well as populations not listed in these pages. The issue will not simply be one of reactively avoiding discriminatory practice, but rather in how to proactively include differences in the improvement of practice and learning for all.

✑ CONTINUED POLITICAL ACTIVITY

An amazing statement made by many educators is that "education is too political." The notion expressed in this phrase is tempting to believe but is simply untrue. Schools are the center of American life, including political life. As a result, the often-heard belief that "good schools are apolitical" is simply not realistic. It never has been and it never will be.

Even with this recognition of the fundamental political nature of public education, one cannot help but believe that the educational leader in the twenty-first century will increasingly find him- or herself at the center of many political struggles. As most people understand, recent proposals for increasing the accountability of schools are much more related to political agendas than they are to educational reform efforts. Since schooling and education are matters of significant emotional as well as practical impact on the lives of most taxpayers and voters, one can hardly assume that pressures to put education at the forefront of election promises and political debate will ever disappear.

The implications of this observation should be clear to the present and future educational leader. In short, schools will always be "in need of repair" according to the ideologies of one political group or another. And that means that those who serve as administrators and supervisors will be called upon consistently to furnish evidence that they are serving the public as efficiently and as effectively as possible. The political dialogue will define in large measure what "effective" and "efficient" means.

⚜ PRESS TOWARD MINIMALISM

The greatest problem with the press toward using common measures and standardized achievement testing as indicators of school effectiveness is that such forms of determining efficiency tend to look toward students' abilities to demonstrate minimal levels of competence. The argument that often goes with such efforts is quite tempting: "After all, if a child cannot demonstrate even the most fundamental command of reading, writing, spelling, and computation, how will he or she ever move on to more complex forms of learning?" The problem is, of course, that defining learning for all students according to attainment of the lowest levels of achievement is likely to have an extremely negative effect on learning at higher levels. In many cases across the nation, students are coached relentlessly so that they will "pass" the statewide achievement tests each year. Unfortunately, this diverts considerable instructional time and other resources to addressing what is actually a non-issue for many students who are able to move well beyond the stated standards. With the attention paid to "passing the state test," little time is available for learning enhancement and enrichment.

The educational leader, therefore, must find ways to walk the line between simply proving that her or his school is "good enough to meet the state expectations" while also ensuring that minimal performance does not become a proxy measure of maximum learning opportunities.

⚜ TRANSFORMATION TO LEARNING COMMUNITIES

Another trend that is likely to have significant impact on those who are educational leaders in this country involves what many are calling the creation of "learning organizations" or "learning communities." Here, the emphasis is on the design of practices and procedures that will focus on the ability of leaders to bring together all who might contribute to the success of an organization. In short, emphasis in the future will be on the importance of creating organizations where quality is derived from the work of all participants being viewed as whole, rather than simply individual parts. In school terms, the creation of "educated children" will be the goal of effective schools rather than simply having desirable outcomes in one or another subject area. Just because students get high math scores will not necessarily mean that their schooling experiences were successful.

Forging the school into a learning community has many challenges for the effective educational leader. For one thing, it means that the leader will work effectively with the staff to create a vision of how the school would become a more effective place for students if everyone would work toward a common goal. Second, if the common goal is to be that all who work in the school would strive to achieve the same desirable outcomes, it is critical that everyone be included in the creation of the vision. That means that learning becomes a goal not only of teachers and administrators, but also of custodians, food service workers, clerks, and anyone else who has the opportunity to affect the nature of practice in the school as a learning community. Further, significant groups outside the walls of the school must also become involved. These include parents, community members without children in schools, business leaders, and others. In short, viewing schools as learning communities requires educational leaders to look at their work in much more inclusive terms than ever before. Traditional images of supervisors and administrators as those who maintain order by controlling teachers and their interactions with students will become much less viable in the future.

❧ INCREASED ATTACKS ON PUBLIC EDUCATION

The radio program of talk-show host (and convicted Watergate-era felon) G. Gordon Liddy rarely went more than a week without some presentation of the shortcomings of what Liddy always referred to sneeringly as "the government schools in this country." He was referring to American public schools. Early in 2006, the ABC News department's weekly show, 20/20, presented a full-hour report by conservative reporter John Stossel to describe the horrible things that are part of public school education in the United States. Included were segments showing out-of-control students playing during a social studies class in Washington, DC, and what seemed like an example of a "typical union meeting" for New York City teachers at Madison Square Garden. The "deplorable state of public education in this country" was presented largely as a result of parents having no choice in where to send their children to school, as well as out-of-control teacher unions.

Add these kinds of reports to numerous inaccurate depictions of public education like the TV show Boston Public, where every other teacher appears to be psychotic and the remainder of the school staff seems to be having illicit affairs with students, and it begins to appear as if there might even be a conspiracy that has been developed to support the abandonment of public schools in this country. The reason for the attacks? Perhaps it is because of a genuine belief that quality education must contain an element of elitism; serving all students under one roof will lead to nothing but chaos. Perhaps, too, for many the underlying issue may be the perceived need to "improve education," either by returning religious values to the curriculum or at least by moving forward the never-ending agenda pushed by conservatives to promote vouchers enabling students to "escape the horrible public schools of the United States."

Whatever the motivation for those who consistently predict the demise of public school in the United States, nothing changes the fact that public schools (and public school administrators and supervisors) are likely to face continuing efforts to discredit the work of those who serve children in "government schools" each day.

◈ SUMMARY

The first three editions of this book noted several different issues assumed to be important areas that would have to be addressed by proactive leaders of the future. These included continued calls for educational reform, increased professionalism of educational leaders, more opportunities for professional development for educators, battles over standards and outcomes, and increased expectations for social roles of schools. This concluding chapter notes a number of additional challenges likely to face educational leaders in the future. The new issues reported in this chapter are not meant to suggest that the problems noted earlier have now been totally resolved. The point is, however, that whatever issues have been viewed as important in the past, the educational leader will always be called upon to face even more complex and challenging demands.

Many of the most perplexing problems to be faced by educational leaders cannot be imagined by most people at this point. For example, in 1979 it would have been inconceivable for anyone to imagine that personal computers would be available to almost anyone who wanted one. Therefore, developing school policies to deal with the inappropriate use of the Internet would have been impossible to foresee. But in a relatively short period of time, what goes on in schools (and society in general) has been totally transformed as a result of one scientific development. In this chapter, a very few issues have been enumerated because they are likely to have a significant impact on the ways in which educational leaders will be able to do their jobs. It is through this type of analysis that it may be possible to identify ways in which proactive behavior will continue to flourish in the next several years.

Appendix
Applying the Concepts Answer Key

Following are the answers to the quizzes found in the *applying the concepts* section at the end of each chapter.

Chapter 1	Chapter 2	Chapter 3
1. b.	1. b.	1. c.
2. c.	2. c.	2. b.
3. d.		

Chapter 4	Chapter 5	Chapter 6
1. b.	1. a.	1. d.
2. c.	2. b.	2. c.
		3. b.
		4. d.

Chapter 7	Chapter 8	Chapter 9
1. b.	1. c.	1. c.
2. c.	2. a.	2. b.
3. a.		3. b.
4. c.		4. c.
		5. c.
		6. d.

Chapter 10

1. c.
2. d.
3. a.

Chapter 11

1. a.
2. d.
3. d.

Chapter 12

1. b.
2. c.
3. d.
4. c.
5. c.

Chapter 13

1. a.
2. c.
3. a.

Chapter 14

1. d.
2. c.
3. a.

Chapter 15

1. c.
2. b.
3. d.
4. c.

Chapter 16

1. d.
2. a.
3. c.
4. b.

Chapter 17

1. c.
2. c.
3. d.
4. d.
5. d.

References

Acheson, Keith A., & Gall, Meredith D. (1987). *Techniques in the clinical supervision of teachers* (2nd ed.) White Plains, NY: Longman.

Alinsky, Saul D. (1971). *Rules for radicals.* New York: Vintage Books.

Anderson, L. W. (1985). Policy implications of research on school time. *School Administrator, 40,* 25–28.

Andrews, P. H., & Baird, J. E. (2005). *Communication for business and the professions* (8th ed.). Long Grove, IL: Waveland Press.

Andrews, Richard, & Smith, Wilma (1991). *Instructional leadership: How principals make a difference.* Alexandria, VA: Association for Supervision and Curriculum Development.

Argyle, M. (1994). *Bodily communication.* London: Routledge.

Argyris, Chris (1965). *Integrating the individual and the organization.* New York: Wiley.

Argyris, Chris (1971). *Management and organization development.* New York: McGraw-Hill.

Armstrong, David G., Henson, Kenneth T., & Savage, Tom V. (1981). *Education: An introduction.* New York: Macmillan.

Austin, G. R. (1979, October). Exemplary schools and the search for effectiveness. *Educational Leadership, 35* (1): 10–14.

Barker, Joel (1996). *Visions.* Videotape production by the author.

Barnett, Bruce (1991). *The educational platform: A developmental activity for preparing moral school leaders.* Paper presented at the Annual Meeting of the American Educational Research Association, Chicago, IL.

Barnett, Bruce (1992). Using alternative assessment measures in educational leadership programs: Educational platforms and portfolios. *Journal of Personnel Evaluation in Education, 6:* 141–151.

Barnett, Bruce, MacQuarrie, Frank O., & Norris, Cynthia J. (eds.) (1991). *The moral imperatives of leadership: A focus on human decency.* Fairfax, VA: National Policy Board for Educational Administration.

Bass, Bernard M. (1960). *Leadership, psychology, and organizational behavior.* New York: Harper and Row.

Beck, Lynn, & Murphy, Joseph (1993). *Understanding the principalship: Metaphorical themes, 1920s–1990s*. New York: Teachers College Press.

Benne, Kenneth D., & Sheats, Paul (1948, Spring). Functional roles of group members. *Journal of Social Issues, 4* (2): 41–49.

Bennett, N., Wise, C., Woods, P.A., and Harvey, J. A. (2003) *Distributed leadership*. Nottingham, England: National College for School Leadership.

Bennis, Warren G., Benne, Kenneth D., & Chin, Robert (1969). *The planning of change* (2nd ed.) New York: Holt, Rinehart, and Winston.

Bennis, Warren, & Nanus, Burt (1985). *Leaders: Strategies for taking charge*. New York: Harper and Row.

Benthal, J., & Polkemus, T. (eds.) (1975). *The body as a medium of communication*. London: Allen Lane.

Bents, R. H., & Howey, Kenneth R. (1981). Staff development: Change in the individual. In Betty Dillon-Peterson (ed.), *Staff development, organization development*. Alexandria, VA: Association for Supervision and Curriculum Development.

Berliner, David, & Tikunoff, William (1976). The California Beginning Teacher Evaluation Study: Overview of the ethnographic study. *Journal of Teacher Education, 27*.

Berliner, David, & Tikunoff, William (1976). The California Beginning Teacher Evaluation Study: Overview of the ethnographic study. *Journal of Teacher Education, 27*.

Bhola, H. S. (1965, October). *The configuration theory of innovation diffusion*. Columbus: The Ohio State University, College of Education.

Biggs, Thomas H., & Justman, Joseph (1952). *Improving instruction through supervision*. New York: Macmillan.

Blake, Robert R., & Adams McCanse, Anne (1991). *Leadership dilemmas—Grid solutions*. Houston: Gulf Publishing.

Blake, Robert R., & Mouton, Jane S. (1985). *The managerial grid III*. Houston: Scientific Methods.

Blake, Robert, & Mouton, Jane (1964). *The managerial grid*. Houston, TX: Gulf Publishing.

Blase, Joseph, & Kirby, Peggy (1992). *Bringing out the best in teachers: What effective principals do*. Thousand Oaks, CA: Corwin.

Block, Peter (1988). *The empowered manager: Positive political skills at work*. San Francisco: Jossey-Bass.

Block, Peter (1993). *Stewardship: Choosing service over self interest*. San Francisco: Jossey-Bass.

Blumberg, Arthur (1974). *Supervisors and teachers: A private cold war*. Boston: Allyn & Bacon.

Bobbitt, Franklin (1918). *The curriculum*. Boston: Houghton Mifflin.

Bolman, Lee G., & Deal, Terrence E. (2002). *Reframing organizations: Artistry, choice, and leadership* (2nd ed.). San Francisco: Jossey-Bass.

Borich, Gary D. (1977). *The appraisal of teaching: Concepts and process*. Reading, MA: Addison-Wesley.

Boulding, Kenneth (1962). *Conflict and defense: A general theory*. New York: Harper and Row.

Bowers, D. G., & Seashore, S. E. (1966). Predicting organizational effectiveness with a four-factor theory of leadership. *Administrative Science Quarterly, 11* (2): 238–263.

Bredeson, Paul (2003). *Design for learning: A new architecture for professional development*. Thousand Oaks, CA: Corwin.

Brimm, J. R., & Tollett, D. J. (1975). How do teachers feel about inservice education? *Educational Leadership, 30* (7): 60–62.

Brookover, W. B., & Lezotte, L. (1980). *Changes in school characteristics coincident with changes in student achievement*. East Lansing: Michigan State University, College of Urban Development.

Burns, James McGregor (1978). *Leadership*. New York: Harper and Row.

Campbell, Roald F., & Gregg, R. (eds.) (1957). *Administrative behavior in education*. New York: Harper.

Capper, Colleen A. (1995). An otherist poststructural perspective of the knowledge base in educational administration. In Robert Donmoyer, Michael Imber, & James Scheurich (eds.), *The knowledge base in educational administration: Multiple perspectives*. Albany, NY: SUNY Press.

Carlson, Robert V. (1996). *Reframing and reform: Perspectives on organization, leadership, and school change*. White Plains, NY: Longman.

Carroll, J. G. (1981). Faculty self-evaluation. In Jason Millman (ed.), *Handbook of teacher evaluation*. Beverly Hills: Sage.

Cartwright, Dorian, & Zander, Alvin (eds.) (1960). *Group dynamics: Research and theory* (2nd ed.). Evanston, IL: Harper and Row.

Cawelti, Gordon, & Reavis, Charles (1980). How well are we providing instructional improvement services? *Educational Leadership, 38*: 236–240.

Cheney, George, Thøger Christensen, Lars, Zorn, Theodore E., Jr., & Ganesh, Shiv (2004). *Organizational Communication in an Age of Globalization: Issues, Reflections, Practices*. Long Grove, IL: Waveland Press.

Chicago Public Schools (2004). Executive summary, proposal for the Educational Leaders Improve Instruction grant. Washington, DC: U.S. Department of Education.

Ciampa, Dan (1992). *Total quality: A user's guide for implementation*. Reading, MA: Addison Wesley.

Clark, David L., & Guba, Egon G. (1975, April). The configurational perspective: A new view of educational knowledge production and utilization. *Educational Researcher, 4* (4): 112–115.

Cogan, Morris (1961). *Supervision at the Harvard-Newton Summer School*. Unpublished paper. Harvard Graduate School of Education.

Cogan, Morris (1973). *Clinical supervision*. Boston: Houghton Mifflin.

Cooley, Charles H. (1909). *Social organization*. New York: Scribner.

Covey, Stephen R. (1991). *Principle-centered leadership*. New York: Simon and Schuster.

Cox, Philip W. L. (1934). *High school administration and supervision*. New York: American Book Company.

Culbertson, Jack A. (1988) A century's quest for a knowledge base. In Norman Boyan (ed.), *Handbook of Research on Educational Administration*. White Plains, NY: Longman.

Daresh, John C. (1987). Research trends in staff development and inservice education. *Journal of Education for Teaching, 13* (1): 3–11.

Darling-Hammond, Linda (2000). Teacher quality and student achievement: A review of state policy evidence. *Education Policy and Analysis Archives, 8* (1).

Dempsey, R. A., & Traverso, H. P. (1983). *Scheduling the secondary school*. Reston, VA: National Association of Secondary School Principals.

Deutsch, Morton (1973). *The resolution of conflict: Constructive and destructive processes*. New Haven, CT: Yale University Press.

Dewey, John (1929). *The sources of a science of education*. New York: Horace Liveright.

Drucker, Peter F. (1967). *The effective executive*. New York: Harper and Brothers.

Duke, Daniel L. (1984). *Teaching: An imperiled profession*. Albany: SUNY Press.

Dwight, Theodore (1835). *The school-master's friend of the committee man's guide*. New York: Roe Lockwood.

Education Commission of the States (2002). *Interstate leadership licensure consortium standards*. Washington, DC: Author.

Eisner, Eliot W. (1979). *The educational imagination*. New York: Macmillan.

Eisner, Elliot W. (1982). An artistic approach to supervision. In Thomas J. Sergiovanni (ed.), *Supervision of teaching* (1982 Yearbook of the Association for Supervision and Curriculum Development). Alexandria, VA: The Association.

Eisner, Elliot W. (1985). *The educational imagination* (2nd ed.). New York: Macmillan.

Ekman, P. (1976). *Telling Lies*. New York: Berkeley Press.

Eliot, E. C. (1914). *City school supervision*. New York: World Book Company.

Etzioni, Amitai (1975). *A comparative analysis of complex organizations* (rev. ed.). New York: Free Press.

Etzioni, Amitai (1990). *The Moral Dimension*. New York: Macmillan.

Fay, Peter, & Doyle, A. G. (1972). Stages of group development. In J. W. Pfeiffer & J. E. Jones (eds.), *The 1982 annual handbook for facilitators, trainers, and consultants*. San Diego: University Associates.

Flanders, Ned A. (1970). *Analyzing teaching behavior*. Reading, MA: Addison-Wesley.

French, J. R. P., & Raven, B. (1961). The bases of social power. In D. Cartwright & A. Zander (eds.), *Group dynamics: Research and theory* (2nd ed.). Evanston, IL: Harper and Row.

Fullan, Michael (1973). Overview of the innovative process and the user. *Interchange, 3*: 1–46.

Fuller, Frances F. (1969). Concerns of teachers: A developmental conceptualization. *American Educational Research Association, 6*: 207–226.

Furnham, Adrian (1999). *Body language at work*. London: Institute of Personnel and Development.

Garman, Noreen B. (1982). The clinical approach to teaching. In Thomas J. Sergiovanni (ed.), *Supervision of teaching* (1982 Yearbook of the Association for Supervision and Curriculum Development). Alexandria, VA: The Association.

Geer, Blanche (1965). Teaching. In E. Sils (ed.), *International encyclopedia of the social sciences*. New York: Free Press.

Getzels, Jacob W., & Guba, Egon G. (1952). A psycho-sociological framework for the study of educational administration. *Harvard Educational Review, 22*: 235–246.

Getzels, Jacob W., & Guba, Egon G. (1957). Social behavior and the administrative process. *The School Review, 65*: 423–441.

Glanz, J. (1998). *Action research: An educational leader's guide to school improvement*. Norwood, MA: Christopher-Gordon.

Glatthorn, Allan A. (1986). How does the school schedule affect the curriculum? In H. J. Walberg & J. W. Keefe (eds.), *Rethinking reform: The principal's dilemma*. Reston, VA: National Association of Secondary School Principals.

Glatthorn, Allan A. (1997). *Differentiated supervision* (2nd ed.) Alexandria, VA: Association for Supervision and Curriculum Development.

Glatthorn, Allan A. (2006). *The principal as curriculum leader* (3rd ed.). Thousand Oaks, CA: Sage Publications.

Glatthorn, Allan A., Whitehead, Bruce M., & Boschee, Floyd (2005). *Curriculum leadership: Development and implementation.* Thousand Oaks, CA: Sage Publications.

Glickman, Carl D. (1992). Introduction: Postmodernism and supervision. In C. Glickman (ed.), *Supervision in transition (1992 Yearbook of the Association for Supervision and Curriculum Development).* Alexandria, VA: The Association.

Glickman, Carl D., Gordon, Stephen P., & Ross-Gordon, Jovita M. (2007). *Supervision of instruction: A developmental approach.* (7th ed.) Boston: Allyn & Bacon.

Goldhammer, Robert (1969). *Clinical supervision.* New York: Holt, Rinehart, and Winston.

Goldhammer, Robert, Anderson, Robert H., & Krajewski, Robert J. (1993). *Clinical supervision: Special methods for the supervision of teachers* (3rd ed.). San Diego: Harcourt, Brace, and Jovanovich.

Good, T. L., & Brophy, J. (2002). *Looking in classrooms* (9th ed.). Boston: Allyn & Bacon.

Gorton, Richard A. (1962). Perceptions of organizational authority: A comparative analysis. *Administrative Science Quarterly, 6* (4).

Gorton, Richard A. (1988). *School leadership and administration: Important concepts, case studies, and simulations* (3rd ed.). Dubuque: Brown.

Gould, R. (1972). The phases of adult life: A study in developmental psychology. *The American Journal of Psychiatry, 129*: 521–531.

Greenleaf, Robert K. (1977). *Servant leadership.* New York: Paulist Press.

Griffiths, Daniel (1982). *Theories: Past, present, and future.* Paper presented at the Fifth International Intervisitation Program, Lagos, Nigeria.

Guskey, Thomas (2000). *Evaluating professional development.* Thousand Oaks, CA: Corwin.

Hackman, M. Z., & Johnson, C. E. (2004). *Leadership: A communication perspective* (4th ed.). Long Grove, IL: Waveland Press.

Hage, Jerald (1965). An axiomatic theory of organizations. *Administrative Science Quarterly,* 10 (3): 289–320.

Hage, Jerald, & Aiken, Michael (1970). *Social change in complex organizations.* New York: Random House.

Hall, Gene (1987). *Taking charge of change.* Alexandria, VA: Association for Supervision and Curriculum Development.

Hall, Gene E., & Hord, Shirley (2001). *Implementing change: Patterns, principles, and potholes.* Boston: Allyn & Bacon.

Hall, Gene E., & Loucks, Susan (1976). *A developmental model for determining whether or not the treatment really is implemented.* Austin: Texas Research and Development Center for Teacher Education.

Hall, Gene E., & Loucks, Susan (1978, September). Teacher concerns as a basis for facilitating and personalizing staff development. *Teachers College Record,* 36–53.

Hallinger, Philip, Leithwood, Kenneth, & Murphy, Joseph (eds.) (1993). *Cognitive perspectives on educational leadership.* New York: Teachers College Press.

Halpin, Andrew W. (1957). A paradigm for research on administrative behavior. In R. F. Campbell & Russell T. Gregg (eds.), *Administrative behavior in education.* Chicago: University of Chicago, Midwest Administrative Center.

Halpin, Andrew W. (1967). *Theory and research in administration.* New York: Macmillan.

Halpin, Andrew W., & Croft, Donald B. (1963). The organizational climate of schools. *Administrator's Notebook*, 11: 1–2.

Halpin, Andrew W., & Winer, J. A. (1957). A factorial study of the leader behavior description questionnaire. In R. M. Stogdill & A. E. Coons (eds.), *Leader behavior: Its description and measurement* (Research Monograph Series No. 88). Columbus: The Ohio State University, Bureau of Business Research.

Hames, C. C., & Joseph, D. H. (1986). *Basic concepts of helping: A holistic approach* (2nd ed.). East Norwalk, CT: Appleton-Century-Crofts.

Hamilton, L. S., & Koretz, D. M. (2002). Tests and their use in test-based accountability systems. In. S. P. Klein (ed.), *Making sense of test-based accountability in education*. Santa Monica, CA: RAND.

Harris, Ben M. (1976). Limits and supplements to formal clinical supervision. *Journal of Research and Development in Education, 9* (2): 85–89.

Havelock, Ronald G. (1969). *Planning for innovation through dissemination and utilization of knowledge*. Ann Arbor, MI: Institute for Social Research, Center for Research on Utilization of Scientific Knowledge.

Havelock, Ronald G. (1972). *Bibliography on knowledge utilization and dissemination*. Ann Arbor, MI: Institute for Social Research, Center for Research on Utilization of Scientific Knowledge.

Havelock, Ronald G. (1973). *Training for change agents*. Ann Arbor, MI: Institute for Social Research, Center for Research and Utilization of Scientific Knowledge.

Heck, Shirley F., & Williams, C. Ray (1984). *The complex roles of the teacher: An ecological perspective*. New York: Teachers College Press.

Hemphill, John K. (1949). *Situational factors in leadership*. Columbus: The Ohio State University Press.

Hemphill, John K., & Coons, A. E. (1957). Development of the leader behavior description questionnaire. In R. M. Stogdill & A. E. Coons (eds.), *Leader behavior: Its description and measurement* (Research Monograph Series 88). Columbus: The Ohio State University, Bureau of Business Research.

Henderson, E. S. (1979). The concept of school-focused inservice education and training. *British Journal of Teacher Education, 5* (1): 17–25.

Henson, Kenneth T. (2006). *Curriculum planning: Integrating Multiculturalism, Constructivism, and Educational Reform* (3rd ed.). Long Grove, IL: Waveland Press.

Hersey, Paul, & Kenneth H. Blanchard (1996). *Management of Organizational Behavior* (7th ed.). Mahwah, NJ: Prentice-Hall.

Herzberg, F. (1966). *Work and the nature of man*. Cleveland: World Publishing.

Hodgkinson, Christopher (1991). *Educational leadership: The moral art*. Albany: SUNY Press.

House, Ernest R. (1974). *The politics of educational innovation*. Berkeley: McCutchan.

House, Robert J. (1973). A path-goal theory of leader effectiveness. In W. Scott, Jr., & L. L. Cummings (eds.), *Readings in organizational behavior and human performance*. Homewood, IL: Irwin.

Howey, Kenneth (1985). Six major functions of staff development: An expanded imperative. *Journal of Teacher Education*, 58–64.

Hoy, Wayne K., & Miskel, Cecil G. (1988). *Educational administration: Theory, research, and practice* (2nd ed.). New York: Random House.

Hughes, Larry W. (1984). Organizing and managing time. In James M. Cooper, (ed.), *Developing skills for instructional supervision*. White Plains, NY: Longman.

Hutson, Harry M. (1981). Inservice best practices: The learnings of general education. *Journal of Research and Development in Education, 14* (2): 277–283.

Jacobs, T. O. (1970). *Leadership and exchange in formal organizations*. Alexandria, VA: Human Resources Research Corporation.

Jamison, Larry W., & Thomas, Kenneth W. (1974). Power and conflict in the teacher-student relationship. *Journal of Applied Behavioral* Science, *10* (3): 326.

Janada, K. F. (1960). Toward the explication of the concept of leadership in terms of the concept of power. *Human Relations, 13*: 345–363.

Jensen, Mary C. (1989). Leading the instructional staff. In Stuart C. Smith & Philip K. Piele (eds.), *School leadership: Handbook for excellence*. Eugene, OR: ERIC Clearinghouse on Educational Management, University of Oregon.

Joftus, S., & Maddox-Dolan, B. (2003). *Left out and left behind: NCLB and the American high school*. Washington, DC: Alliance for Excellent Education.

Joyce, Bruce, & Showers, Beverly (1988). *Student achievement through staff development*. White Plains, NY: Longman.

Jung, Carl G. (1923). Psychological types. In Jacob Jolande (ed.) (1970), *Psychological reflections: A new anthology of the writings on C. J. Jung*. Princeton: Princeton University Press.

Katz, D., & Kahn, R. L. (1978). *The social psychology of organizations* (2nd ed.). New York: Wiley.

Kelly, George (1965). *A theory of personality: The psychology of personal constructs*. New York: Norton.

Killian, Jane (2002). *Assessing impact: Evaluating staff development*. Oxford, OH, National Staff Development Council.

Kimmelman, Paul L. (2006). *Implementing NCLB: Creating a knowledge framework to support school improvement*. Thousand Oaks, CA: Corwin.

Knowles, Malcolm S. (1970). *The modern practice of adult education*. New York: Association Press.

Kochran, T. A., Schmidt, S. S., & DeCotiis, T. A. (1975). Superior-subordinate relations: Leadership and headship. *Human Relations, 28*: 279–294.

Kormanski, Chuck (1999). *The team: Explorations in group process*. Denver: Love Publishing.

Kouzes, J. M., & Posner, B. Z. (1987). *The leadership challenge*. San Francisco: Jossey-Bass.

Kunkel, Richard C., & Tucker, Susan (1977). *A perception-based model of program evaluation: A values-oriented theory*. Paper presented at the Annual Meeting of the American Educational Research Association, New York.

Lawrence, Gordon (1974). *Patterns of effective inservice*. Tallahassee: Florida Department of Education.

Lawrence, Gordon (1982). *People types and tiger stripes: A practical guide to learning styles*. Gainesville, FL: Center for Applications of Psychological Types.

Leithwood, K. (1989). *Expert problem solving*. Albany: SUNY Press.

Leithwood, K., & Montgomery, D. (1986). *Improving principal effectiveness: The principal profile*. Toronto: OISE Press.

Leithwood, K., & Steinbach, R. (1995). *Expert problem solving: Evidence from school and district leaders*. Albany: SUNY Press.

Levinson, Daniel (1978). *The seasons of a man's life*. New York: Knopf.

Lieberman, Anne, & Miller, Lynne (1984). *Teachers, their world, and their work: Implications for school improvement*. Alexandria, VA: Association for Supervision and Curriculum Development.

Lindstrom, P. M., & Speck, Marsha (2004). *The principal as professional development leader*. Thousand Oaks, CA: Corwin.

Lipham, James M. (1965). Leadership and administration. In Daniel Griffiths (ed.), *Behavioral science and educational administration*. Chicago: National Society for the Study of Education.

Lipham, James M. (1981). *Effective principal, effective school*. Reston, VA: National Association of Secondary School Principals.

Lipham, James M., & Hoeh, James A. (1974). *The principalship: Foundations and functions*. New York: Harper and Row.

Lippitt, G. (1969). *Organizational renewal*. New York: Appleton-Century-Crofts.

Lippitt, R., Watson, J., & Westley, B. (1958). *The dynamics of planned change* New York: Harcourt Brace Jovanovich.

Littrell, Janet, & Foster, William (1995). The myth of a knowledge base in administration. In Robert Donmoyer, Michael Imber, & James Scheurich (eds.), *The knowledge base in educational administration: Multiple perspectives*. Albany: SUNY Press.

Liu, Ching-Jen (1984). *An identification of principals' instructional leadership behavior in effective high schools*. Unpublished Ed.D. dissertation, The University of Cincinnati.

Loevinger, J. (1976). *Ego development*. San Francisco: Jossey-Bass.

Lortie, Dan C. (1975). *Schoolteacher*. Chicago: University of Chicago Press.

Lovell, John T., & Phelps, M. S. (1976). *Supervision in Tennessee: A study of perceptions of teachers, principals, and supervisors*. Murfreesboro: Tennessee Association for Supervision and Curriculum Development.

Lovell, John T., & Wiles, Kimball (1983). *Supervision for better schools* (5th ed.). Englewood Cliffs, NJ: Prentice-Hall.

Lunenburg, Fred C., & Ornstein, Allan C. (2004). *Educational administration: Concepts and practices* (4th ed.). Belmont, CA: Wadsworth/Thomson Learning

Marion, Russ. (2002). *Leadership in education: Organizational theory for the practitioner*. Long Grove, IL: Waveland Press.

Maslow, A. H. (1970). *Motivation and personality* (2nd ed.) New York: Harper and Row.

Massachusetts Bay Company in New England: Records of the Governor and the Company. (1642). (Vol. II).

McDonald, Joseph P. (1992). *Teaching: Making sense of an uncertain craft*. New York: Teachers College Press.

McGregor, Douglas (1960). *The human side of enterprise*. New York: McGraw-Hill.

McLaren, Peter (1989). *Life in schools: An introduction to critical pedagogy in the foundations of education*. White Plains, NY: Longman.

McLaughlin, Milbrey (1976). Implementation as mutual adaptation: Change in classroom organization. *Teachers College Record, 77*: 339–351.

McLaughlin, Milbrey, & Berman, Paul (1977). Retooling staff development in an era of decline. *Educational Leadership, 34*: 21–28.

McLaughlin, Milbrey, & Marsh, David D. (1978). Staff development and school change. *Teachers College Record, 80* (1): 69–94.

Miles, Matthew B. (1965). Planned change and organizational health: Figure and ground. *Change processes in the public schools*. Eugene: University of Oregon, Center for the Advanced Study of Educational Administration.

Morgan, Gareth (1987). *Images of organizations*. Beverly Hills, CA: Sage.

Morgan, Gareth (1996). *Images of organizations* (2nd ed.). Thousand Oaks, CA: Sage.

Mosher, Robert L., & Purpel, David E. (1972). *Supervision: The reluctant profession*. Boston: Houghton Mifflin.

Myers, Isabel Briggs, & Briggs, Katherine (1962). *The Myers-Briggs Type Indicator.* Princeton: Educational Testing Service.

National Education Association, Department of Superintendence (1930). *The superintendent survey supervision* (Yearbook 8). Washington, DC: Authors.

National Policy Board for Educational Administration (1989). *Improving the preparation of school administrators: An agenda for reform.* Charlottesville, VA: NPBEA.

Nicholson, A. M., Joyce, Bruce R., Parker, D. W., & Waterman, F. T. (1976). *The literature of inservice education: An analytic review.* Palo Alto, CA: Stanford Center for Research and Development in Teaching.

Oberg, Antoinette (1986). Using construct theory as a basis for research into teacher professional development. *Journal of Curriculum Studies, 19* (1): 55–65.

Oliva, P. F., & Pawlas, G. E. (2004). *Supervision for today's schools* (7th ed.). New York: Wiley.

Olmstead, Michael S., & Hare, A. Paul (1978). *The small group* (2nd ed.) New York: Random House.

Orfield, G., & Kornhaber, M. L. (eds.) (2001). *Raising standards or raising barriers?* New York: Century Foundation Press.

Owens, Robert G. (1987). *Organizational behavior in education* (3rd ed.) Englewood Cliffs, NJ: Prentice-Hall.

Owens, Robert G. (1998). *Organizational behavior in education* (5th ed.) Upper Saddle River, NJ: Prentice-Hall.

Owens, Robert G., & Valesky, Thomas (2007). *Organizational Behavior in Education* (9th ed.). Boston: Allyn & Bacon.

Palonsky, Stuart B. (1986). *900 shows a year: A look at teaching from a teacher's side of the desk.* New York: Random House.

Patterson, Jerry L. (1993). *Leadership for tomorrow's schools.* Alexandria, VA: Association for Supervision and Curriculum Development.

Paul, Douglas (1977). Change processes at the elementary, secondary, and post-secondary levels. In J. Culbertson & N. Nash (eds.), *Linking processes in educational improvement.* Columbus: University Council for Educational Administration.

Payne, William H. (1875). *Chapters on school administration.* New York: Wilson Hinkle and Company.

Peabody, Robert L. (1962).Perceptions of organizational authority: A comparative analysis. *Administrative Science Quarterly, 6* (4): 460–461.

Peters, T. J., & Waterman, R. H. (1982). *In search of excellence.* New York: Harper and Row.

Playko, Marsha A. (1991). *The voyage to leadership: Journeys of four teachers.* Unpublished Ph.D. dissertation, The Ohio State University.

Porter, L. W., & Lawler, E. (1965). *Managerial attitudes and performance.* Homewood, IL: Irwin.

Prestine, N. A., & LeGrand, B. (1991). Cognitive learning theory and the preparation of educational administrators: Implications for practice and policy. *Educational Administration Quarterly, 18* (1): 16–25.

Pugach, Marleen C., & Johnson, Lawrence J. (1995). *Collaborative practitioners, collaborative schools.* Denver: Love Publishing.

Reddin, W. J. (1967). The 3-D management style theory. *Training and Development Journal, 21,* 8–17.

Reddin, W. J. (1970). *Managerial effectiveness.* New York: McGraw-Hill.

Redding, W. C. (1972). *Communication within the organization.* New York: Industrial Communications Council.

Reilly, A. J., & Jones, J. E. (1974). Team building. In J. W. Pfeiffer & J. E. Jones (eds.), *The 1974 annual handbook for facilitators, trainers, and consultants.* San Diego: University Associates.

Resser, Clayton (1973). *Management: Functions and modern concepts.* Chicago: Scott, Foresman.

Ritz, W. C., & Cashell, J. G. (1980, October). "Cold War" between supervisors and teachers? *Educational Leadership, 38*: 77–78.

Rodgers, Frederick A. (1976). Past and future of teaching: You've come a long way. *Educational Leadership, 34*: 97–99.

Rogers, E. M. (1962). *Diffusion of innovations.* New York: The Free Press of Glencoe.

Rogers, E. M., & Shoemaker, F. F. (1971). *Communication of innovations: A cross-cultural approach.* New York: Free Press.

Rokeach, Milton (1971). *Beliefs, attitudes, and values: A theory of organization and change.* San Francisco: Jossey-Bass.

Rubin, Louis J. (1985). *Artistry in teaching.* New York: Random House.

Russell, D., & Hunter, M. (1980). *Planning for effective instruction.* Los Angeles: University Elementary School.

Ryan, B., & Gross, N. (1943). The diffusion of hybrid seed corn in two Iowa communities. *Rural Sociology, 8*: 15–24.

Schmuck, Richard A., & Miles, Matthew B. (1971). *Organizational development in schools.* Palo Alto, CA: National Press Books.

Schön, Donald A. (1983). *The reflective practitioner: How professionals think in action.* New York: Basic Books.

Schubert, William H. (1986). *Curriculum: Perspectives, paradigm, and possibility.* New York: Macmillan.

Scriven, Michael (1967). The methodology of evaluation. In Robert E. Stake (ed.), *Curriculum evaluation.* American Educational Research Association Monograph Series on Evaluation. Chicago: Rand McNally.

Senge, Peter (1990). *The fifth discipline.* New York: Doubleday.

Sergiovanni, Thomas J. (1990). *Value-added leadership.* San Diego: Harcourt Brace Jovanovich.

Sergiovanni, Thomas J. (ed.) (1982). *Supervision of teaching.* (Yearbook of the Association for Supervision and Curriculum Development). Alexandria, VA: The Association.

Sergiovanni, Thomas J., & Starratt, Robert J. (1988). *Supervision: Human perspectives* (3rd ed.). New York: McGraw-Hill.

Sergiovanni, Thomas J., & Starratt, Robert J. (2007). *Supervision: A redefinition* (7th ed). New York: McGraw-Hill.

Shakeshaft, Charol (1987). *Women in educational administration.* Beverly Hills, CA: Sage Publications.

Sheehy, Gail T. (1976). Passages: *Predictable crises in adult life.* New York: Dutton.

Simon, Herbert A. (1945). *Administrative behavior.* New York: Macmillan.

Southworth, Geoff (2004). *Primary school leadership in context: Leading small, medium, and large sized schools.* New York: Routledge Falmer.

Speck, Marsha, & Knipe. E. (2001). *Why can't we get it right? Professional development in our schools.* Thousand Oaks, CA: Corwin.

Spillane, James P. (2006). *Distributed Leadership.* San Francisco: Jossey-Bass.

Spillman, Russell (1975, Summer). The nature of communication. *The Administrator, 5* (4): 4–9.

Sprinthall, N. A., & Thies-Sprinthall, L. (1983). The need for a theoretical framework in educating teachers: A cognitive development perspective. In Kenneth R. Howey & W. E. Gardner (eds.), *The education of teachers: A look ahead.* White Plains, NY: Longman.

Starratt, Robert J. (1996). *Transforming educational administration: Meaning, community, and excellence.* New York: McGraw-Hill.

Stogdill, Ralph M. (1974). *Handbook of leadership: A survey of theory and research.* New York: Free Press.

Sunderman, Gail L., Kim, James S., & Orfield, Gary (2005). *NCLB meets school realities: Lessons from the field.* Thousand Oaks, CA: Corwin.

Swenson, Thomas I. (1981). The state of the art in inservice education and staff development. *Journal of Research and Development in Education, 15* (1): 2–7.

Tannenbaum, R., Weshler, I. R., & Massarik, F. (1961). *Leadership and organizations.* New York: McGraw-Hill.

Taylor, Frederick W. (1916). *Principles of scientific management.* Paper presented to the Cleveland Industrial League.

The Holmes Group (1986). *Tomorrow's teachers: A report of the Holmes Group.* East Lansing, MI: Authors.

Thelen, Herbert A. (1954). *Dynamics of groups at work.* Chicago: University of Chicago Press.

Thurston, Paul, Clift, Renee, & Schacht, Marshall (1993). Preparing leaders for change-oriented schools. *Phi Delta Kappan, 75*: 3, pp. 259–264.

Tom, Alan R. (1984). *Teaching as a moral craft.* White Plains, NY: Longman.

Tuckman, B. W., & Jensen, M. A. C. (1977). Stages of small group development revisited. *Group and Organization Studies, 2* (4): 419–426.

Tyler, Ralph W. (1950). *Basic principles of curriculum and instruction.* Chicago: University of Chicago Press.

Unruh, A., & Turner, H. E. (1970). *Supervision for one and innovation.* Boston: Houghton-Mifflin.

Villers, Raymond (1960). *Dynamic management in industry.* Englewood Cliffs, NJ: Prentice-Hall.

Vroom, V. (1994). *Work and motivation.* San Francisco: Jossey-Bass.

Waller, Willard (1932). *The sociology of teaching.* New York: Russell and Russell.

Walton, Mary (1986). *The Deming management method.* New York: Perigree Press.

Watson, Goodwin (ed.) (1966). Resistance to change. *Concepts for social change.* Washington, DC: National Training Laboratories.

Wayne, A. J., & Youngs, P. (2003). Teacher characteristics and student achievement gains: A review. *Review of Educational Research, 73,* 89–122.

Weber, James R. (1989). Leading the instructional program. In Stuart C. Smith & Philip K. Piele (eds.), *School leadership: Handbook for excellence* (2nd ed.). Eugene: ERIC Clearinghouse for Educational Management, University of Oregon.

Weber, Max (1947). *The theory of social and economic organization* (Talcott Parsons, Translator). Glencoe, IL: The Free Press.

Weller, Richard (ed.) (1977). *Humanistic education: Visions and realities.* Berkeley: McCutchan.

Wickerman, James P. (1864). *School economy: A treatise on the preparation, organization, employments, government, and authorities of schools.* New York: Lippincott.

Wiles, Kimball (1967). *Supervision for better schools* (3rd ed.). Englewood Cliffs, NJ: Prentice-Hall.

Wilmore, B. (2002). *Principal leadership.* Thousand Oaks, CA: Corwin.

Wood, Fred, & Thompson, Steven R. (1980). Guidelines for better staff development. *Educational Leadership, 37:* 374–378.

Woods, Philip A., Bennett, Nigel, Harvey, Janet A., & Wise, Christine (2004). *Educational Management, Administration, and Leadership, 43:* 4, pp. 439–457.

Worthen, Blaine R., & Sanders, James R. (1987). *Educational evaluation: Alternative approaches and practical guidelines.* White Plains, NY: Longman.

Wynn, Richard, & Guditus, Charles W. (1984). *Team management: Leadership by consensus.* Columbus, OH: Merrill.

Young, J. M., & Heichberger, R. L. (1975, Fall).Teacher preparations of an effective school supervision and evaluation program. *Education, 96:* 10–19.

Yukl, Gary A. (1997). *Leadership in organizations* (4th ed.) Englewood Cliffs, NJ: Prentice-Hall.

Zaltman, Gerald; Duncan, Robert, & Holbeck, Jonny (1973). *Innovations and organizations.* New York: Wiley-Interscience.

Index